The Devil's Book
Charles I, The *Book of Sports* and Puritanism in Tudor and Early Stuart England

'A rich telling of an important story of developing tensions within English Protestantism ... a well conceived and very well executed study ... I can warmly commend this book ...'

John Morrill, Professor of British and Irish History, University of Cambridge

'Well-researched, cogent, extremely readable and likely to become the standard work upon its subject.'

Ronald Hutton, Professor of History, Department of Historical Studies, Bristol University

This book takes a fresh look at the controversy surrounding the publication of the *Book of Sports* and the cultural battle over the tension between Sunday observance and traditional revelry in pre-civil war England. Alistair Dougall shows how a new form of sabbatarianism became the hallmark of radical Protestants who sought to impose their beliefs on society and to suppress all Sunday recreations. The book also makes an important contribution to the ongoing debate surrounding the causes of division in English society which led to the outbreak of civil war in 1642.

Alistair Dougall taught for four years at Southampton University before joining the Godolphin School in Salisbury, where he is Head of Sixth Form and teaches history.

The Devil's Book

Charles I, the *Book of Sports* and Puritanism in Tudor and Early Stuart England

Alistair Dougall

UNIVERSITY
of
EXETER
PRESS

First published in 2011 by
University of Exeter Press
Reed Hall, Streatham Drive
Exeter EX4 4QR
UK

www.exeterpress.co.uk

© Alistair Dougall 2011

The right of Alistair Dougall to be identified
as author of this work has been asserted by him in accordance with
the Copyright, Designs and Patents Acts 1988.

British Library Cataloguing in Publication Data
A catalogue record for this book is available
from the British Library.

ISBN 978 0 85989 856 0

Typeset in Sabon, 10 on 12 by
Carnegie Book Production, Lancaster
Printed in Great Britain by
TJ International, Padstow

To my parents

Contents

List of illustrations	viii
Acknowledgements	ix
Abbreviations	xi
Chronology	xii
Glossary	xv
Introduction	1
1 'Vain, stupid, profane games': Medieval attitudes to the playing of sports on the Sabbath and other holy days	7
2 The impact of the break with Rome	25
3 The reign of Elizabeth I and the battle over the Lord's Day	39
4 James I's 'dancing book' and the politicisation of 'Saint Sabbath'	66
5 The *Book of Sports* and the reign of Charles I: From a 'pious Statute' to 'bloody civil war'	100
6 Enforcement and reaction: Choosing between the 'Commandments of God and Man'	126
Conclusion	160
Appendix: The text of the 1633 *Book of Sports*	165
Notes and references	169
Bibliography	203
Index	222

Illustrations

The illustrations appear between pages 118 and 119

1 Engraving showing the Devil encouraging a man to play a game of bowls with Cupid
2 Handwritten verse in a copy of the 1618 *Book of Sports*
3 Title page of Thomas Young's *Dies Dominica* (1639)
4 Title page of the 1633 *Book of Sports*
5 First page of the 1618 *Book of Sports*
6 Charles I's instructions to print his 'Declaration Concerninge Recreations on the Lords Day after Eveninge prayer'
7 Satirical engraving of Archbishop Laud and Henry Burton, 1641
8 Burning of the Book of Sports by the common hangman in May 1643 on the orders of Parliament

Acknowledgements

I am very conscious that I owe a huge debt of thanks to many people for encouraging me, supporting me and advising me over an extended period of time as I undertook the research and writing to complete this book.

I should like to thank the staff of the Bodleian Library, the British Library, the Devon Record Office, the National Archives, the Somerset Record Office, and Southampton University Library for all their help. In particular, I should like to thank Susan Laithwaite of the Devon Record Office and Philip Hocking of the Somerset Record Office – who gave me invaluable assistance in researching sixteenth- and seventeenth-century court orders against wakes and ales – and Paul Holden, the collections manager at Lanhydrock House, Cornwall.

Many colleagues and friends have given me their advice, interest and support. In particular, my heartfelt thanks go to: Daniel and Susan Bedingfield, Professor George Bernard, Dr Alastair Duke, Dr Brian Golding, Dr Marjorie Huntley, Matthew Huntley, and Professor Kevin Sharpe. My greatest debt of gratitude is owed to my friend and mentor, Professor Mark Stoyle. Mark has been an enormous inspiration to me ever since I was fortunate to be an undergraduate student of his many years ago. He has been a wonderful mentor ever since and has given me enormous encouragement and invaluable advice. I greatly value the friendship of both Mark and his wife, Lynn. I will forever be in their debt.

During the course of both researching and writing this book, I experienced various setbacks. These included my house being flooded within weeks of starting my research and, on another occasion, my house being struck by lightning, ironically while I was working one Sunday afternoon. At some points I did wonder if someone was trying to tell me something! While undertaking my research, I came across a passage in Edward Brerewood's treatise on the Sabbath, in which he wrote: 'I grow weary, & have already both dulled my penne and my selfe.' I confess that this struck a chord at the time, and I am therefore grateful to the people who gave me the moral support to keep going. I owe sincere thanks to my family and friends: Neil, Jane, Bill, Sarah, Laura, Alan, Mary, Alex and

Eddie; and to my many colleagues and friends at The Godolphin School, Salisbury. Above all, I want to thank my parents for giving me so much in life and for their unwavering love and support.

Abbreviations

CSPD	*Calendar State Papers Domestic.*
CSPV	*Calendar State Papers Venetian.*
DRO	Devon Record Office, Exeter.
EHR	*English Historical Review.*
JEH	*Journal of Ecclesiastical History.*
P&P	*Past and Present.*
REED	*Records of Early English Drama.*
SP	State Papers.
SRO	Somerset Record Office, Taunton.
TRHS	*Transactions of the Royal Historical Society.*

Chronology

1543	*The King's Book* (*A necessary doctrine and erudicion for any chrysten man*) published.
1552	Act for keeping Holy and Fasting Days passed.
	Act of Uniformity passed (which made attendance at church on Sundays a legal requirement).
1558	Act of Uniformity passed (reinstated the legal requirement for people to attend their parish church on Sundays).
1563	*Book of Homilies* endorsed by Convocation.
1570	Alexander Nowell's *Catechism* published.
1583	Gallery at Paris Garden collapsed.
1584	Elizabeth I vetoed Sabbath observance bill.
1587	Purging of the Commission of Peace in Lancashire.
1595	Nicholas Bownd's *The Doctrine of the Sabbath* published.
1599	Richard Greenham's *A Treatise of the Sabbath* published.
	Thomas Rogers launched attack on puritan sabbatarianism.
1603	Death of Elizabeth I and accession of James I.
	May, James I issued a proclamation against *unlawful* pastimes on Sundays.
1606	Bill introduced for 'the better observing ... of the Sabbath'.
1614	Another Sabbath observance bill introduced.
1616	Justice Edward Bromley issued order banning recreations on Sundays in Lancashire.
1617	*August,* James I petitioned by people in Lancashire to nullify Bromley's order.
	August, James I's *Declaration to his Subjects, Concerning Lawful Sports to Be Used* issued for Lancashire.

1618	*May*, James I's amended *Declaration* published for the whole realm.
	June, trial and imprisonment of John Traske.
1621	Sabbath observance bill passed by both Houses but then vetoed by James I.
	Bishop Bayly of Bangor imprisoned 'for disputing malapertly with the king on the Sabbath'.
1625	Death of James I and accession of Charles I.
	Charles I signed an Act against abuses committed on Sundays.
1628	Theophilus Brabourne's *A Discourse Upon the Sabbath Day* published.
1631	Theophilus Brabourne's *A Defence of that most Ancient, and Sacred ordinance of Gods the Sabbath Day* published with a dedication to Charles I.
1632	Baron Denham and Lord Chief Justice Richardson issued order suppressing ales in Somerset and instructed the order to be read out in parish churches.
1633	William Prynne's *Histrio-mastix* published.
	February, 1633 order suppressing ales read out in Somerset parish churches.
	February, Sherfield case before the Star Chamber.
	August, William Laud appointed Archbishop of Canterbury.
	August, under direct instruction from Charles I, Richardson revoked the 1632 order suppressing ales in Somerset.
	August, twenty-five Somerset justices petitioned the king to suppress ales in the county.
	October, Laud wrote to Bishop Piers on the king's instructions asking for a report on the status and value of wakes in Somerset.
	October, Charles I's *Declaration to his Subjects, Concerning Lawful Sports to Be Used* published.
	November, Bishop Piers reported back to Laud on wakes and ales in Somerset.
1635	Francis White's *A Treatise of the Sabbath Day* published.
	Henry Burton's *A Brief Answer to a Late Treatise on the Sabbath Day* published.

1636	Henry Burton's *A Divine Tragedie Lately Acted* published.
	Peter Heylyn's *The History of the Sabbath* published.
	John Pocklington's *Sunday No Sabbath* published.
1637	Francis White's *An Examination and Confutation of a Lawless Pamphlet* published.
1641	*September*, Commons passed bill banning dancing and sports on Sundays.
1643	*May*, Parliament ordered the burning of the *Book of Sports* by the common hangman.
1644	*April*, Parliament passed ordinance prohibiting any recreations on Sundays.
1645	*January*, execution of Archbishop Laud.
1649	*January*, execution of Charles I.
1650	Act passed banning dancing on Sundays.
1657	Act passed banning all types of sports and recreations on Sundays.
1660	*May*, Restoration of the Monarchy.

Glossary

Ale An 'ale' usually denoted a festival held, partially at least, in order to raise funds. Church-ales were among the most common type of ale. As the name suggests, ale would be drunk on these occasions. An ale would usually also be an occasion for people to dance and play a variety of sports.

Bear-baiting The sport of setting dogs to attack a bear chained to a stake.

Bearward The keeper of a bear or bears used for bear baiting or to perform tricks as public entertainment.

Bid-ale An ale or entertainment for the general benefit of an individual, to which a general invitation or 'bidding' was given. Bid-ales were generally informal and held when good weather could be expected.

Bowling Playing at bowls.

Bride-ale An ale to raise money for newly-weds. Also, a wedding feast or ale-drinking at a wedding.

Bull-baiting The action of baiting a tethered bull with dogs. Although this was primarily a very popular sport, it was also undertaken by people in the belief that baiting made the meat of the bull more tender.

Caliver A kind of musket.

Cambuc A forerunner of modern golf.

Carding Card-playing.

Church ales Church ales were among the most common type of ale. They were organised by churchwardens and were principally designed, as the name suggests, to raise money for the upkeep and repair of the parish church. Whereas bid-ales and help-ales were generally informal and held when good weather could be expected, church-ales tended to be larger affairs and were often held at Whitsun or on Easter Sunday itself. Consequently, they were sometimes referred to as 'Whitsun-ales' or 'Easter-ales'.

Clerk ale   An ale-drinking for the benefit of the parish clerk.

Closh   A game with a ball or bowl and pins; similar to nine pins or skittles.

Club ball   A generic term to describe a game in which a ball is struck by a club or bat. Also, a forerunner of cricket.

Cock-fighting   The sport of making cocks fight each other. Spectators would gamble on which cock would win.

Coursing   The sport of chasing hares and other game with dogs, especially greyhounds.

Dicing   Playing or gambling with dice.

Easter-ale   The name sometimes given to a church ale which was held at Easter time.

Half-bowl   A game played with a hemisphere of wood and fifteen small conical-shaped pins.

Handball   A game resembling Fives.

Help-ale   An ale held to raise funds for someone who had fallen on hard times. Also, an ale held in celebration of the completion of some work (such as bringing in the harvest or haymaking) done with the help of neighbours. They were generally informal and held when good weather could be expected.

Hobby horse   The figure of a horse fastened about the waist of one of the participants in a morris dance who then mimics the movement of a lively horse.

Interlude   Another term for a stage play.

Kailes or kayles   A version of skittles or nine pins.

Kitling   A version of skittles or nine pins; also called 'kittle-pins' or 'kettle-pins'.

Leaping   An acrobatic sport involving springing from the ground or other standing place: leaping and turning in the air with the heels over the head. It was like tumbling, but could also involve leaping or jumping through hoops.

Loggats   A game similar to nine pins or skittles.

Lady of the May   Also called 'Queen of the May': girl or young woman chosen to be 'queen' of May games and festivities.

Lord of the May   A young man chosen to preside over the May games and festivities.

Lord of Misrule A mock title of dignity given to the boy or man appointed to preside over some festive occasions.

Madding pole Another term for a maypole.

May games Festivity and sports associated with the first of May, although they were often held in the months of June and July as well as in May.

May-ale An ale held as part of celebrations associated with May Day. They often took place in the months of June and July and not just in May.

Maypole A high pole, painted with spiral stripes of different colours and decked with flowers, set up on a village green or other open space for people to dance around.

Morris dancing A grotesque dance performed by men in fancy costume, usually representing characters from the Robin Hood legend.

Pall mall Also called 'paille-maille'. A forerunner of croquet. A game in which a boxwood ball was struck with a mallet through a long alley of iron arches. The winner was the player who could drive the ball through the alley with the fewest number of strokes.

Paris Garden A bear-garden in Southwark where bears were baited for public entertainment.

Pins Nine-pins or skittles.

Pitching the bar The throwing of a wooden or metal bar.

Playing at the caitch Another term for tennis (real tennis).

Queckboard A game most probably similar to checkers or draughts.

Quoits or coits The throwing of a flat disc of stone or metal – similar to a discus, although horseshoes were also used.

Ringdance A round dance.

Running at quintain Running to a stake or stout post set as a marker.

Rushbearings An annual ceremony held (particular in the north of England) which involved carrying rushes and garlands to the parish church and decorating the walls with them or strewing them on the floor of the church.

Scot-ales An ale held at which ale was drunk at the invitation of the lord of the manor or some other official where a forced contribution was levied for the ale drunk. They were another form of ale held to raise money for the community but, unlike church ales, most scot-ales carried some form of compulsion to contribute.

Shooting Often another term for archery.

Shovegroat Another term for shovel-board: a game in which a coin or other disc is driven by a blow with the hand along a polished table, board or floor.

Stoolball A forerunner of cricket.

Summer games Festivities held during the summer where there would be dancing, games and sports. Also known as 'May games'.

Summer pole Another term for a maypole.

Tables Another term for backgammon.

Tennis Real tennis.

Throwing at cocks A sport where a cock would be tied to a post and players would then throws sticks or cudgels at it until it was killed, with the person administering the fatal blow winning the game and the dead bird.

Throwing the sledge Throwing a heavy hammer or sledgehammer.

Tilting Jousting: charging on horseback with a lance against an opponent.

Vaulting Vaulting was similar to leaping but it entailed jumping onto or over an object. It could, for example, entail vaulting on to or over a horse.

Wake A communal feast which was often called a 'wake' and sometimes just called a 'church ale', and which was held in many parishes to commemorate the dedication day of the parish church. Wakes could be held on the actual dedication day of the church in honour of its patron saint or on the Sunday nearest to the relevant saint's day. However, where the saint's day was later in the year, wakes and church ales were most often held sometime between Easter and the end of summer, although they could take place at any convenient time when money was needed for the church.

Whitsun-ale The name sometimes given to a church ale which was held at Whitsun.

Introduction

On his return from a visit to Scotland in 1617, James I was presented with a petition by people in Lancashire who resented attempts by magistrates there to stop them playing their traditional sports on Sundays. The king responded by issuing a declaration licensing the playing of certain sports on Sundays and published this declaration nationally the following year. It met with opposition, particularly from puritans who were actively engaged in a campaign to reform both the Church and society. As part of that campaign, they wanted the Lord's Day to be strictly observed and devoted wholly to religious duties. In 1633, following an order by Somerset magistrates banning traditional Sunday revels, James' son and successor, Charles I, instructed the Somerset bench to revoke its order and then reissued his own version of his father's so-called *Book of Sports*. Unlike James, who, in the face of opposition, had prudently decided not to enforce his Declaration, Charles was determined that *his* Declaration would be enforced and required that it should be read in parish churches throughout England. This decision created resentment and opposition far beyond the ranks of the puritans.

Writing in 1930 about the controversy surrounding the issue of Sunday observance in early seventeenth-century England, J.R. Tanner declared that: 'the Sabbatarian Controversy is vastly more important than it appears to be at first sight.'[1] Most histories of the period make at least some reference to contemporary divisions over Sunday observance and to the controversial publication of the *Book of Sports*.[2] It is widely acknowledged that the question of how Sunday was observed and whether or not any form of recreation should be allowed on Sundays was an issue that created bitter and serious divisions within English society. Yet, although the *Book of Sports* and the debate surrounding it is seen as important, it has often not been given the prominence that it deserves.[3] In 1988 Kenneth Parker published an important work on early modern English sabbatarianism in which he sought to trace its origins back to medieval scholastic theology, and argued that there was a broad consensus on the issue in the Elizabethan and Jacobean Church. As part of his study, Parker looked at issues surrounding the *Book of Sports* in the context of his examination of the wider question of Sunday observance in England. One of the main thrusts of his argument was that the sabbatarianism espoused by early modern puritans was a mainstream tenet of the established Church. Indeed, Parker claimed that, far from the puritans breaking with the past, it was the followers of Archbishop Laud who were being innovative in asserting that the fourth commandment was not morally binding, and he accused the Laudians of using the *Book of Sports* as part of a campaign against the puritans in an attempt to portray their views as both new and dangerous.[4] Several historians have taken issue with Parker's thesis, but no in-depth study of the *Book of Sports* has been undertaken in recent years and there are aspects of Parker's work that have remained largely unchallenged.[5]

As the following chapters demonstrate, although Laudians did exaggerate and caricature puritan beliefs in order to make them seem even more extreme than they actually were, they were nonetheless right to identify the innovative and radical nature of puritan sabbatarianism. Far from being merely a continuation or development of a long sabbatarian tradition within the English Church, the sabbatarianism which emerged during the late sixteenth and early seventeenth century was new and extreme. The puritans had a radically different view of Sunday observance from that which had been traditionally held by the English Church. At both national and local level, puritans represented an increasingly uncomfortable challenge to both ecclesiastical and royal authority in that they sought to engineer changes to both the Church and wider society. Their attempts to put an end to sports and revels, which the common people had enjoyed on Sunday afternoons for centuries, brought the puritans increasingly into conflict with the Church hierarchy and with the Crown; both regarded such attempts as challenging their respective jurisdictions and authority. The issue of Sunday recreations consequently became a cultural battleground, with radical reformers and established authority fighting not just over the question of sports and Sunday observance, but over issues of authority and power in early Stuart England.

Much of this book concerns the nature of puritan sabbatarianism and the divisions which were caused by the puritans' attempts to suppress traditional revelry. Given that the following chapters refer frequently to puritans and their beliefs, it is important to address the thorny issue of what, precisely, contemporaries understood by the term 'puritan'. Historians have long struggled to find an acceptable definition of this word. Indeed, because of its nebulous nature some have even argued that the term should not be used at all. Yet, although hard to define satisfactorily, it continues to be widely used and, in the absence of any better alternative, so it should be. Even though it is impossible to provide an all-encompassing definition, it would be perverse to avoid using the word in a book about early Stuart society, particularly given its widespread use by contemporaries, many of whom themselves had a very clear idea of what they meant by it.[6]

The problem with trying to define 'puritan' is that the puritans did not belong to a separate, distinct organisation. Although separatist groups were to emerge later in the seventeenth century, during the reigns of Elizabeth I, James I and Charles I puritans were very much part of the established Church, even if, to varying degrees, they wanted to reform it. The early seventeenth-century Church of England was a broad church whose membership, as John Coffey and Paul Lim have observed, 'ranged from church papists and high churchmen, through conformist Calvinists, to moderate Puritans and radical Puritans'.[7] Even among puritans themselves there were differences and varying degrees of radicalism, which is why it is difficult to define them. They were not members of an external, clearly distinct group. Nor did they form a distinct sect or monolithic group within the Church.

Puritans believed in the Calvinist doctrine of predestination: that is to say, that God had predestined certain individuals, a godly elect, for salvation. They were also vehemently anti-Catholic. Yet these factors alone did not distinguish them from their fellow church members. The Church of England's theology was, broadly speaking, Calvinist, and the consensus of scholarly opinion is that most of the Church hierarchy and the majority of the clergy and laity themselves believed in the doctrine of predestination. Similarly, most English Protestants were staunchly anti-Catholic. What distinguished the puritan members of the Church from their fellow Protestants was, essentially, two things: their desire to reform both the Church and society along godly lines and the zeal with which they held their beliefs. It was not that their beliefs were different from many of their fellow Protestants, it was the degree of their conviction and their belief in the need for greater change in both Church and society that marked them out. In the words of the Elizabethan pamphleteer, Perceval Wiburn, they were the 'hotter sorte of Protestants'.[8] Their intense religious beliefs governed and coloured their lives to a much greater degree than was true of most of their contemporaries, and they saw themselves as part of a godly elect with a duty to bring about the moral reform of the ungodly majority and to purge the Church of what they saw as the vestiges of its Catholic past. To varying degrees, they believed that the Church of England, as established by the Elizabethan Settlement, was still too 'popish' in its liturgy, ceremony, doctrine and structure. They deplored the use of images and of rituals like the signing of the cross at baptism, bowing at the name of Jesus and kneeling to receive communion. All of this smacked too much of popery. Even here, though, the puritans differed in the intensity of their hostility. The more moderate puritans, while disapproving, were by and large prepared to conform. The more extreme puritans not only condemned these perceived trappings of Catholicism in favour of a much simpler form of worship without the traditional vestments and ceremonies, but also wanted to see a radical restructuring of the Church itself in which the episcopacy would be abolished and a presbyterian church would be established, governed instead by lay elders.

The puritans put enormous emphasis on studying scripture and on godly preaching. They favoured a simpler style of church service which centred around the sermon. As this book will demonstrate, another characteristic of the puritans was their fervent belief in a rigid form of sabbatarianism which required people to devote Sunday entirely to worship, prayer and religious duties, and which did not allow for any form of recreation on the Lord's Day. There were many non-puritans who also wished to see an end to the disorder often attendant on traditional Sunday revelry and some non-puritans who wanted to see the Lord's Day more properly observed. There were, therefore, sabbatarians who were not puritan, but there were no puritans who were not also sabbatarian, and it is argued in this book that a new – far more hard-line – form of sabbatarianism developed during the late sixteenth and early seventeenth century; one which was a characteristic of puritan belief.

The puritans sought reform not only of religion but also of society: of people's morals and behaviour. They were hostile to the traditional popular culture, which was at odds with the way they believed a godly world should be. Consequently, many puritans were actively involved in attempts to suppress traditional festivity, and they gained a reputation as kill-joys. As William Hunt has well observed:

> A man of irreproachable personal piety who nevertheless has no objection to his neighbours' boozing on the Sabbath or fornicating in haylofts is not a Puritan. A Puritan who minds his own business is a contradiction in terms.[9]

H.L. Mencken once defined puritanism as 'the haunting fear that someone, somewhere, may be happy'.[10] This is probably unfair to many puritans who were motivated by sincere religious conviction and a desire for good. While there were, no doubt, sombre puritans who suspected that any form of levity was the product of some sort of vice, others knew how to enjoy themselves. As is discussed in chapter six, the puritan MP, Sir Thomas Barrington, hosted morris dancers and other revellers at his house. While he may have disapproved of public festivity, leading as it often did to drunken, unruly behaviour, and would certainly have disapproved of revels held on Sundays, he was nonetheless happy to see his household enjoy their festivities in the controlled conditions of his own home.[11] Yet, when it came to traditional revelry among the common people, most puritans severely disapproved, seeing such revelry as papist or pagan in origin and as an occasion of temptation and sin. Although it has been argued that Philip

Stubbes was not a radical puritan because he defended the episcopacy and rejected any form of presbyterianism, he was nonetheless vehement in his opposition to traditional festivity. As is discussed in chapter three, he bitterly attacked dancing, wakes, May games and other forms of popular revelry. His condemnation of the traditional festive culture was typical of his fellow puritans.[12]

The clash between the puritans and those ordinary people who enjoyed and valued their traditional culture helped to mark out the former and to shape their identity. It should be stressed, indeed, that the very term 'puritan' was originally a term of abuse used scornfully and often indiscriminately by ordinary village and townspeople to describe and attack those zealously Protestant ministers and others who were seeking to impose their strict religious views upon them. Given that 'puritan' was a pejorative term, puritans themselves rarely used it and instead tended to speak of themselves as 'the godly', 'children of God', 'the people of the Lord', 'professors', 'true gospellers', 'God's saints' or 'the elect'.[13] As Patrick Collinson has commented, puritanism 'was not a thing identifiable in itself, but one half of a stressful relationship'.[14] Many ordinary people bitterly resented the self-styled godly, whom they saw as threatening their traditional way of life, and godly ministers and others who attempted to intervene to stop their revels were often subjected to foul-mouthed abuse and damned as 'scurvy puritans' or worse.[15] As Coffey and Lim have observed, the puritans reacted by developing 'an embattled sense of identity' and creating their own networks.[16] The antipathy exhibited towards the puritans only served to highlight and increase divisions and to strengthen the sense of identity among the puritans who, even though they had a range of differing views on liturgical, doctrinal and organisational issues, nonetheless shared a common spiritual and cultural outlook.[17]

In examining the impact of puritan belief on traditional festivity, this book considers the nature and importance of Sunday revelry in Tudor and early Stuart England, and explores how and why wakes and ales, and the various sports traditionally enjoyed by people after church on Sundays, came under such attack and became a matter of major political concern during this period. As it is important to look at these issues in their proper context, the first chapter examines the role played by traditional revels in medieval society and attitudes to Sunday observance in late medieval England. Chapter two considers the impact of the English Reformation and the enduring popularity of Sunday recreations in the mid-sixteenth century. The third chapter examines the attitudes of the Elizabethan Church to Sunday observance and explores in detail the emergence, nature and impact of the new form of sabbatarianism espoused by radical puritans. Chapter four looks at the importance of puritan sabbatarianism in terms of the cultural divisions within Jacobean society, analyses the reasons behind James I's decision to enter the debate by publishing the first *Book of Sports*, and assesses popular and elite reactions to its publication. Chapter five, in particular, challenges not only the notion that it was the Laudians' view of sabbatarianism that broke with the past, but also – in examining the reasons for the publication of the 1633 Declaration – challenges the all-too-widely-accepted idea that it was Archbishop Laud who was the prime mover behind both the decision to publish and then to enforce the 1633 *Book of Sports*. As the chapter explains, the evidence suggests that it was Charles I himself who took the lead and that Laud was indeed, as he later claimed, just following his master's instructions. The final chapter examines the nature and impact of the enforcement of the Caroline *Book of Sports*; the extent to which reaction to it increased opposition to Charles' policies; and how divisions over traditional recreations helped to determine allegiance in the Civil War.

This study underscores the crucial importance of the *Book of Sports* and the whole sabbatarian controversy to our understanding of early Stuart England. As Tanner observed, these matters are far more important than some historians appear to have appreciated. It is hard to underestimate their significance when considering the religious and cultural divisions in English society during the reign of Charles I. It is important to acknowledge the challenge that puritan sabbatarianism presented, both to traditional ways of life and to the established Church and state. It is also important to appreciate why puritan sabbatarianism was resisted and how the resulting tensions helped to contribute to a bloody civil war.

1

'Vain, stupid, profane games'
Medieval attitudes to the playing of sports on the Sabbath and other holy days

Long before the Reformation and the later emergence of English puritanism, the perceived dangers and evils of idleness, drinking and traditional Sunday revels were the focus of condemnation from some English moralists. Writing in the early fifteenth century, the anonymous author of *Jacob's Well* condemned as guilty of the sin of sloth those people who spent their leisure time hunting, wrestling, going to wakes, dancing, drinking in taverns, and revelling and rioting on holy days and who neglected attending church and giving proper service to God.[1] He asserted that 'idleness' such as this led to the vices of pride, gluttony and lechery. People, he claimed, would mix in evil company, squander their goods, think evil thoughts and succumb to 'wykkyd desires'. Moreover, he concluded, since people usually indulged in these idle pastimes on Sundays and other holy days, they were guilty of compounding matters by 'defouling the halyday, in synne & evyll werkys'.

Other literature of the period similarly highlighted the moral dangers various pastimes enjoyed by large sections of the population. Many 'ydell dedys' were denounced, with drinking, sports and all forms of gambling being particularly condemned.[2] Some of this criticism was motivated by secular concerns. There was an anxiety that servants and apprentices who lost money through gambling would subsequently turn to stealing from their masters and that drinking and playing sports could lead to crime and violence. Royal proclamations and acts of Parliament also repeatedly stressed the importance for the defence of the country for men to practise their archery. Again and again, authority voiced its concern that archery practice was being neglected as people indulged in various other games and sports. Such pastimes were criticised by some as being immoral. There were also concerns that games should not be played in or around the parish church, the sanctity of which should be respected. Furthermore, there was a strong belief in pre-Reformation England that Sunday and other holy days should be properly observed by people refraining from work and fulfilling their religious duties. Yet, though there were moralists who called for a strict form of Sunday observance which would not allow for sports and revels on a Sunday, they were in a minority and did not represent the views of either the mainstream Church or of the state. Sabbatarianism was not a major issue at this time and did not have the prominence that it was to acquire in the late sixteenth and early seventeenth centuries, when it was to cause serious social divisions which were to lead the Crown to become involved in the debate over the regulation of Sunday revelry and to publish the *Book of Sports*.

In order to understand the later debate surrounding Sunday revels in its proper context, it is important to consider how Sunday was observed in the later Middle Ages; and how people spent their leisure time, and which sports they indulged in on Sundays and holy days. How did those in authority in Medieval England react to such pursuits? What were the secular and religious reasons behind attempts to suppress certain sports; and how successful were such attempts at suppression? Contemporary sources which discuss sports and popular entertainment in this period are limited; consequently, the importance that ordinary individuals attached to sports on the one hand and to the observance of Sunday and holy days on the other is difficult to gauge precisely.[3] As is so often the case, the voice of the ordinary man and woman is silent. Inevitably, we have to make assumptions based on indirect evidence. For example, the fact that acts and proclamations outlawing certain games had to be repeatedly made suggests that, despite legislation and persistent exhortation, people continued to play such games. They needed to be urged repeatedly to refrain from certain pastimes and not to neglect their archery practice. However, it remains difficult to ascertain the extent to which people indulged in sports and the degree to which archery or Sunday observance was actually neglected.

The ritual year

Much has already been written on the liturgical and agricultural calendars in the medieval period and on how these intertwined and determined the pace and pattern of life.[4] England's economy was an agrarian one and the vast bulk of people were involved in agriculture in some form or other. Consequently, the time which could be given over to sports and festivity was, in part, determined by the agricultural cycle: the changing seasons and the times when it was necessary to plough, sow and harvest and to take produce and livestock to markets.[5] The Church recognised this in setting the other calendar which determined the pattern of people's lives: the liturgical calendar. Time was to be given over to work, but time also had to be given over to God: to worship and prayer and to observing the Sabbath and a myriad of other feast days. The liturgical year was in tune with the agricultural cycle and its effect was to roughly divide the year in half. This is because, coinciding with the agricultural year's growing season, the first 'half' of the year, from December to June, was crammed with major festivals and holy days. These included Advent, the twelve days of Christmas, Epiphany, Candlemas, Shrovetide, Easter, Ascension, Whitsun, Midsummer and Corpus Christi. By contrast, the second 'half' of the year was comparatively lacking in major festivals and was instead commemorated largely through saints' days, many of which had only local significance. Unlike the major festivals celebrated between December and June, very few of these were commemorated nationwide.[6] Yet, contemporaries would not have seen the year as being thus divided. Eamon Duffy has rightly warned against viewing the second half of the liturgical year as 'secular' in contrast to the 'ritualistic' first half. The people of the later Middle Ages would not have regarded any period of the liturgical year as 'secular'.[7] It is nonetheless legitimate to contrast the two 'halves' of the year. The period from December to June described in the shorthand of some historians as the 'ritual half' of the year, contained all the principal Church festivals, whereas the months from July to November saw few nationwide festivals or commemorations.

Everyone was affected by the seasonal observances of the liturgical calendar. For example, it was not possible to marry during the forty days of Lent or the four weeks of Advent. Fasting was obligatory throughout Lent and on nearly thirty other days during the course of the year. However, as well as fast days there were, of course, also feast days; and it was at times of festival that most sports and other pastimes such as dancing were pursued.[8] The liturgical calendar was peppered with all manner of feast and saints' days in addition to the major Church festivals, but these should be distinguished from the *obligatory* feast days or *festa ferianda*. Sunday was always a *festa ferianda* and the majority of the other obligatory feast days fell in the period from December to June. The *festa ferianda* were holy days of obligation on which people were required to refrain more or less completely from servile work and were obliged to keep the Sunday pattern of attending matins, Mass and evensong.[9] The degree to which certain holy days were observed varied. Some required a total cessation of work – with the exception of feeding livestock, milking cows or the necessity of saving crops at harvest time – and others only a partial abstention from work. There was inevitable tension over the status of holy days and how they should be observed. Landlords and employers wanted tenants and employees to work as much as possible, while workers relished the prospect of a day free from toil.[10]

Although the majority of *festa ferianda* were celebrated in the 'ritual' half of the year, others such as the Feast of the Assumption, the Feast of

St Luke and the Feast of the Archangel Michael – or Michaelmas – were commemorated in the other half. There were also many feast days celebrated during this second half of the year which were not *festa ferianda* and which did not have the same national significance but on which people nonetheless indulged in sports and games. For example, most parishes would celebrate the feast day of the saint to whom their church was dedicated. Such celebrations would often take place on the Sunday nearest to the relevant saint's day. This prompts the question of how important the observance of Sundays and other holy days of obligation was in medieval society and what attitudes were to the playing of sports on such days.

Observing Sunday and other *festa ferianda*

It was on Sunday that Christ had risen from the dead and on Sunday that the Holy Spirit had come to the Apostles. Consequently, commemorating as it did the renewal of the world through Christ's resurrection, Sunday replaced the Sabbath of the Old Testament as the Christian day of worship. However, it was not until after the conversion of the Emperor Constantine that it became possible to oblige people to observe Sunday as a day of rest from work. Constantine decreed that, with the exception of farmers cultivating their fields, there should be a total public rest from work on Sunday. Subsequently, conscious that simply requiring people to refrain from work could lead to idleness, 'the beginning of all vice,' the Church applied the Old Testament fourth commandment by demanding that the day be kept holy.[11] The Church felt threatened by the fact that, on Sundays, the vast majority of people indulged in celebrations which were often very unchristian in nature. Anxious that Christians might be tempted to indulge in wicked pursuits themselves, the early Church set aside Sunday as a day of worship as well as rest.[12] Parishioners were expected to hear Mass in its entirety and to fulfil their spiritual duties properly.[13] Putting the weight of the Old Testament Sabbath commandment behind the state's decrees concerning rest from work on Sunday, the Church now required that Sunday should be kept holy in the Old Testament sense. All servile work, including farming, was forbidden. Instead, the day had to be given over to worship and contemplation. Although feasts such as Christmas and Ascension Day were seen to be significantly more important than the ordinary Sunday, Sunday was nonetheless thereafter the most important holy day.[14]

Although some moralists decried them, the medieval Church itself did not condemn pastimes held on Sundays provided they did not prevent the laity from attending church. Indeed, Sunday revels were often an occasion to raise funds for the parish church. However, working on Sundays was condemned. Throughout the medieval period, people were required to refrain from servile labour for the whole of Sunday. Yet, over time the definition of servile labour was refined to permit various tasks, such as writing, which was allowed if it was not done for profit, and a small amount of sewing or sweeping or the repairing of a break in a hedge.[15] Servile work was permissible if done for pious reasons, such as caring for the destitute or carting materials for the building or repairing of churches or monasteries.[16] Necessary works such as the cooking of food, the feeding of livestock or the harvesting of crops threatened by an imminent storm were also permitted.[17] Nonetheless, for the main part, the laity were required to observe Sunday and other holy days of obligation by resting from worldly pursuits and attending Mass. Medieval moralists castigated people for misusing the Lord's Day by either working or playing sports, and urged them to observe Sunday and the important feasts of the year with due reverence and devotion. 'Yf thou be no prest nother clerk, but on[e] of the peple,' a fifteenth-century tract on the Decalogue declared, 'thenne bysy thee in the halyday to here prechynge of Godes worde'.[18] Writing in the early fourteenth century, Robert Mannyng of Brunne wrote that people were obliged to observe holy days properly, and stated that:

> Of al the festys that yn holy chyrche are,
> Holy sunday men oght to spare;
> Holy sunday ys byfore allefre
> That euer yt were, or euer shal be.[19]

Mannyng took a clear sabbatarian line and asserted that, although the pope had authority to alter the liturgical calendar and change the days on which other feasts and saints' days were celebrated,

> ... he may, thurgh no resun,
> The sunday puttyn vp no dowun;
> Tharfore the sunday specyaly
> ys hyest to halew, and most wurthy
> ... For hyt ys goddys ownë day.[20]

The fifteenth-century treatise, *Dives and Pauper*, similarly declared that Sunday and other holy days should be hallowed properly and that people should so manage their working days that they did not then need to break the holy days.[21] It stated that 'Sonday is our lordis day & is mest halwyd,' and that people should refrain from worldly things on Sundays and spend the day in giving to the Church, hearing God's word and in meditation and prayer.[22] In his dialogue with Dives, Pauper, a mendicant preacher, condemned those who did servile work on the Sabbath.[23] While accepting that some works done for pious motives were permitted on holy days, Pauper stated that even these works should not be undertaken on Sundays or on great feast days unless absolutely necessary. As with other medieval treatises, *Dives and Pauper* asserted that of all the church's feast days, 'the Sonday is mest solempne & holy for the grete dedis and wondris that God dede in the Sonday'.[24] Easter Sunday and Whitsunday were regarded as more important than ordinary Sundays and *Dives and Pauper* acknowledged that major feasts such as Christmas Day and Epiphany were similarly commemorated more solemnly than ordinary Sundays. Yet, given that feasts such as Christmas could fall on any day of the week, it stated that there was no day of the week as solem in itself as Sunday.[25]

The best known fifteenth-century English manual of religious instruction, John Mirk's *Instructions for Parish Priests*, similarly made it clear that people were required to keep holy days by going to church and refraining from work:

> The halyday only ordeynet was,
> To here goddes serues and the mas,
> And spene [spend] that day in holynes,
> And leue alle other bysynes.[26]

In 1362, the Archbishop of Canterbury condemned the fact that people did not honour God on Sundays as they should, complaining that:

> that which was prepared as a summary of devotion is made into a heap of dissipation, since upon these holy-days the tavern is rather worshipped than the Church, gluttony and drunkenness are more abundant than tears and prayers, men are busied rather with wantonness and contumely than with leisure of contemplation.[27]

Yet, even if some moralists and churchmen criticised people for their failure to fulfil their religious duties, unlike the later puritan sabbatarians, most did not rule out recreations altogether but merely those that prevented people from attending church and from fulfilling their religious duties.

Reference was often made to disasters and misfortunes being visited upon those who, either by working or otherwise neglecting their spiritual duties, failed to observe Sundays and holy days properly. It was said that St Hugh, Bishop of Lincoln, had himself witnessed a miracle of bread being broken and flowing with blood, the dough for which had been kneaded on a Sunday. This was taken as a sign of God's displeasure at servile work being done on the Sabbath.[28] Similarly, it was claimed that attempts to fell a tree on a Sunday caused blood to flow from it and that, as the tree was struck, a voice damned the person who had ordered the felling on such a holy day. The young man who cut the tree died very soon afterwards and the monk who had ordered that it should be felled was said to have disappeared without trace.[29] *Jacob's Well* tells of a man who often either missed or was late for Mass and who failed to pay attention when he did attend. When he died and prayers were said for his soul, the crucifix on the funeral bier covered its ears with its hands and a voice from above told the congregation:

> this cursyd man wolde neuere for slauthe heryn my woord, ... [nor] heryn my seruyse in holy cherche deuoutly; ... Therfore, myn ymage on the cros stoppyth his erys, to schewe you that I, god, stoppe myn erys in heuene, that I here no prayere, prayed for hym in holy cherche. Therfore, prayeth no more for hym, for he is dampnyd.[30]

It is important to note, however, that these are all assertions about God's displeasure directed towards people who worked on Sundays or who failed to attend church as they should have done and are not about whether or not people should indulge in recreations once they have fulfilled their religious duties. This is an important distinction.

To what extent did people observe the Church's requirement to keep Sunday and other *festa ferianda*? A fourteenth-century Dominican, John Bromyard, lamented that not only did few people abstain from worldly pursuits on Sundays and holy days, but that they also failed to fulfil their spiritual obligations:

> They get up late, and come late to church, and wish to be so little there, that they will urge the priest to be quick because they have a friend coming to dinner ... Even the short time that they cannot help remaining in the church they spend in unnecessary talk, forgetting that the house of God is the house of prayer. Then they go away to dinner or to the tavern, and there they are in no hurry, for some spend the whole rest of the day and even till late at night, like the Amalecites eating and drinking and as it were keeping a festival day.

Yet, although some people did work on Sundays and holy days in contravention of the Church's teaching, this was not as prevalent a problem as some contemporaries seemed to suggest. Barbara Harvey has shown how, in the eleventh century, *festa ferianda* were marked by virtually complete abstention from servile labour. The economy remained overwhelmingly agrarian in nature throughout the medieval period. Up until the twelfth century, labouring on the land meant that the vast bulk of people were working under conditions of maximum immobility and that the traditional patterns of work and leisure were maintained and respected. However, the subsequent growth of towns led to a change in attitudes. As towns expanded and the labour force became comparatively more mobile, attitudes began to change for a significant section of society. Moreover, the scarcity of labour in the wake of the Black Death forced at least a temporary change in practices.[31] Immediately following the ravages of the Black Death, more work was done on feast days than had previously been countenanced. Despite the exhortations of theologians and moralists, more and more goods were carried on Sundays and feast days, and many Sunday and feast day markets were held.[32] Indeed, a statute of 1402, perhaps both acknowledging and attempting to discourage work on Sundays and other holy days, prohibited the payment of labourers for feast days and vigils.[33] However, it would seem that the old practices of observing *festa ferianda* were soon re-established. Harvey has pointed out that Henry VI's builders at Eton observed much the same holy days as Henry III's men had done when building his palace at Westminster two centuries earlier.[34] She also cites the fact that the local bishop permitted the parishioners of St Dominic, in Cornwall, to move their dedication festival, which fell in the harvest season, to a more convenient date so that they could commemorate it with suitable reverence.[35] Most farmers did largely refrain from working in the field on *festa ferianda* and, even if many craftsmen and shopkeepers worked on the eve of a feast day, they too nonetheless kept the day itself as a holiday.[36]

Non-attendance at church was the most common charge recorded in court records under the category of irreligious behaviour for the years immediately before the English Reformation. Yet such charges were relatively infrequent, suggesting that the day of rest continued to be widely observed. For example, only 26 people were accused of non-attendance in Suffolk in 1499 and only 25 in Hampshire in 1527.[37] Even if this does not reflect the true numbers who failed to attend, it almost certainly indicates that there was no great concern over Sunday trading, otherwise one would expect to find more allegations being made. Certainly, some people did work on *festa ferianda* and they were condemned by churchmen and others for doing so.[38] Although the authorities wanted to prevent people from working on holy days, the moralists were just as concerned about the other activities that people pursued on such days. For them, it was not sufficient for people to stop work, they had also to observe the holy days properly by fulfilling their spiritual duties. Idleness and devoting time to drinking, dancing and playing sports on these enforced days of rest were to be discouraged. Moralists believed that drinking and playing sports could lead to sin, which was even more serious when committed on a holy day. They urged people to reject worldly pastimes and:

> To here goddes serues and the mas,
> And spene [spend] that day in holynes.[39]

Idleness, sports and games: Sunday and holy days outside church

Throughout the late medieval period there was concern about people being idle and about the likelihood that idleness would lead to debauchery, gambling, drinking and crime.[40] In his discussion of sloth, the fourth deadly sin, Mannyng wrote disapprovingly of people who, instead of fulfilling their religious duties on holy days, spent their time eating and gambling:

> Yuf hyt be nat then redy, hys dyner,
> Take furthe the chesse or the tabler;
> So shal he pley tyl hyt be none,
> And Goddys seruyse be al done.
> Alas wykkédly he dyspendyth
> Alle the lyfe that God hum sendyth![41]

Gambling was regarded as pernicious because it led to the sin of covetousness and caused people who were losing money to slander God and his saints. It set a bad example for others and encouraged people to waste their time when they could be doing good works.[42] The many other sports and games that people indulged in on feast days similarly met with disapproval in some quarters. Not only were many associated with gambling, they provided a temptation to miss church services and, with the attendant drinking, could lead people to utter profanities and to become violent.[43] Mannyng condemned dances and summer games for leading people to sin. A Gloucestershire monk preaching in the mid-fifteenth century similarly condemned the 'vain, stupid, profane games' played at midsummer and the attendant heavy drinking.[44]

All manner of sports were played in the late medieval period including football, handball, tennis, bowling, archery, wrestling, quoits and running. People would also amuse themselves through singing, dancing, leaping and vaulting, as well as by playing a variety of board games including chess and backgammon, or 'tables,' and other games of chance such as dice and cards.[45] Bull- and bear-baiting were also common, as was cock fighting. Sports such as archery, running and wrestling were seen to have some military benefit because they kept men fit and prepared for war. For this reason, the practice of archery was positively encouraged by the state. Practising archery was not criticised by the moralists, but many other sports were frowned upon by writers like Mannyng who thought they distracted people from the proper observance of holy days. For, it was indeed on Sundays and holy days that people had the greatest opportunity to play sports.

Holy days occurred throughout the year, with most of the major feasts falling between December and June. These provided opportunities for celebration and for the pursuit of various sports and games. In addition, the summer months of May, June and July afforded the opportunity for parishes across the country to hold festivities and communal celebrations. Some parishes celebrated on May Day itself. Many others held festivities on different dates during the course of the following two months.[46] Even when held in June or July, these celebrations were sometimes known as 'May-ales' or 'May games', but they were also often called 'summer games' or 'church ales'. An 'ale' usually denoted a festival held, partially at least, in order to raise funds. Church ales were among the most common type of ale. They were organised by churchwardens and were principally designed, as the name suggests, in order to raise money for the upkeep and repair of the parish church. Indeed, they were an important source of income for parish churches and could raise considerable amounts. In the early sixteenth century in Stogursey in Somerset the Whitsun church ale raised more than £6 a year.[47] Bride-ales were also held to raise money for newly-weds, and help-ales would often be held to raise funds for someone who had fallen on hard times.[48] Scot-ales were another form of ale held to raise money for the community but, unlike church ales, it seems that most scot-ales carried some form of compulsion to contribute.[49]

A strong ale would be brewed for these occasions and, in the case of church ales, the parishioners would buy the ale and drink it, with the profit on each sale going into the parish coffers.[50] In addition to providing ale at these events, parishioners were often also offered meat, cheese, eggs and other food.[51] Indeed, it is clear that, although many people attended the various types of 'charity ale' in order to contribute money to the church or other worthy causes, people also went to socialise: to drink, eat, dance and play games.[52] The church ale was an important opportunity for a communal celebration, often helping to reinforce neighbourly bonds and social relationships.[53] Some parishes appear not to have held such events at all, but the surviving evidence suggests that the vast majority of rural parishes did so. Many parishes held a church ale every year, while some only did so in years when money was needed for a specific purpose.[54] Others held ales frequently. For example, in Elverton and Okebrook in Derbyshire there were as many as four church ales a year.[55] Ales were most popular in rural areas, but rarely held in towns.[56]

Whereas bid-ales and help-ales were generally informal and held when good weather could be expected, church ales tended to be larger affairs and were often held at Whitsun or on Easter Sunday itself.[57] Consequently, they were sometimes referred to as 'Whitsun-ales' or 'Easter-ales'.[58] Often called a 'church ale' and sometimes referred to as a 'wake,' a communal feast was held in many parishes to commemorate the dedication day of the parish church. These could be held on the actual dedication day of the church in honour of its patron saint or on the Sunday nearest to the relevant saint's day. However, where the saint's day was later in the year, wakes and church ales were most often held sometime between Easter and the end of summer, although they could take place at any convenient time when money was needed for the church.[59]

Ales and wakes had, then, both secular and religious dimensions. They were often used to raise money for the church and to commemorate its dedication day. Usually held on Sundays and other holy days, they also took place on important feast days such as Easter Sunday and Whitsun, or Pentecost, Sunday. But they were also important social occasions when parishioners could meet, drink and play sports together. Thus, they both had a religious significance and afforded an opportunity for substantial merry-making. A number of drinking cups from the period illustrate how these secular and religious aspects overlapped. For example, one cup has the following couplet inscribed around its rim:

> In the name of the Trinitie
> Fill the kup and drinke to me.

Another says:

> Sayn denis yt es me dere
> For hes lof drenk and mak gud cher.[60]

By the end of the fifteenth century church ales were a regular method of raising funds in most parishes, and they were well-attended and popular.[61] They were occasions for people to play games and drink, often to excess. Indeed, people frequently got drunk at such events. The fifteenth-century ballad, *Romance of Merline*, speaks of a woman who:

> With neighbours to the ale went,
> Long she sat and did amiss
> That drunken she was I wiss.[62]

Fuelled by drink, violence and crime would often follow.[63] Indeed, although we are forced to rely principally on court records for evidence, it is clear that the mixture of alcohol and aggressive sport often resulted in injuries and even deaths. A study investigating 66 thirteenth-century court cases involving crimes connected to sport and recreation found that as many as 51 involved the death of one or more of the participants or spectators.[64] Although it is impossible to determine how representative such cases were of people's behaviour at ales and wakes, such instances clearly fed the concern of many in authority that these events could lead to disorder.

Given that heavy drinking was common at such events, and the fact that ales and wakes were usually held in either the church-house or the churchyard, and sometimes even in the church itself, they were severely disapproved of by many moralists.[65] Since they were mostly held on Sundays and other holy days, when people could have been devoting their time to matters spiritual, the playing of sports, dancing and drinking was the source of much indignation among such moralists. Some sneered at the fact that ales were supposedly held for charitable purposes, claiming that this was just a mask for ill-living and merry-making. Although they were often genuinely used to raise money for the local church, some churchmen objected to their abuse. In 1257, for example, the Bishop of Salisbury condemned as immoral any gathering of ten or more men for drinking, observing that such drinking bouts were sometimes given a veil of respectability 'by a change of name called charity scot-ales'.[66] Even seemingly straightforward games which did not involving gambling met with disapproval as they too could cause people to utter scandalous oaths, speak ill of others and profane the holy day.[67] Mirk condemned people:

> For schotynge, for wrastelynge & other play,
> For goynge to the ale on halyday,
> For syngyne, for roytynge & such fare,
> That ofte the sowle doth myche care.[68]

The author of *Jacob's Well* similarly rebuked those who misspent their time in 'ydell dedys', and condemned people who 'gon to wakys & to wrestlynges, to daunsynges ... to reuell ... on the holy-dayes'.[69] In *Handlyng Synne*, Mannyng asserted that:

> Halyday was made for preyere,
> ... Yyf thou euer ...
> Hauntust tauerne, or were to any pere
> To pley at the ches or at the tablere,
> Specyaly before the noun
> whan goddys seruyse owyth to be doun
> Hyt ys agens the comaundment
> And holy cherches asent.[70]

One medieval preacher complained that, no sooner was Mass finished on a Sunday or other holy day, than people would be:

Soone aftir at the ale, bollynge and synginge, with many idil wordis, as lesynggis, bacbitinggis, and scornyngis, ... with al the countenaunce of lecherie, chidingis, and figtingis, with many other synnes; makinge the holi daye a synful daye. And so it semeth now a daies that the holi daye may be clepid [called] the sory day. For of alle the daies in the yeer, the holidayes ben moost cursidli dispensid in the develis servyce in dispite of God, and alle his seyntis in hevene ... It is wondre that god suffrith the peple to lyve up on erthe.[71]

Moralists demanded that the laity should attend Mass and, thereafter, should continue to keep the Sabbath holy. People were called on to repeat the sermon to household members who had been unable to go to the service themselves and to spend the day doing other good deeds. They were not to spend the rest of the day in idle sport:

> men schulde not be idil, but as besi on the holi day about the soule, as men ben on the werk day about the bodi.[72]

There was particular concern that the enticement of drinking and playing sports on the day of rest from work might encourage people to miss divine service altogether. In *Jacob's Well*, for example, the failure to hear divine service in favour of such pursuits was denounced as 'poisoning people in sloth'.[73] In 1447 the Bishop of Exeter complained of youths playing games around the Cathedral, especially when they did so 'in tyme of dyvyne service'.[74] Between 1527 and 1530 a number of people were brought before the court in the manor of Amberley, West Sussex, for encouraging immorality by allowing people to play quoits during the time of divine service and permitting people to play bowls and tennis during vespers.[75] *Handlyng Synne* asserted that it was forbidden to play such games 'whyle the prest stondeth at messe'.[76] Yet, it is important to note that in all these instances the authorities were concerned with the fact that the use of recreations was either preventing people from attending church or was interrupting church services for others. They do not appear to be concerned with the use of recreations *per se*, but merely with the fact that they were sometimes preventing people from attending divine service. They were not demonstrating the sabbatarian views that were to be espoused by later puritan sabbatarians.[77]

Nonetheless, moves were made to protect the sanctity of the church and to prevent secular recreation compromising that sanctity. It was a common practice to hold church ales and wakes in the churchyard or in the church-house, which was often within the enclosure of the churchyard.[78] Some ales and games were even held in the church itself.[79] Edward I had passed a statute commanding that 'neither Fairs nor Markets be kept in Church-Yards for the Honour of the Church'.[80] The holding of sports and ales within the consecrated grounds of the church offended moralists such as Mirk, who insisted:

> Also wyth-ynne chyrche & chyrchhay
> Do rygt thus as I the say;
> Songe and cry and such fare,

> For to stynte thow schalt not spare;
> Castynge of axtre & eke of ston,
> Sofere hem there to vse non.
> Bal and bares and suche play,
> Out of chyrcheyorde put a-way;
> ... For cryst hym-self techeth vs
> That holy chyrche ys hys hows
> That ys made for no thynge elles
> But for to praye In, as the boke telles.[81]

Mannyng similarly complained that it was sacrilegious to hold 'swyche shames' as wrestling and summer games in the church and churchyard.[82] In 1287 the Bishop of Exeter ordered that 'no one should presume to carry on wrestling, dances or other improper sports in churchyards'.[83] It is important to note here that the bishop wanted to prevent such activities taking place in churchyards and was against 'improper' sports; he was not trying to prevent sports taking place on Sundays altogether and, presumably, in banning 'improper' sports, he was content for archery to continue. Others insisted that people should 'make no jangeling, rowning [chattering], no cry, no din in church nor in churchyard ... no dances, no worldly songs, no interludes, no castings of the stone, steracles [performances], no playing at the ball, nor other idle japes and plays.'[84]

The suppression of games and sports

The playing of sports on *festa ferianda* clearly offended medieval moralists, but attempts to suppress recreations were often the product of secular concerns about social order rather than a response to moralistic outrage. Indeed, the attempts to suppress a wide variety of sports are very instructive. They suggest that secular motives and concern about possible disorder lay behind the outlawing of certain games rather than religious concerns that people should observe holy days properly. They also indicate that many sports continued to be practised and enjoyed by a large section of the population, despite legislation against them and despite the condemnation of theologians.

As early as the reign of Edward III, the Crown attempted to force all able-bodied men to use their holiday leisure to good purpose by stipulating that they should practise archery on Sunday and other holy days. In a royal proclamation of 1365 they were forbidden 'to meddle in hurling of stones, loggats and quoits, handball, football, club ball, cambuc, cock fighting or other vain games of no value'.[85] It is clear that the proclamation was not motivated by worries about prophaning the sabbath or other holy days. Rather it was born out of a concern that English men should maintain the archery skills that had brought England victory on the battle field and which were vital to the country's defence. Rather than setting aside holy days exclusively for worship, men were required to use such days to practise their archery. In 1388, Edward's successor, Richard II, made these requirements statutory when he passed an Act which ordered that:

> Servants and Labourers shall have Bows and Arrows, and use the same the Sundays and Holydays, and leave all playing at Tennis or Football, and other Games called Coits, Dice, Casting of the Stone, Kailes [skittles], and other such importune Games.[86]

Thereafter, a succession of proclamations were made and acts passed ordering men not to play such games, and to use Sundays and other feast days to practise their archery.[87] Numerous proclamations and acts emphasised the importance of archery, 'whiche is & hathe ben a greate suertie & defence of this realme'.[88] In 1514, for example, Henry VIII enacted a statute which reminded people that:

> by the fete & exercise of the subjettys of thys ... Realme in shotyng in long bowes ther hath contynually growen & bene wythin the same grete noumber & multytude of good Archars whych hath not only defendyd this realme & the subjectys thereof ... but also wyth lytell noumbre and puyssance in regard have done many noble actys & dyscomfytures of Warre agaynst the infydeles & other, And furthermore subdued and reducyd dyvers & many regyons & countrees to their due obeysaunce to the grete honour fame & surety of thys Realme.[89]

Proclamations and acts repeatedly expressed fears that archery was being neglected and at risk of being 'for evermore ... decayed and destroyed'.[90] Consequently, again and again, the government outlawed all manner of games including tennis, closh, quoits and various games of chance. Most of them specifically cited the promotion of archery as the reason for outlawing such games. Only the 1477 statute of Edward IV and Henry VIII's act of 1514 referred to the playing of such games as profaning holy days.[91] Edward IV's statute spoke of people who played a variety of unlawful games such as 'Closh, Kailes, Half-Bowl' and 'Queckboard' as being: 'such evil disposed Persons that doubt not to offend God in not observing their Holy Days'.[92] Yet even this statute ordered that every able-bodied man 'should use his bow' instead of playing such games, suggesting that keeping feast days holy was not its primary concern. Moreover, it cited other, purely secular reasons for outlawing other sports. Many of these sports led to gambling and thus, the statute claimed, impoverished people. People frequently gambled on the outcome of tennis matches. There was a fear that consequent gambling losses could induce some people to turn to crime in order to obtain the resources needed to pay off debts.[93] Indeed, the statute asserted that 'many Murders, Robberies, and other heinous Felonies' were linked to such activities.[94] In attacking worldly pursuits on holy days, theologians themselves also often linked drinking and sports to violence and crime. Even though Edward IV's statute referred to the observance of holy days, it is clear that it was nonetheless mainly concerned with the secular consequences of playing unlawful games: the neglect of archery and the risks of impoverishment, leading to crime. The 1514 act referred to the 'hygh displeasure of Almyghty God' being incurred by those who played unlawful games and did not hear 'the devyne servyce ... on holy and festivall dayes'. However, it too referred to the fact that 'Impoverysshment hath ensued and many heynous murders robberies & felonys' and concentrated on the neglect of archery.[95] Certainly, all the other proclamations and statutes which concerned themselves with unlawful games appear to have done so for purely secular reasons. Apart from the 1477 and 1514 statutes, no others referred to the observance of holy days.

That said, those secular reasons were not as straightforward as they might at first appear. Many of the proclamations and acts referred specifically to 'servants,' 'labourers' and 'apprentices'.[96] Indeed, the actions of young people, including apprentices and servants, were examined particularly closely when it came to jurors deciding whether to report offences.[97] This appears to have been due largely to concern over how they spent their free time and, more especially, to fears about the risks of disorder following drinking and gambling. Such concerns – again, secular and practical more than religious – were clearly enunciated in the act of 1477. The crown, jurors and local officials were all concerned that servants and the labouring poor should not squander their resources on alcohol or gambling.[98] Drunkenness could lead to violence and, in any event, might result in people being incapable of work.[99] Injury in sport might similarly lead to an incapacity to work. Worse still, loss of money through gambling could encourage young men to turn to crime and even to steal from their masters in order to get the necessary money to pay back creditors.[100] At least part of the motivation behind the moves to suppress games was, therefore, to prevent disorder and to control the activities of young people. More specifically, in the words of the Bishop of Exeter, who complained in 1477 of sports being played during divine service, people in authority were concerned to control the activities of the 'yong people of the ... comminalte'.[101] Several kings, including Henry VII and Henry VIII, themselves enjoyed playing tennis, but they clearly did not want the ordinary people to indulge in the game. Moves against sports were therefore, in part at least, attempts to keep people in their place.

The enduring popularity of sports

Despite the views expressed in *Handlyng Synne* and *Jacob's Well* and by moralists such as Mirk, many priests not only permitted wakes and ales and the playing of sports on *festa ferianda*, but were themselves actively involved in them. Given that so much has to be based on cases that actually reached the courts or on the reactions of those opposed to 'unlawful games,' it is impossible to know with absolute certainty how extensively traditional sports and pastimes were pursued. Nonetheless, it is clear that many clergymen both encouraged and participated in sports and games held in May and other festivals. In the thirteenth century, the Bishop of Lincoln criticised priests for encouraging 'games which they call the bringing-in of summer and autumn'.[102] Although it is doubtful that his disapproval extended to archery, he clearly disapproved of May games and such like and felt the need to try to stop his clergy from condoning them. That Mirk felt it necessary to tell priests that they had to forego 'hawkyng, huntynge and dawnsynge,' and not get involved in 'Wrastelynge & schotynge & such man*er* game,' again suggests that many priests were indulging in such activities.[103]

Proclamations had to be made repeatedly and numerous acts had to be passed ordering men to desist from 'unlawful games' and to practise their archery. This itself is a powerful indication that archery was indeed being neglected and that many people continued to spend their Sundays and holy days playing a wide range of sports and games, despite laws to the contrary. Henry VIII's proclamation of May 1526 itself acknowledged that the many 'good acts and provisions for longbows and archery notwithstanding, ... unlawful games be ... continually used and exercised in this realm'.[104] When the Bishop of Exeter complained of the unlawful games played by young people in the Cathedral cloister, the Mayor of Exeter replied that playing ball in churchyards and other ecclesiastical places was common elsewhere.[105] The continuing need for statutes outlawing games and the comments of the Mayor of Exeter illustrate that, despite such measures and despite the condemnation of moralists, the popularity of these games persisted. Theologians had criticised popular culture since the earliest days of the Church. The fact that such condemnation continued throughout the Middle Ages merely serves to highlight the remarkable resilience of that culture and the popularity of sports and of wakes and ales.[106] Indeed, the fact that so many wakes and ales continued to be held in this period and that the majority of them appear to have been held in the church-house or in the churchyard suggests that, while a number of moralists did speak out against them, large numbers of priests and churchwardens gave indirect if not explicit support to the celebrations and sports enjoyed by large sections of the populace on Sundays and holy days. Despite condemnation from some churchmen, the late medieval Church tolerated traditional revels and festivity provided that church services were not disrupted and that the sanctity of church buildings and churchyards was generally respected.[107] Similarly, secular authority neither espoused nor sought to enforce strict sabbatarianism in pre-Reformation England. The sabbatarianism of later puritans was not a mainstream principle of the medieval Church and it did not enjoy the long pedigree that they were later to claim.

2

The impact of the break with Rome

The concerns voiced by late medieval moralists over how the sabbath should be observed found considerably greater expression during the course of the sixteenth century. This was due, in large part, to the emergence of English puritanism in the final decades of the century when a new, fundamentalist form of sabbatarianism emerged. To understand these developments and the impact of puritan sabbatarianism it is important to first examine the impact of the break with Rome and the early English Reformation, and the changing attitudes to the Sabbath and holy days and to traditional festivity. The mid-Tudor period was a time of momentous change and a time of considerable instability: there were fundamental and unsettling reversals in religious policy coupled with an increased threat of disorder and rebellion. Consequently, both because of changing religious attitudes and because of anxieties about social order, traditional pastimes became a major focus of concern.

The status of Sunday in Henrician, Edwardian and Marian England

Many early Protestant reformers challenged the Catholic Church's teaching on the Sabbath. They claimed that the fourth commandment applied to the Jewish Sabbath only and that the Catholic Church was wrong to teach that Christians should sanctify Sunday in the same way: by setting it apart and fulfilling spiritual duties prescribed by the Church of Rome. Luther declared: 'If anyone sets up the observance of Sunday upon a Jewish foundation, then I order you to work on it, to ride on it, to dance on it, to feast on it.'[1] Instead of treating the fourth commandment literally, Luther applied an allegorical interpretation, claiming that Christians should internalise the Sabbath and rest from sin every single day. Although Calvin also rejected Catholic teaching on the Sabbath and claimed that God required people to rest from sin at all times rather than superstitiously observe a specific day of rest, he nonetheless maintained that it was practical for Christians to set aside a particular time to worship collectively. He therefore saw merit in appointing a day in the week for such worship. Yet, while he acknowledged that Sunday was designated as the Lord's Day to commemorate the day of Christ's resurrection, for him there was no obligation to keep Sunday as the day of worship.[2] The English reformer, William Tyndale, similarly rejected the concept that Christians were morally bound by any day, declaring:

> We be Lordes over the Saboth and may yet chaunge it into the monday or any other day, as we see neede ... Neither was there any cause to chaunge it from Saterday then to put difference betwene us and the Jews, and least we should become servauntes unto the day after their superstition. Neyther needed we any holyday at all, if the people myght be taught without it.[3]

Henry VIII's break with Rome was made for political rather than religious reasons. Henry was a religious conservative: reluctant to make sweeping changes to religious rituals and customs and averse to embracing the teachings of the Protestant reformers. Nonetheless, under Henry the Church's teachings concerning Sunday and holy days of obligation were modified. Indeed, as early as 1536, in his first injunctions as head of the Church, Henry responded to complaints in the Commons about the excessive number of holy days and to claims that they encouraged idleness, riot and excess. He abolished a large number of holy days and ordered that all dedication feasts of parish churches should be held on the first Sunday in October. Although many wakes were already held on this day, many more took place at other times during the summer months, providing the opportunity for neighbouring parishes to reciprocate hospitality and entertainment. The 1536 articles prohibited such festivities and any rest from labour during the harvest period, from the beginning of July through to the end of September, except on Sundays and four dates dedicated to the Virgin Mary and the apostles. Yet, in spite of this injunction, wakes continued to be held during these months and, as the Bishop of Exeter complained in 1539, many labourers continued to refrain from working on saints' days.[4] The Pilgrimage of Grace and the serious threat that it had posed to Henry may have made him reluctant to enforce the 1536 injunctions. In any event, wakes continued to be held in the summer months and Henry's order against them appears to have been largely ignored.

The Church and Crown nonetheless continued to address the question of Sunday observance and the nature of the Sabbath in greater detail. In 1539 Convocation issued a book of ceremonies, which stipulated that:

> Sundays are to be continued and employed in the service of God, to hear the word preached, to give thanks for the benefits which

we receive daily. And that day is much to be regarded, ... it is a memorial of Christ's resurrection: whereby we ought to be stirred to rest our minds from earthly things to heavenly contemplations of Christ's glorified nature[5]

1543 saw the publication of *A Necessary Doctrine and Erudition for any Christian Man*, popularly known as *The King's Book*.[6] This claimed that the ten commandments were moral commandments that were binding on both Jews and Christians alike, save for the fourth commandment which was partly ceremonial and only partly moral. It declared that the requirement to rest from bodily labour on the seventh day was only ceremonial and applied exclusively to the Jews. Yet, the commandment was morally binding insofar as it provided for a perpetual spiritual rest from sin. *The King's Book* stated that:

as concernyng the spirituall rest ... that is to saye, reste frome the carnall workes of the fleshe, and all maner of synne, this precept is morall, and remayneth styll, and byndeth them that belong unto Christe: and not for every seventh day onely, but for all dayes, houres, and tymes. For at all tymes we be bounde to rest, from fulfyllynge of oure owne carnall wylle and pleasure, and from all synes and euyll desires[7]

In speaking of a spiritual rest from sin, *The King's Book* therefore adopted a position similar to that of the early reformers. In doing so, it also rejected the concept that was to be so fundamental to later puritan belief: that the fourth commandment was literally binding on all Christians. It did, however, steer something of a middle course in that, having repudiated the morally binding nature of the Sabbath, it nonetheless went on to advance the traditional idea that the Church had ordained that Sunday should be devoted wholly to God's service through church attendance, public and private prayer, visiting the sick, instructing children in the faith and in other pious works. It declared that Saturday, the Jewish Sabbath, had been succeeded by Sunday in commemoration of Christ's resurrection. Furthermore, it stated that there were 'many other holy & festivall daies, which the church hath ordained, from tyme to tyme'. Christians should devote these days, like Sundays, entirely to worship and spiritual works. *The King's Book* therefore specifically retained the custom of observing holy days appointed by the Church, although it warned against becoming overly superstitious about such observance and expressly permitted works of necessity on Sundays and holy days. These included working to save corn or cattle that were in danger of destruction and fighting for king and country when commanded to do so. However, although it permitted necessary work it expressly prohibited Sunday pastimes, declaring that people who '(as is commonly used) passe the tyme, either in idelnes, in glotony, in ryot, or other vaine, or idel pastime, do breake this commandement'. Indeed, it held that it was preferable for men to labour in the fields on Sundays rather than to be idle at home and for women to spin wool rather than 'to lose their tyme in leapyng or daunsyng, and other ydell wantonness'. This represented a departure from the old traditions in that, despite the fact that pastimes had been commonly used on Sundays and holy days, such pastimes were now condemned to the extent that even ordinary work was preferable to them.[8]

Sunday pastimes were further condemned in Edward VI's injunctions of 1547. These referred to Sunday as 'the holy day' and declared that it was 'at first beginning, godly instituted and ordained, that the people should that day give themselves wholly to God'. Underlining the regime's desire to introduce godly reforms, it stated that:

> whereas in our time, God is more offended than pleased, more dishonoured that honoured, upon the holy day, because of idleness, pride, drunkenness, quarrelling, and brawling, which are most used in such days ... therefore all the king's faithful and loving subjects shall from henceforth celebrate and keep their holy day according to God's holy will and pleasure.

It is clear from this that *The King's Book* had not succeeded in altering the way in which many people spent their Sundays. Thus the people were again enjoined to spend the day in attending church, hearing God's word, praying, receiving the sacraments and in visiting the sick. Although Sunday was to be devoted entirely to God, the injunctions nonetheless allowed for working during harvest time on Sunday and holy days. In permitting this, the injunctions pointedly rejected Catholic teaching against labouring on these days by stating that:

> if, for any scrupulosity or grudge of conscience, men should superstitiously abstain from working upon these days, ... they should grievously offend and displease God.[9]

Writing in 1549, John Hooper – a hard-line Protestant who had been in exile, had returned to England on the death of Henry VIII and who later became Bishop of Gloucester under Edward VI – stated that, through the words of Saint Paul, God had expressly commanded that Christians should observe Sunday as their Sabbath. Hooper maintained that those who failed to devote the day wholly to God were breaking the fourth commandment and condemned those who revelled on the Lord's Day, stating that it was:

to breeke the Sabboth not to ceasse from doing of ile, but to abuse the rest, and eace of the Sabboth, in sporties, games, and pastimes, keeping of merkettes, and feres upon the Sabbothe is to abuse the Sabboth.[10]

In 1552 an *Act for keeping Holy and Fasting Days* emphasised that certain days were appointed as holy days for the sole purpose of honouring God and edifying the people:

> this is to say, separated from all profane use, and dedicated and appointed, not unto any saint or creature, but only unto God and his true worship.[11]

It expressly stated that the time and number of holy days was not prescribed by Scripture, but was the prerogative of the Church to determine. It ordained that the approved holy days comprised every Sunday in the year plus twenty-seven additional holy days. Although it had forbidden the 'profane use' of such days and required people to abstain from bodily labour, it nonetheless declared that:

> it shall be lawful to every ... person or persons, of what estate, degree, or condition he or they may be, upon the holy days aforesaid; in harvest or at any other time of the year when necessity shall require, to labour, to ride, fish or work, any kind of work, at their free wills and pleasure.[12]

It is clear from the Edwardian legislation that, while the regime wanted to put an end to the veneration of saints and to what it saw as the superstitious celebration of many holy days, it also wanted to ensure that Sunday was properly observed. Indeed, although it had long been the teaching of the Church that the laity should attend church on Sundays and holy days of obligation, under Edward VI's second Act of Uniformity they were for the first time required to do so by law. This statutory requirement underscored the Christian's duty to devote Sunday to God's worship, but it also sought to ensure that people attended the parish church at least once a week. Thus, they would be exposed to the new religion: a church service in English and the preaching of the Protestant faith.

Mary I succeeded to the throne determined to re-establish the Catholic Faith within England and, by the time of the dissolution of her first parliament in December 1553, Edward's religious legislation had been repealed, including the 1552 Act of Uniformity and the legal requirement to attend church on Sundays. Protestant services ceased to be legal on 20 December 1553.[13]

Sports and pastimes in Henrician, Edwardian and Marian England

Given the Henrician and Edwardian legislation relating to the status and observing of Sundays and holy days, what were the attitudes and practice of both officialdom and people concerning Sunday pastimes during this period?

As in medieval times, the majority of people had no time for recreation except on Sundays and holy days. For most people, Sunday was the day after pay-day and their only free day of the week.[14] With the reduction in the number of holy days, Sunday became *the* day of leisure to an even greater extent than it had been before. Consequently, people sought to make the most of it. It was the usual day for stage plays and bear-baitings and was also the day when people would go drinking in alehouses and pursue a wide range of recreations.[15]

A series of statutes and proclamations had long prohibited servants and labourers from indulging in various sports in an attempt both to encourage able-bodied men to spend their Sunday afternoons practising archery and to prevent gambling and disorderly behaviour. In 1541 another act was passed, which claimed that the playing of a wide variety of games, including new games invented in order to frustrate the intentions of the earlier statutes, had resulted in archery becoming 'sore decayed'. The statute claimed that the sidelining of archery in favour of other, more popular sports was putting bowyers and fletchers out of work and forcing them to seek employment in other countries, where they were passing on their skills to potential enemies to the detriment of the realm. It further stated that the gambling associated with the playing of unlawful games had impoverished people and led them to commit acts of robbery and murder. Moreover, it claimed that the such games enticed people away from attending church and had led to 'the devyne service of God by such misdoers and holye and festyvall dayes nor heard or solemnpnized, to the high displeasure of Almyghtie God'. Although this statute – like Henry VIII's earlier statute of 1514 – spoke of God's displeasure at the failure to solemnise Sundays and holy days, it referred specifically to the fact that the playing of sports kept people from hearing divine service on those days. It was the failure to go to church that was principally objected to. Sports were not condemned as profanations in themselves.[16] The Act was not a piece of sabbatarian legislation; it was primarily concerned with secular issues surrounding unlawful games: their tendency to impoverish people and lead them into crime and the fact that archery practice was being neglected.

The Act required able-bodied adult males to practise archery and to keep a longbow and arrows in their houses. Fathers of boys aged between seven and seventeen also had to provide them with a bow and arrows and to 'bringe them upp in shotinge'. The Act prohibited anyone from keeping a house, garden or alley where unlawful games were played and listed the prohibited games as including bowls, quoits, closh, kailes (nine pins), loggats (the same as nine pins, but using bones), half-bowl, tennis, dice, cards, tables (backgammon) and 'any unlawful newe game' which might be subsequently invented to bypass the statute. Whereas previous acts had banned servants, apprentices and labourers from playing such sports, the scope of this act was widened to embrace a broader range of occupations, including artificers, husbandmen, mariners, fishermen, watermen and any servingmen. Thus, the vast majority of adult males were prohibited from playing nearly every conceivable game – except archery – at all times and in all places, with the exception of Christmas time when they were allowed to play games in their master's house provided they had his permission. Only noblemen and gentlemen who had property with a yearly value of £100 or more could licence the playing of cards, dice, tables, bowls or tennis within the confines of their own houses, gardens or orchards.[17]

Despite its provisions and despite heavy fines for breaching the statute, the 1541 Act was no more successful than earlier statutes had been in preventing people from playing unlawful games in their free time. It was equally unsuccessful in halting the decline of archery. As the need for repeated legislation promoting it demonstrates, the practice of archery had been much neglected for generations, and during the mid-late sixteenth century it went into permanent decline. Archery had a proud history and the skill of English archers had been central to many historic military victories in previous centuries. It was therefore regarded as essential for men to maintain their archery skills and thereby keep themselves fit for war. England's historic victory at Agincourt back in 1415 had raised English archery to almost mythical status and a nostalgic attitude towards archery had persisted long after it had ceased to be of any real military significance.[18] It had therefore been common for churchwardens to erect butts for parishioners to practise archery after Sunday service, with the clergy often sanctioning it by their presence and frequently taking part themselves.[19]

Although the gun as a weapon of war soon displaced the bow and arrow, many in England remained reluctant to acknowledge that its day had passed. Writers such as Thomas Elyot and Roger Ascham continued passionately to advocate the practice of archery. Elyot maintained that no other form of exercise could compare to archery, which made men fit and strong and was better exercise than tennis, bowling, pins or any other sport.[20] Ascham wrote a whole treatise on archery in which he enthusiastically lauded its benefits, claiming that it led to bodily health, quickness of mind and the ability to help defend the country.[21] He described it as being 'a pastime holesome and equall for euerye parte of the bodye' and praised the skill of English archers in winning historic victories on the battlefield.[22] Bishop Latimer saw archery as:

a gift of God that he hath given us to excel all other nations withal. It hath been God's instrument whereby he hath given us many victories against our enemies.

Bemoaning the neglect of archery, he added: 'now we have taken up whoring in towns, instead of shooting in the fields.[23] Later, preaching before Edward VI, Latimer commended archery as 'a worthy game, a wholesome kind of exercise, and much commended in physic'.[24] Yet, despite such sentiments, archery continued to decline and the longbow, which had enjoyed an almost mystical place in the national psyche, came to be known disparagingly as the 'country weapon'. The forces mustered in 1588 to combat the threat of a Spanish invasion counted no bowmen at all among the 6,000 trained men and only 800 out of the 4,000 untrained men.[25] In war, the longbow gave way to the gun and, in recreation, it gave way to more fashionable sports.

Among the most popular sports were bowling, tennis, football, dicing, carding, dancing, bear-baitings and cockfights. Bowling had been practised since the Middle Ages, both on greens and in bowling alleys. It was popular at all social levels. Henry VIII had a bowling alley built at his palace of Whitehall while many wealthy people had bowling greens laid down in their gardens.[26] Despite the legislation that prohibited them from playing it, bowling was also widely enjoyed by the lower orders. While many public bowling greens closed in the wake of the 1541 statute, many alehouses had bowling alleys annexed to them and they continued to contravene the act.[27] Whereas the gentry played a rather sedate form of bowls, or lawn bowling, on their bowling greens, these wooden alleys saw a more rowdy sort of game: nine pins or skittles which, Elyot stated, was 'to be utterly abiected of al noble men'.[28] The gambling and unruly behaviour that accompanied these games was a major factor in their prohibition and in the condemnation of them by moralists. Writing in 1550, Robert Crowley attacked the large number of illegal bowling alleys in London and the idle men who frequented them and gambled away their goods, and declared that hell awaited both them and those who failed to close down such places.[29] Nonetheless, despite such condemnation and the laws against it, the popularity of bowling continued to grow, leading Stephen Gosson to complain in 1579 that 'common bowling alleys are privy moths that eat up the credit of many idle citizens'.[30]

Like bowling, tennis was very popular among the nobility and gentry, and Henry VIII, who in his youth was a keen tennis player, had tennis courts built at the palace of Whitehall. Tennis was also fashionable at the universities and in many towns, where a number of public, enclosed courts were built. Again, although the 1541 Act allowed the wealthy to have their own private courts, the legislation provided for fines to be imposed for every day that the public courts remained open.[31] The Act sought to prevent the common people from playing tennis because tennis was the occasion of much gambling. Moreover, as with attempts to suppress other popular sports, the prohibition of tennis playing among the commonality was also designed to reinforce the social hierarchy and to keep people in their place. Certain games were deemed to be the prerogative of the higher social classes. A strictly hierarchical society demanded a hierarchy of pastimes, with certain games being deemed unsuitable for the lower orders.[32]

One sport that was exclusive to the lower classes was football. Football had little in common with today's game. It was a mass ball-game with virtually no rules and with no limit to the number of players on either side. Whole villages or sizeable teams from rival parts of a single parish would challenge each other to what was frequently an extremely rough contest, which, if it involved neighbouring parishes, often spread out over several miles of countryside. Football could be very violent and frequently resulted in broken limbs, even fatalities. It often led to fierce arguments and fights and was frowned upon by many merchants because the injuries sustained and the disruption it caused often led to working days being lost.[33] It was regarded with contempt by Elyot and the propertied classes generally as:

> nothinge but beastly furie and exstreme violence; whereof procedeth hurte, and consequently rancour and malice do remaine with them that be wounded; wherefore it is to be put in perpetuall silence.[34]

Although football was often played on Sundays, it was traditionally most widely played on Shrove Tuesday. Neither the nobility nor the gentry played it and, although it did sometimes prevent people from attending church services, its designation as an unlawful game was neither primarily an attempt to ensure proper Sabbath observance nor to reinforce social demarcation. Rather, it was prohibited primarily because of the violence associated with it and the consequent anxieties about social disorder.[35]

Animal baiting and cockfights regularly took place on Sundays. These brutal sports were extremely popular and were the occasions of much gambling. The most common form of animal baiting was bear-baiting, but dogs also baited bulls and badgers for public amusement. The widespread nature of this barbarous sport is evidenced by the observation of Erasmus during Henry VIII's reign that there were 'many herds of bears maintained in this country for the purpose of baiting'.[36] Writing towards the end of the sixteenth century, the German traveller, Paul Hentzner, described the gruesome spectacle in which bulls and bears were tied up and then set upon by dogs:

> There is a place built in the form of a theatre, which serves for baiting of bulls and bears; they are fastened behind, and then worried by

great English bull-dogs; but not without risk to the dogs, from the horns of the one and the teeth of the other; and it sometimes happens they are killed on the spot; fresh ones immediately supplied in the places of those that are wounded and tired. To this entertainment there often follows that of whipping a blinded bear, which is performed by five or six men standing circularly with whips, which they exercise upon him without any mercy, as he cannot escape because of his chain; he defends himself with all his force and skill, throwing down all that come within his reach, and are not active enough to get out of it, and tearing the whips out of their hands, and breaking them.

Another observer, Robert Laneham, writing in 1575, described the horror of how:

if [a bear] were bitten in one place ... he would pinch in another to get free; that if he were taken once, then by what shift with biting, with clawing, with roaring, with tossing, and tumbling, he would work and wind himself from them; and when he was loose, to shake his ears twice or thrice with the blood and the slaver hanging about his physiognomy.[37]

While some later Elizabethan moralists were to condemn bear-baiting for its cruelty, in the mid-sixteenth century few acknowledged the barbarity of the sport. Indeed, bear-baitings were popular among the elite as well as the populace at large. Mary I attended a bear-baiting with her husband, Philip of Spain, and when Mary visited her sister, Elizabeth, at Hatfield House, they watched a performance of bear-baiting together after Mass and 'their highnesses were right well content'.[38] Yet, even before the flood of complaint literature in the 1580s, bear-baiting was condemned. Crowley attacked as fools those who squandered their money watching baitings every Sunday when they should have given money to the poor instead.[39]

Cock-fighting and throwing at cocks were other similarly cruel sports which, while popular among the common people, were also enjoyed by the highest in the land, as is evidenced by Henry VIII's building of a cock-pit at his palace of Whitehall.[40] The custom of throwing at cocks involved tying a cock to a post with a rope several feet long and then charging people to throw sticks and cudgels at it until it was killed, with the person administering the fatal blow winning the dead bird. Thomas More boasted, in later years, that he had been skilled at this sport in his childhood.[41] As with many other sports of the day, cockfights and throwing at cocks were intrinsically linked with gambling and could often lead to heated exchanges and violence. Consequently, they were not deemed to be suitable pastimes for the common people and, along with football and many other sports, they were officially classified as unlawful games.

A recurring theme in considering the prohibition of various sports is that of gambling. Gambling among the lower orders was disapproved of by those in authority who feared that servants and workers who lost money through gambling would turn to crime in order to recover their losses. Indeed, the 1541 Act claimed that 'manye haynous murders robberies and fellonyes were committed and done' as a result of the impoverishment caused by gambling over unlawful games.[42] As poverty increased during the sixteenth century, concerns about gaming and its implications for social order also grew. In the sixteenth century the number of court presentments for illegal gambling dramatically increased.[43] Of course, it was not just games associated with gambling which were frowned upon; dicing and cards were themselves understandably attacked and prohibited. These games of chance were expressly forbidden by the 1541 Act, as they had been in earlier statutes.

Dancing was another popular pastime. It was especially practised at ales and wakes, and at May games and summer games generally. Although dancing was not yet attacked as vehemently or as persistently as it was to be later in the century, dancing on Sundays nonetheless came in for criticism. *The King's Book* described dancing as 'idell wantonnesse' and declared that even bodily labour on a Sunday was less sinful than dancing.[44] However, the 1541 statute neither condemned nor prohibited dancing and some people saw merit in dancing as a good, wholesome recreation.[45] In any event, dancing on Sundays after church remained a popular pastime despite censure from some quarters.

Ales, wakes and May games continued to be popular well into the sixteenth century; and Henry VIII's attempt to move all wakes to the first Sunday in October was a dismal failure. However, during the reign of Edward VI the number of summer games across the country did diminish dramatically. Although neither the government nor the Church hierarchy issued any formal orders against such festivities, there is some evidence of official hostility towards them. In 1547 the royal visitors to the West Country banned church ales 'because it hath byn declared unto us that many inconveniencies hath come by them'.[46] As Ronald Hutton observes, the term used is ambiguous and could refer to a religious issue such as a desire to separate profane celebrations from holy places, given that many ales took place in churchyards and church houses. There were certainly concerns that holy places should be properly respected, as Edward's statute against fighting in churches and churchyards demonstrates.[47] However, it seems more likely that the 'inconveniences' reported referred to disturbances and that the move was made as a practical measure to avoid disorder or to prevent assemblies that might breed rebellion.[48] Indeed, even before the Western Rebellion of 1549 there had been disturbances in the West Country in 1547 and 1548, suggesting that the authorities had cause to fear the possible consequences of popular assemblies.[49] It should be noted, too, that Kett's Rebellion in East Anglia began at just such an assembly, when the townspeople of Wymondham in Norfolk gathered together with neighbouring villagers for a performance of a play in the summer of 1549.[50]

Due to the paucity of the surviving evidence it is not clear whether the royal visitors on other circuits adopted a policy on ales similar to the one adopted in the West Country. However, a study of parishes for which comprehensive accounts for this period survive suggests that, whereas ales had been held regularly in parishes across most of southern England in the mid-1540s, after 1549 they occurred in just a handful of communities. This was not true of central Oxfordshire where it would appear that ales continued to flourish, but that may simply be because officials there had a more lenient policy towards them.[51] Elsewhere, Edward's reign saw moves against other traditional celebrations. In 1549, for example, having already encouraged property-owners to discipline servants who attended May games, the Corporation of London issued an order prohibiting youths from attending such games altogether. In the same year a Protestant preacher denounced as an idol the huge maypole that had stood in Cornhill for many years and incited his congregation to destroy it.[52] When, in 1553, a brightly coloured maypole was brought into Fenchurch accompanied by a troupe of morris dancers, the Lord Mayor had the pole cut up.[53] These events demonstrate that some moves were made to suppress May games and the use of maypoles even before they became the objects of vehement puritan attack.

Although traditional festivities clearly declined during Edward's reign, they did not stop altogether. Despite their decline, ales continued to be held in some parishes and, although there were moves to suppress May games and revels in London and elsewhere, it is clear from the writings of John Hooper, from Edward's injunctions and from other surviving records that they still took place in various parishes. Moreover, certain aspects of traditional revelry continued to flourish at court where, for example, 'Lords of Misrule' and the use of 'hobby horses' were as popular during Edward's reign as they had been during that of his father. Nonetheless, there was a general stifling of popular celebration, whether through fear of disorder or as part of a move to institute a more godly society. Even as early as 1552 John Caius could look back longingly to 'the old world, when this country was called Merry England'.[54]

With the death of Edward and the restoration of the Catholic faith under Mary, most of the traditional customs enjoyed a complete revival. Church ales, for example, rapidly reappeared across much of England, except in the north-east, where they had never been widely held, and in the south-east of England where radical Protestantism was strongest.[55]

Given that Mary's government did not actively promote these popular festivities, their immediate revival suggests that it had been difficult to hold them under the previous regime. It is also testament to their enduring popularity, and indicates their deep links with the old religion in the minds of the people. On a more practical level, given the importance of ales as a source of revenue for parish funds, their rapid re-emergence may reflect how much they were needed to help to raise funds needed to meet the considerable expense of restoring Catholic worship. Rood screens, altars and tabernacles had been removed from parish churches during Edward's reign, and these now needed replacing together with chalices and vestments.

The restoration of traditional festivity was largely spontaneous and was certainly not official government or Church policy. Indeed in 1554, Mary's Bishop of London, Edmund Bonner, issued Articles for his diocese that opposed both work and recreation on Sundays and holy days and inquired of the London clergy:

> Whether there have been any men, women, or children of the age of fourteen or above, who upon Sundays or holydays have gone a-hunting or hawking, [or to] bear-baiting, games and other plays, [or to] disport or pastimes.[56]

However, the revival of summer games was so marked that it is clear that most bishops did not adopt or enforce Bonner's injunction and traditional pastimes were broadly tolerated.[57] It is true that Mary's Privy Council banned all May games in Kent in 1555, but this was almost certainly because, following Wyatt's rebellion in Kent, the government feared that the convening of large numbers of people at any games ran the risk of occasioning a further instance of rebellion.[58] Indeed, in the same year Mary passed an Act which voided licences granted under Henry VIII's 1541 Act to allow bowling, tennis, dicing and other 'unlawful' games in certain houses across the country on the grounds that:

> divers & many unlawfull Assemblies, Conventicles Sedicions & Conspiracies have & bene daily secretly practised by ydle & misruled person repairing to such places.[59]

Nonetheless, the Privy Council did not issue a national prohibition of the seasonal festivities and, with the exception of Kent, it did not ban ales or Sunday sports.

The mid-Tudor period saw a fluctuation in the use of ales and other traditional revelry and, for a variety of reasons, there were moves to suppress such festivity in certain parts of the country. Such attempts at suppression were clearly often made because of concerns about potential disorder, but some were instigated by reformers seeking to establish a more godly society. Yet, such attempts had little impact at this time. It was during the reign of Elizabeth I that the calls for change increased and reformers began to clamour ever more loudly for the imposition of much stricter Sunday observance.

3

The reign of Elizabeth I and the battle over the Lord's Day

Traditional attitudes to popular festivity and to Sunday observance both came under severe attack during the reign of Elizabeth I, when the very nature of the Sabbath and the question of any form of recreation on Sundays became the focus of an increasing number of radical Protestant polemics. Kenneth Parker has argued that the doctrine of a morally binding Sabbath was well established in England long before the Reformation and that the strident sabbatarianism of many puritans in the 1580s and 1590s was not an innovation but merely an elaboration of established, orthodox thinking regarding the Sabbath.[1] The early Christian Church had indeed taught that the fourth commandment obliged Christians to keep Sunday holy and moralists called for stricter Sabbath observance well before the Reformation. In that sense, the sabbatarianism of the late sixteenth century did have roots in the Middle Ages. However, Parker underestimates the significance of late sixteenth-century puritan sabbatarianism and the extent to which puritans developed and promoted a different type of sabbatarian doctrine.[2] The 1580s and 1590s saw the development of a new, far more fundamentalist sabbatarianism and an outpouring of doctrinal and increasingly polemical works which went much further than the Church's traditional stance. The numerous catechisms and works of complaint literature that poured forth not only turned up the volume of protest against perceived Sabbath profanations, but also set out detailed arguments for the morally binding nature of the fourth commandment. They introduced complex, reasoned theological arguments for the moral imperative of strict Sunday observance, and also argued against the keeping of other holy days on the grounds that, unlike the Sabbath, those days had not been ordained for sanctification by God. In this they departed from pre-Reformation thinking and presented a challenge to the authority of the Church and its right to appoint holy days. They were at odds with the Church hierarchy, which was far more concerned with church attendance than it was with how people spent their day after the service was over.

Recreations and popular pastimes came under more sustained and comprehensive attack than ever before: on both religious and secular grounds. Puritan writers equated popular culture and Sabbath violation with popery and with paganism, and called on lawmakers and law enforcers to stamp out irreligious pastimes and to force people to devote Sundays entirely to God. Attempts to suppress Sunday revels were, in part, also due to increasing anxieties over the possibility of disorder. Concern for social order grew steadily greater towards the end of the sixteenth century as the country experienced rising inflation coupled with significant population growth. This in turn led to a frightening increase in the numbers of people descending into poverty. There was a growing clamour for reforms to control the way that people conducted their lives, and those calls came both from those keen to reform society on religious grounds and from people concerned by the increasing poverty and the threat of disorder that it seemed to presage. Attitudes to the poor and to the concepts of charity and social provision also began to change. Alongside sabbatarian zeal and religious desires for moral reform, these factors played a significant role in leading many JPs and municipal authorities to attempt to restrict popular festivity.

The status of Sunday under Elizabeth I

Elizabeth I's Act of Uniformity (1559) reinstated the legal requirement for people to attend their parish church on Sundays. Elizabeth's injunctions set out the obligations for Sunday observance: namely, that people should attend church and hear the Word of God preached, that they should pray, repent of their sins, receive the sacraments and visit the sick, 'using all soberness and godly conversation'.[3] The Injunctions granted people permission to work on Sundays during harvest time, essentially restating the position set down in the 1547 Injunctions. In 1560 Richard Cox, Bishop of Ely, wrote *Interpretations and Further Considerations of Certain Injunctions*, in which he amplified on Elizabeth's Injunctions by declaring that no shops should be open and no craftsmen should go about their worldly affairs on Sundays. However, he accepted that many fairs and markets were held on Sundays and stipulated only that 'there be no shewing of any wares before the service be done'.[4] It was this concern that people should not miss divine service on Sunday that was most marked in all the pronouncements of the leading Elizabethan clergy. They were far more concerned about this than they were about how people spent the remainder of the Sabbath. Archbishop Parker's Visitation Articles of 1560 enquired of the clergy:

> whether be in your parishes any inn-keeper or ale-wives, that admit any resort to their houses in time of common prayer; any that commonly absent themselves from their own church, or otherwise idly or lewdly profaneth the Sabbath day.[5]

Although Parker's Articles made this rather ambiguous reference to profaning the Sabbath, the emphasis was clearly on ensuring that people attended divine service and that they should not be encouraged to do otherwise.

The *Book of Homilies* that Convocation endorsed in 1563 is unusual in that it is one of the few officially sanctioned publications of Elizabeth's reign that appears to be markedly sabbatarian in content. The book was issued as a collection of homilies to be used by parish clergy who did not have a sermon prepared. The *Homily of the Place and Time of Prayer* held that, in two respects, Christians were not bound to keep the Sabbath as strictly as the Jews were. Firstly, repeating the assertions of *The King's Book* and the Injunctions of 1547 and 1559, it stated that Christians were permitted to work on Sundays in times of great necessity. Secondly, it declared that, although Christians kept the first day, the Sunday, as their Sabbath in honour of Christ's resurrection, in all other respects the fourth commandment applied to Christians and that:

> God hath given expresse charge to al men, that upon the Sabbath daye, whiche is nowe our Sundaye, they shoulde ceasse from all wekely and workeday labour ... Gods obedient people should use the Sunday holyly ... and also give themselves wholly to heavenly exercises of Gods true religion and service.[6]

It went on to condemn the 'wicked boldness' of those Christians who failed to hallow Sunday by either working on Sundays without necessity or giving themselves over to their own pleasures and diversions instead of devoting the day to God. Indeed, the *Homily* declared that those who pursued their own amusement were worse transgressors than those who worked on the Sabbath because:

> they wyll not rest in holyness, as God commaundeth: but they rest in ungodlynesse, and in fylthynes, praunsyng in their pryde, prankyng and prickyng, poyntyng and payntyng themselves, to be gorgeous and gay ... They rest in wantonnesse, in toyishe talkyng, in fylthy fleshlynesse, so that it doth to evidently appeare that God is more dishonoured, and the Devyll better served on the Sunday, then upon al the dayes in the weke beside.[7]

The *Homily of the Place and Time of Prayer* therefore appears to disapprove of revelry on Sundays. Yet, the homily does not actually prohibit sports, dancing or other Sunday pastimes as such. It is the debauchery and disorder often associated with traditional revelry that is actually being attacked. Furthermore, the criticism of Sunday working and merry-making comprises a very small section of the whole sermon, the vast bulk of which is taken up in exhorting people to go to church on Sundays. The *Homily of the Place and Time of Prayer* has been described as 'an officially sanctioned sabbatarian doctrine' which provided the foundation on which puritans such as Nicholas Bownd subsequently constructed their own uncompromising sabbatarian arguments.[8] Yet, while the homily is disapproving of those who worked and engaged in 'debauchery' on Sundays, such disapproval must be put in context. As the title of the homily makes clear, it is concerned with 'the place and time of prayer' and is given over almost exclusively to the issue of church attendance. It is peppered with references to how people should 'assemble together' in church on Sundays. The very paragraph that attacks those who work or indulge in 'fylthy fleshlynesse' on Sundays speaks of people who 'do not resort together to celebrate and magnifie Gods blessed Name, in quiet holynesse and godlye reverence'. The seemingly unambiguous condemnation of Sunday merry-making is therefore not all that it appears when put in its proper context. The homily is concerned with church-going and it is the hearing of divine service that is stressed. While devoting the day to 'fleshly' pursuits rather than to God is disapproved of, a complete reading of the homily suggests that this is because such pursuits either prevented people from going to church or hindered them from concentrating fully when in church. The sports and festivities that traditionally took place after Sunday service are neither explicitly attacked nor forbidden.

In addition to endorsing the *Book of Homilies*, the Convocation of 1563 also decided that 'there should be authorised one perfect Catechism for the bringing up of the youth in godliness, in the schools of the whole realm' and it subsequently approved *A Catechism* by Alexander Nowell, Dean of St Pauls.[9] Nowell's *Catechism*, which, after several revisions, was finally published in 1570, held that, although the outward rest required by the fourth commandment applied only to the Jews, Christians were perpetually bound by the Commandment to:

> assemble together to hear the doctrine of Christ, to yield confession of their faith, to make openly public prayers to God, to celebrate and retain the memory of God's work and benefits, and to use the mysteries that he hath left us.[10]

Therefore, the catechism again stressed the requirement to attend church. Although Nowell's *Catechism* has been described as a 'source of sabbatarian teaching', it is not strongly sabbatarian in the way that later puritan works were to be.[11] The *Catechism* declared that people should meditate on God's works every day but that 'for our negligence and weakness' sake, one certain day is, by public order, appointed for this matter'. Nowell held that Sunday was ordained for public worship by the Church as a matter of practicality and not by God under the fourth commandment. He stated that men should yield themselves 'wholly to God's governance' and should refrain from working on Sundays, and that servants should be allowed to rest from labour on the Sabbath. The reasons given for providing rest for servants were so that they too could worship and pray and, on a purely practical level, that it was:

> also profitable for the masters themselves that servants should sometimes rest between their workings, that, after respiting their work awhile, they may return more fresh and lusty to it again.[12]

Nowell's catechism required people to 'rest from worldly business' and to 'express a certain form and figure of the spiritual rest' in which:

> we crucify our flesh, we bridle the froward desires and motions of our heart, restraining our own nature, that we may obey the will of God.[13]

Nonetheless, although the catechism called for people to rest from worldly business and set out the necessity for public worship on Sunday, it made no specific reference to Sunday recreations after church. Given also that it stated that Sunday was appointed for public worship 'by public order' it would be wrong to regard Nowell's *Catechism* as an overtly or strongly sabbatarian publication. In endorsing it, the bishops were affirming the requirement of people to refrain from work and to attend church once a week, and the Church's right to appoint the day of worship. They were not adopting a hard-line, stridently sabbatarian doctrine.

It has been argued that the Elizabethan bishops promoted sabbatarian doctrine through the *Homilies*, Nowell's *Catechism*, Bible marginalia and through Visitation Articles, and that this provided the foundation on which later sabbatarians built.[14] This is not the case. The *Homilies*, Parker's Visitation Articles and Cox's *Interpretations* of the Queen's 1559 Injunctions were primarily concerned with church attendance. Furthermore, Nowell's *Catechism* suggested that the Christian's Sunday Sabbath was not divinely instituted but was instead ordained 'by public order'. The Elizabethan episcopacy as a body did not promote a morally-binding Sabbath which demanded that people devote the day wholly to God to the exclusion of everything else. Although, some did have strong sabbatarian beliefs and disapproved of Sunday pastimes, they were in a minority. The few examples of senior churchmen attacking Sunday recreations are found in the later rather than the early Elizabethan period. For example, in 1575 Bishop Cooper of Winchester ordered the suppression of 'church ales, May games, morris dances and other vain pastimes'.[15] In 1584 Cooper again instructed his clergy to ban morris dancing and other 'heathenish and ungodly customs'. Yet, Cooper was responding to a report that they were taking place during divine service and keeping people from church; so it was the issue of church attendance rather than the pastimes themselves that prompted Cooper's order.[16] Indeed, although Cooper did not approve of the likes of morris dancing, he was not against recreations on the Sabbath *per se* and later wrote defending the playing of bowls on Sunday.[17] Of those bishops who did attack games and pastimes, all but two did so either because they were keeping people from church or because they were taking place in the church or churchyard. Archbishop Grindal, for example, prohibited feasts and dances in the church and churchyard and dances, games, piping and plays were subsequently banned in churches and graveyards by the bishops of Winchester, Worcester, Chester, Lichfield, Lincoln, Chichester, Hereford and London and the Archdeacons of Middlesex and Oxford.[18]

Church attendance was important to both the Church and the Crown. Under Edward and Elizabeth it had been made compulsory so that people would hear the Protestant faith preached. It was important to deter recusancy and to convert people to Protestantism. Around 1590, for example, a report commissioned by the Bishop of Chester on conditions in Lancashire, which had the largest proportion of Catholics of any county, complained that:

> the lords daie is generallie prophaned with unlawful trade & marketts, with heathenish and popishe pastimes, some tendinge to the norrishinge of Idolatrous Supersticion, others to increas of horedome & dronkenness, all purposlie maynteyned & countenanced by ye Gentrye and better sortt, for the hinderance & defacying of the Religious & holie excercyses of the Sabaoth.

Both the government and the Church hierarchy were keen to convert Lancashire's many Catholics to Protestantism and to discourage anything that might keep them from attending church.[19] Indeed, in 1592 the Privy Council ordered that 'May gaimes, morryce daunces, plaies, bearebaytinges, ales and other like pastimes' should be banned 'on the Sondaie or Holydaie at the tyme of Divine Service' because they were being used by people who were 'evill affected in religion, purposlie ... to drawe the people from the service of God'.[20] Even if people did not stay away from church because of adherence to the old faith and customs, absenteeism from church increased with the growth of the population as the alehouse became an increasingly attractive alternative meeting place. Others missed church because they were obliged to work on Sundays. Indeed, as many as a fifth of the population in Kent regularly failed to attend church in the late sixteenth century.[21] For the Church hierarchy, therefore, it was the issue of church attendance that was of greatest importance when considering the question of Sabbath observance.

For some, though, pastimes were themselves an issue. For example, even though he did not seek to prevent the laity from attending May games, Richard Barnes, the Bishop of Durham, prohibited his clergy from doing so. Some senior clergymen, such as the Archdeacon of Middlesex, saw 'any kind of work or pastime whatsoever' as a violation of the Lord's Day. Nonetheless, only two Elizabethan bishops condemned traditional festivities outright.[22] Richard Cox of Ely attacked Sunday merry-making, declaring in his 1579 visitation articles:

> Because the Saboth day is so fondly abused ... in feasting and making good chere, in wanton daunsing, in lewd maygames sometyme continuing riotously with Piping all whole nightes in barnes and such odde places, both younge men and women out of their fathers and masters howses, I charge all my parishes within my Dioces, and charge the Churchwardens, Sidemen, and ministers to see that no such disorders be kept upon the Sabaoth day, commonly called the Sundayes.[23]

The only other of Elizabeth's bishops to condemn Sunday pastimes was Coldwell of Salisbury who, in 1595, attacked church ales as 'minstrelsie, daunsing, and drinking, ... under colour thereby to procure some contribution towards the repairing of their church'. He condemned them as 'great abuses in prophaning the Lordes Sabbaoth consecrated wholie to his service' and as a 'great prophanation of that daie and the manifest contempt and dishonour of almightie God'.[24]

Yet, these bishops were unusual. Most other senior churchmen tolerated or even supported traditional pastimes, provided that they did not interfere with church attendance or take place on church property. In 1586, for example, the vice-chancellor and heads of colleges at Cambridge University declared that Sunday sports and plays were lawful provided that they did not hinder religion and they rebuked a minister for preaching against them.[25] In 1602 the vice-chancellor of Oxford argued that the moral obligation to observe the Sabbath only applied to the time spent in divine service and that games and festivities were permitted once the church service was over.[26] None of Elizabeth's bishops published any tracts against traditional merry-making. Indeed, in the early 1590s the queen's most senior cleric, Archbishop Whitgift, paid for a pageant at his palace in Croydon that included scenes of 'Maying' and 'country dances'.[27] Whitgift himself enjoyed playing bowls after church on Sunday afternoons and was even defended in doing so by Bishop Cooper of Winchester, who declared that:

> for your iesting at the Bishop for bowling upon the Sabboth, you must understande that the best expositor of the Sabboth, which is

Christ, hath saide, that the Sabboth was made for man, and not man for the Sabboth: and man may have his meate dressed for his health upon the Sabboth, and why may he not then have some convenient exercise of the body, for the health of the body?[28]

As a body, the Church hierarchy was clearly not sabbatarian. With some notable exceptions, it was tolerant of Sunday pastimes provided that they did not prevent people from attending church and, by so doing, did not challenge the Church's authority. Indeed, contrary to later puritan sabbatarians, who elevated the observance of the Lord's Day and attacked the observance of many other holy days, the Church hierarchy sought to protect its authority by arguing that it maintained the right to establish additional holy days for spiritual labours.[29] Whereas many puritans argued for the right to work on every day except Sunday, senior churchmen sought to prevent people from working on other holy days.[30] Moreover, in 1560 a new list of holy days was issued which was considerably longer than that issued in 1552, even though the requirements concerning observance continued to apply only to the feasts that had been permitted under Edward VI.[31]

As for Elizabeth I herself, while she expected people to attend church services, she was even more relaxed than most of her prelates about how people spent the rest of their Sunday. Unlike her successors, James I and Charles I, Elizabeth chose not to publicly declare her support for lawful Sunday pastimes and thus avoided needlessly antagonising the growing number of rabidly sabbatarian puritans. Nonetheless, through her actions she demonstrated both her support for and her delight in sports and traditional festivities, and provided a poor example of Sabbath observance. Elizabeth enjoyed watching courtiers and servants play tennis, and planned, but never finished, a new tennis court at Windsor.[32] She also had her own bearward and attended bear-baitings throughout her reign both for her own amusement and as entertainment for foreign dignitaries.[33] Furthermore, clearly not sharing the concern of some of her bishops to separate the sacred from the secular, in 1561 the Queen even allowed a wrestling match to take place in her chapel.[34] Elizabeth's Privy Council frequently met on Sundays and, throughout her reign, she enjoyed dancing and watching plays, jousts and other entertainments after Sunday church. In 1575, for example, she visited Kenilworth Castle where, after attending Sunday service, she was entertained with morris dancing, tilting, plays and a banquet.[35] Unlike Edward VI and Mary I, who took no active part in May celebrations, Elizabeth herself loved to dance on May Day and did so well into her old age.[36] In 1589, Elizabeth's Privy Council intervened to stop puritans in Banbury from taking down maypoles and from prohibiting May festivities, declaring that it saw:

noe cause that those pastimes of recreacion, being not used at unlawful tymes as one the Sabboth day in tyme of Dyvyne Service, and in disordered and riotous sorte, should be forbidden the people.[37]

Provided people attended church and did not cause public disorder the Queen and her Privy Council were not hostile to parish revels or to Sunday festivity.

The Queen's support for ales and Sunday revels is further evidenced by her decision in 1569 to grant a licence to a London poulterer who had 'fallen into decay' to organise Sunday sports to raise money for his family. The games which were sanctioned included archery, leaping, running, wrestling, throwing the sledge and pitching the bar, and they were to be held on up to nine separate Sundays.[38] Indeed, the Queen's evident support for Sunday revelry was such that she prompted the puritan, William Fuller, to dare to openly criticise her. In 1586, Fuller complained:

I fear, O gracious sovereign, that your Majesty hath too little used so to sanctify the Lord's Sabbaths; for if you had, things could never have gone on as now they do; and how do your Majesty's people sanctify it? How? Alas, alas, they (by all likelihoods) do without punishment offend God more at that day than in any other day in the week.[39]

In 1572 Elizabeth issued proclamations which repeated her father's prohibition on unlawful games and called for the maintenance of archery.[40] However, these proclamations were not concerned with Sunday observance but were motivated by a concern to avoid gambling among the common people and to avoid the disorder and crime which was frequently associated with such games. Indeed, the licence that the Queen granted to the impecunious poulterer demonstrates not only how popular Sunday sports were, but also, given the large numbers which attended such events, the concerns of those in authority for the maintenance of public order. In granting the licence, Elizabeth instructed the constables of Middlesex 'considering that great resorte of people in lyke to come thereunto' to ensure 'the preservation of the quene's majestie's peace'.[41] In 1578 the Privy Council instructed JPs in Cheshire to ban the holding of wakes, where 'people doe assemble them selves under pretence of chering and feasting ... where they doe for the moste parte no good exerecise, but fall to intemperate drinking and tipling ... and other wicked disorders'. Yet, no reference was made to Sunday observance at all and the instruction to the JPs explicitly stated that, 'it is not meante that honeste exercises and pastimes or any good exercises for the body, to be had at fitte and convenient tymes, shalbe taken awaie'.[42] As for archery, although the

Queen included this in the games sanctioned by the 1569 licence and issued a proclamation enforcing its maintenance, the promotion of shooting with bows and arrows was by now almost certainly intended simply to keep men fit and out of trouble and not because archery was still regarded as militarily important. Indeed, by 1595 Elizabeth was instructing the authorities in Buckinghamshire 'to convert all the bows in the trained bands unto muskets and calivers ... and to see that they may be trained and taught to use their pieces'.[43]

If final proof were needed that Elizabeth was not herself sympathetic to sabbatarianism, the Queen vetoed a series of Parliamentary bills which sought to promote and enforce stricter Sunday observance. In part, this was to protect the royal prerogative and to prevent Parliament from meddling in matters of religion and because of Elizabeth's unwillingness to alienate her Catholic subjects. However, it also reflected her own views. She consistently rejected such measures and never instigated or promoted any sabbatarian legislation herself. Preaching at the opening of parliament in 1563, Alexander Nowell urged MPs to legislate to enforce church attendance, declaring that:

> the Lord's day, which now is so diversly abused, is to be looked unto: for on that day, taverns, alehouses, and other unruly places be full, but the Lord's house empty.[44]

However, despite Nowell's exhortation to legislate against such abuses, a bill drafted along these lines failed to pass through parliament. A series of bills followed in the 1571, 1572, 1576 and 1581 sessions of parliament. All of these bills were concerned with church attendance and were targeted at recusant Catholics and could not therefore be described as sabbatarian bills. In any event, none of them received the royal assent. Whereas the earlier parliaments focussed on church attendance, the Parliament of 1584 did concern itself with the question of how people spent Sunday and drafted a bill for 'the better and more reverent observing of the Sabbath Day'. This stipulated that there should be:

> no unlawful games, pleyes, bearebaitinges, wakes, ringegames and such lyke hawkinge huntinge or rowinge with bardges uppon the Sundaye for common cawses during the tyme of service or sermon.[45]

This bill was drafted in the wake of the tragedy at a bear-baiting in the Paris Garden in London on Sunday 13 January 1583, when a gallery collapsed killing at least eight people and injuring many others. Lord Burghley, who backed the 1584 Sabbath observance bill, was horrified by the events at the Paris Garden and told the Lord Mayor of London:

'I think it very convenient to have both that [bear-baiting] and other like prophane assemblies prohibited on the Saboth daie.'[46] The bill was passed by both houses in March 1585, but was vetoed by Elizabeth. Although this bill was certainly more sabbatarian in nature than the previous bills, it too referred to pastimes being pursued 'duringe the tyme of service or sermon'. In 1601, Parliament considered four further bills that concerned the sabbath and included provisions for enforcing attendance at church and suppressing Sunday trading. None of them concerned Sunday pastimes and none of them passed into law.[47] Nonetheless, even though they were primarily concerned with church attendance, the fact that Elizabeth's later parliaments debated a series of bills that sought to promote better Sunday observance is important. The passion of some MPs in advocating these measures from the 1580s through to the beginning of the following century reflected the change in the religious climate. Strident, puritan voices were now calling for proper sabbath observance and an end to all abuses and profanations of the Lord's Day.

Late sixteenth-century sabbatarianism and the puritan attack on the day of leisure

The debate at the Dedham Conference held in the early 1580s is an early indication of the breakdown of consensus on Sabbath observance. Clergy from surrounding parishes met at Dedham to debate matters of theology and serious divisions soon emerged about the moral nature of the fourth commandment and the nature of rest on the Sabbath.[48] During the 1580s and 1590s Sabbath observance became the subject of heated debate.[49] Indeed, Nicholas Bownd himself asserted that 'this argument of the Sabbath is full of controuersie, aboue many other points of diuinitie'.[50] These years saw the publication of a large number of works calling for ever-stricter adherence to worship and spiritual duties on Sundays. They focussed on perceived abuses of the Sabbath and on the legitimacy of many activities pursued on Sundays, rather than on the narrow issue of church attendance which was the main concern of the Church hierarchy. Sabbath violations were frequently equated with the most heinous of crimes and those in authority were called upon to punish offenders. Holy days were attacked, and the concept that the Church had the right to appoint such days or to move the day of the Sabbath was challenged. These writers and their adherents elevated the Sabbath as never before: as the 'Lord's Day', to be spent wholly in His service and they challenged the traditional Sunday of the English people. There had, of course, been moralists who had condemned idleness and revelry on Sundays well before the Reformation, and who had called on people to devote the day entirely to God. However, they had also wanted people to devote holy days to spiritual duties as well and had not challenged the Church's right to appoint such days or to determine the day on which the Sabbath was celebrated. With the drastic reduction in the number of holy days following the Reformation, Sunday had become an even more highly valued day of leisure to the ordinary people at the very time that it was becoming increasingly significant to those radical Protestants who were pushing for reform within England and in the way the English people spent their lives.

Much has already been written about the outpouring of complaint literature during the 1580s and 1590s: about the numerous works which discussed the nature of the Sabbath and its observance, and which attacked the various pastimes pursued by the masses. Amongst the most influential were the works of Richard Greenham and Nicholas Bownd, which were crucial in polarising attitudes to traditional Sunday revelry. Greenham wrote *A Treatise of the Sabbath* in about 1590. It was extremely influential and led Thomas Fuller to conclude that 'no book in that age made greater impression on people's practice'.[51] It was circulated in manuscript for a number of years before finally being published in 1599. The manuscript version almost certainly prompted Greenham's step-son, Nicholas Bownd, to write his own *Doctrine of the Sabbath*, which was published in 1595. Despite Fuller's claims for Greenham's *Treatise*, Bownd's *Doctrine* had an even greater impact on the sabbatarian debate. Greenham and Bownd analysed the nature of the Sabbath and how it should be observed in great detail, and they were among the most learned exponents of puritan sabbatarian thinking. Both men challenged the position set out in the Injunctions of Edward VI and Elizabeth I and declared that it was wrong to work on the Sabbath even in harvest time, because it was forbidden by God and because to do so denied the bodily rest that men needed after labouring the other six days of the week.[52] They accepted that works of necessity were permitted on Sundays, but defined 'necessity' very narrowly to include only extreme situations of immediate danger such as a house fire.[53] Greenham declared that Sunday should be devoted wholly to God and that men should rise early to avoid idleness and spend the entire day in prayer, meditation and in hearing and discussing God's word. Whereas the government and Church authorities had been concerned with church attendance, Greenham was concerned with how the whole day was spent and insisted that no pastimes of any kind were permissible on the Sabbath. He maintained that 'unlawfull ... phrophane and idle pleasures' were always wrong and were especially so on the Sabbath. However, he went further and declared that even:

> recreations, as in themselves are lawfull, and may lawfully bee vsed of the children of God in their time and place; as those of shooting, training vp of souldiers, and such like, all which their pleasures carie profit either present, or in time to come, to the Church or common wealth, wee denie not simply that their places, but thinke them

conuenient, and commendable ... Howbeit, the Sabboth day is no fit time for these vses.[54]

In holding that not even archery was to be practised on Sundays, Greenham contradicted the various acts passed over many years to promote its maintenance. In so doing, and in condemning harvest work on the Sabbath, Greenham therefore directly challenged the legitimacy of the acts and injunctions that expressly permitted such activities. He was uncompromising in his belief that Sunday had to be devoted entirely to God's worship:

> Is not the Sabbath the harvest time and the market day for the soule, wherein wee should gather in whilest the sunne shineth, wherein wee should be very diligent, whilest our gaine is promised, wherein wee must provide for living and maintenance, and lay up store, laying all pleasure aside until the time to come?[55]

Bownd extended the attack on the *status quo* by denouncing the concept of holy days and declaring that to 'have adioyned so many other daies ... and made them equal with *the seventh* in sanctifying of them' was nothing short of popery.[56] In doing so Bownd was, like Greenham, at odds with the established Church, which retained its right to appoint additional holy days. Moreover, in denying the holy nature of such days he was also developing a doctrine that pre-Reformation sabbatarians had not advocated. William Perkins similarly attacked the continued use of holy days in the post-Reformation Church, asserting that:

> God alone hath this priuiledge, to have a Sabboth consecrated vnto him: and therefore all holy dayes dedicated to whatsoeuer eyther Angell or Saint are vnlawfull: howsoeuer the Church of Rome haue imposed the obseruation of them vpon many people.[57]

For both Bownd and Perkins, the Sabbath was to be elevated above all other days. No so-called holy day was either equal to it or should be allowed to compete with it. Bownd held that the Apostles had appointed Sunday as the Christians' Sabbath in recognition of Christ's resurrection. However, he rejected the name 'Sunday' as profane and heathen and stated that it should be called by its 'right name religiously, *the Lord's day*'.[58] The Lord's Day was just that: the day belonging to the Lord in which all things should be devoted to Him. Therefore, workers and servants had to give the day entirely to God, and masters were obliged to allow them to do so. Indeed, Bownd asserted that fathers and masters had a duty to punish children and servants who disobeyed God's commandment to refrain from work on the Lord's Day:

which if they neglect to doe, the sinne of the children, and of the servants shall kindle the fire of Gods wrath against them, the flame of which shall breake out to the destruction of the fathers, and masters also, because they have their part in the sin, by not keeping them in obedience vnto God, who he placed vnder them for the same purpose.[59]

Bownd made clear that those in positions of government had an even greater obligation to enforce Sabbath observance 'because their authoritie is greater to commaund, and their power mightier to punish them that doe disobey'.[60]

As for Sunday pastimes, Bownd, like Greenham, ruled them out completely and insisted that men should not hunt, fence or play tennis or bowls on the Lord's Day and that they 'must not come to Church with their bowes and arrows in their hands'.[61] The fourth commandment demanded more than simply refraining from work and people were not free to indulge in 'all kinde of pleasure and delights'.[62] He roundly condemned interludes, stage plays, animal baitings, cockfights and other sports pursued on Sundays.[63] He was particularly damning of May games and the setting up of maypoles, which he described as 'the unfruitful workes of Aitheisme among the Heathen, from whence they spring, or Idolatrie among the Papists, in which they grew vp'.[64] All these things were sinful at any time, Bownd declared, but far more so when indulged in on the Lord's Day. He made a point of stating that he was not against all forms of recreation, but all recreation was forbidden on the Sabbath. Bownd therefore advised people to pursue lawful recreations at another time and called upon those in government 'to give some time to their children and servants, for their honest recreation, upon other dayes'.[65]

The themes covered by Greenham and Bownd are found repeatedly in the many works that poured forth from radical Protestants in the latter part of Elizabeth's reign: the elevation of the Lord's Day; the attack on other holy days; the condemnation of all work on Sundays; the call on those in authority to enforce God's law; the threat of divine punishment if Sabbath abuses continued; and the condemnation of all manner of pastimes and of traditional revelry.[66] Vociferous attacks were made on popular pastimes and there were repeated demands to have them suppressed. Playing and singing on the Lord's Day were regarded by George Estye and many others as even worse than working, and numerous writers complained, as Thomas Lovell did, about the way in which so many people in England failed to observe the Sabbath:

> as if it were consecrated to the abhominable idole of fleshly pleasure, rather then to the true service of the almighty God: for if there be any match made for the triall of any mastrie, or meeting for merriment

(as they terme it) either between town & town, or neighbour & neighbour, or if there be any keeping ales, either for ye maintenance of the Church, or for some that are fallen into decay. When must these be tried ... but upon the Saboth Day?[67]

The puritans naturally shared the hierarchy's concern about church attendance and writer after writer railed against the fact that taverns and playhouses were full when churches were comparatively empty. John Field complained that: 'there is not Taverne or Alehouse, if the drink be strong, that lacketh any company: there is no Dicing house, Bowling alley, Cock Pit, or Theater, that can be found empty.'[68] John Stockwood protested to the Lord Mayor of London that such places were 'blocks layde in [the] way' of people on their way to church, and Humphrey Roberts complained that:

a great many, yea: I may say (a mulititude) come neither at service, sermon, nor any other godly exercise in the Church: But upon the Sabaoth Day resorte rather to Bearebaytying, Bulbaytyng, Dauncing, fenceplaying and such likewayn exercises, then to the church.[69]

Yet, the attacks on popular pastimes went way beyond the fact that they kept people from attending church. Perkins asserted that it was wrong 'to vse iests, sports, banketting' or anything else which would hinder people from spending the entire day in God's service, and Adam Hill complained that people misspent their time in 'idle pastimes' when they should be spending the whole day in prayer and meditation.[70] Leonard Wright protested that the Lord's Day was being grievously abused, 'as though it had been ordeyned to serve Bacchus and Venus'.[71] Numerous other writers condemned pastimes for keeping people from devoting the whole day to spiritual duties. William Kethe, for example, denounced the fact that 'the multitude do most shamefully prophane the Sabboth day, & have altered the very name thereof, so as where god calleth it his holy sabaoth, the multitude call it there revelyng day'.[72]

Adam Hill, George Gifford, Arthur Dent, Philip Stubbes and Hugh Roberts were among the many complaint writers who denounced bear-baiting, bowling, tennis, football, stage plays, dicing, playing cards and tables, drinking, piping, dancing, May games, ales and wakes and all manner of other sports and festivity as profanations of the Sabbath.[73] Some went further still and denounced many popular sports as being intrinsically immoral, regardless of which day of the week they were indulged in. Stubbes claimed, for example, that football was 'a bloody and murthering practice' which was more like 'a friendly kinde of fight ... then a felowly sporte or pastime' and which 'withdraweth us from godlines, either upon ye Sabaoth, or any other day els'. Stubbes also attacked bear-baiting for being intrinsically cruel, asking: 'what Christian heart can take pleasure to see one poore beast to rent, teare, and kill another, and all for his foolish pleasure?'[74] John Field similarly described it as a 'cruell and lothsome exercise', and Bownd condemned the barbarity of baitings and cockfights that fed people's 'affections with the crueltie of one creature against another to no purpose'.[75] One of the most popular pastimes, drinking, was also one of those most condemned. In the early days of the Reformation, English Protestants had gathered at alehouses on Sundays and holy days for bible readings, and they would sit and drink ale before going to hear their sermons.[76] However, by the 1580s radical Protestants were denouncing alehouses for enticing people away from religion. They condemned Sunday drinking as a breach of the fourth commandment, and also attacked drunkenness for causing men to break the seventh commandment. Drunkenness was cited as a sign of damnation and as 'deadly venim, and ranke poyson to the soule', which aroused lust in men and led them into committing adultery.[77] Some accepted that drink taken in moderation or for medicinal purposes was not sinful, but overindulgence was condemned for damaging the body and for leading men into blasphemy, violence and shameful lusts.[78]

The puritan reformers were particularly offended by dancing. They were forced to accept that dancing was not in itself intrinsically evil as the Bible contained many examples of holy men and women dancing. They therefore distinguished contemporary, mixed dancing from that recorded in the Bible, where, they observed, the men danced separately from the women. They also pointed out that when David and godly women like Miriam and Judith danced, they did so 'for ioy in thanks to god', and their dances were 'spirituall, religious, and godlie, not after our hopping, and leapings, & interminglings men with women'.[79] The 'deuelish dauncing' of men and women together was 'the nurce of much naughtiness', which lured participants and onlookers alike into sin.[80] In typical robust style, Stubbes asked:

> what clipping, what culling, what kissing and bussing, what smouching & slabbering one of another, what filthie groping and uncleane handling is not practised euery wher in these dauncings?

and he declared that mixed dancing 'is euill in it self'.[81] The dangers of mixed dancing were a constant theme among late sixteenth-century puritans. They warned that such dances were 'nourishments and prouocations unto lusts and wantonnesse' as they 'stirre up and inflame the hearts of men'.[82] Indeed, Christopher Fetherstone claimed that even if some people met their future spouses through dancing, most dancing led to adultery instead of marriage, and that most people who went dancing were unchaste and ungodly.[83] Dancing on the Sabbath was vehemently attacked as 'a foule abuse on the Lordes day', and churchwardens were criticised for allowing people to indulge in 'lasciuious' dancing after divine service.[84] Wandering minstrels were also blamed for keeping people away from Sunday service: 'for they pipe away all our audience in many places: so pleasaunt a thing is it to daunce after the Diuell.'[85]

Music and dancing were, of course, very common at ales and wakes, and these too came under severe attack from the puritan polemicists. They had a bad reputation for debauchery, as Richard Carew recorded in his *Survey of Cornwall*, noting that ales were known for 'a multitude of abuses, to wit, idlenes, drunkennesse, lasciuiousnes, vaine disports of minstrelsie, dauncing, and disorderly night-watchings'.[86] Stubbes acknowledged the neighbourliness of wakes to which 'freendes and kyns-folk farre and neer are inuited', but claimed that the excess at wakes was such that people would spend the whole of the following week 'in drunkennesse, whoredome, gluttony, and other filthie sodomiticall exercises'.[87] Ales were an important source of income for the parish church, often raising large sums of money to repair the church and to buy service books, plate and vestments. This was acknowledged by some of the puritan writers. Indeed, Thomas Lovell highlighted the fact that the revelry associated with ales attracted young people and thus got them to contribute to church funds, which they otherwise would be unlikely to do. Nonetheless, Lovell disapproved of using ales for this purpose, claiming that it was wrong to maintain the parish churches through the use of 'filthie sporte'.[88] Stubbes similarly condemned the dependence on ales, asking: 'do they think that the Lorde will have his howse build with drunkennesse, gluttony and such like abhominations?' Instead, Stubbes insisted, it would be better for everyone to be made to contribute towards the upkeep of the church according to their ability to pay.[89]

Many church ales were held in the summer months after May Day, and 'May games' and 'silver games' often formed part of the celebrations.[90] These games, too, were roundly denounced by the complaint writers: not only because they profaned the Sabbath, but also because they led people into committing sins of the flesh and acts of idolatry, thereby occasioning breaches of three of the ten commandments. Morris, maypole and hobbyhorse dancing were commonly used in these festivities, to the outrage of puritans who regarded them as idolatrous.[91] Morris dancers dancing 'naked in nettes' were said to be a major 'enticement unto naughtines' and the maypole, sometimes referred to contemptuously as the 'mischievous pole' and 'madding pole', was seen as a pagan symbol and was denounced as a 'stinking idol'.[92] The use of maypoles was even attacked as a needless waste of valuable timber. Hugh Roberts declared that God had not created trees for them to be cut down and used 'to satisfie mens fleshly lustes', and described 'may-polers' as 'caterpillars to the commonwealth' for destroying the best quality trees and depriving the country of good building timber.[93] May celebrations were deeply disapproved of by the complaint writers, who saw them as occasions of excessive drinking and sexual licence. Christopher Fetherstone claimed that the May custom of going into the woods to collect garlands to adorn houses and maypoles simply provided young men and women with an opportunity for fornication, and he wrote that in one instance 'of tenne maidens which went to set May, ... nine of them came home with childe'.[94] Stubbes put the numbers even higher, claiming that those who went 'a-maying' behaved like heathens and 'that fortie, threescore, or a hundred maides going to the wood over night, there have scaresly the thirde part of them returned home again undefiled'.[95] Despite such assertions the demographic evidence suggests that there was no rise in the number of either legitimate or illegitimate pregnancies associated with May celebrations.[96] Nevertheless, those attending May games were accused of drunken, wanton behaviour and the revelry was said to be 'the cause of strife & tumult, & sometime of murther also'.[97] Inevitably, with large numbers of people gathering and consuming great quantities of alcohol, arguments and brawling were not uncommon and, religion aside, May games did raise legitimate concerns over the potential for disorder.

The complaint writers argued that popular culture was ungodly and repeatedly claimed that it stemmed from both paganism and popery, and that Catholics were using traditional festivity to lure people away from Protestantism.[98] For example, John Terry maintained that the Church of Rome had deliberately tried to prevent people from hearing God's word by distracting people with diverting pastimes, and John Field declared that all the Sabbath abuses sprang from the idolatries of Catholics, who 'cared not what deuice took place, what pastime were used, though therein the diuell himselfe were served, so they might keep the people quiet and occupied in ignorance'.[99] John Northbrooke claimed that the Pope had invented holy days 'to traine up the people in ignorance and idlenesse ... in loitering and vaine pastimes', and Hugh Roberts said that the Pope was behind the setting up of maypoles: using them to 'pervert' people 'to go after *Baal*, and to like better of the *Masse*'.[100] These writers called repeatedly for all Sabbath abuses to be stamped out and for the suppression of the 'heathen' and 'papist' pastimes that so many people evidently enjoyed. They compared England to Sodom and Gomorrah and threatened that God's wrath would be visited upon the country if those in authority did not act:

> the Lord hath threatened to poure out his wrathful indignation upon such as polute his Saboth. If we wil not be obedient unto him to hallowe it: then shall he set fire uppon the gates of our Cities and townes and it shall burn up our houses and no man shall be able to quench it.[101]

To reinforce these warnings they pointed to disasters that they said had befallen Sabbath-breakers. It was claimed, for example, that a man received fatal injuries while playing football on a Sunday, that the staging of plays had brought plague to London and, most famously of all, that the collapse of scaffolding which killed several spectators during a Sunday bear-baiting in London's Paris Garden was an act of divine judgment 'both for the punishment of these present prophaners of the Lordes day, ... & also [to] informe and warne us'.[102]

During the latter part of Elizabeth's reign, then, traditional pastimes came under attack as never before. A new, more strident form of sabbatarianism emerged which went far beyond concerns about church attendance and which elevated the Sabbath and sought the suppression of all Sunday recreations. With the population of the country growing and at a time of dramatic increases in inflation and poverty, these writings fuelled concerns about the dangers of disorder and polarised attitudes towards traditional revelry. Attitudes towards charity and poor-relief also began to change, and traditional ales came under pressure. In some areas of the country local magistrates took measures to ban revels and tensions grew between those who saw them as either wrong or dangerous and those who valued their traditional way of life and sought to defend their day of leisure.

The suppression of traditional revelry

The revival of church ales and other traditional revelry that had taken place under Mary was sustained well into the 1560s. Although Edward VI's accession had seen a dramatic reduction in the number of such festivities, Elizabeth's accession did not have the same effect and they continued to thrive into the early years of her reign. Maypoles and morris dancing were commonplace and ales prospered. They were particularly popular in the West Country and in the Midlands, but took place in many parishes elsewhere and extended into the North West and South East of England. Wakes and ales remained a communal celebration that helped to bring communities together and also provided the opportunity to extend hospitality to neighbouring parishes. At Whitsun in 1561, for example, ten parishes gathered for a communal feast at Northill in Bedfordshire.[103] However, during the late 1560s the traditional parish revels went into a considerable and steady decline until, by the beginning of the seventeenth century, they were largely confined to the West Country and parishes in the Thames Valley and the surrounding area.[104] Whereas entries for the payment of morris dancers, maypoles, drinking cups and the ingredients to brew ales were previously common features in many churchwardens' accounts, they became rare in many areas after the 1570s.[105] Such was the decline in popular festivals in some areas that, by 1576, William Harrison was able to write that:

the superfluous numbers of idle waks, guilds, fraternities, church-ales, helpe-ales and soule-ales, called also dirge-ales, with the heathenish rioting at bride-ales, are well diminished and laid aside.[106]

The decline in traditional revels in this period was due to a combination of factors. In part, they were suppressed for religious reasons: because, as the puritan divines vociferously claimed, they were thought to be ungodly and the occasions of sinful behaviour. However, there were secular reasons for their prohibition too, as local justices feared that they would lead to crime and disorder. Some revels simply withered on the vine because the poor rate came to be regarded as a more efficient and attractive way of raising funds, and attitudes to hospitality and charity began to change. All these factors were at play and combined to bring about the end of wakes and ales in many areas.

The sixteenth century was a period of enormous change. The break with Rome, followed by the Edwardian reformation and the Marian counter-reformation, had led to fundamental and unsettling religious changes which had, in part, politicised traditional revelry. Although many parishes were deeply attached to their old festive customs, as is evidenced by their rapid revival under Mary and their persistence into the early years of Elizabeth's reign, the reversals of policy towards them in the mid-Tudor period had at least raised questions about their permissibility. The fact that traditional festivities had frequently been the occasion for disorder and had even been the starting point for rebellion only served to increase concerns about the desirability of such events. Indeed, as the century progressed inflation, poverty and the size of the population all increased, and anxieties about social order steadily grew. The 1590s in particular saw considerable poverty in many areas compounded by poor harvests and food shortages.

High levels of unemployment and vagrancy served to increase fears about criminality and disorder. Such fears prompted moves by many authorities towards greater social control. Even in areas where puritanism was not a factor, anxiety about potential social unrest prompted attempts to curb disorderly and immoral conduct. In many other areas of the country the desire of radical Protestants to reform society and create a truly godly community was a factor behind moves to control misbehaviour. Indeed, attempts to suppress alehouses and popular revelry were most intense in areas where puritanism was strongest.[107] Puritan writers fuelled people's concerns about social order by repeatedly highlighting the dangers of 'slotheful idlenesse' and of allowing people – particularly young men – the licence to do as they wished in their free time.[108] Idleness was said to lead to 'many inconueniences' and idleness in youths 'would quickly flame evyll deedes'.[109] Adam Hill claimed that idleness was the root cause of 'many fraies and bloodsheds' in London and, arguing that it led men to commit theft, he concluded that 'idlenesse causeth pouerty, pouerty famin, & famin causeth robbery'.[110] Many non-puritans made similar links and were deeply concerned by the rising numbers of the poor and by the way in which young people led their lives. These concerns helped to make popular revelry a contentious issue.

It was generally agreed that young people needed controlling. The age of adolescence was perceived as threatening to many in society and was described variously as a 'dark' and 'dangerous age' and as 'the worst and most dangerous time of all'. The violent and rowdy nature of youths was frequently commented upon and, in part, prompted the passing of The Statute of Artificers of 1563, which condemned 'the unadvised rashness and licentious manner of youth'. Young people's promiscuity was also frequently remarked on. Young men were said to be 'carried with a more headlong force unto vice, lust, and vaine pleasures of the flesh', and so were in 'need of straiter discipline, more carefull watching ... harder bridling, and more diligent instruction by the word of God'.[111] The question of sexual licence was of concern for secular as well as religious reasons, as it could lead to the birth of illegitimate children and, consequently, to the making of greater demands upon the poor rates.[112] Young people were also closely associated with traditional festivity, because the youth of a community would frequently take the lead in organising May games.[113] These games were perceived as occasions of debauchery which led to large numbers of illegitimate births. Although the demographic evidence does not support such perceptions, it was perceptions that mattered in determining attitudes towards revels, and many people regarded them as occasions of bawdiness and violence, when a mixture of high spirits and alcohol often spilled over into disorder.[114]

Wakes and ales were also threatened by changing attitudes towards poverty. With the increase in anxiety over social order, the poor came to be feared both as a drain on parish resources and as a potential threat to law and order. The crisis of the 1590s created massive unemployment and privation and placed enormous pressures on parish communities, which, under successive pieces of Tudor legislation, carried the burden of providing poor relief. The large numbers of unemployed who left their own communities in search of work were treated like criminals and outcasts, as parishes sought to avoid the onerous responsibility of providing for them. The economic and demographic problems of the 1590s created tensions between parishes, as neighbouring communities clashed over their respective responsibilities for the poor in their area.[115] Consequently, concepts of reciprocal entertainment between parishes began to change. Communities in many areas began to rely on rates, rents and pew-rates as a means of raising funds in place of ales and traditional revels. However, the imposition of rates by an Act of Parliament in 1572 was initially applied only erratically and the gradual move towards systematic poor relief cannot therefore fully explain the decline in fund-raising by communal festivity.[116] All the evidence suggests that the decline in traditional revels was due to a combination of factors. Social polarization resulting from spiralling inflation, the growth of poverty and increased fears of social unrest combined with the desires of religious enthusiasts to stamp out immoral, unruly behaviour and the profanation of the Sabbath and to reform England into a godly society. These concerns, both secular and religious, led to attempts across the country to suppress traditional games and festivals.

Local elites in various parts of the country took measures to suppress popular pastimes and to enforce Sunday observance. In 1578, for example, the authorities in Leicester ordered the public reading of the statute forbidding unlawful games and subsequently announced the imposition of fines on alehouses and other places where such games were played. In London, people who played football were threatened with imprisonment in 1572. Football was prohibited in the Royal Exchange in 1576 and banned from the City altogether four years later. In Southampton, the court leet sought the appointment of officials to arrest men hosting and playing illegal games, and imposed a curfew on artisans and servants in order to stop them drinking and gambling the night away in taverns.[117] In 1598, justices of the peace in Bodmin, Cornwall, ordered householders to prevent their children and servants from going to alehouses and from playing unlawful games. In Cheshire there was a campaign against summer games, and in Essex, a carpenter was presented at court for keeping 'evil rule in his house ... and dancing and other unlawful games', even though dancing was not an unlawful game under the statutes.[118]

Even in the West Country, where wakes and ales were most firmly rooted, there were moves to ban them in both Devon and Somerset during the 1590s. Having already forbidden ales from being held on Sundays, at the quarter sessions in July 1595 the Devon justices made an order banning Sunday May games as well and stipulated that ales would have to take place during daylight hours and without music or dancing. They justified the order by claiming that the revels caused 'the dishonour of Almighty God, increase of bastardy and of dissolute life and very many other mischiefs'. The alleged disorders nonetheless continued and, in January 1600, the Devon JPs banned church ales altogether on the grounds that they led to 'many inconveniences, which with modesty cannot be expressed'.[119] In neighbouring Somerset, the justices banned ales completely in 1594 and again in 1596. In part they did so to prevent ales from being misused. A Somerset gentleman, Humphrey Sydenham, had been accused of poaching royal deer and he held a series of lavish ales to raise money to finance his defence. The county bench were apparently determined to stop him raising funds in this way and consequently prohibited ales altogether. However, the religious zeal of some of the justices was also almost certainly a factor behind the decision to ban ales. One of the judges, Sir John Popham, was from a family who were notable patrons of puritan ministers. He regarded ales as 'licentious' events and sought support for their prohibition from Sir Francis Hastings who was also well known for his puritan sympathies. Indeed, Hastings bequeathed money to five Somerset parishes in his will on condition that they would never hold any ales, which, he claimed, profaned the Sabbath, led to drunkenness and riot and trained youth in licentiousness.[120] Both secular and religious motivations therefore lay behind the decision to ban ales in Somerset.

Elsewhere there were clearly concerns about the profanation of the Sabbath. In 1579, for example, a High Commission issued orders for the whole of Lancashire banning:

pipers and minstrels playing, making and frequenting bear-baiting and bull-baiting on the Sabbath days, or upon any other days in time of divine service; and also against superstitious ringing of bells, wakes and common feasts.[121]

Given that Lancashire contained more Catholics than any other English county, it is unsurprising that an order should have been issued which spoke of 'superstitious' bell-ringing and which outlawed pastimes that might keep people from the Protestant Sunday service. Yet, the order went further than this in that it related to the Sabbath generally and not just to the time of the church service and it prohibited wakes and other 'common feasts' altogether. Indeed, although national laws did not require such stringency, in 1588 jurors in Manchester were ordered to present at court anyone who kept 'wakes, fairs, markets, bear-baitings, bull-baitings, greenes, alleys, may-games, piping and dancing, hunting and gaming, upon the Sabbath day'.[122] That same year ten men were presented for bear-baiting on the Lord's Day and, in 1592, justices warned the licensee of an alehouse not to allow breaches of the Sabbath day by permitting wakes, markets, bowling, cock-fighting, bear-baitings or May games.[123]

In parts of the country Elizabeth's reign saw a dramatic increase in the number of presentments and punishments for playing games on Sundays and for Sabbath offences generally, particularly during the crisis years of the 1590s. Between 1591 and 1592 there were just four presentments for non-attendance at church and for perceived profanations of the Sabbath in the Vale of Gloucester compared with a yearly average of ten such presentments in the years 1594, 1595, 1596 and 1597, which rose to thirteen in 1599 and in 1600. Most of these concerned people working on the Sabbath, particularly during divine service. However, people were also prosecuted for playing sports and revelling, as in 1597 when a group of apprentices in Tewkesbury were prosecuted for playing stoolball during service time and, in 1599, when a Twyning man was prosecuted for playing the pipes 'on Sabbath days in time of prayer'.[124] During the

1590s the grand jury in Essex presented people for permitting the playing of shovegroat during divine service, for allowing children and servants to play 'shovel board' on a Sunday and for 'disorder and dancing' on the Sabbath during the time of divine service. In Cheshire several men were similarly presented at the Quarter Sessions in October 1602 for bowling on a Sunday 'at time of divine service and sermon'.[125]

In Lincoln, the issues of sabbath observance and popular revelry divided the city corporation. A powerful puritanical faction called for strict enforcement of the Sabbath and sought to ban May games and maypoles. The rival faction on the council vigorously opposed these measures and actively supported May games and the setting up of maypoles.[126] Indeed, maypoles, which had historically been communal symbols whose erection had been a community activity, became a symbol of the struggle taking place between those who were seeking to stamp out popular revelry and those who enjoyed and sought to defend it. Lincoln was just one of a number of cities that banned maypoles. Doncaster, Banbury, Canterbury, Bristol, Leicester and Shrewsbury all imposed similar bans, often leading to clashes with sections of the local community. The resulting controversy in Banbury, which prompted the intervention of the Privy Council to support 'pastimes of recreation' has already been referred to. In Shrewsbury, in 1588, the authorities banned the traditional maypole and several members of the Shearmen's Guild were jailed when they opposed the order and struggled with the officials taking down the pole. The banning of the maypole in Canterbury in the same year prompted a group of morris dancers to dance outside the mayor's house in protest. When celebrations became too riotous in Leicester in 1599, the mayor had the maypole broken and then had one reveller imprisoned for helping to fix the broken shaft back together and for denouncing the mayor for what he had done. A few years later the city's corporation issued an order banning maypoles permanently because 'the multitude of rude and disorderly persons' who attended the maypole caused 'manifold inconveniences and disorders'.[127]

Although maypoles were just one aspect of popular culture, in a sense they were representative of traditional festivity as a whole. The taking down of maypoles symbolised a general attack on traditional revelry. This could well explain the tragic incident in May 1572 when a man was shot and killed as he and a number of others tried to take away the maypole standing on the green in the Sussex village of Warbleton. The man was from a neighbouring village and he may have been trying to steal the maypole as a trophy rather than to destroy it as something ungodly. The incident nonetheless illustrates the importance of maypoles to many local communities.[128] Those who resented the attacks on traditional festivity and were very protective of its most potent symbol: the maypole. Indeed, in order to protect their maypoles, some men attached the royal coat of arms to them in the hope that they would then appear to be sanctioned by the Queen and suggesting, also, that an attack on the maypole was an act of treason.[129]

The hostile reaction to the taking down of maypoles is an indication of the strong attachment that people felt towards their sports and pastimes. The moves to suppress them and to enforce strict sabbath observance were widely resented. In Deighton in Yorkshire, the curate was beaten and stabbed when he tried to stop a man from bowling in the churchyard on May Day in 1575. Many people objected to the enforcement of sabbath observance and no doubt sympathised with the Ramsgate boatman who complained in 1581 that 'it was never merry England since we were impressed to come to the church', and with Ann Carter of Maldon, Essex, who told the constable charging her with working on a Sunday that 'if he would provide one to do her work she would go to church'.[130] By the mid-1580s the word 'puritan' was being used to mean a 'kill-joy'. In his 1585 treatise *Nobody is My Name*, John Deacon's character 'Everybody' enquired of the puritanical 'Nobody';

> Why? Would you not have men to bee merrie and drive awaye the time in good fellowshippe? I perceive you are one of those Puritanes, who allow neither of pastime nor pleasure. Surelie you are the strangest people that euer I hard of.[131]

Many people still clung to their traditional pastimes in the face of the attempts to put an end to them. The ban on ales had to be repeated frequently in both Devon and Somerset, as they continued to be held in defiance of the orders against them.[132] Similarly, despite the various orders made 'to inhibit the outrageous playe at footeball' in London during the 1570s and 1580s, in 1593 the Common Council was forced to acknowledge that football was still being played and was creating 'divers great ryotts'. Indeed, football was apparently being played 'in everie part' of London in 1599, to the extent that people 'can hardlie passe through the streets'. The fact that numerous orders against it had to be issued well into the seventeenth century demonstrates its continuing popularity.[133]

While football was very much a game for the lower orders, other aspects of popular culture were both tolerated and supported by those higher up the social scale. Many churchwardens and parish clergy were indifferent towards the attempts to enforce sabbath observance and some notably failed to observe it themselves. In 1591, for example, two Tewkesbury men appeared before the church court for 'playing at tables on a Sunday at the time of evening prayer'. One of them had been a churchwarden a year earlier and the other became churchwarden three years later.[134] The curate of Rufford, Lancashire, was accused of dancing on Sundays and holy days; the vicar of Normanton in Rutland was caught playing backgammon on a Sunday and, in 1597, two ministers in the Norwich diocese were cited for playing unlawful games.[135] In Essex, the churchwardens at White Notley missed divine service in order to help set up a maypole, and at Rudgwick in Sussex several of the parish's most prosperous residents were among those who erected a maypole in the churchyard.[136]

By the end of the sixteenth century two opposing sides were emerging: those who actively defended popular culture and those who were trying to suppress it for a combination of religious and secular reasons. The issues of sabbath observance and traditional festivity were becoming contentious, political matters in a way and to an extent that they had not been before the Reformation and the emergence of puritanism. For most of Elizabeth's reign the outpouring of complaint literature went virtually unanswered. George Puttenham was one of the earliest writers to defend orderly Sunday recreations. In 1579, he presented the queen with a set of verses in which he said that it was wrong to 'forbid peasants their country sport'. As the volume of condemnation of traditional festivity was turned up towards the end of the reign, so a number of works appeared which lent support to popular revelry. In 1598, for example, John Stow wrote in nostalgic terms about the many May customs and summer games that had once been so popular in London. In his *Survey of Cornwall*, Richard Carew stressed the communal and bonding nature of church ales, and the playwright John Marston produced plays which romanticised English summer festivities.

Indeed, by the end of Elizabeth's reign there was a significant reaction against the many attacks on traditional pastimes.[137] In addition to the appearance of works that celebrated traditional revelry, the 1590s saw the beginning of a doctrinal challenge to the sabbatarianism espoused by the puritan divines. Although apparently motivated as much by a personal vendetta as by religious conviction, Thomas Rogers, the rector of Horringer in Suffolk, targeted the puritan sabbatarians in a sermon he gave in December 1599, in which he described the concept of a morally binding sabbath as 'anti-christian and unsound'. At the same time, Archbishop Whitgift moved to suppress Bownd's *Doctrine of the Sabbath*. The remaining copies of Bownd's book were called in and, in 1600, the Lord Chief Justice banned the publishing of any further copies.[138] The attempts to suppress Bownd's work only served to stimulate demand and made the way for a second and larger edition in 1606. Nonetheless, the fact that it came under attack and was banned by the Church hierarchy is a powerful indication of the polarisation that had taken place over the issues of Church authority and sabbath observance. The Church wanted to maintain the prerogative of determining doctrine and rejected the strict sabbatarian views of the likes of Bownd, Greenham and Perkins.

The preceding years had seen the development of a new, more strident and rigorous form of sabbatarianism and an unprecedented attack on traditional festivity, both in print and on the ground. The traditional view that once people had attended church they could then do what they liked on Sunday was now under attack and threatened as never before. The sabbatarians had mounted a challenge not only to a people attached to their revelry but also to the government of the Church itself. As Christopher Hill put it, whereas 'sabbatarianism of a sort had previously been part of the common protestant heritage' from the 1590s 'it becomes the shibboleth of the puritans, and the spokesmen of the hierarchy came to attack it'.[139]

4

James I's 'dancing book' and the politicisation of 'Saint Sabbath'

Under James I there was a dramatic change in royal policy, with the publication of the King's *Declaration to his Subjects, Concerning Lawful Sports to be Used* and the licensing of Sunday recreation by the Crown that the Declaration represented. During his reign, Sunday sports became more and more politicised, increasing polarisation and divisions in early Stuart society.

Thomas Rogers and his attack on Bownd and puritan sabbatarianism

In 1607 Thomas Rogers renewed his attack on puritan sabbatarianism. In his preface to a revised edition of his *Catholic Doctrine of the Church of England*, Rogers accused puritans of using the printed word to disseminate 'their sabbath speculations', and warned that theirs was a new and insidious view of the Sabbath and that, if it went unchallenged, 'unsound opinions and paradoxes will so poison many, as the whole church and commonweal will find the danger'. He attacked puritans for denying the Church's authority to stipulate any holy days other than the Lord's Day and accused them of using the issue of the Sabbath to subvert the authority of the episcopacy.[1] Declaring that puritans had: 'set up a new idol, their Saint Sabbath', he stressed the fact that puritan sabbatarianism was a break from the past. He argued that, in concentrating on the Lord's Day, the puritans had opened the way for licentiousness and profanity on other holy days and that they had 'introduced a new, and more than either Jewish or popish superstition into the land'. Rogers maintained that puritans treated the Lord's Day as the Jewish Sabbath, describing them as 'demi-Jews' who had abandoned all Jewish ceremonial law except in regard to the Sabbath.[2]

Rogers stated that puritan preachers had claimed that doing any servile work on Sundays was tantamount to murder and playing bowls on Sunday was as great a sin as killing a man or as a father cutting the throat of his own child.[3] He blamed Bownd's *Doctrine of the Sabbath* for promoting this new sabbatarianism and claimed that this new doctrine, which 'had taken deep impression in men's hearts', had spread across the whole of England.[4] Rogers went on to claim credit for revealing Bownd's sabbatarian errors; for Archbishop Whitgift's calling in of the remaining copies of Bownd's book; and for prompting Lord Chief Justice Popham to forbid any more copies being published. He argued that the actions of Whitgift and Popham demonstrated that puritan sabbatarianism was contrary to the doctrine of the Church and the law of the land and 'tendeth unto schism in the one, and sedition in the other'.[5]

In the preface to the second edition of his *Doctrine of the Sabbath*, Bownd claimed not to have known who was behind the suppression of the first edition.[6] It is likely, though, that Rogers was at least partly responsible for bringing it to the attention of the Church hierarchy and for highlighting its challenge to their authority.[7] Rogers, a Suffolk minister eager for advancement, was probably partly motivated by ambition and a desire to make a name for himself as a loyal son of the Church and, in part, by a desire to damage the reputation of Bownd, who was another Suffolk cleric and a potential rival for promotion.[8] Rogers relished opportunities to snipe at godly preachers, who he saw as a threat to the Church's authority and who he also suspected might seek to hinder his preferment within the Church. Rogers may have seized on the opportunity to attack Bownd in his sermon of December 1599 by exploiting the fact that Bownd's book had been dedicated to Robert Devereux, the Earl of Essex. Essex had left his command in Ireland in September 1599 and, by the time of Roger's anti-sabbatarian sermon, Essex was viewed with suspicion by the government and was under virtual house arrest. Two works dedicated to Essex had already been suppressed by the authorities, who might have moved to suppress Bownd's book both because it challenged the Church's right to determine holy days of obligation and because they feared sedition among Essex's supporters.[9] Yet, even if Rogers' motivations are suspect, it would be wrong to dismiss all of his claims about puritan sabbatarianism; many of which were well-founded.

Rogers certainly exaggerated his claims in his attack on puritan sabbatarianism. Many of the extreme, judaical attitudes that Rogers ascribed to 'our English Sabbatarians' cannot be found in Bownd's work.[10] Indeed, Bownd counselled against falling 'into the extremity of the Jewes' who prepared their meat before the Sabbath and would not light a fire on the day itself.[11] Nonetheless, Bownd and other puritans did censure all recreation and work on the Lord's Day and they demanded that the day be totally devoted to God. They argued for the morally binding nature of the Sabbath and denied the Church's right to determine which day should be observed as the Christian Sabbath. They insisted that there should be no other holy days, and that the other six days of the week should be devoted to work. Given that the Church authorities concentrated on church attendance and did not condemn recreation on the Sabbath as such, and that they maintained their right to appoint other holy days, puritan sabbatarianism *was* an innovation, as Rogers claimed. Rogers nonetheless ascribed beliefs to the puritans that many did not hold, and portrayed their sabbatarianism as even more extreme than it was. In doing so, he characterized it in a way that was to be exploited by Peter Heylyn and others in the reign of Charles I. Yet, although Rogers distorted puritan sabbatarianism, his view that it was something new and went beyond the hitherto orthodox beliefs surrounding Sabbath observance was correct.

Rogers' attack on puritan sabbatarianism had two important consequences. Insofar as it led to the suppression of Bownd's *Doctrine of the Sabbath*, it increased demand for Bownd's second edition in 1606. His attack also identified Bownd and puritans generally with extreme sabbatarian ideas and deepened the divide in the debate over Sunday observance.[12] Sabbatarianism had become an issue of considerable contention by the beginning of James' reign, but, in Lancashire, it had been a source of conflict as far back as the 1580s.[13]

Lancashire and the battle for hearts and minds

Lancashire is crucial to any study of the sabbatarian question in early modern England. Lancashire had the largest proportion of Catholics of any English county.[14] Lancashire's high degree of recusancy was of considerable concern to the government, and during much of Elizabeth's reign, the extent of local Catholicism was seen as much more important than the potential problems that puritanism might cause in the county.[15] Recusants did not acknowledge the monarch as head of the Church and their loyalty to the Crown was therefore regarded as suspect. The Protestant reformation had made little discernible impact in Lancashire, although there were centres of Protestantism at Manchester and some other towns; and Lancashire's Protestants tended to be particularly radical – possibly because so many Catholics were concentrated in Lancashire. Despite these centres of Protestantism, vast regions of the county remained defiantly Catholic.[16] Writing to the Privy Council in 1574, the Earl of Derby described Lancashire as 'the very sink of Popery where more unlawful acts have been committed and more unlawful persons held secret than in any other part of the realm'. The government feared sedition among Catholics, and among Lancashire Catholics in particular; giving the conversion of Lancashire Catholics a high priority, it encouraged Protestant preachers to target the county.[17] In the 1570s and 1580s, when puritanism was seen by some in the Church hierarchy as a growing threat to its authority, the strength of Catholicism in Lancashire was seen as a continuing threat to the stability of the realm. For these reasons puritan preachers were sent into Lancashire: both to convert Catholics and to try to get puritan preachers out of southern England, where they might challenge the interests of the Church.[18] In 1577 Bishop Aylmer of London, keen to rid London of puritan clergy, concluded that 'They might be profitably employed in Lancashire ... and other such like barbarous counties, to draw the people from Papism and gross ignorance.'[19] The government and Church hierarchy were wary of the power and influence of puritan preaching in the South East, where Protestantism was well established. However, in Lancashire, where Catholicism remained entrenched and was seen as a greater threat, they sought actively to use preaching to convert the population.

In 1583 the Privy Council instructed the Bishop of Chester:

> to appoint some learned and godly ministers to repair unto such places where it shall be needful, to instruct the people the better to know their duty towards God and her Majesty's laws and to reduce them to such conformitie as we desire.[20]

Sir Francis Walsingham also told the Earl of Derby that 'diligent and public preaching' was the surest way to stamp out recusancy.[21] In 1584 monthly meetings or preaching 'Exercises' were established in the diocese of Chester, designed to bring people to the Protestant faith.[22] The Privy Council not only backed this scheme but also specifically requested that the Bishop of Chester should involve a number of prominent puritan clergy including Edward Fleetwood, William Langley, Richard Midgley and John Caldwell. Puritan ministers dominated the preaching Exercises.

Such was the government's concern about the potential for sedition and the strength of Catholicism in Lancashire that it was the only county where 'Queen's Preachers' were appointed to convert Catholics.[23] In 1599 four Queen's Preachers were appointed in Lancashire 'for the needful instruction of the simple and ignorant in the knowledge of their duties to God and Her Majesty'.[24] The Preachers were to live and work in areas that were staunchly Catholic and, through preaching, were to entice locals away from the old religion to which they seemed to be so firmly wedded. Three of the first four Queen's Preachers were puritan clerics: Richard Midgley, William Harrison and William Forster. Significantly, earlier, in 1587, the Privy Council had engineered a purging of the Commission of the Peace in Lancashire. This also favoured the puritan party and increased the influence of the staunchly Protestant Salford bench. Indeed, from 1587 onwards, the circuit of sessions began at Manchester: the most puritan town in Lancashire.[25]

These moves are important in considering the issue of Sabbath observance and recreation, because they help to explain why sabbatarianism became a source of conflict in Lancashire as early as the late sixteenth century. It was a county in which many people were wedded to a traditional way of life and to traditional festivities, as well as to the old religion. In an attempt to stamp out the embedded recusancy, the Crown gave puritans prominent positions and authority both as magistrates and within the Church. Given that puritans were increasingly espousing a more extreme form of sabbatarianism, clashes over this issue were bound to occur.

Church attendance was particularly important in a diocese with such a large population of recusants. Consequently, the Church authorities were keen to stop anything that might dissuade people from going to church on Sundays. In 1579 Bishop Chaderton of Chester, the Earl of Derby, the Earl of Huntingdon and other members of the Ecclesiastical Commission issued an order prohibiting Sunday pastimes, including wakes, piping and minstrelsy on Sunday 'or vppon any other dayes in time of divine service or sermons'.[26] The Salford magistrates moved dutifully to suppress 'those Lewde sportes, tending to no other ende but to stir opp our freiyle natures to wantonness'.[27] Displaying something of the judaical approach to Sabbath observance that Rogers later accused the puritans of, the puritan JP, Edmund Assheton, encouraged such suppression and pointed out that the Christian Sabbath was 'called in Scriptures the Lords day, and [it] was not lawfull under the old lawe to carrye a pitcher of water on the Sabbath ... but it was Deathe'.[28] However, the Church hierarchy was primarily concerned with the question of church attendance, as evidenced further by Bishop Chaderton's suggestion that markets and fairs should be prohibited until after morning prayer.[29]

The purging of the Commission of the Peace in 1587 was masterminded by the puritan, Edward Fleetwood, and gave puritan JPs in Lancashire considerably greater influence than before. The Salford magistrates were far more radically Protestant than most of their counterparts elsewhere in the county. From 1587 they were able to set the agenda and tone of the Quarter Sessions. This change saw an immediate increase in indictments for recusancy. Fleetwood and others also seized the opportunity provided by the removal of a dozen conservative JPs from the Commission of the Peace and the new dominance enjoyed by the puritan faction to formulate an order to regulate sabbath observance entitled the 'Enormities of the Sabbath'.[30] The 'Enormities of the Sabbath' condemned as 'dysorders of the Sabbath' all wakes, bear-baitings, bull-baitings, Ales and May Games held on the Sabbath, together with piping and dancing and unlawful gaming generally. It gave discretionary powers to officials to present sabbath breakers at the Quarter Sessions.[31] The 'Enormities of the Sabbath' was drafted after the puritan purge of the Commission in 1587, and it is therefore likely that the puritans and their new form of zealous sabbatarianism provided the driving force behind this order.[32] Most of the episcopal and secular orders concerning sabbath abuses issued in the Chester diocese in the late sixteenth and early seventeenth centuries stipulated or implied that recreations were prohibited only until after evening prayer.[33] They were primarily concerned with church attendance and were relaxed about recreations taking place after church. The 'Enormities of the Sabbath' order represented a more hard-line approach to the enforcement of Sabbath observance and beyond the issue of church attendance.

Despite the 'Enormities of the Sabbath' order, Sunday recreations remained popular and persisted in many Lancashire communities. Various presentments were made at the Quarter Sessions for carrying rushes to church, piping, bear-baiting and other recreations on Sundays.[34] In 1590, seventeen Lancashire preachers complained to the bishop that:

> Wackes, Ales, Greenes, Maigames, Rushbearinges, Bearebaites, Doveales, Bondfires, all maner vnlawfull Gaming, Piping and Daunsinge, and such like, are in all places freely exercised vppon ye Sabboth[35]

These seventeen preachers were puritans.[36] Bishop Chaderton sent a summary of their complaint to the High Commission, and the civil authorities as well as the preachers appear to have been concerned that profaning the Sabbath represented a social as well as a religious threat in that it discouraged church attendance.[37] The puritan strictures on sabbath observance were nonetheless something new and it is important to note that their moves to enforce a stricter observance followed in the wake of the puritans' greater control of local affairs. In 1592, for example, the Quarter Sessions bound alehouse keepers not to entertain people who 'uphold disorders on the Sabbath day as wakes, fairs, markets, bearbaits, bullbaits, greens, ales, May games, hunting, bowling, cockfighting, or such like'.[38]

The attempts to suppress popular recreations on Sundays were resented by many of the people in Lancashire.[39] Despite, or because of, the orders against such practices, presentments for Sabbath abuses increased markedly.[40] People were presented at law and church courts for having minstrels play on the Sabbath, for keeping wakes, holding May games and for bowling and bull-baiting on the Sabbath.[41] Possibly due to the resentment over attempts by the godly to suppress Sunday recreations, some people even threw stones at church windows during divine service 'to the disquietinge of the congregation'.[42] Attitudes were polarising. Matters came to a head when James I progressed through Lancashire on his return from Scotland in 1617 and was asked to intervene to prevent the increasing suppression of Sunday recreations.

The events surrounding the first 'Declaration of Sports'

On 8 August 1616, at the instigation of a number of puritan JPs, Justice Edward Bromley sitting at the Assizes in Lancaster, issued orders designed to enforce stricter Sabbath observance in the county. Bromley's orders decreed:

> That theare bee no pipinge, Dancinge, bowlinge, beare or bull batinge or any other profanacion upon any Saboth Day in any parte of the Day or upon any festival day in tyme of Devyne service.[43]

These orders sought to prevent such activities at *any* time during the whole of the Sabbath, including the period after divine service when such recreations normally took place. The orders also required that these measures be enforced by the JPs and that parish ministers should read out the orders every quarter to their parishioners 'that they may the better bee remembred and observed by the parishioners'.[44] This is a remarkable example of the Lancashire magistrates, with the help of the Assize judge, moving to enforce a much stricter sabbath observance than was generally the case. Again, the evidence suggests that the justices were motivated by puritan zeal. They appear to have included the puritans: Edmund Fleetwood, James Anderton, John Bradshaw and Richard Ashton, together with some other clerical JPs who had come from the group of King's Preachers appointed by Robert Cecil before 1601.[45] The 1616 orders were, then, the culmination of attempts by an influential group of puritans to introduce a much stricter form of sabbath observance.

Godly JPs and clerics had used the fear of popery during the years of threat from Spain to purge the Commission of the Peace and to then pursue a sabbatarian campaign within the county.[46] Puritan preaching had not, though, made great inroads into converting Catholics in Lancashire. Indeed, puritan attitudes, not least towards Sabbath observance, had possibly even increased Catholic antipathy towards them. Although the Lancashire preachers had appeared useful to the government in the 1580s and 1590s as Protestant propagandists, by the time of the 1616 orders the government's view of them had changed. The threat of Spanish invasion was long over and the potential danger of Lancashire's Catholics had receded. Conversely, Lancashire's puritans, and the radical Protestantism that they espoused, had come to be seen as a potential threat by both the government and the Church hierarchy.[47]

There was a crucial difference in the attitude to Sabbath observance between the church hierarchy in Lancashire and the county's pro-puritan magistrates. In 1617, the Visitation Articles of Thomas Morton, the new bishop of Chester, asked whether:

any Rush bearings, Bul-baitings, Beare-baitings, Maygames, Morrice-dances, Ales or such like prophane Passetimes, or Assemblies on the Sabbath be used on the Sabbath to the hindrance of Praiers, Sermons, or other godly exercises.

The bishop wanted to know of any abuses that hindered 'Praiers, Sermons, or other godly exercises'. That same year, Warrington justices ordered that:

no person uppon anie parte of the Sabbath day shall ... use anie shuteinge, bowleinge, diceinge, cardinge, ball playinge, drinking, or anie other unlawfull games.[48]

Therefore, while the bishop was concerned about sermons and services being interrupted or missed because of people's Sunday recreations, the magistrates sought to go much further. They were trying to ban recreations on Sundays altogether, regardless of whether people had already been to church or not. This is a crucial difference. The order of the Warrington justices was a sabbatarian order in the puritan mould.[49]

In August 1617 James I returned from a visit to Scotland and passed through Lancashire, where he was to be entertained by Sir Richard Hoghton at Hoghton Tower. On his progress to Hoghton, the king was petitioned by a group of Lancashire tradesmen, servants and peasants who complained that the magistrates' orders were preventing them from pursuing their traditional and hitherto lawful recreations on Sundays. They asked the king to nullify the orders. On hearing this, and with the encouragement of various courtiers, James decided in favour of the petitioners and made a 'speech about libertie to pipeing and honest recreation'.[50] He then continued with his journey to Hoghton Tower, where on the following Sunday he himself attended a rushbearing and piping in the afternoon, and later watched some country dances.[51] On that same Sunday, 17 August, an unruly mob seemingly took advantage of James' pronouncement and piped and danced noisily during service time outside a nearby parish church, to the disgust of the worshippers inside.[52] Clearly, such activities went beyond what the Church authorities could countenance, as people were here failing to attend church and were instead indulging in recreations during service time itself, as well as apparently taunting the churchgoers. Bishop Morton duly informed the king of these events and James 'utterly disfavoured any thoughts or intention of encouraging such prophaneness'. He left it to Morton to punish the offenders. The ring leader was duly fined and the piper was put in the stocks and 'laid by the heeles'.[53]

Some of the king's attendants felt that the reaction to the revellers had been too harsh and that they had only been seeking 'some innocent recreation for servants and other inferior people on the Lords day and Holy dayes, whose laborious callings deprived them of it at all other times'. They prevailed upon the king to look kindly on the question of people's Sunday recreation, which they claimed 'was the general desire of most of that Country'.[54] James decided to consult Bishop Morton in order to see how he could satisfy people's desire for honest recreation 'without endangering his liberty to be turned into Licentiousness'.[55] Morton considered the issue and drew up draft regulations, which he then presented to the king, who approved them after making some minor amendments to 'alter them from the words of a Bishop, to the words of a King'.[56] James then issued the amended draft that day, 27 August 1617, as a 'Declaration' setting out the conditions upon which certain sports would be allowed on Sundays. The King's 'Declaration to His Subiects concerning lawfull sports to be used' represented a major shift in Crown policy. Elizabeth I had enjoyed May games and favoured Sunday recreations, provided that her people attended church as required. However, although she gave tacit support to such recreations, Elizabeth never made any public declaration on the matter, and shrewdly refrained from getting embroiled in this increasingly contentious issue. By formally pronouncing on the matter of Sunday recreation, James now involved the Crown in the debate.

Referring to the Lancashire magistrates' order, the 1617 Declaration criticised 'some puritans and precise people' for 'prohibitinge & unlawfull punishinge of our good people for usinge theire lawfull recreations & honest exercises upon sondaies and other holidaies after the afternoone sermone or service'. It described Lancashire as being 'too much infected' with puritans as well as Catholics. It claimed that, there were signs that many Lancashire Catholics were showing signs of reform, but that the attempts to suppress Sunday recreations were preventing:

> the conversion of manie whom theire preists will take occasion heareby to vex perswading them that no honest myrth or recreacion is lawfull or tollerable in our religion which cannot but breede a great discontentment in peoples harts.[57]

As well as discouraging many Catholics from converting, the Declaration also stated that the prohibitions against Sunday sports 'barreth the common & meane sort of people from usinge such exercises as make theire bodies more able for warrs'.[58] Not only would recreation keep men fit, it would also keep people from drinking in alehouses where they might indulge in 'ydle & discontented speeches'. The suppression of Sunday recreations therefore hindered the conversion of Catholics, risked driving men into alehouses to indulge in seditious talk, and could make men less fit to fight, to the detriment of the country in the event of war. James' Declaration also acknowledged that Sundays and holy days were the only days when people had time to exercise.

James used his Declaration to state the official view of the Crown on the matter of Sunday recreation: people should not be prevented or discouraged from lawful recreation on Sunday after divine service. Again, church attendance was of crucial concern and the liberty to indulge in recreation was only granted to those who had first attended their parish church. James stated in the Declaration:

> Wee likewise straightlie comand that everie person shall resorte to theire owne parishe Church to heare devine service & eich parish by its selfe to use the said recreation after the service.

Whether or not this actually meant that people could only attend recreations in their own parish, or whether they could attend others provided that they went to the relevant parish church first was later to become the subject of some debate. Those who had been to church were expressly allowed to take part in:

> Pypinge Dansinge either men or women archerie for men leaping valtinge or anie such harmeles recreation & the women to have leave to Carrie rushes to the Church for the decoringe of it according to theire ould Custome.

Bear- and bull-baiting, interludes [plays] and bowling were to remain unlawful, and anyone taking part in recreations before divine service would be 'sharplie punishe[d]'.[59] The Declaration was directed to be published in all the parishes within the diocese, just as Justice Bromley had required his 1616 orders to be read to parishioners. Bishop Morton further instructed that he should be informed of any people who inclined 'to a kind of Judaisme by neither eatinge meate themselves nor sufferinge others to dress it upon the Lords day'. He also issued instructions that afternoon sermons should not be more than an hour long in order to give parishioners time to enjoy the recreations permitted them by virtue of the King's Declaration.[60]

The Declaration instructed that puritans who failed to conform should be exiled from the county, and denied the liberty of Sunday recreation to Catholics and others who did not attend church. In that sense, it was even-handed in that it had implications for Catholics as well as puritans within the county. Yet, given it concerned recreations on Sundays and expressly attacked the orders of the puritan magistrates who had sought to ban them, James was clearly using the document to put the puritans 'in their place'. He and Morton regarded attempts to suppress all Sunday pastimes as an unwelcome, novel intervention, and the official position of the Crown was now clearly to support lawful recreation on Sunday after church.

The 1617 Declaration was issued for the County of Lancashire, but James decided later that the Declaration should 'with a few words thereunto added ... be published to all our Subiects'.[61] On 24 May 1618 he duly published an amended version for the whole realm. The 1618 *Book of Sports* was essentially the same as the earlier version. However, in addition to sanctioning dancing, leaping, vaulting and archery and 'other such harmlesse Recreation', it also explicitly allowed 'May Games, Whitson Ales, and Morrisdances, and the setting up of Maypoles'.[62] This was almost calculated to upset the puritans, many of whom regarded the maypole in particular as a symbol of idolatry. Again, the king required his declaration to be published in parish churches across the country.

The genesis of the 1618 *Book of Sports*

Although the events surrounding the publication of the 1617 Declaration have been well documented, it is not clear why James issued his national Declaration of 1618. Kenneth Parker has offered the trial of John Traske as a possible reason for the national extension of the Declaration.[63] Traske was the leader of a sect of judaizing Christians who held that, just as it was for the Jews, Saturday and not Sunday was also the Sabbath for Christians, and that Christians should observe it as strictly as the Jews observed their own Sabbath. The views of Traske and his followers were treated dismissively at first, but, after he wrote 'presumptious letters to the Kinge', the government's attitude to Traske changed. Traske was now viewed as 'a dangerous person' and was tried in the Star Chamber. On 19 June 1618 Traske was fined £1,000 and sentenced to life imprisonment. It was further ordered that he should 'bee whipped from the prison of the Fleete to the Pallace of Westminster with a paper on his head ... then to bee sett on the Pillory and to have one of his ears nayled to the Pillory'. To signify 'that hee broached Jewish opinion', it was decreed that Traske should then 'bee burnte in the forhead with the letter J' before being 'whipped from the Fleete into Cheapside ... sett in the Pillory and have his other Eare nayled thereunto'. Traske was duly punished and branded sometime between 23 and 30 June.[64] Traske's trial and the discussions surrounding it may indeed have played a part in the national extension of the Declaration, but not, as Parker suggests, because it was what prompted James to issue the Declaration nationally, but because, as McDowell argues, the trial was a way of legitimating the Declaration's publication. The 1618 *Book of Sports* was issued in May 1618; the month *before* Traske's sentencing and public punishment. The government sought to use Traske's punishment as a tactic to undermine the puritan opposition to the *Book of Sports* and to stigmatise puritan sabbatarians as Jews.[65] James appears to have used the national extension of his Declaration and Traske's trial and punishment in an attempt to stamp out strict sabbatarianism altogether and to counter what he had come to see as a potential threat to royal authority.

James personally favoured moderate recreation and had no objection to what he saw as suitable, honest sports being enjoyed on Sundays. He himself was happy to conduct business and to indulge in revelry on Sundays. His Privy Council, like Elizabeth's, met every Sunday morning.[66] On one occasion, when the court was preparing to move the next day, the Lord Mayor of London tried to stop the king's carriages going through the City on Sunday during Divine Service; James sent the Mayor a warrant commanding him to let the carriages proceed.[67] Masques and plays were performed frequently at court on Sundays, and the marriage of James' daughter, Elizabeth, to Frederick of the Palatinate took place on Shrove Sunday, 1613 and was followed by 'dancing, masking, and revelling'.[68]

James was a passionate huntsman and was reported to 'love the chase above all the pleasures of this world, living in the saddle for six hours on end'.[69] He not only hunted deer on horseback, but also used beagles to hunt rabbits and even used cormorants to hunt fish.[70] James also enjoyed attending races between royal footmen and those of his nobles. These races could be over distances of fifteen or twenty miles and the king was reported as taking 'pleasure in being present at such sports'.[71] He also attended bear- and bull-baitings and even introduced the baiting of bears by lions.[72]

James saw many recreations as 'conuenient and lawfull' and set out his views on sports at some length in *Basilikon Doron*. He recommended bodily exercises and games as necessary to keep a man fit and 'exercise his engine, which surely with idlenesse will ruste and become blunt'. He condemned football as being 'meeter for laming, then making able the vsers thereof', but encouraged:

> running, leaping, wrestling, fencing, dancing, and playing at the caitch or tennise, archerie, palle maillé, and such like other faire and pleasant field-games.

Although he favoured bodily exercise over 'sitting house-pastimes', James explicitly refused to condemn them, stating that he did not agree 'with the curiositie of some learned men in our age, in forbidding cardes, dice, and other such like games of hazard'. He said that he respected such 'godly men', but that they were mistaken in equating such games with casting a lot and that, although they should be played in moderation, playing at cards or tables was lawful.[73] James even went on to appoint someone to license people to 'keep several numbers of Bowling Allies, Tennis Courts, and Such Like Places of Honest Recreation'. In all, some thirty-one bowling alleys were licensed, along with fourteen tennis courts and forty gaming houses.[74]

It is clear, then, that James looked benevolently upon those who wanted to indulge in healthy exercise or in what he regarded as harmless recreation. This does not, though, necessarily explain why he decided to issue the Declaration of Sports. Fourteen years earlier, on 7 May 1603, James had issued a proclamation in which he had declared:

> And for that we are informed, that there hath bene heretofore great neglect in this Kingdome of keeping the Sabbbath day: For better observing of the same, and avoiding of all impious prophanation of it, wee do straightly charge and commaund, that no Beare-bayting, Bul-bayting, Enterludes, common Playes, or other like disordered or unlawful Exercises or Pastimes be frequented, kept or used, at any time hereafter upon any Sabbath day.[75]

It is interesting that, on his coming to the throne, James decided to issue a proclamation in which he talked about the profanation of the Sabbath. The fact that the proclamation was issued at the beginning of May could suggest some connection with the onset of the season for May and summer games. Nonetheless, the proclamation did no more than repeat the established position of the Crown and Church in relation to baitings, the performance of plays for the masses, and the practice of *unlawful* games on Sundays. On 23 May 1603 a set of instructions was issued to constables ordering them 'not to suffer the Sabbath day to be profaned with bearbaiting, piping, dancing, bowling and other unlawful games and exercises, according to the King's proclamation'.[76] Yet, the king's proclamation had made no reference to piping and dancing. In seeking to ban piping and dancing on Sundays and to classify piping and dancing as unlawful, the instructions, which were most probably issued by justices who either innocently or wilfully misinterpreted James' proclamation, went much further than the proclamation itself. They did not accurately reflect the terms of James' proclamation, which was not the sabbatarian document that some have suggested.[77] Consequently, James' subsequent *Book of Sports* was entirely consistent with his 1603 proclamation and with his own views.

James had long associated moves to suppress Sunday pastimes with radical Protestantism and he appears to have reacted increasingly against this. Before his accession to the English throne, James had already crossed swords with godly ministers who had tried to suppress Sunday recreations in Scotland. In 1599 a band of English comic players stayed in Edinburgh to perform their comedies. Fearing 'the profanitie that was to ensue, speciallie the profanation of the Sabbath day', church ministers called the Kirk into session and passed an order forbidding people from attending the plays and instructing ministers to publicise the order from their pulpits. James had earlier granted the players a warrant to lodge in the city and saw the Kirk's decision as a challenge to his earlier warrant and to his authority. He told the Kirk's representatives that he had issued the warrant granting the players a house in the city so 'that the people might resort to their comedies' and he instructed the Kirk to reconvene and rescind its order, telling them 'Yee are not the interpreters of my lawes'.[78] For James, the issue was one of jurisdiction and power rather than public morality.[79] This gives us some insight into the issues behind the Declaration of Sports, where James sent a message to godly preachers and magistrates not to encroach upon the Crown's authority in trying to regulate social behaviour. Indeed, this episode has considerable parallels with events surrounding his Declaration of Sports. After James' intervention, the Kirk reconvened and duly voted to rescind its earlier order. However, several ministers made it clear that they would not publish the fact that the order had been reversed and that they were not prepared 'to justifie the thing they had done, or ellis they could not goe to a pulpit'. When James' reaction was sought, he responded: 'Lett them nather speeke good nor evill in the mater, but leave it as dead.' As with his later Declaration, having asserted his authority and rebuked the ministers, James was prepared to let the matter drop rather than make a major issue of it by trying to enforce his order in the face of opposition.[80]

James' experiences in Scotland predisposed him to link the support of traditional revelry with the maintenance of royal authority.[81] From August 1582 until June 1583 the young king, had been held captive by a group of Scottish lords led by Lord Ruthven. They were backed by the Kirk. Dance was an abomination to the Kirk and, while James was under the control of the 'Ruthven raiders', court pastimes were suppressed and he was without any musicians.[82] James' reaction to the Kirk's later attempt to stop the performances of the English players is thus even more understandable: he saw moves by the godly to restrict traditional pastimes as an encroachment on his prerogative and he was prepared to link the Crown ever more firmly with traditional recreation in defiance of moves to suppress it.

Furthermore, James regarded traditional pastimes as a way of alleviating tensions in society and of providing people with a harmless distraction, thereby discouraging them from discussing politics and seditious talk. James' policy embodied Juvenal's maxim that the people desire only 'bread and circuses': keep them amused and they will be less likely to cause trouble. In *Basilikon Doron* James wrote that the common people were prone 'to iudge and speake rashly of their Prince' and to help prevent this and

> to allure them to a common amitie among themselves, certaine dayes in the yeere would be appointed, for delighting the people with publicke spectacles of all honest games, and exercise of armes:

as also for conueeing of neighbours, for entertaining friendship and heartlinesse, by honest feasting and merrinesse.[83]

In the Declaration of Sports, James similarly warned that to deny people honest recreation on Sunday would lead them to 'set up filthy tiplings and drunkennesse, and [breed] a number of idle and discontented speeches in their Alehouses'.[84] Puritan attempts to suppress Sunday recreations were therefore a usurpation of royal authority and a potential threat to social order. James did not, of course, approve of the riotous behaviour that prompted many magistrates to support the suppression of traditional revelry; but he was concerned that, if denied a sensible 'escape valve', people could resort to drinking and talking in alehouses which might encourage sedition.

James had no love for the puritans. He did not share their views on recreation and his experiences in Scotland had given him cause to be suspicious of the 'godly'. James was recorded in 1605 as having 'most bitterly inveighed against the Puritans' and as having declared 'that he would hazard his Crown but he would suppress those malicious spirits'.[85] In *Basilikon Doron*, James had called puritans 'verie pestes in the Church and Common-weale ... breathing nothing but sedition and calumnies'. Describing them as 'phanaticke spirits', he advised his son that he should 'suffer not the principals of them to brooke your land, if ye like to sit at reste'.[86] After the Hampton Court Conference in 1604, James ridiculed the puritans and claimed that in his arguments with them he had 'pepperid theaime ... soundlie'. When he addressed Parliament shortly afterwards, he described puritans as 'a sect rather than a Religion' and stated that they should not 'be suffred in any wel governed Commonwealth'.[87] At the Hampton Court Conference itself James had nonetheless recognised the usefulness of puritan preachers in trying to deal with recusancy in Lancashire and had said that no severe measures would be taken against puritan ministers in that county.[88] However, by 1617 the Lancashire puritan preachers had become an increasing nuisance, and their attempts to suppress recreations and impose their own form of Sunday observance were believed to be undermining attempts to get Catholics to convert.[89] In his Declaration, James voiced his irritation about this and spoke of 'puritanes & precise people' as an 'infestation'.[90]

While we cannot know for certain what prompted James to extend the Declaration nationally in 1618, it seems clear that he wanted to reassert royal authority by supporting traditional festivity and, at the same time, to attack puritans within the kingdom. He was exasperated by what he saw as their attempts to encroach upon his prerogative. For him, the question of Sunday recreation had become as much a political as a moral issue and he decided to firmly identify the Crown with traditional festivity and to publicly reject puritan sabbatarianism.

In his Declaration – or *Book of Sports*, as it came to be called – James associated strict sabbatarianism with puritanism, and he was correct to do so. Their form of sabbatarianism, which included denying the right of the Church to appoint holy days of obligation, was non-conformist in that sense and their strictures on Sabbath observance went far beyond mere concerns over church attendance. However, by allying the Crown so clearly with those who supported traditional festivity – and by attacking puritan sabbatarianism and associating people who sought to suppress such festivity with the puritans – James' Declaration politicised the question of Sunday observance and recreations to a far greater degree than ever before. It outraged even moderate puritans, who felt strongly about Sabbath observance but had hitherto regarded themselves as conformists. It also troubled magistrates and others who were concerned about social order.

Reaction to the 1618 'Dancing Book'

Many people were scandalised by the licence given to Sunday recreations while others delighted in the royal sanctioning of their traditional pastimes and cited the King's Declaration in support of their revelry. There are examples of several ministers refusing to publish the 'Dancing Book', as its opponents called it. In Lancashire, a number of ministers refused to read it in their churches, believing that it sanctioned the profanation of the Lord's Day. They were duly reported for failing to comply with the Declaration.[91] William Clough, the vicar of Bramham in Yorkshire, preached on the fourth commandment in August 1619 and was reported as saying:

> Nowe in deed the king of Heauen doth bid you keepe his Sabboath and reuerens his sanctuarie. Nowe the king of England is a mortall man and he bids you break it. Chuse whether of them you will followe.

He ended by declaring that: 'in the ould and Auncient tymes Kings were subiect to the Lawes of preists, And not preistes to the Lawes of Kinges'.[92] One London minister read out the Declaration, followed by the ten commandments and then told his congregation that they had heard both the commandments of God and of man and then instructed them that they should 'Obey which you please'.[93] The vicar of Horninghold was similarly reported as quoting passages of scripture 'in opposition to the King's Book of Recreations on the Lord's Day'.[94] Some ministers apparently disagreed with the Declaration but read it anyway because they felt obliged to obey their king; others read it and, having done so, then preached against it.[95] Others, such as William Gouge, a staunchly puritan minister at Blackfriars, simply refused to read it at all.[96] However, while there are several of examples like these, there is no evidence to suggest that opposition to the Declaration's publication was widespread among the clergy.

Bishop Bayly of Bangor most probably disapproved of the Declaration. While the circumstances are unclear, in 1621 the bishop was sent to Fleet Prison 'for disputing malapertly with the king on the Sabbath'.[97] Bayly had puritan leanings and had already incurred disfavour by making accusations of popery against some members of the Privy Council. His brief imprisonment in 1621 may well have been due, in part at least, to his taking issue with the king over the *Book of Sports*.[98] However, given the timing, it is more likely that it was connected to the attempts in Parliament to push through a sabbatarian bill banning Sunday recreations, which was itself contrary to the Declaration.[99] In *The Practice of Pietie*, Bayly had stated that allowing people to profane the Sabbath without being punished was a hindrance to piety and, although he allowed for recreation insofar as it made men fitter in mind and body to serve God, he maintained that 'Man was not created for sports, playes, and recreation: but zealously to serue God'. Bayly further questioned:

> whether Dancing, Stage-playing, Masking, Carding, Dicing, Tabling, Chesse-playing, Bowling, Shooting, Beare-baiting, Carowsing, Tipling, and such other fooleries of Robin-Hood, Morrice-dances, Wakes and May-games, be exercises that God will blesse and allow on the Sabboth day.[100]

In any event, Archbishop Abbot himself appeared to be unhappy about the Declaration as he refused to have it read in his presence when he attended the parish church at Croydon on the day that it was meant to be read to parishioners there.[101] An examination of fifteen sets of visitation articles issued between 1618 and 1620 found no example of ecclesiastical officials enforcing the reading of the *Book of Sports*.[102] However, even though Archbishop Abbot and Bishop Bayly may have disapproved of it, the lack of reference to the Declaration in these visitation articles cannot be taken to denote disapproval on the part of the episcopate generally, as they would have been primarily concerned with the question of church attendance rather than recreations after church. Indeed, Francis Godwin, Bishop of Hereford, declared that the Sabbath was in part ordained 'for the reliefe of nature by rest as of the body soe of the minde which is recreation' and enquired 'whether any person have taken upon them to hinder honest and seemely recreation upon sondayes and holidayes'. He also enquired 'whether the minister doe not defer the afternoone service unseasonably for the debarring or hindering of fit recreation?' and 'whether you know if any preacher that impugneth or inveigheth against as unlawfull the exercise of such things as tend to honest and fit recreations upon the sabboth or upon holidays or doth machinate any thing to the hindrance of them'.[103]

Godwin's orders are undated, but appear to have been made in the early 1620s. He, at least, issued orders which suggest support for the *Book of Sports*. He clearly wanted to know if ministers were prolonging services or were otherwise trying to prevent people's recreations on Sundays.

In certain quarters, the issue of the *Book of Sports* served to polarise attitudes. In one Northampton parish, for example, a puritan woman was presented for scolding servants who had claimed that they 'must play upon the Sabboth days and holidays and obey the king's laws in that point or else be hanged'. Reprimanding the servants, the woman declared that 'they might choose whether the king should hang them for not obeying him or the devil burn them for so breaking the sabbath'. She went on to condemn the *Book of Sports*, saying that 'she does not think it lawful, let others do what they list'.[104] If others did not share the Northampton servants' belief that the king actually required them to play sports on Sundays, many clearly understood that he had sanctioned their doing so. In 1622 in Exeter, for example, a constable who tried to stop men playing trap-ball was met with defiance and told that 'they played att noe unlawfull game and that the King [himself] did allowe it'.[105] Five parishioners in the Wiltshire parish of Keevil similarly, and successfully, claimed that they were entitled to dance after evening prayer according to 'the king's book', and in Marlborough a parishioner cited the 'king's book' when challenged for taking part in 'sport or merriment' on Midsummer day in 1618.[106]

The Declaration highlighted the division on the issue of Sabbath observance. When the minister at Fuston in Yorkshire preached against it and tried to stop the traditional rushbearing he provoked a fracas in the church.[107] Indeed, while many people seized on the Declaration as a means of protecting their traditional recreations in the face of attempts to suppress them, others cited it as encouraging vice and disorder. A copy of the 1618 Declaration survives in the library at Lanhydrock, the Cornish seat of the staunchly puritan Robartes family. Reflecting the abhorrence with which puritans greeted the Declaration's publication, the final page of the Lanhydrock copy of the *Book of Sports* contains the following anonymous composition:

> Alas yf euer men should so far blinded be
> Not only to Comminde but Command villanie
> Must God & our soules be rob'd by proclamation
> To drive off God is to undoe ye nation
> When to divide ye dayess made lawfull by ye Lawes
> Flesh doth take more than God Experience showes
> And who but must esteem't a double wrong
> To have Gods seruice short, our Riots long.

The annotations on the Lanhydrock copy are not dated and, even though it is a copy of the 1618 Declaration, given that it is the only version of the *Book of Sports* in the Lanhydrock library and therefore, possibly, in the Robartes family's possession at the time, it may be that the verse was written after Charles I reissued the *Book of Sports* in 1633. It nonetheless underscores the deep feelings and fears aroused by the *Book of Sports* and its potential to cause serious division and to 'undoe ye nation' in terms of religious and social cohesion.[108]

Without doubt, such cohesion was under evident strain. In November 1618 it was reported that, while parishioners were at prayer at Albrighton, Staffordshire, a mob gathered in the churchyard beating drums and firing guns and shouting 'Come out, ye Puritans, come out'; and at nearby Lea Marston some people, impatient to begin their revelry, left church before the service had ended in order to begin drinking and dancing.[109] These events illustrate the tensions between those who wanted strict Sunday observance and those who wanted to enjoy traditional festivity. Perhaps the best example of this is the dispute in 1618 between Sir Edward Montagu and John Williams, which was triggered by Montagu's attempts to interfere in the holding of a wake.

In July 1618 Sir Edward Montagu and Sir Thomas Brook, both puritan JPs, wrote to the constables of Grafton Underwood, where a wake was due to be held. Seeking to put the strictest possible interpretation on the King's Declaration, they instructed the constables that it was 'the King's Majesty's pleasure that all such shall be presented and sharply punished that shall use any lawfull recreations before the end of divine services on Sundays' and further demanded that anyone present at the festivities who lived in another parish should either leave or be punished. In so doing, Montagu and Brook were targeting a group of musicians who were to attend from nearby parishes. They also prohibited the unlicensed selling of ale. The vicar of Grafton Underwood was John Williams, himself a recently appointed JP who eschewed the puritanism of Montagu and Brook. Williams was to go on to become Bishop of Lincoln and Lord Keeper. When the constable, Robert Reeve, attempted to enforce Montagu's warrant, Williams read it out to the people assembled in the churchyard and instructed the alewives sell their ale regardless of the warrant. Williams, who regarded Reeve as a 'tumultuous and schismatical constable', later claimed that the warrant was 'opposite to the meaning of his Majesty's declaration' and criticised the constable for arguing:

> 1. That the King's declaration was a bolstering up of sin and breach of the Sabbath. 2. That his Majesty therefore ought to be prayed for, that God would give him an understanding heart. 3. That the observation of the Sabbath in religious worship must be continued for twenty-four hours. 4. That he and such as he can keep the Sabbath thus, when they are fast asleep; and the like.[110]

Williams therefore defied Montagu's warrant, which he clearly saw as a work of puritan meddling in the community's traditional revelry: revelry that he believed had the king's blessing. Williams therefore ordered that fiddlers should be permitted to play and even demanded that 'if there were none in the town, they should be sent for'. Again, linking attempts to suppress sports with puritanism, Williams told the people attending the feast from other parishes that: 'You honest men that are come to the town, you shall use your pastimes and your sports, for I will have no such precise doings in this town.'[111]

Williams' actions infuriated Montagu, who bitterly resented the challenge to his authority, even though it was he who had taken it upon himself to issue orders concerning Williams' parish. The dispute divided the Northamptonshire gentry. Sir Arthur Throckmorton, Sir John Pickering and Sir Thomas Crewe backed Montagu. Sir Francis Fane and Sir John Isham supported Williams.[112] Williams' supporters believed that there was nothing wrong with honest recreation after church and that people like Montagu were seeking to suppress such recreation because of their puritanical views, and where Montagu wanted to apply the Declaration very narrowly, they sought to give it the most generous and widest interpretation. They argued, for example, that the Declaration did not mean that a person could only attend festivities in his own parish, but that a person could take part in recreations in any parish so long as he had first attended the church there: 'where he is at church, he is for that day as of that parish.'[113] Montagu's supporters, referring to the circumstances in Lancashire that had led to the Declaration, held that the king would countenance:

> many things in the remote places of his Realm which he will not do in the centre of his Kingdom; for many things may become the borders and skirts, as gardes of many colours, which will disgrace the heart of the garment.

Whereas they could accept that such liberty might be necessary in areas such as Lancashire, where there was a justifiable desire not to alienate the large Catholic community, they felt that such licence was not appropriate elsewhere. Moreover, they were concerned about the potential for violence and stressed the fact that disorders frequently occurred at feasts.[114] Montagu claimed that Williams' actions had encouraged 'people in other towns ... to use disorderly courses'.[115] Indeed, it was claimed that some of the men playing with cudgels at the Grafton wake had 'had their heads broke, and the blood ran out'.[116] Montagu later argued that 'the mistaking and misinterpreting of the King's Majesty's Declaration concerning recreations on the Sunday hath begotten many disorders and great assemblies'. He clearly felt that the Declaration gave magistrates power to keep people in their respective parishes and that 'there never was so good a device to keep the people in order, especially upon Sundays'.[117]

The dispute between the two sides became something of a *cause célèbre*, with repercussions at court as well as within the county of Northampton. The king was informed of the events and Montagu was told that 'the whole council, man by man,' supported Williams' actions. Conversely, on 17 September 1618 Throckmorton wrote to Montagu saying that 'the great Judges' had ruled in Montagu's favour.[118] However, a letter from Sir Charles Montagu to Sir Edward dated 11 November 1618 shows that the matter remained unresolved. Indeed, it suggests that Montagu had been unsuccessful in gaining the support he had sought from Lord Chief Justice Sir Henry Hobart, who was said to be 'but cold in it'.[119] The evidence suggests that Montagu's actions did not enjoy much support at court and that, in the end, Williams carried the day.[120] This episode highlights the controversial nature of the 1618 *Book of Sports* and the divisions among important sections of society on the question of Sunday recreation and its implications for Sunday observance and social order. Given this, it is no surprise that the question of Sunday observance was raised in Parliament at various times during James' reign.

Parliament and the question of Sabbath observance

James I, like Elizabeth I before him, resisted moves by Parliament to meddle in religious policy; yet MPs persistently tried to enforce stricter Sabbath observance. Several parliamentary bills were introduced that sought to suppress drinking and other recreations on Sundays. The MPs who promoted and supported these bills did so for social and economic reasons as well as moral and religious ones. While many MPs spoke about Sunday recreations as profanations of the Lord's Day and gave a strong moral tone to their speeches, other emphasised the threat to social order of drinking and festivities on Sunday. Indeed, even the puritan MP, Francis Hastings, seemed to be as concerned about the likelihood of violence resulting from drinking at church ales as he was about the ungodly nature of the festivities themselves. Although many MPs were willing to lend their support to legislation which sought to achieve the moral reformation of the population, many did so only because they regarded the 'vices' that they were seeking to regulate as a threat to social order. Yet, the radical Protestant members of the Commons were motivated by more than just the desire to achieve good order and peaceful government. They pressed for laws to keep the Sabbath and to suppress drunkenness and other 'sins' out of religious fervour and a desire to achieve moral reform.[121] Attempts were made time and again in successive Parliaments to enforce stricter Sabbath observance. However, to the frustration of the zealous MPs and magistrates who wanted legislation to ban wakes, ales, May games, dancing and other recreations on Sundays, none of the bills introduced ever made it onto the statute book.[122]

In his *Doctrine of the Sabbath* published in 1604, George Widley spoke approvingly of James' proclamation of the previous year in which James had prohibited certain recreations on Sundays, and Widley called for laws to be enacted to force people to keep the Sabbath holy. For Widley and like-minded Protestants, the king's 1603 proclamation was only a first, but insufficient, step. Legislation was needed: 'for Gods Lawes to many are but as cobwebs to the great flyes, which they easily breake, without they be strengthened by the Princes lawes'.[123] Many MPs clearly shared Widley's views and differed from the king on how the Sabbath should be observed. This is illustrated by the fact that, whereas the Privy Council met on Sundays, in 1604 the Commons refused to hold a meeting with members of the Lords because it was scheduled to be held on a Sunday.[124]

In January 1606, Sir Francis Evers introduced a bill 'for the better observing and keeping holy the Sabbath day or Sundays'.[125] The bill stated that, contrary to James' 1603 proclamation, the Sabbath was being:

> many times prophaned and neclected by a disorderly sort of people in using and exercising bear-baytinges, bulbaytinges, Stage playes, morrice daunces hunting, coursing, hawking, churchales, daunsing, rushbearing, maygames, whitsonales, outhurlinges, inhurlinges wakes and dyvers other unlawfull games, assemblies and pastimes in and upon the Sabbaoth dayes or sundayes.[126]

The bill was designed to prohibit all such activities on Sundays and sought to impose heavy fines on offenders and to punish defaulters by having them put in the stocks for three hours on a Sunday. It found considerable support among MPs and passed through all stages in the Commons within three weeks without a division. The MP, Nicholas Fuller called upon the king and the Lords to support the bill, but it did not make it through the Lords. It is possible that it failed through lack of support from the Crown.[127]

In the 1614 Parliament, Fuller reintroduced the 1606 bill, or a version of it, with support from Sir Edward Montagu.[128] The bill was the first bill passed by the Commons in the 1614 Parliament, which indicates the importance already being attached to the question of Sabbath observance by many MPs.[129] The details that were recorded of the Commons debate give an indication of the thinking of at least some of the MPs who supported the bill. Some sought to widen the scope of the 1614 bill. Football was frequently played on Sundays and attracted large numbers of people. It caused many people to miss church and frequently led to violence; as in Great Bedwyn in Wiltshire, where several players and 'beholders' were fined for 'certain boxes and blows one against another at the football play on a Sabboth day'.[130] Football had long concerned both moralists and magistrates and one MP tried to have it added to the prohibited games in the bill. For others, the bill was insufficiently sabbatarian and they wanted to prevent any form of recreation and work on Sundays altogether.[131] Even if some wanted it to go further than it did, MPs approved of the bill. The 1614 bill faired better in the Lords than the 1606 bill had done. It is not clear whether or not the 1614 bill was identical to that of 1606. Either it was the same, but the mood in the Lords had changed to such an extent that they looked upon it more favourably than before, or it was not and some changes had made it more palatable to the peers. Unsurprisingly given his puritan sympathies, the bill was backed by Lord Saye and Sele, who declared that the Sabbath 'is as much broken by recreations and sportes as the businesses of a mans callinge'.[132] The Bishop of Lincoln, Richard Neile, also supported the bill, declaring that 'I think that there is noe man that regardes the glory of God and Keepinge of the Sabbaoth day holy but doth like well this bill'. However, Neile wanted the bill to be changed in order expressly to allow people 'to worke in tyme of harvest' in accordance with the Edwardian statute of 1552.[133] Neile evidently did not share the radical sabbatarianism of the puritans, who were against work of any description being undertaken on Sundays.

Not all the bishops supported the bill. James Montagu, the Bishop of Bath and Wells, spoke against it, in contrast to the backing given to it by his brother, Sir Edward, in the Lower House.[134] He took issue with the claim of the bill's supporters that dancing profaned the Sabbath, arguing that 'we finde in the scripture that dancinge is lawfull, for David danced before the Arke, naye the Jews did recreate on the Sabbaothe day and we cannot be stricter in observinge these things than they were'. He went on to state: 'that dancinge cannot be proved vnlawfull by the scripture nor any such exercise vpon the sabbaoth day wherin there is neither labour vsed nor profainenes committed'. He accepted that lawful recreation could be abused by 'wantonnes and deliciousnes' and could consequently profane the Lord's Day, but argued that Sunday recreations such as leaping and dancing were not in themselves unlawful or sinful.[135] The 1614 bill enjoyed considerably more support than its predecessor. At the end of May, the Archbishop of York reported that the Lords' Committee set up to consider the bill 'did hold the Drift and Purpose thereof to be good, and to tend to the Glory of God'.[136] However, he announced that some unspecified details needed changing and a conference was subsequently held between twenty-five members of the Lords' committee and fifty from the Commons committee to discuss suggested amendments.[137] At the conference, Bishop Montagu again argued against the bill and stated that 'to take away all recreation is ... contrary to the divine rule it selfe'. He pointed out that even Calvinist Geneva allowed pall-mall, tennis and other recreations after evening prayer and said that 'those recreations that neyther breake rest nor sanctification ... are lawfull and may be vsed'.[138] However, the Bishop of Oxford felt that the bill did not go far enough and wanted to see it also exclude all servile work and all buying and selling on Sundays. George Abbot, the Archbishop of Canterbury, personally backed the bill and stressed the fact that 'in the Scriptures ... God punished his people for nothinge more than the neglect of sanctifyinge his Sabbaoth'. He assured the members of both committees that 'though some Lordes spake against partes of the bill' they did not dislike it and said that 'they are most gladde to imbrace it'.[139] Most did indeed seem willing to embrace the bill, but Parliament was dissolved before the amended bill could be passed by both Houses and so the bill died.

Parliament did not meet again until 1621, when, for a third time, MPs tried to introduce a bill to make ales, May games and other Sunday recreations unlawful. However, this time they were doing so in the knowledge that such activities had been sanctioned by the king. Nonetheless, MPs once again tried to meddle in religious matters. Indeed, the Declaration may have spurred some of them on to do so. A mere two days after the Commons had commenced business, Sir Walter Earle MP reintroduced the 1614 bill, described as:

> An Act for keeping holy the Saboth-daye. Whereby all assemblyes at Church Ales, Dancing, May-games, etc., were made unlawfull.[140]

Hill has suggested that the bill may have been aimed directly against the *Book of Sports* because it prohibited dancing and May games on the Sabbath. However, since the 1606 bill and, most probably, the 1614 bill did so as well, it seems unlikely that the King's Declaration was being targeted specifically. That said, the Declaration had polarised attitudes and had strengthened the feeling of antipathy of some MPs towards Sunday recreations. The Devonshire MP, George Chudleigh, said that he would not support the bill if the intention was to oppose the king's Declaration, but he clearly had no love for the Declaration since he went on to say that:

> when his Majesty shall be informed by the experience of the justices of the peace in the country that it hath done more harm by increasing profaneness than it hath done good in converting papists, I doubt not but he will be pleased to call it in again.[141]

If the Declaration had served to harden the attitudes of some MPs and strengthened their desire to curb Sunday recreations, others used it to justify their opposition to the bill and to criticise those seeking to ban traditional recreations. The MP for Shaftesbury, Thomas Shepherd, argued that the bill 'was against the King's Book' and claimed that, when properly translated, many of the psalms did not begin with the call to 'rejoice' but began with the phrase 'dance ye'.[142] He asserted that: 'the Kinge by his edict hath given leave to his subiects to daunce', and went on to denounce the bill's backers:

> Saying it savored of the spirit of a puritan, exclaiming against justices of the peace in the country for favouring them, taxing the House, saying they made laws which were gins and snares for papists but not so much as a mousetrap for a puritan, etc.[143]

Shepherd linked the bill to puritanism and challenged the bill's premise by asserting that 'David biddeth us dance', claiming both royal and divine sanction for such recreation.[144] Shepherd asserted that the moves against recreation not only contravened the King's wishes but also flew in the face of 'the greifes and cries of the people'.[145]

The content and tone of Shepherd's attack caused uproar. John Pym called Shepherd a 'pertubator of the peace' and accused him of wanting JPs to be 'protectors of those that disobey the orders of the church'. He denied that Parliament was making laws against the 'King's Book' and accused Shepherd of manufacturing a division among MPs 'by intimating that [the bill] was occasioned by some puritans'.[146] Others accused Shepherd of 'abusing God's word' and claimed that by approving 'our maypole dancing by David's example he shewed his profaneness'.[147] Shepherd was viewed by some as 'a base, jesuited papist'.[148] Seemingly acknowledging the important implications of overtly linking puritanism with the attempt to suppress lawful games, Sir Edward Coke declared: 'He hath sett a fire in religion and the state'.[149] Shepherd was censured and expelled from the Commons as an 'unworthy member', and Pym claimed that Shepherd was 'seekeing to bring us into the ill opinion of the kinge … [by] sayinge that we went about to make a lawe in the face of his Majestie opposite to his Royall iudgement declared in printe'.[150] The bill, if passed, would indeed have been contrary to the King's Declaration, which, contrary to Pym's suggestion, did not contradict the King's proclamation of 1603. The proclamation had not outlawed ales, dancing or May games on Sundays and the Declaration had specifically sanctioned such activities. The bill, though, sought to make church ales, dancing and May games unlawful and therefore did contradict the king's stated views.[151] Although James accepted Shepherd's censure, he nonetheless appeared to support much of what Shepherd had said. The Secretary of State, George Calvert, reported that as the Commons had censured:

> one who spake against the Puritan Bill, because that Bill was directly against a Decree of his owne, … [the king] would have us carefull howe we gave passage to that Bill And as we had stricken with the

right hand against Papists soe we would strike with the left against Puritans.[152]

The King's message confirms that he saw the bill as the work of puritans and regarded it as contrary to his Declaration. He also urged the Commons to be even-handed, wanting the puritans to be treated equally with papists, just as he had in the Declaration itself, where he called on church authorities to 'convince & reforme' Catholics and to 'take the like straight order with all the Puritans and Precisians'.[153] Despite the king's evident displeasure over the bill, the Commons pressed forward with it, and it was passed by both Houses. James then vetoed it. Given James' earlier statement and the fact that the bill defied his Declaration, this was of little surprise. It may have been James' veto, though, that caused Bishop Bayly to argue with the king over Sabbath observance: an argument that landed him in gaol.[154]

Despite the veto, when Parliament met again in 1624 MPs promptly reintroduced the 1621 bill.[155] This bill was similarly passed by both Houses only to be vetoed by the king once again. James again made it clear that it was contrary to his Declaration. Claiming that he 'did not love to doe contradictory things', he pointed out that he had 'published a declaration in print for the allowance of some exercises after evening prayer'.[156] Oddly, James described bull- and bear-baiting as lawful recreations, even though these were specifically condemned in both his 1603 proclamation and his Declaration.[157] James went on to make clear that he did not object to people 'going to other parishes to make merry'. This had, of course, been a major point of dispute between Montagu and Williams, and the fact that James now seemed to sanction both bull- and bear-baiting and the prospect of people going to neighbouring parishes to take part in recreations on Sundays, indicates his increasing exasperation with those who wanted to suppress traditional pastimes through stricter sabbatarian legislation. Indeed, he stated that he would not assent to a bill:

> which is but to give the puritans their will, who thinke all consists of two sermons a day and will allow noe recreacon to poor men that labour hard all weeke long to ease themselves on the Sunday.[158]

Once again, James identified the attempts to suppress Sunday recreation with puritanism and made clear his opposition.

Nonetheless, although James prevented Parliament from passing this legislation and cited his Declaration as a reason for doing so, he did not try to enforce the Declaration itself. This may well be because Archbishop Abbot was against it.

The Jacobean Church and Sunday recreation

Only a couple of Jacobean bishops wrote works which in any way supported puritan sabbatarianism, and only a handful condemned Sunday pastimes. Most of those who did were concerned with the question of church attendance. Bishop Bayly is exceptional in that he does appear to have been a strict sabbatarian. In *The Practice of Pietie*, he argued that Sunday was the Christian Sabbath, instituted by Christ, and that Christians were bound to keep it holy and that, indeed, 'the Moralitie of [the fourth commandment], as of the rest of the Commandements, is more religiously to be kept as under the Gospel, than of the Iews under the Law'.[159] Bayly condemned recreations on Sundays and cited examples of divine punishment being visited upon people for profaning the Sabbath. These included fires which destroyed much of Stratford-upon-Avon and Tiverton and which, Bayly claimed, were sent to punish the people of those towns for profaning the Lord's Day.[160] Despite this, Bayly was appointed Bishop of Bangor in 1616. Nonetheless, his sabbatarian views were to land him in trouble, as we have seen, when he argued with the king over the question of Sabbath observance, most probably following James' vetoing of the sabbatarian bill of 1621.[161] Lancelot Andrewes, Bishop of Winchester, had also written about the fourth commandment and wanted Sunday to be properly observed. Yet, although he was against people working and trading on Sundays and may have been more sabbatarian than most of his brother bishops, as Paul Welsby observes, 'the list of things which Andrewes stated to be unlawful on the Sabbath was plainly more conservative than that given by Bownd or Greenham.'[162] Moreover, it is possible that Andrewes was involved in drafting the Lancashire Declaration of Sports as he was in attendance on James at the time.[163] There is no evidence that Andrewes was critical of the *Book of Sports*.[164]

In 1603, following James' proclamation of that year, the Bishops of Llandaff and Bristol both issued Visitation Articles which asked whether people in their dioceses were indulging in games on Sundays. Yet, both sets of Articles speak only of 'unlawful games,' and so did not rule out games or recreations which were deemed to be lawful.[165] It is important to distinguish between 'unlawful games', which some bishops were concerned about, and popular pastimes generally, which most were not.[166] In 1606, Thomas Jegon, Archdeacon of Norwich, asked if innkeepers and householders 'suffer any plaies or games ... upon any Sunday' and, in 1607, Thomas Matthew, Archbishop of York enquired whether parishioners used 'Rush-bearings, Bull-baytinge, Beare-baitings, May-games, Morice-dancers, Ailes or such like prophane pastimes ... on the sabbath'. However, Jegon enquired if Sunday games were allowed 'before evening praier be cleane done in that Parish' and Matthew's Visitation Articles asked whether 'prophane pastimes' were being used on the Sabbath 'to the hindrance of Prayers, Sermons, or other godly exercises'.[167] Similarly, James Montagu, Bishop of Bath and Wells, and Bishop Vaughan of London were simply concerned that *unlawful* games should not be held on Sundays and that festivity should not prevent people from attending divine service. Many, like Archbishop Bancroft also wanted to ensure that church ales should not be held in the church or churchyard.[168] In other words, although they were concerned that recreations should not be held in the vicinity of the church and should not prevent people from going to church on Sunday, they did not seek to prevent Sunday recreations altogether. Indeed, nearly all the bishops allowed for the use of lawful recreations after church.

Nonetheless, although puritan sabbatarianism was much stricter than the traditional sabbatarianism of the English Church, it did find some support among a few senior churchmen. Puritan sabbatarianism had now existed for some time and it would be surprising if it had not influenced at least some senior members of the Church. Bishop Bayly clearly embraced the stricter view of Sabbath observance. John King, Bishop of London, also seemed to disapprove of revelry 'whereby the Sabbaoth or Holy-day is prophaned, and the people led away to much lewdnesse'.[169] Furthermore, although Bishop Montagu had argued against the 1614 bill, Archbishop Abbot and the Bishops of Lincoln and Oxford had supported it.[170] Nonetheless, Jacobean Visitation Articles, including Abbot's, were mostly concerned about preventing people from working and trading on Sundays and preventing festivity from interrupting church services rather than prohibiting Sunday revelry altogether.[171]

The Lancashire Declaration of 1617 had to be read in all the churches in Lancashire, but ministers in churches elsewhere were not made to read the 1618 Declaration. This may well have been due to the influence or intervention of Archbishop Abbot. He was at a parish church in Croydon on the day that the declaration was to be read there and he refused to allow it.[172] Abbot had, of course, supported the 1614 bill and his evident lack of support for the Declaration may have persuaded James not to enforce it. James was nothing if not prudent and clearly saw more merit in allowing his Declaration to stand without actively trying to enforce its publication. It was reported that James decided to 'wink at' Abbot's failure to publish the Declaration.[173] In other words, he decided to 'turn a blind eye'.

Although both Archbishop Abbot and Bishop Bayly appear to have disapproved of the Declaration, there is no evidence of any large-scale opposition among the bishops. On the contrary, some were clearly supportive. Following James' 1617 Declaration, Morton, Bishop of Chester, instructed that afternoon sermons should be no longer than an hour long in order to prevent preachers from trying to sabotage the king's declaration.[174] In similar vein, following the 1618 Declaration, the

Visitation Articles of Francis Godwin, Bishop of Hereford, asked 'whether the minister doe not defer the afternoon service unseasonably for the debarring or hindering of fit recreation?' Godwin also stated that, as well as public worship, the Sabbath was ordained 'for the reliefe of nature by rest as of the body soe of the minde which is recreation' and enquired if 'any person have taken upon them to hinder honest and seemely recreation upon Sondayes'.[175] Although this is the only example of overt episcopal enforcement of the 1618 Declaration, the fact that other visitation articles did not incorporate such enforcement is not a sign of opposition.

The debate dramatised

Despite the politicisation of Sunday recreation during James' reign, the Jacobean period saw relatively few theological works published on the question of Sabbath observance. A clutch of books were written espousing puritan sabbatarianism in much the same vein as the puritan works of the late Elizabethan period: attacking wakes, ales, May games, dancing and other pastimes on Sundays.[176] William Harrison's *Difference of Hearers* (1614) is typical of these, declaring that 'pleasure is the baite of sinne' and attacking 'lascivious dancing, riotous gaming, wanton sports & prophane pastimes on the Sabboth day'.[177] These works added to the far more numerous Elizabethan polemics attacking traditional festivity, prompting Robert Burton to write in the 1620s that 'these sports have many oppugners, whole volumes writ against them'.[178] As divisions on the issue became more apparent, works attacking puritan sabbatarianism and defending traditional festivity also began to appear. In addition to Rogers' *Catholic Doctrine*, Thomas Broad published his *Three Questions Answered*, in which he declared that 'there is scarce any point of doctrine more controverted, then the doctrine of the Sabbath' and went on to dispute Bownd's version of sabbatarianism.[179] Even more support was given to traditional festivities by poets and playwrights. Given that many puritans were vehemently opposed to interludes and plays, it is of little surprise that they were targeted by playwrights, but it nonetheless highlights the increasingly apparent divisions in early Stuart society.

Thomas Dekker was unusual in that he used plays to attack traditional festivity. Dekker indirectly criticised James' support for traditional festivity in his play, *If This Be not a Good Play, the Devil Is in It*. Written in 1612, the play associates revelry with the Devil and, at first, has the character of the king, Alfonso, declaring that the Sabbath will be devoted entirely to God: 'Sacred is that and hye; / And who prophanes one houre in that, shall dye.' This may well be a reference to James' 1603 proclamation, which no doubt encouraged English puritans to believe that James intended to follow a much stricter sabbatarian course than Elizabeth had done, even if they misinterpreted the scope of the proclamation. Their subsequent sense of disappointment, even betrayal, is reflected in Dekker's play, as Alfonso later abandons his earlier stance and, instead, indulges himself and his court in May games and other revelry, taking his kingdom to the verge of ruin as a result.[180]

Unlike Dekker, most writers wrote in support of traditional pastimes, and ridiculed those who sought to suppress them. In 1612 a play entitled *The Merry Devil of Edmonton* gave a positive portrayal of the function of popular pastimes and, in 1614, several poets collaborated to produce a collection of poems called *The Shepheards Pie*, which celebrated ales, maypoles, dancing and other traditional revelry.[181] Ben Jonson wrote a number of plays which similarly fêted traditional festivity and lampooned puritans. His prologue to *Bartholomew Fair* (1614) referred to the puritans as James' 'land's faction' and spoke of their 'zealous noise'. He caricatured puritans savagely in the form of Zeal-of-the-land-Busy, who attacked ales, dancing and May games. Busy was ridiculed as a self-righteous hypocrite who railed against innocent, popular pastimes, describing himself as someone who 'sitteth here to prophesy the destruction of fairs and May-games, wakes and Whitsun-ales, and doth sigh and groan, for the reformation of these abuses'.[182]

In *Pleasure Reconciled to Virtue* (1618), Jonson took the opposite view from Dekker of James' perceived change in policy and indirectly praised the *Book of Sports*. He depicted James as Hercules, first preventing excess in merrymaking and preventing riotous behaviour and then restraining people who attempted to suppress sport altogether.[183] The anonymous poem, *Pasquils Palinodia*, printed in 1619, took a nostalgic approach, lamenting an idyllic England that it feared was lost and linking it with traditional festivity; the underlying message being that such festivity had to be protected and embraced in order to re-establish a prosperous England that was at peace with itself:

> Happy the age and harmless were the dayes,
> (For then true love and amity was found,)
> When every village did a May-pole raise,
> And Whitson-ales, and May-games did abound ...
> ... But since the summer-poles were overthrowne,
> And all good sports and merryments decayed,
> How times and men are chang'd.[184]

Plays and poems not only celebrated traditional festivity and attacked puritans for seeking to suppress it; some also targeted magistrates who tried to ban revels. Magistrates in Middlesex had made increasing attempts to curb traditional pastimes and Jonson criticised them too in *Bartholomew Fair* in the guise of Justice Overdo. Overdo, as the name suggests, was portrayed as a busy-body who had no sense of proportion.

All too easily outraged by people's behaviour, he suspected crime, disorder and all manner of 'enormities' at every turn. He was portrayed as a pompous buffoon who continually overreacted and misjudged people and their motives.[185] Jonson's attack on the magistrates is understandable given that traditional revelry was under threat from JPs who were concerned that revelry would lead to disorder.

Maintaining social order and the polarisation within society

Magistrates across the country were anxious to avoid disorder. Many of them saw wakes and ales as dangerous, as they often led to drunkenness and violence. Writing in 1611, Thomas Coryate, praised church ales as 'feasts of charity ... breeding love betwixt neighbors & ... raising of a stocke for the supporting and maintenance of our Church'. A supporter of ales, Coryate nonetheless accepted that they were often the occasions of 'abuses' such as 'drunkennesse, gluttonie, swearing, lasciuiousnesse' and 'brawling, picking of quarrels'.[186] Indeed, in Lancashire the eve of May Day was known as 'mischief night'.[187] There were many examples of drunkenness and violence at revels of various types held on Sundays. For example, in 1614, and again in 1615, fighting broke out at May games held in the Worcestershire village of Longdon involving men from neighbouring parishes. In 1616, a William Jeffries attempted to stop morris dancing taking place on Sundays in Longdon by trying to arrest the minstrel. His attempts to punish the minstrel under the vagrancy laws led to the threat that Jeffries would have his neck broken down the stairs.[188] Of course, court records only record instances where disorder occurred and it can be assumed that many ales took place without any violence. Nonetheless, violence frequently occurred at festivities and was sometimes serious, as in 1615 when two Devonshire ales ended in manslaughter.[189] Coryate condemned such disorder, but called for the abuses to be stamped out rather than the ales themselves. Many magistrates took a different view and wanted to put a stop to the revels themselves. Following the manslaughters in Devon, on 24 July 1615 the Assize Court at Exeter complained of 'the continual profanation of God's Sabbath at these and other like such unlawful meetings', and ordered that, because 'of the infinite number of inconveniences daily arising by means of revels, Church-ales, and bull baitings, that all such revels, Church-ales, and bull-baitings be from henceforth utterly suppressed'.[190] This order is interesting in that, while it condemned 'inconveniences' seen at revels, it also referred to the 'profanation of God's Sabbath'. This raises the issue of what motivated civic authorities in their attempts to suppress revelry.

It is clear that magistrates in Lancashire were subject to a strong puritan influence, and JPs elsewhere in the country were too. At the very least, as is evidenced in the order of the Exeter assizes, they sometimes cited religious grounds to justify orders suppressing revelry which, for secular reasons, they feared would cause disorder. Certainly, a number of puritan ministers put pressure on justices to stop wakes and ales. In 1618, for example, Edmund Rudyard called on Sir William Bowyer and other Staffordshire justices 'to look into the weighty and burdensome charge that lieth upon you as you are public magistrates'. He wrote that God had put them 'in place and authoritie to punish such greivous sinnes' as 'lasciuious and unchaste (mixt) dauncings, with diuers other abuses being common: as the horrible profanation of the Lords Saboth' and called upon them to demonstrate their 'hatred and lothing of sinne'.[191]

No doubt many magistrates wanted to ban revels because they feared disorder, but the evidence suggests that, particularly in certain parts of the country, many also had religious motives and wanted to stop what they saw as immoral behaviour and the profanation of the Sabbath. In 1611, for example, the Mayor of Salisbury tried to prevent the traditional Midsummer Eve festivity because that year it fell upon a Sunday.[192] That year the Corporation of Chester voted to reschedule its midsummer show because it fell on a Sunday.[193] Elsewhere, municipal authorities moved other feasts and events like annual elections to prevent them taking place on the Lord's Day.[194] In 1611 the Common Council of London claimed that apprentices were living riotously by, among other things, spending their time in dancing, playing tennis and bowls 'and other exercises unfitt for their degrees and calling to the high displeasure of almightie God'.[195] In 1622 the entire bench of Devon's JPs defied James' Declaration of Sports and, citing complaints surrounding the holding of church ales, declared that their order prohibiting them still stood. Two years later the Somerset JPs similarly confirmed earlier orders banning church ales.[196]

There is no doubt that in various parts of the country, despite James' Declaration, traditional festivity was under attack from local magistrates, many of whom not only feared disorder but also appear to have been influenced by the new strain of puritan sabbatarianism. The issue of Sunday pastimes continued to become politicised and to polarise attitudes. This is clear from episodes like the one that occurred in Stratford in 1619 when the Bailiff of Stratford and Alderman Henry Smith had the town's maypole taken down. This caused a riot, and about forty supporters of the maypole then defied the authorities and erected another maypole. Satirical libels were then distributed attacking the town's puritan governing faction. One of them spoke of 'the old bitinge and young sucking Puritans of Stratford' and another accused them of using their positions in local government to their own ends.[197] In 1624, people in Guildford were furious when the town's mayor pulled down their maypole even though they had attached to it 'the armes of his Majestie'.[198] The maypole therefore retained its role as a totem symbolising the struggle between those who wanted traditional festivity preserved and those who wanted to ban it.

During the course of James' reign traditional festivity declined in many parts of the country. Puritans became closely associated with the attacks on popular pastimes, but they were aided by many magistrates motivated by fears of disorder. These were not, though, the only reasons for their decline. Economic factors were also at play. For many parishes church ales were simply becoming less economically viable, as receipts from them did not keep pace with the rising cost of providing food and drink and many parishes instead introduced a system of parochial rates in order to maintain the church.[199] Ales continued to be used to raise money in many places, as in Wells, where an ale was held in 1607 to maintain the steeple and bells of St Cuthbert's.[200] However, traditional festivity was struggling to survive as a means of raising money in other parts of the country. The move away from using ales was sometimes a halting one. At Thatcham in Berkshire, for example, the traditional ale had been abandoned in favour of rating, only to be revived again in 1617 and then held annually until 1621, when Thatcham moved finally and permanently to a system of rates to raise funds.[201] This see-sawing between fund-raising ales and a system of rates also reflected the tensions within society: the enduring popularity of traditional festivity among sections of society and the desire of others to see them ended or replaced for whatever reason. The very fact that the Devonshire and Somerset JPs had to reissue their orders against ales is testimony to their continuing use.[202]

By the end of James' reign there was a serious division in society over the issue of popular pastimes traditionally enjoyed on Sundays. Rogers' *Catholic Doctrine* and the MP, Thomas Shepherd, had both pointed the finger at puritans for pushing forward a new kind of sabbatarianism and they were right to do so. James I's Declaration of Sports had similarly linked puritanism to the suppression of traditional festivity. A new, far stricter and wide-ranging form of sabbatarianism was indeed at work and influenced many MPs and magistrates into trying to suppress traditional revelry. Many ordinary people resented the attack on what they saw as their traditional way of life and blamed the puritans. For example, a new minister at Wylye who was apparently in all other respects a conformist in church ceremony and discipline was condemned by a woman parishioner as a puritan when he began a campaign against drunkenness, sexual immorality and dancing:

> We had a good parson here before but now we have a puritan ... I would we had kept our old parson, for he never did dislike with (games and dancing) ... These proud puritans are up at the top now but I hope they will have a time to come as fast down as ever they came up.[203]

James' Declaration of Sports had attempted to draw a line under puritan sabbatarianism and to protect the traditional rights of ordinary people to revelry after church on Sundays. He had tried to put puritans in their place and to prevent them from encroaching on what he regarded as areas of royal authority. However, he did not enforce the reading of the Declaration and, although he vetoed attempts in Parliament to pass sabbatarian legislation which ran contrary to his Declaration, various magistrates and puritan ministers continued their war against traditional revelry. During the reign of his son, Charles I, the battle lines were to become even more clearly marked as Charles and his supporters sought to bring about the happy time that the parishioner from Wylye hoped for.

5

The *Book of Sports* and the reign of Charles I
From a 'pious Statute' to 'bloody civil war'

Looking back at the bloody civil wars that had torn England apart in the 1640s, Richard Baxter claimed that: 'The Warre was begun in our streets before the King or Parliament had any Armies', adding that: 'The hatred of the Puritans, and the Parliament Reformation, inflamed the ignorant, drunken, and ungodly rout ... even before the Warres.'[1] There is no doubt that, long before the country descended into physical conflict, tensions in Caroline society increased between the 'godly' puritans and those who they viewed as 'ungodly' people resistant to reformation. It is now widely accepted that arguments over religion and fears from both sides about perceived and potential religious changes were among the major factors that led to the Civil War and religious belief was a major factor in determining allegiance in the war.[2] Baxter claimed that:

> the generality of the People through the Land ... who were then called Puritans ... that used to talk of God, and Heaven, and Scripture, ... and spend the Lord's Day in Religious Exercises ... the main Body of this sort of men, both Preachers and People, adhered to the Parliament. And on the other side, the Gentry that were not so precise and strict against an Oath, or Gaming, or Plays, or Drinking, nor troubled themselves so much about the Ministers and People that were for the King's Book, for Dancing and Recreations on the Lord's Day; ... and which ordinarily spoke against this strictness and preciseness in Religion, and this strict observation of the Lord's Day ... the main body of these were against Parliament.[3]

Religious divisions were at the root of many of the problems facing the regime on the eve of civil war, and tensions over the question of Sabbath observance and Charles I's decision to reissue and then enforce the *Book of Sports* played their part. Fuller claimed that many contemporaries even believed that the *Book of Sports* and the profanation of the Lord's Day 'was a principal procurer of God's anger, since poured out on this land, in a long and bloody civil war'.[4] After it was over, many even viewed the war, which had 'rent the bowels of England', as divine punishment for the licensing of Sunday recreations that had taken place so many years before. This underscores the *Book of Sports'* profound impact on sections of English society.[5] Allegiance in the war was, for many people, determined by religious convictions; and the serious differences over Sabbath observance had become a matter of real contention during Charles' reign. Indeed, in 1641, John Ley observed that the Sabbath had:

> become as a Ball, betwixt two Racketts bandied this way and that way, by mutuall contradiction, not onely betwixt the godly and the profane (which is no newes) but among many of those who are in no mean accompt in the Church of God.[6]

This last point is significant in that Charles I's *Book of Sports* not only outraged puritans, but also distressed many otherwise moderate, mainstream Protestants. Indeed, it provoked considerable opposition and, as Kevin Sharpe has claimed, 'more than any other of [Charles I's] injunctions it raised opponents, who were not natural enemies to the church'.[7] At the time that the Declaration was reissued its opponents had no platform from which to speak out, as Parliament was not sitting and printed works were subject to censorship. When Parliament did sit again in 1640 and control of the printing presses was lost, the lasting resentment felt towards the *Book of Sports* by significant sections of English society became all too evident. Why, then, did Charles I reissue his father's *Book of Sports* and why did it provoke so much more opposition and trouble for the Crown?

1625

For many radical Protestants, Charles I's reign got off to a promising start. Both Elizabeth I and James I had resisted attempts by MPs to meddle in religious policy and had blocked moves to pass legislation on Sunday observance.[8] However, in the last Parliament of his father's reign, the so-called 'Prince's Parliament', the then Prince Charles had lent his support to the bill for better Sabbath observance, which his father subsequently vetoed. While Charles' was most probably motivated to do so for political advantage rather than through religious conviction, as Charles and Buckingham were eager for Parliament to support war against Spain and were currying favour with MPs.[9] Given Charles' support for the bill in the 1624 Parliament, it is not surprising that MPs anticipated his support for a bill for better Sabbath observance when the new king's first Parliament met in 1625. Indeed, they decided against incorporating a suggested amendment to the bill, resolving instead to reintroduce the 1624 bill without any alterations on the basis that 'it past both Houses the last Parliament in this manner, and the Kinge beinge then a Member of the Upper House gave his voice to it and therefore is not like to denye his assent now, unless it receive alteration'.[10] Both Houses duly passed the bill 'for the further Reformation of Sundry Abuses committed on the Lords Day, commonly called Sunday' and, this time, it did indeed receive royal assent.[11] Charles' supported the 1624 bill and gave his assent to the 1625 Act because he hoped to be rewarded by MPs voting for much-needed revenues.[12] However, in doing so, Charles was not approving sabbatarian legislation. Although he enacted legislation concerning the observing of the Lord's Day which his two predecessors had refused to do, the 1625 Act was not 'sabbatarian' in the puritan sense of the word. The terms of the 1625 Act were the same as those of the 1624 bill and, those terms were entirely in keeping with James I's *Book of Sports*, which had so offended the puritan sabbatarians.[13] The 1625 statute described 'the holy keeping of the Lord's day' as 'a principal part of the true service of God' and stated that the Lord's Day:

> in very many places of this realm hath been and now is profaned and neglected by a disorderly sort of people, in exercising and frequenting bear-baiting, bull-baiting, interludes, common plays and other unlawful exercises and pastimes upon the Lord's day.

It went on to complain of 'quarrels, bloodsheds, and other great inconveniences' resulting from people going '*out of their own parishes*' to attend 'such disordered and unlawful exercises and pastimes, *neglecting divine service* both in their own parishes and elsewhere'. The Act prohibited any 'meetings, assemblies, or concourse of people *out of their own parishes* on the Lord's day ... for any sports and pastimes whatsoever' and also banned people, even within their own parishes, from using 'bear-baiting, bull-baiting, interludes, common plays, or other unlawful exercises and pastimes'.[14] These are important points. Firstly, in addition to voicing obvious concerns over disorder, the Act specifically referred to people 'neglecting divine service', once again highlighting the concern that people should attend church on Sunday. Secondly, although bear- and bull-baiting, plays and 'other *unlawful* exercises' were prohibited completely on Sundays, all lawful sports and pastimes were denied people only if they exercised them 'out of their own parishes'. In other words, the Act did not contradict James I's *Book of Sports* and was, therefore, no more sabbatarian than his Declaration had been.

The 1625 Act is nonetheless important in that it was the first piece of legislation which had been passed concerning recreations on Sundays since the reign of Elizabeth I, and many zealous Protestants saw it as a significant and positive step. Walter Yonge recorded in his diary: 'a good bill passed the house for observation of the Sabbath' and William Prynne referred to it as 'the pious Statute'.[15] Henry Burton described the Act as 'an auspicious beginning, promising a religious gracious Raigne'. Indeed, he was so impressed that he called Charles 'our pious King Charles, whose raigne hath bene honoured with a religious Law for the better keeping of the Lords day' and referred to the Act as 'the prime gemme in his Royall diadem; ... which deserves to be writen in golden characters'.[16] Yet, either through wishful thinking or because they deliberately sought to exploit ambiguities in the statute's wording, they misinterpreted the Act. The Act ruled out 'any sports or pastimes whatsoever' for people outside their own parishes and only prohibited people from indulging in 'unlawful exercises' within their own parishes, but it did not stipulate which exercises were lawful. Puritan commentators exploited this fact to assert that it outlawed recreations which it patently did not. Prynne, for example, referred to the 'unlawful exercise, sport, or pastime [referred to] within the pious statute' and added: 'within which there is no question, but dancing is included'.[17] Similarly, William Twisse, despite referring to the clause about people being forbidden to come out of their own parishes, nonetheless claimed that the statute meant 'that all sports and pastimes are prophanations of our Christian Sabbath ... in the judgement of the whole Parliament consisting of the Kings Majesty the head thereof'.[18] Burton also asserted that 'it is plaine, that all manner of sports and pastimes are unlawful on the Lords day ... And therefore dancing, maygames, morrices, and the like ... are unlawfull.'[19] In fact, by referring to unlawful pastimes, the Act clearly implied that other pastimes were perfectly lawful, provided people used them in their own parishes and did not neglect divine service.

James I's *Book of Sports* had expressly allowed dancing, piping, leaping and vaulting and other 'such harmelesse Recreation' on Sundays after church, including May games, whitsun ales, morris dances and setting up maypoles.[20] Although James had wisely thought better of enforcing his Declaration, he had not revoked it. Therefore, the recreations listed in the 1618 Declaration remained lawful. This enabled Charles I to assent to the 1625 bill without any risk of nullifying the 1618 Declaration. Nonetheless, the fact that the Act did not specify which recreations were lawful enabled the likes of Prynne and Twisse to make false assertions about the recreations prohibited. At least one modern historian has misconstrued the 1625 Act, mistakenly claiming that it 'effectively reversed the 1618 Declaration of Sports and banned Sunday recreations'.[21] It did no such thing. Ronald Hutton and Esther Cope both observe that the statute did not specify which sports were lawful and that the identity of these 'lawful pastimes' remained ambiguous. However, given that the 1618

Declaration had made clear which sports were lawful, there were no real grounds for conflicting interpretations.[22] The likes of Yonge and Prynne nonetheless stated that the Act was more sabbatarian than it actually was and exploited it to support attempts to suppress traditional recreations. In 1628 Parliament passed another Act 'for the further reformation of sundry abuses committed on the Lord's day', which also got royal assent.[23] This Act made no reference to recreations, but prohibited the driving of cattle, the carrying of goods, and the slaughtering of animals on Sundays. Together, the two Acts, which did seek to enforce stricter Sunday observance, albeit to a limited degree, may have encouraged both puritans and JPs concerned about social order to make further moves to suppress gatherings and recreations on Sundays.

1625–1633

Although it is impossible to establish a causal link between the passing of the 1625 Act and a decline in recreations, it is clear that traditional merry-making experienced a decline in some parts of the country in the years following its enactment. Church ales ended in Bere Regis in Dorset, and other traditional festivities stopped in Alton in Hampshire and in the Cotswold town of Dursley.[24] These were all areas where Sunday revelry had been long established. The cessation of traditional pastimes in the first two years of Charles' reign may have been connected to the passing of the 1625 statute. Certainly, the pressure to suppress revels continued in some quarters. Writing in 1629, Samuel Bachiler warned of God's wrath being visited upon people for their sins and called upon magistrates:

> to looke to good order in your Townes ... that prophane liberty bee not given to breake the Sabboths, ... for heathenish May-games and Whitsunales (as they call their mad sports).[25]

Various orders were made by judges on the Western Circuit who were seeking to suppress wakes and ales in the counties of Dorset, Somerset and Devon; and in Bristol, in 1628, the corporation ordered the destruction of a maypole that had been set up in the city.[26]

Yet, although moves were made in some areas to suppress ales and other traditional revelry, elsewhere they continued to thrive. Baxter, who was a child when the 1625 Act was passed, recalled how, in his Shropshire village of Eaton Constantine:

> the Reader read the Common-Prayer briefly, and the rest of the Day even till dark Nights almost, except Eating time, was spent in Dancing under a May-pole and a great Tree, not far from Father's Door; where all the Town did meet together.

Baxter was a member of a godly, respectable family. Yet, the Baxters were unable to influence or restrain the revellers and Baxter recorded how, while they were trying to read the scriptures, they had to do so to the sound outside of 'the great disturbance of the Tabor and Pipe and Noise in the Street'. Even though one of the minstrels was a tenant of Baxter's father, his father was nonetheless unable to restrain him. Indeed, the revellers called Baxter's father a 'puritan' for trying to intervene. They clearly wanted to enjoy their merriment without interference and linked the attack on their traditional revelry with puritanism.[27]

Traditional revelry also enjoyed support from a number of writers. In a delightful book written in 1626 about the pattern of life in early seventeenth-century England, Nicholas Breton took the reader through the rituals and 'speciall dayes' of the year, and wrote approvingly of 'the youth of the Country mak[ing] ready for the Morris-Dance' in April and of 'the tall young Oke [being] cut downe for the Maypole' in May.[28] Michael Drayton celebrated an idealised rural life in *The Muses Elizium* (1630), in which he too wrote approvingly about traditional pastimes. He wrote about two youths impressing girls with their dancing and celebrated the fact that the youths indulged in traditional sports:

> To throw the Sledge, to pitch the Barre,
> To wrestle and to Run,
> They all the Youth exceld so farre,
> That still the Prize they wonne.[29]

Other writers engaged in the ongoing theological debate with the puritan sabbatarians. Thomas Broad published a further work defending the anti-sabbatarian position, and Edward Brerewood produced two works in which he insisted that the fourth commandment was only partially morally binding. Brerewood stated that the Lord's Day had been instituted by the Church and that it did not have to be observed in the same way or with the same rigour as the Jewish Sabbath had been.[30]

In comparison to the small number of works that appeared at this time attacking puritan sabbatarianism, several more works were published condemning recreations on Sundays and supporting the rigid sabbatarianism that radical English Protestants had come to adopt. In his 1625 *Declaration of the Christian Sabbath*, Robert Cleaver attacked 'the adversaries of the Sabbath'. He denied that his fellow sabbatarians' beliefs were 'Innovations & Novelties', insisting that the Church had always taught that the fourth commandment was a moral and perpetual precept.[31] Similarly, far from accepting that his sabbatarianism was anything new, Richard Byfield claimed that it was the idea that the fourth commandment was not moral and perpetual which was 'novel and adulterous'.[32] Edward Elton also argued for the moral nature of the fourth commandment, and attacked the use of recreations on Sundays. He accepted that there were:

> such moouings of the body as bee honest and moderate, and carry with them an honest and delightfull exercise of the minde, and serue to the refreshing of the body and minde, as Shooting, Tennis-playing, Stooleball-playing, Wrestling, Running and such like.

However, he maintained that, when such recreations were used on the Sabbath, 'especially in time of divine service', then the Sabbath was turned from a day of 'holy rest' into one of 'carnal rest'.[33] Robert Bolton, writing in 1626, attacked the baiting of animals and exhorted his readers to: 'bathe not thy recreations in blood'. He also argued against recreations that encouraged people to waste time, complaining that thousands of people indulged in recreations, 'wherein they very vnworthily and wofully waste the fat and marrow, as it were, of deare and precious time.[34] Henry Burton attacked those who:

> eyther idle or trifle out the Lords day impertinently, or such as prophane it with carnall pleasures, as ... reuelling and ryoting, playes and enterludes ... & many such vnchristianlike prophane pastimes.[35]

Griffith Williams not only maintained that the fourth commandment was a moral precept and applied to the Christian Sabbath, but also stated that Christians were obliged to sanctify the Lord's Day even more strictly than the Jews did their own Sabbath.[36] It is clear from this that Williams' sabbatarianism went well beyond the teachings of the Church. He held that recreations, which were honest and lawful at other times, were unlawful on the Lord's Day and demanded that anyone using sports on Sunday should be punished. He singled out dancing, dicing, bowling, shooting, tipling and May games for particular condemnation and said that those who sought to justify such profaneness were speaking 'what the Deuill puts in their mouthes'.[37]

Of all the sabbatarian works which appeared during the early years of Charles' rule, two books in particular angered the authorities and prompted them to act: Theophilus Brabourne's, *A Defence of the most Ancient, and Sacred ordinance of Gods, the Sabbath Day*, and William Prynne's, *Histrio-mastix*. Brabourne had published an earlier *Discourse vpon the Sabbath Day* in 1628, in which he argued that the fourth commandment was morally binding to the extent that the seventh day, Saturday, remained the Sabbath Day and that the 'Lord's Day' had never replaced it.[38] Brabourne's *Discourse* caused little stir. However, in 1632 Brabourne published his *Defence of that most Ancient, and Sacred ordinance of Gods, the Sabbath Day*, and this got him into hot water. Brabourne's *Defence* was a huge tome, in which he set out at much greater length his argument that the fourth commandment was a moral and perpetual law and that Christians should observe Saturday rather than Sunday as their Sabbath.[39] He condemned the Church for sanctifying the Lord's Day as the Sabbath day and attacked the 'absurdity' of people arguing about preserving the moral law when they were failing to defend God's Sabbath itself.[40] Arguing that the Lord's Day was not the true Sabbath, Brabourne criticised puritan sabbatarians who claimed that God cursed people who prophaned the Lord's Day and who wrote books describing 'many remarkable iudgements of God, which haue befalne the profaners of the Lords day'. He stated that no one could ascertan God's will by simply judging events, arguing that, if that were the case, then logically the loss of the Palatinate to the Catholic Holy Roman Emperor would have been God's will.[41] Unlike his earlier *Discourse*, Brabourne dedicated his *Defence* to the king and it was this dedication that was to get him into real trouble.

Brabourne's dedication called on Charles I to accept that the Sabbath was prescribed in the moral law and that Saturday was still the 'Lord's Sabbath'. He called on Charles to act to stop the Saturday Sabbath from being condemned as Jewish and ceremonial and from being 'prophaned & trampled vnderfoote'.[42] Brabourne told Charles that, as king, he was *obliged* to protect and uphold the fourth commandment, and called on him to revive the 'old law, a long time dead' and to proclaim Saturday as the Sabbath as it used to be. Quoting from 2 Kings 5:13, he told the king: 'If it were a great thing, which the Lord requireth of thee, wouldest thou not have done it?.'[43] At the end of his long treatise, Brabourne again called on the king to change the law and restore the Lord's Sabbath.[44] Charles I was offended by the fact that Brabourne had dedicated such an unorthodox work to him and resented Brabourne's presumption in telling him what his obligations were. Heylyn claimed that Charles felt the dedication was 'so lewd an impudence' and recorded that, 'fearing to be thought the Patron of a doctrine so abhorrent from all Christian piety, [Charles] gave Order for the Author to be censured in the High Commission'.[45] Brabourne was duly examined before the High Commission, charged with disseminating 'erroneous, heretical, and judaical opinions'.[46] As an indication of Charles' considerable displeasure over the dedication, and to underscore his rejection of Brabourne's argument, the prosecution against Brabourne was led by the king's advocate. After being tried in the presence of several bishops and privy councillors and being subjected to lengthy interrogation, Brabourne 'began to stagger in his former opinion' and finally admitted his errors.[47] The king then commissioned Francis White, Bishop of Ely, to write a work attacking and correcting Brabourne's errors. White duly produced two works, one in 1635 and the other in 1637, which attacked Brabourne's 'pestilent, and subtile Treatise', challenged Brabourne's 'Sabbatarian Error' and argued against Saturday being the Christian Sabbath and against the moral and perpetual nature of the fourth commandment.[48]

Both contemporaries and later historians have maintained that the publication of Brabourne's book was one of the key factors behind the republication of the *Book of Sports* in 1633. Heylyn claimed that this was the case and, according to Prynne, Laud cited 'a Booke set out by Theophilus Brabourne' as one of three reasons behind the reissuing of the *Book of Sports*, the other two being events in Somerset and 'a generall and superstitious opinion conceived of [the Lord's Day]'[49] L'Estrange also suggested that the reissuing of the *Book of Sports* was prompted by 'a potent tendency in many to Judaisme, occasioned by the dangerous Doctrine and Positions of several Puritans, especially of one Theophilus Brabourne'.[50] Brabourne's book certainly seems to have played a part in the decision to reissue the Book of Sports, if for no other reason than because its challenge to the king to act may have helped to convince Charles that the matter of Sunday observance needed to be clarified once more. In his diary entry recording the publication of the 1633 Declaration, Thomas Crosfield recorded that it was 'conceived to be published to the opposition of some doctrine taught by some of our divines'.[51] Crosfield may well have been referring here to Brabourne's *Defence*. Certainly, Heylyn, Prynne, L'Estrange and, apparently, even Laud himself cited it as one of the reasons behind the Declaration's publication. Brabourne's book and its impertinent dedication pushed the whole question of Sabbath observance up the political agenda. However, Brabourne's *Defence* was devoted entirely to arguing the case for the perpetual and moral nature of the fourth commandment and of the Saturday Sabbath and did not discuss the issue of recreations, which was the subject of the Declaration. Therefore, Brabourne's work alone cannot explain why Charles reissued his father's *Book of Sports*.

The other work that caused enormous controversy and that *did* address the issue of Sunday recreations was William Prynne's *Histrio-mastix*, and Crosfield may have had this in mind as well when he referred to the doctrine being taught by certain divines. Hutton makes the interesting suggestion that *Histrio-mastix* was far more likely to have prompted Charles to reissue the declaration than was Brabourne's work.[52] Certainly, the content of *Histrio-mastix* was more directly relevant to the question of recreations than was Brabourne's book, even though that related to Sabboth observance. Brabourne's *Defence* was cited by contemporaries, including Laud, who cited it at his own trial, yet *Histrio-mastix* was not similarly cited. It may, of course, be that it did not influence Charles I's decision to reissue the *Book of Sports*, but it could also be that Laud did not want to antagonise Prynne, who was prosecuting him, by linking

Prynne's work to the publication of the Declaration, and that Prynne himself did not want his work associated with it. Given the subject matter and the impact of *Histrio-mastix*, it is certainly possible, even probable, that it too influenced Charles' decision to act.

Much has been written about *Histrio-mastix* and its attack on stage plays, which was the main focus of the treatise, and about the implied criticism of the queen performing in court masques. However, Prynne also attacked traditional recreations. Indeed, Prynne himself later wrote how he:

> did in my Histrio-mastix ... produce the Decrees, Laws, Statutes, Canons of many Christian Emperours, kings ... and Resolutions of Fathers, Casuists, Schoolmen, and Protestant Divines Forraign and Domestick, to prove the unlawfulnesse of Stage Plays, Revels, Dancing, Gaming, Sports and Pastimes on the Lords day.[53]

In *Histrio-mastix* Prynne condemned mixed dancing and May games as 'sinfull, wicked, unchristian pastimes'.[54] He attacked dancing as 'the Devils procession', arguing that it led to adultery and that 'As many paces as man maketh in Dancing, so many paces doth he make to Hell'.[55] Referring back to the 1625 statute, Prynne misleadingly claimed that the Act 'intended to suppresse dancing on the Lords-day'.[56] Prynne argued that the dances recorded in the Bible:

> were no ordinary daily recreations, practised at every feast or meeting, upon every Lords-day, ... upon no other occasion but for mirth or laughter sake, to passe away the time, or to satiate mens unruly lusts ... as all our moderne dances are.

He added that dancing in scripture never took place in an alehouse 'much lesse at any may-pole, wake or Church-ale'.[57]

Histrio-mastix outraged the authorities, particularly since it insulted the queen by describing women actors as 'notorious whores', and because of the invective it directed at the Church hierarchy. The Venetian ambassador recorded that *Histrio-mastix* contained 'scandalous and biting remarks, about the civil and ecclesiastical government of [t]his kingdom'.[58] Prynne's formal expulsion from Lincoln's Inn also declared that *Histrio-mastix* contained 'divers incitements of ... [the] people to sedition'.[59] In 1634 Prynne was fined and imprisoned and further punished by being placed in the pillory and having both his ears cropped. His book *Histrio-mastix* was 'burnt by the Common Hangman'.[60] *Histrio-mastix* added to the controversy over Sunday pastimes and served to push the issue even higher up the ecclesiastical and political agenda. Although it may also have contributed to Charles I's decision to reissue his father's

Book of Sports, the main factor behind this decision was neither the works of Brabourne nor Prynne but the controversy surrounding attempts to suppress revels in Somerset, which came to a head in 1633. To quote Thomas Fuller: 'Pass we now from the pen to the practical part of the sabbatarian difference.'[61]

West Country ales and the Somerset controversy

Just as it was events in one English county, Lancashire, that led James I to issue the first *Book of Sports* in 1618, so too it was the events in another English county, Somerset, that led his son, Charles I, to issue his own version of the *Book of Sports* in 1633; although this time with more far-reaching consequences. Thomas Barnes described Somerset as a 'predominantly puritan' county, but puritan in the sense of being orthodox Calvinist and staunchly anti-Catholic. There were relatively few of the 'precisor sort' of clergy in Somerset and even fewer 'Laudian clergy'. In religious terms, the county was essentially moderate, orthodox and conservative.[62] Traditional festivity was popular among large sections of the Somerset people, as is evidenced by the need for repeated orders which sought to suppress them. As for the justices who made such orders, although a handful, like John Harington, were zealous puritans, most appear to have been motivated by concerns about possible disorder rather than religious zeal.[63] Certainly, the judges on the Western Circuit issued repeated orders against wakes and ales, but it is important to distinguish between those issued in Somerset and those issued in the neighbouring county of Devon.[64] In Somerset, orders against wakes and ales were issued in 1594, 1608, 1612, 1624, 1628 and 1632, but none of them, with the possible exception of the 1628 order, appear to have been made on any religious grounds whatsoever. However, in Devon, where puritanism was a far stronger force and where the bench seems to have been influenced by zealous puritans very early on, a number of the orders were made specifically to prevent people from profaning the Sabbath. The Devon bench issued orders in 1595, 1600, 1607, 1615, 1622 and 1627, and the orders of 1595, 1615 and 1622 were both clearly concerned to prevent profanations of the Sabbath as well as preventing disorders.[65]

In 1595 the justices at the Quarter Sessions in Devon issued an order against revels, arguing that they not only led to 'sundry disorders, and abuses', but also caused 'great prophaness of the Lords Sabath, [and] the dishoner of Almighty god'. The order stipulated that no ales, revels or May games should be held 'upon the Sabathe at any tyme of the daye'.[66] In January 1600 the justices in Devon again ordered that 'Church-Ales and Revells shall bee hence forth utterly suppressed', but this time they made no mention at all of the Sabbath or any concerns about irreligion, although they did refer to 'many enormities' having occurred at two recent ales, suggesting that the order was prompted by concerns about disorder.[67] However, in July 1615 the Devon justices issued an order that 'church-ales, and Bull-baitings be from henceforth utterly suppressed'. Citing 'severall manslaughters committed at two church-ales' in Devon earlier that month, it also referred to 'further advertisements given now unto the Court of the continuall prophanation of Gods Sabbath, at these and other such like unlawfull meetings'.[68] As with the 1595 order, the justices were concerned about the irreligious nature of revels held on Sundays as well as the danger of disorder arising from them. In 1622 the Devon Bench issued a further order, citing a 'greate disorder' at an ale held at Ashburton 'to the great dishonour of Almightie God, prophanacion of the Sabboth and the withdrawinge of many well disposed persons from good and godlie exercises'.[69] In July 1627 at the Assizes held in Exeter, Chief Baron Walker and Sir John Denham confirmed the previous orders made against ales and complained of 'the infinite number of inconveniences daily arising by means of Revels, Church-Ales, Clerk-Ales and publicke Ales' and ordered that they should all be 'utterly suppressed'. They further instructed that, 'to the end that this Order may be better observed', every minister 'shall publish it yearely in his Parish Church'.[70] Yet, even though this order was to be published in parish churches, it was not concerned with questions of irreligion, but with maintaining order and avoiding 'inconveniences'. Nonetheless, in Devon where the puritan influence was strong, several orders *were* sabbatarian in nature. This was not the case in Somerset.

The distinction between Devon and Somerset is an important one because it underscores the point that it was where puritans influenced on the judiciary that orders suppressing ales were motivated by religious belief. The fact that orders demonstrating concerns about irreligion were not issued in areas where puritan influence was weak suggests that it is wrong to deny a link between puritanism and the new form of sabbatarianism that had emerged from the later Elizabethan period onwards. In his analysis of the orders of the Western Circuit, Parker glosses over such distinctions. For example, he asserts without distinguishing between the Devon and Somerset orders, that 'regulations issued in 1594, 1600, 1607, 1615, 1624, 1628, 1631 reflected concern over the irreligious nature of [wakes]', when most of those orders made no reference to irreligion at all. The 1594 order issued at the Sessions held at Bridgwater, stated that 'no Church-Ale be admitted to be kept within any part of this shiere', but gave no reason for the order. It neither mentioned concerns over disorder nor any matters of religion.[71] In 1608 the justices in Somerset renewed the 1594 order, with additional prohibitions on bull- and bear-baiting, and did so in response to an especially rowdy church ale that had recently taken place.[72] Again, no reference to irreligion or Sabbath profanation was made. The 1612 order against ales similarly made no reference to the Sabbath or religion generally. Indeed, it implied that the only reason for the order was the 'dearth of Corne' that year.[73] Similarly, the Somerset justices order of 1624 gave no reasons for suppressing ales.[74] The order issued at the Devon Assizes in 1627 had also been issued at the Summer Assizes in Dorset in 1627. Following this, six Somerset clergymen petitioned Denham, requesting him to make a similar order at the Assizes held in Somerset in 1628, which he duly did.[75] This order was also to be published in parish churches. Barnes has described this order as the only Somerset order against church ales that was made 'ostensibly on religious grounds'. However, Barnes claims that this order was made on religious grounds simply because the vocation of the petitioners 'would indicate religious intent'.[76] Yet, although the petitioners were clergymen, the petition made no religious references at all; it simply asked Denham to grant an order similar to the 1627 order 'for the suppressing of the like Ales and disorders in this county of Somerset'.

The situation in Somerset was, then, very different from that in Devon, where, reflecting the puritan sabbatarianism of the Devonian godly, orders were made suppressing ales expressly to prevent the profanation of the Lord's Day. Even if the ministers who petitioned Denham in 1628 were motivated by religion, none of the Somerset orders, including the 1628 order itself, made any reference to profaning the Lord's Day or any other form of irreligion, whereas they all made some reference to 'disorders', 'inconveniences' or 'enormities' resulting from the holding of ales and revels. Given the non-sabbatarian nature of the Somerset orders compared to some of those made in Devon, it is ironic that it was events in Somerset, and not Devon, which were to lead to the reissuing of the *Book of Sports*.

Judges on the Western Circuit made numerous orders to suppress revels. The fact that such orders had to be issued repeatedly is a testament to the continuing popularity and use of wakes and ales in many areas. Indeed, preaching before the Western Circuit judges sitting in Exeter in 1642, Thomas Trescott railed against church ales, 'Bacchanalian Revellings, and Heathenish May-games' which prophaned the Sabbath and bemoaned their enduring popularity, declaring that they were 'yet in some places ... more zealously observed ... than either the Lawes of God, or the King'. Referring to the 1627 'wholesome order ... for the suppressing of Church-Ales and Revells', he said that it was like the engraving of a tombstone in that it was 'quite worn out' and he called on the judges once again to act to suppress ales, adding that action was what was needed as, even though 'we may preach against these disorders so long, till we spit out our very Lungs; ... Our words shall be but wind.'[77] Just as wakes and ales continued in parts of Devon, despite the many orders against them, so too they continued to be popular and to take place in many Somerset parishes, prompting calls for further moves to suppress them.

At the Somerset Assizes held at Taunton Castle on 19 March 1632 Baron Denham and Lord Chief Justice Richardson issued yet another order suppressing ales and revels. Referring to the many earlier orders, it declared that it was 'agayne ordered by the court in regard of the infinite number of inconveniences dayly arisinge by meanes of revels, church ales, clarkes ales, and other publique ales, [that they] be utterly from henceforth suppressed'.[78] As with the previous Somerset orders, the 1632 order did not prohibit revels on religious or sabbatarian grounds, but on the grounds that disorder often resulted from the holding of such events. Indeed, Prynne later claimed that the 1632 order was made at the behest of Somerset JPs after 'many persons [were] indicted for murthering Bastard children begotten at Wakes and Revels, with sundry other grand disorders occasioned by these intemperate meetings'.[79] As the 1628 order had done, this order stated that it should be read by the minister in every Somerset parish annually on the first Sunday in February and again on the two Sundays before Easter. In itself the 1632 order was not unusual. It merely repeated the prohibition of ales and revels made in earlier orders, and the instruction that it should be published in parish churches followed a similar instruction made some years before without causing any particular fuss. However, the 1632 order prompted considerable controversy because it became embroiled in matters of local politics and personal rivalries.[80]

In accordance with the Judges' instructions, the 1632 order was duly read out in parish churches throughout Somerset in February 1633. William Laud, who became Archbishop of Canterbury in August of that year, objected to this, as he saw it as encroaching on diocesan jurisdiction. As Bishop of London, Laud had clashed with the Lord Mayor of London over the issue of jurisdiction. In April 1629 the then Lord Mayor, Richard Deane, had issued an order which prohibited people from profaning the Sabbath by carrying and selling goods on Sundays. Laud had regarded this order as interfering with his jurisdiction as bishop and had written on his copy of the order: 'The Lord Mayor of London his Warrant against breakers of the Sabbath, My jurisdiction interessed.'[81] When the new Lord Mayor, Nicholas Rainton, stopped a woman from selling apples within St Paul's churchyard on a Sunday, Laud reproached Rainton for usurping his jurisdiction, threatened to report him to the king and insisted that the woman should continue to sell apples in the churchyard 'notwithstanding [the Lord Mayor's] Command to the contrary'.[82]

Given Laud's predisposition to jealously guard ecclesiastical jurisdiction, it is not surprising that he resented the fact that the 1632 Somerset order was to be read from the pulpits. Yet, when Laud had been Bishop of Bath and Wells, he had not reacted to the fact that judges had instructed that the 1628 order should be read in parish churches. However, unlike the 1632 order, the requirement to publish the 1628 order was probably never enforced. A rubric in the Prayer Book ordered ministers not to publish anything in church except that which had been commanded by either the king or the diocesan bishop. Although Chief Justice Richardson may have believed that he could exercise that authority on the king's behalf, Laud took a different view.[83] Indeed, Richardson's involvement seems to have been crucial in that the reading of his order in parishes in February 1633 coincided with Laud and Richardson clashing over the sentencing of Henry Sherfield in the Star Chamber. Sherfield, the Recorder of Salisbury, had been furious at the failure to remove a stained glass window from the local church of St Edmund's Church, which depicted the Creation and which Sherfield regarded as idolatrous. He had wanted the window removed, but the Bishop of Salisbury had intervened to prevent its removal. Sherfield had then taken matters into his own hands by smashing the window with a pikestaff. Sherfield was brought before the Star Chamber in February 1633, the very month in which the order against ales was published in Somerset's parish churches. The judges all agreed on Sherfield's guilt, but disagreed on the severity of the sentence that should be meted out to him. Laud, who was less concerned with the act of inconoclasm and more concerned about the fact that Sherfield had defied the bishop's authority, wanted Sherfield to be fined £1,000 and to be dismissed as Recorder of Salisbury. Laud was particularly protective of Church authority and often suspected judges of being behind challenges to that authority.[84] In calling for this sentence, Laud took the opportunity to voice his dislike of lawyers. Richardson, a leading judge, voted for a more lenient sentence, thus voting against Laud. In the end, Sherfield escaped with a fine of £500 and the costs of repairing the window, much to Laud's annoyance.[85] This episode resulted in bad blood between Laud and Richardson at the very time that the Somerset order was being read in parish churches.

Laud's antipathy towards Richardson coupled with his objection to judicial encroachment on ecclesiastical jurisdiction prompted him to move against Richardson. He complained to the king that Richardson's instructions to the Somerset clergy to publish the order usurped ecclesiastical jurisdiction. Charles agreed with Laud and instructed Richardson to revoke all orders prohibiting church ales at the next assizes. Richardson responded in a foolhardy, petulant way by revoking the orders at the Dorset assizes, but failing to do the same at the Somerset assizes, in direct contravention of the royal instruction to do so. Having failed to revoke the order, Richardson then reprimanded a constable who had the temerity to ask whether the orders against ales were to remain in force.[86] Barnes has demonstrated that Richardson's behaviour was motivated by a personal rivalry between him and Sir Robert Phelips, a prominent figure in Somerset society. Phelips had been one of a group of MPs who had made trouble for the government in parliament some years earlier and he had fallen out of favour as a result. He was anxious to regain royal approval and to retain his elevated status within county politics.[87] Indeed, in April 1633 Phelips had written a letter to Sir John Coke, Secretary of State to Charles I, in which he had said: 'God knows his heart, how right it is set to serve and obey his Majesty.'[88] Phelips was also smarting from the fact that, at the assizes in 1632, Richardson had thrown out a prosecution that Phelips was avidly pursuing. Richardson's handling of that case had led to a bitter falling out between the two men.[89] Consequently, in an attempt to settle old scores and, also, to try to prove himself a loyal subject and to obtain social and political advancement, Phelips decided to exploit Richardson's failure to revoke the Somerset orders against ales.

Whether or not Phelips was himself the informant, news reached the king of Richardson's failure to revoke the orders at the Somerset assizes and, on 2 May 1633, Charles wrote to Phelips and two other Somerset justices, informing them that he had learned that the holding of wakes had been hindered and instructing them to provide him with a full report on Richardson's actions. In his letter, Charles told them that they and the other justices should ensure that disorders did not occur at wakes, but also confirmed 'that the people after evening prayer may use suche decent & sober recreations as are fitt'.[90] Phelips seized on this opportunity to take his revenge on Richardson. In a report which Phelips drafted, he and his two fellow justices told Charles of Richardson's disobedience and of his failure to revoke the orders. They also informed the king about the past suppression of church ales in the county and went on to extol the virtues of ales and revels, telling Charles that such gatherings served 'to nourishe acquaintance and affecion amongst them, eache parishe at those times, mutually entertayninge one another, with arguments of love, freedome, and hospitality'.[91] Charles then personally ordered Richardson to revoke the orders against ales at the next Somerset assizes, which were to be held in August 1633. This Richardson did, but his manner of doing so was extremely ill-judged and displayed extraordinary bad grace.

Before revoking the order, Richardson went out of his way to give an account of the earlier orders made against ales and to highlight the disorders that ales had led to. He then told the court that 'some ill affected persons had misinformed his Majestie concerning this Order, who had given him an expresse command to reverse it'. He then incited the Somerset gentry to petition the king, telling them 'that if the Justices of Peace would truly informe His Majesty would give Order to revive it'.[92] After the court session was over, Richardson went even further and got twenty-five justices to sign a petition to the king requesting the suppression of ales, claiming that that summer had seen revels lead to 'Disorders of prophanation of the Lords-day, riotous tipling, contempt of authorities, quarrels, murders, &c'.[93] This may be a reference to a riot at an ale held at Coleford in May 1633, when eighteen rioters, all from neighbouring parishes, were arrested and several people were injured. There is no other record of any serious church ale disorder in Somerset between 1625 and 1640, which suggests that the justices may have both exploited and possibly exaggerated the trouble at Coleford.[94] Some JPs evidently signed the petition because they genuinely wanted ales suppressed, either on grounds of order or of religion. Some, such as John Harington and John Symes, were sincere puritans who were opposed to ales on religious grounds. Indeed, unlike any of the earlier Somerset orders themselves, the petition referred to the Lord's Day being profaned. Others, though, appear to have signed the petition because of their opposition to Phelips and his faction. Barnes has suggested that the twenty-four justices who did not sign the petition were either loyal partisans of Phelips' or men who either wanted to stay in or to obtain royal favour, and were unwilling to put their name to a petition which appeared to question the king's judgement. However, while local politics were certainly involved, some of those justices may have decided not to sign the petition simply because they shared the sentiments about the value of ales that Phelips had expressed in his earlier report to the king, and genuinely did not want to see them suppressed.[95]

Phelips immediately wrote to the king informing him of Richardson's extraordinary actions and observing that they 'laid an aspercon upon your Majesties direccons for there revocacon'.[96] Charles reacted by instructing that Richardson should be examined by Archbishop Laud, Lord Keeper Coventry, the Lord Privy Seal and the Earl Marshall. After their lordships had conducted their enquiry, the climax of these events occurred when Richardson was brought before the full Privy Council to be comprehensively rebuked in the presence of the king himself. It would appear that Laud was particularly fierce and that he gave Richardson 'such a rattle for his former Contempt ...' that he came out blubbering and complaining, 'That he had been almost choaked with a pair of Lawn Sleeves'.[97]

Richardson's career was ruined. Although he retained his position of Chief Justice, he was disgraced by being moved to ride the Home Circuit, which was by far the least prestigious of the six assize circuits. Julian Davies has suggested that the mutual antipathy between Laud and Richardson has been exaggerated and points to the fact that, not long after the Somerset controversy, Richardson assisted Laud by sending him the names of non-conformists. However, given Richardson's greatly diminished status after his removal from the Western Circuit, it seems far more likely that this was the action of a humbled, broken man and a sign of his attempts to get back into favour rather than an indication that all was well between them.[98] The other, far more important, result of these events was that, on 18 October 1633, Charles I reissued his father's *Declaration to his Subiects, Concerning Lawfull Sports*.

The Caroline *Book of Sports*

There has been much debate over whether the decision to reissue the *Book of Sports* in 1633 was inspired by Archbishop Laud or by the king himself. Contemporaries such as William Prynne and Henry Burton claimed that Laud was responsible, whereas Francis White, Peter Heylyn and Christopher Dow alleged that it was Charles who decided to reissue the Declaration.[99] Similarly, historians such as Thomas Barnes, Kenneth Parker and Richard Cust have suggested that Laud persuaded Charles to reissue the *Book of Sports*, whereas others such as Kevin Sharpe and Julian Davies have argued that it was Charles' own decision to do so.[100] Certainly, the events in Somerset and the argument between justices there about the merits and demerits of revels brought the issue to the fore, and Phelips' correspondence with the king and the petition of the justices made Charles all too aware of the continuing debate surrounding wakes and ales. Indeed, the petition that the twenty-five justices sent to Charles I in August 1633 not only informed him of the disorders associated with ales and of the justices' desire that they should be suppressed, but also explicitly asked the king for a declaration to clarify matters, for the petitioners wrote:

> May it therefore please your most excellent Majesty to grant us some more particular declaracon herein, that your Majesties commaund in that behalfe may not be thought to extend any further then to the upholding of civill feasting between neighbour and neighbour in their parishes, and the orderly and reasonable use of manly exercises and activities, which we all shalbe most ready to maintaine. And that we have your Majesties favoure and allowance to suppresse all the forementioned unlawfull Assemblies of Church Ales, Clerks Ales, and Bidd Ales.[101]

It is clear that the justices hoped that the king would issue a declaration which, while allowing a degree of communal feasting and celebration, would place strict limits on such festivities and would ban the ales which they claimed led to disorder. However, in asking the king for a declaration, the justices were to get much more than they had bargained for. This petition may be regarded as one of the most significant documents in the entire controversy as it not only appeared to question Charles' judgement in ordering Richardson to revoke his 1632 order, but it also invited Charles to issue a formal declaration setting out his position on the whole question of ales and traditional revels. It seems very likely that it was this which encouraged Charles to think seriously about reissuing his father's Declaration. Brabourne's *Defence* and Prynne's *Histrio-mastix* had also served to push the question of Sabbath observance up the political agenda; and the controversy over these contentious works may well have added to Charles' desire to clarify the place of sports on the Sabbath, and to reassert the royal authority. Given that most government business was conducted by word of mouth, it is impossible to know all of the reasons behind the decision to reissue the *Book of Sports* or whose idea it actually was. There are, though, grounds to suggest that it did indeed emanate from the king himself rather than from Laud.

Following the justices' petition, Charles commanded Laud to write to William Piers, Bishop of Bath and Wells, to ask him to enquire of ministers in his diocese who were 'best affected to ye Church & goverment' how recent wakes had been conducted and whether they had been the occasion of any disorders. This Laud did on 4 October 1633. In his letter to Piers, Laud explicitly stated that he had been commanded by the king to write to Piers with this request. Despite Laud's assertion, several historians have nonetheless claimed that this was in fact Laud's idea and that Laud wanted Piers to provide a report that would justify the reissuing of the *Book of Sports*; a course of action upon which Laud was already determined. Parker argues, without any hard evidence, that as early as September 1633 Laud suggested that the king should reissue the *Book of Sports*, but that Charles was not persuaded that such a move was necessary and that it was Charles' uncertainty that prompted him to ask Laud to collect more information.[102] While it is possible that Laud was the prime mover, there is no evidence at all that this was the case. Given the justices' previous petition to the king and their request for a declaration of some kind from him, and given Charles' earlier correspondence with Phelips, there seems every reason to believe Laud when he claimed to be writing on Charles' instructions. Indeed, although Laud did become closely involved in Richardson's later chastisement, the initial impetus for punishing Richardson for his attempts to suppress revels came from Phelips and not from Laud. The godly Dorset diarist, William Whiteway, had recorded in June 1633 that 'Whitsonales and May games were this yeare much countenanced by speciall order from the Court in which Sir Robert Philips and Sir Charles Barkley of Somersetshire were very forward'.[103] He made no reference to Laud.

In his letter to Piers, Laud told the bishop that the king believed that disorders 'may & ought to be prevented by the care of the Justices of Peace, & yet leave the Feasts themselves to be kept, for the Neighbourly meetings & Recreacions of the people, of which he would not have them debarred under any frivolous pretences'.[104] This mirrors the views that Charles had expressed in his own letter to Phelips in May 1633, which suggests that Laud's letter to Piers was indeed the king's idea. Laud added that Charles had been informed, presumably by Phelips, that puritans were behind the attempts in Somerset to suppress wakes in the county. The petition from the twenty-five justices that referred to profanations of the Lord's Day can only have served to have reinforced that view. Charles had come to link the puritans with sabbatarianism and the attempts to ban traditional revels in Somerset even if, in fact, some of the justices were more concerned about disorder and the puritan influence there was minimal.

On receipt of Laud's letter, Bishop Piers chose seventy-two Somerset ministers to consult in order to ascertain their views on the value of wakes.

1. A seventeenth-century engraving showing the Devil encouraging a man – representing Mammon, the personification of greed – to play a game of bowls with Cupid, who represents desire. The prize is the fool's cap held aloft by Fortune, who is standing by the jack at the end of the bowling green. (From Francis Quarles, *Emblemes* (London, 1635), p. 40. Reproduced by kind permission of The British Library)

*That y[e] ever men should so far blinded be
Not only to [commend] but command villanie
Must God & our soules be robd by proclamation
To divide off God is to undoe y[e] nation
when to divide y[e] day is made lawfull by y[e] Lawes
flesh doth take more than God experience shewes
And who but must esteem[e] it a double wrong
To have Gods service short, our Riots long.*

2. The handwritten verse in the copy of the 1618 *Book of Sports* held in the library at Lanhydrock, the Cornish seat of the puritan Robartes family. The verse is not dated and may have been written in response to the 1618 Declaration, or much later as a response to its republication in 1633. It is clearly critical of the *Book of Sports*, suggesting that it commanded villainy and restricted worship in order to facilitate riots. (Reproduced by kind permission of the National Trust/Lanhydrock)

3. The title page of Thomas Young's *Dies Dominica* (1639): the left-hand column shows people fulfilling their religious duties on the Sabbath: praying, hearing sermons, meditating, visiting the sick, and doing charitable works. The right-hand column shows other people drinking, dancing, gambling, feasting and working in the fields. It neatly sums up the cultural divide between those who wanted to suppress traditional revels and reform society and those who resisted such moves and wanted to protect their traditional way of life. (Reproduced by kind permission of the British Library)

THE KINGS
MAIESTIES
DECLARATION to
His Subiects,

CONCERNING
lawfull SPORTS to
bee vſed.

Imprinted at LONDON by
Robert Barker, Printer to the Kings
moſt Excellent Maieſtie: And by
the Aſſignes of *Iohn Bill*.

M.DC.XXXIII.

4. The title page of the 1633 *Book of Sports*. (Reproduced by kind permission of the British Library)

I

By the King. & B.L.

Hereas vpon Our returne the laſt yeere out of Scotland, Wee did publiſh Our pleaſure touching the recreations of Our people in thoſe parts vnder Our hand: For ſome cauſes Vs thereunto moouing, We haue thought good to command theſe Our directions then giuen in Lancaſhire with a few words thereunto added, and moſt appliable to theſe parts of Our Realmes, to be publiſhed to all Our Subiects.

Whereas We did iuſtly in Our Progreſſe through Lancaſhire, rebuke

A 3

5. The first page of the 1618 *Book of Sports* held in the library at Lanhydrock, the Cornish seat of the puritan Robartes family. Next to the words 'By the King' has been written '& B.L.' This is most probably a reference to 'Bishop Laud'. Laud was Archbishop of Canterbury by the time that the 1633 *Book of Sports* was issued. Assuming that the handwritten insertion does indeed refer to Laud, it is not clear why 'B.L.' has been written rather than 'A.L.'. (Reproduced by kind permission of the National Trust/Lanhydrock)

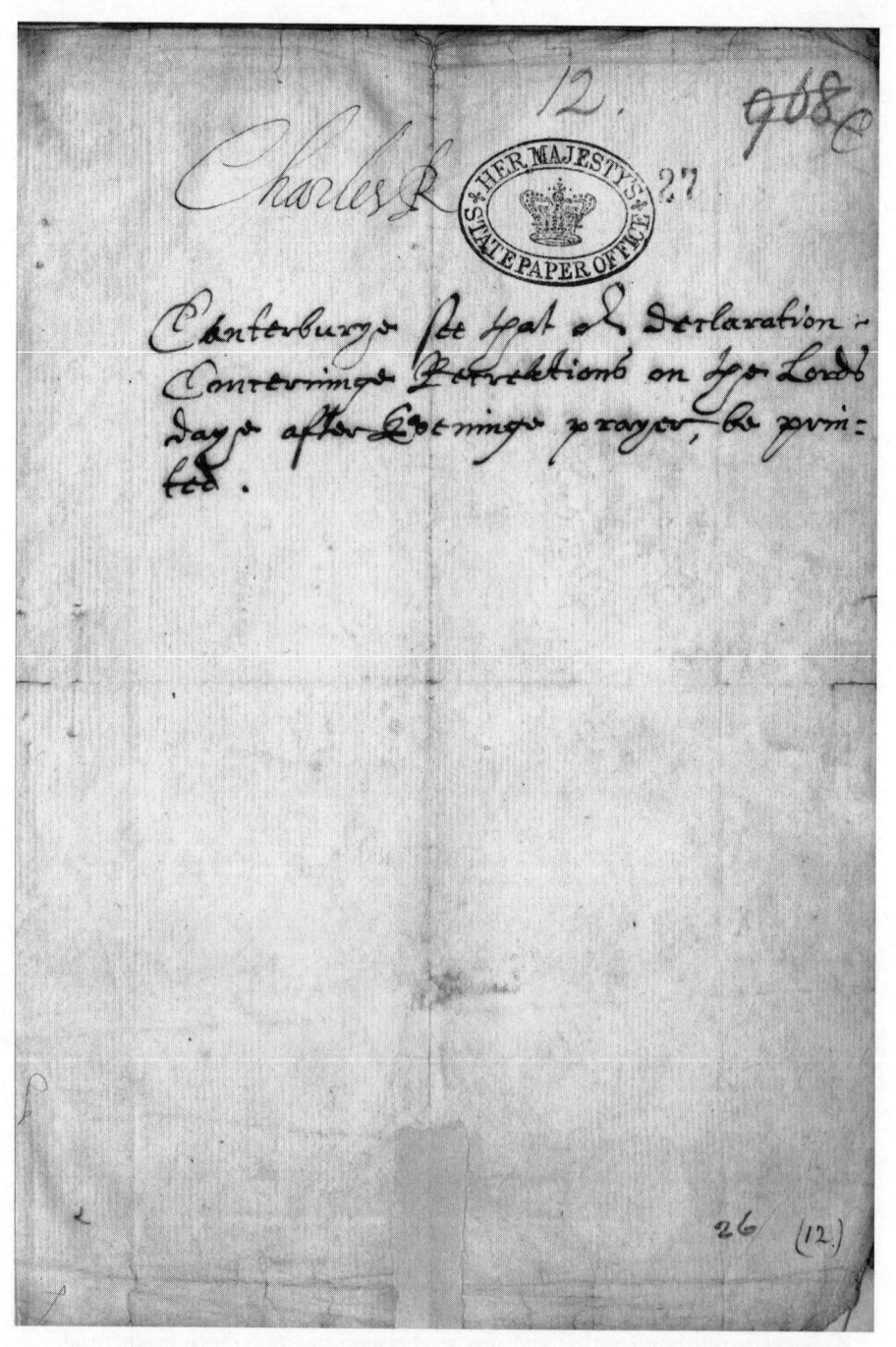

Charles R

Canterbury: See that ye Declaration Concerninge Recreations on ye Lords day after Eveninge prayer, be printed.

6. Charles I's instructions to print his 'Declaration Concerninge Recreations on the Lords Day after Eveninge prayer'. These undated instructions are written in Laud's handwriting and are signed by the king. (SP 16/248 No. 12. Reproduced by kind permission of The National Archive)

7. Archbishop Laud and Henry Burton, 1641. This satire uses the same imagery as *The Bishops Potion*, although that has Laud vomiting up not only *Sunday No Sabbath* – as is also shown in this engraving – but the *Book of Sports* as well. (BM Satire 412. Reproduced by kind permission of the British Museum)

8. The burning of the *Book of Sports* by the common hangman in May 1643 on the orders of Parliament. (From John Vicars, *A sight of ye trans-actions of these latter years* (London, 1646), p. 21. Reproduced by kind permission of The British Library)

Laud's letter had made clear the response that he was expecting and hoping for and Piers did not disappoint: either in the ministers he chose to consult or in his findings. On 5 November he wrote back to Laud and informed him that, having consulted 'the Gravest of my Clergy, and such as stand best affected to the Church and Governement' he had ascertained:

> First, that they [i.e. wakes] have bin kept not only this last yeere, but also for many yeares before, as long as they have lived in their serverall parishes without any Disorders. Secondly, that upon the Feast dayes, (which are for the most part every where upon Sundayes) the service of the Church hath bene more solemnly performed, and the church hath ben better frequented both in ye forenoones, and in ye afternoons, then upon any other Sunday in the yeere. Thirdly, that they have not knowen, nor heard of any disorders in the Neighbouringe Townes, where the like Feasts are kept. Fourthly, that the People doe very much desire the continuance of these Feasts. Lastly, that all these Ministers are of opinion, that it is fitt and convenient these Feast dayes should be continued, for a memorial of the Dedications of their severall churches, for the civilizinge of people, for their lawfull recreations, for the composinge of differences by occasion of the meetinge of friends, for the increase of love and amity, as beinge Feasts of charity, for the reliefe of the poore.[105]

Piers added that 'the cheifest cause of the dislike of these Feasts amongste the preciser sort is, because they are kept upon Sundayes, which they never call but Sabbath dayes, upon which they would have noe manner of recreation'. He also warned that ministers were worried that if people were denied 'their honest and lawfull recreations upon Sundayes after eveninge prayer' they would go 'either unto tipling houses, and there upon their ale-benches talk of matters of the Church or State; or else into conventicles.' In other words, wakes were a way of keeping people out of mischief.

Although Laud's letter had specifically asked about wakes, Piers also talked about ales, pointing out that, in the past, they had been a valuable way of raising money and had been used to help the poor and to finance the repair of church buildings. However, he said that, 'Concerninge Church-ales, I find that in some places the people have bin perswaded to leave them off, in other places they have bin put downe by the Judges and Justices; soe that now there are very few of them left.'[106] Ales were indeed in decline in many places across England, as they were gradually being replaced by a system of rates. They were also liable to be suppressed by justices who feared disorders arising from them and, in the case of puritans, by those who saw them as irreligious. Indeed, the justices' petition to Charles in August 1633 made it clear that the orders that the judges had issued against ales in the years prior to 1633 had meant that 'the sayd Assemblies have for the most part for a long time been foreborne and not used'.[107] Piers similarly reported that in parts of Somerset ales were in decline. However, ales continued to be held in some parts of the county and feasts of dedication, more commonly known as 'wakes', appeared to be thriving:

> The Feasts of Dedications are more generall, and generally they are called Feast-dayes, but in diverse places they are called revell-dayes; they are not knowne amongst the ignorant people by the name of Feasts of Dedication; but all scholars acknowledge them to be in ye memory of their severall Dedications.

Piers also stated that feasts of dedication 'have bin kept not only this last yeere, but also for many yeares before, as long as they have lived in their serverall parishes'. As testament to the enduring popularity of wakes, Piers told Laud that, when the constables of some Somerset parishes had come from the Assizes two years previously and had 'told their Neighboures that the Judges would put downe these Feasts, they answeared that it was very hard, if they could not entertayne their kindred and Friends once in a yeere, ... and they sayd they would endure the Judges penaltyes rather than they would break off their Feast Dayes.'[108]

Piers' report would have been useful in justifying the reissuing of the *Book of Sports*, yet Charles did not wait to receive the report before publishing his Declaration on 18 October. Barnes and Parker could be right in claiming that, in the meantime, Laud had succeeded in persuading Charles to reissue the Declaration. However, this claim does not sit easily with Parker's suggestion that Charles had not been persuaded earlier that it was necessary to reissue the Declaration and had consequently insisted that Laud should get a report from Piers first about the value of wakes. It seems just as likely that Charles made the decision to publish his *Book of Sports* independently of Laud. Indeed, Laud himself subsequently denied responsibility. He denied that he had procured the Declaration and insisted that 'the king commanded the printing of it'.[109] During his trial he produced a warrant signed by Charles I which instructed: 'Canterburye, see that our declaration concerninge Recreations on the Lords daye after Eveninge prayer, be printed.'[110] Davies refers to this very puzzling document, but only gives half the story. Although he points out that the order was signed by the king, he fails to add that the order itself was written in Laud's handwriting.[111] Prynne claimed that Laud had written it and had then got Charles to sign it so that he could later deny responsibility.[112] However, Laud was perfectly willing to acknowledge his responsibility for other controversial policy initiatives, so his denial in this instance should be taken seriously.[113] It is highly improbable that

Laud ever thought that he might one day have to justify himself in open court and would need documentary evidence to support his denial of responsibility. It is tempting to speculate about the origins of such an interesting document, but impossible to be certain about them. It is of no surprise that Prynne should have wanted to use the document against Laud, but the document itself cannot be conclusive evidence either way given that it was both written by Laud and signed by the king.

Laud himself did not indulge in recreations and, although he was concerned to protect ecclesiastical jurisdiction, in other respects he was not a champion of revelry. In 1637, for example, he moved to prevent a parish feast from being held in a church.[114] Although he condemned 'those men who stand so strictly upon the morality of the Sabbath, [and] do by a gross and carnal Sabbatization, three times outgo the superstition of the Jew', he was nonetheless very clear about the need to 'shun profaneness' and believed that the 'apostolical universal tradition settled the Lord's day for holy and public worship'.[115] Laud personally observed the Lord's Day very strictly and he persuaded Charles I to move meetings of the Privy Council from Sunday mornings to Sunday afternoons.[116] Moreover, unlike some other bishops, Laud did not enforce the 1633 *Book of Sports* at all rigorously.[117] If it had been his policy, one would have expected him to have been one of its fiercest enforcers.

Charles I was also a rather austere figure. Although the king was a keen hunter and competitive tennis player, unlike his father he was not someone who easily appreciated traditional revelry.[118] Yet there are facets of his character and beliefs that suggest he needed no persuasion from Laud to reissue the *Book of Sports*. Charles had a deep dislike for and distrust of puritans and he saw their attacks on recreations and their attempts to enforce a stricter Sabbath observance as dangerous, unwelcome interventions in both Church and society. Moreover, Charles did not regard the fourth commandment as a moral and perpetual precept. On the question of whether the same authority that had instituted Sunday as the Christian Sabbath had also instituted Easter, Charles declared that 'it will not be found in Scripture where Saturday is discharged to be kept or turned into ... Sunday ... whereof it must be the Church's authority that changed the one (and) instituted the other.'[119] Charles was certainly no sabbatarian and he regularly held both council meetings and attended masques on Sundays.[120]

Nonetheless, many contemporaries accused Laud of being behind the reissuing of the *Book of Sports*. In Cambridge in July 1634, for example, James Priest was accused of saying that 'some scoruey popish Bishop haith got a toleration for boyes to play vppon the Sabbath day after Euening prayer' and that 'if th' Kinge did vunderstand him selfe he woold not suffere it, but he is ouer ruled by his servants'.[121] The puritan Robartes family of Lanhydrock in Cornwall also appeared to believe that Laud was behind the *Book of Sports*. On the title page of their copy of the Declaration, the printed words 'By the King' are accompanied by a handwritten '& B.L'., which is most probably a reference to 'Bishop Laud'.[122] *The Bishops Potion*, published in 1641, is an imaginary dialogue between Laud and his physician in which Laud declared he was 'diseased in all parts' and was then administered an emetic by his doctor. He at once proceeded to vomit, and the first book that he spewed out was the *Book of Sports*, which Laud told his doctor was 'the Book for Pastimes on the Sunday, which I caused to be made'.[123] Prynne and Burton were among the most prominent puritans who blamed Laud for the publication of the Declaration.

The fact Laud was attacked in this way is of little surprise. It was a long-standing convention to attack a monarch's advisers instead of the monarch himself and it would have been far riskier for them to have accused Charles directly. In some respects, the association by his enemies of Laud with the *Book of Sports* has parallels with 'the Laudian myth' that he was also responsible for the Scottish Prayer Book. In his analysis of the genesis of the Scottish Prayer Book of 1637, Gordon Donaldson concludes that the initial changes made to the English Prayer Book emanated from Charles I personally and not from Laud. Although Laud was consulted and was involved in discussions surrounding the Prayer Book, Donaldson argues that it is misleading to see it as 'Laud's Liturgy'. Indeed, Laud had wanted to see the introduction of the English liturgy into Scotland rather than a different Prayer Book, and responsibility for the Scottish Prayer Book lay with the Scottish bishops and not Laud. Yet, some time after its publication, the myth emerged that Laud had been behind the Prayer Book. Interestingly, given Prynne's later claims concerning the king's instructions to print the *Book of Sports*, Donaldson points out that one of the reasons for the attribution of the Scottish Prayer Book to Laud was the fact that alterations made to the 1636 draft of the Prayer Book were in Laud's handwriting. Donaldson concludes, contrary to the assertion of Laud's enemies – who were naturally reluctant to blame the king directly – that this was simply because Laud had been acting as a clerk, giving effect to decisions made, on representations from Scotland, by the king. Unfortunately for Laud, the draft in his handwriting came into the possession of his enemies, who saw it as proof that he had been responsible for the new liturgy.[124] In a similar way, the fact that Charles' signed instructions to print the *Book of Sports* were in Laud's handwriting was all the evidence that Prynne and others needed to hold Laud responsible.

Even though some saw Laud's hand in the issuing of the 1633 *Book of Sports*, many contemporaries accepted that it was indeed the king who was responsible for its republication.[125] Leah Marcus has floated the intriguing possibility that Charles may have reissued the *Book of Sports* because he was trying to emulate his father, suggesting that, when he travelled to

Scotland for his coronation in June 1633, he was replicating his father's journey of 1617. Marcus suggests that:

> as though to emphasize his ceremonial repetition of his father's progress, in connection with the event Charles reissued Jacobean proclamations designed to restore the countryside: the *Book of Sports* and the order commanding gentry and aristocrats back to their rural estates to keep hospitality in the traditional fashion.[126]

At first sight this suggestion seems a slightly far-fetched one, yet there may well be some mileage in it. It used to be argued that there was little evidence of Charles' personal involvement in his royal proclamations, and contemporary claims about the role of first Buckingham and then Laud in the king's printed statements went largely unchallenged.[127] More recently, historians have recognised Charles' close interest in such matters and his particular interest in what his own father had published. Indeed, Charles I closely followed what his father had done and annotated and corrected some of James' writings. Charles' speeches and proclamations frequently echoed his father's phraseology and Charles appears to have used his father's *Workes* as a pattern for his own kingship.[128] Charles' *Book of Sports* itself clearly drew on that of his father.[129] It may be that Charles' decision to reissue it when he did was just coincidence, but given his keen interest in his father's writings and actions, it is highly probable that Charles would have consulted records of what James had done when he journeyed to Scotland in 1617 when planning his own visit to Scotland in 1633. Charles would then have been reminded of events in Lancashire on James' return and of his decision to issue the first *Book of Sports*. Therefore Charles' letter to Phelips on 2 May 1633, written shortly before his visit to Scotland, may well have been written at a time when his father's actions concerning Sunday festivities were fresh in his mind.[130]

Whatever prompted Charles to issue his own Declaration of Sports, his correspondence with Phelips demonstrates his interest and involvement in the Somerset ales controversy. Charles had also been personally affronted by Brabourne's epistle dedicatory and had instructed White and Heylyn to write works attacking Brabourne and puritan sabbatarianism, demonstrating his own involvement in the sabbatarian debate.[131] Both White and Heylyn moreover insisted that the *Book of Sports* stemmed from Charles himself. There is every reason to believe that Charles decided that he would not only reissue his father's Declaration but that, unlike his father, he would have it enforced and ensure that it was published in parish churches across the land. Charles was well aware of the power of the pulpit, and told his son many years later that 'people are governed by the pulpit more than the sword in times of peace'.[132]

We can never know for certain whether the idea of reissuing the *Book of Sports* came from Charles or Laud. Yet Charles' letter to Phelips in May 1633, the Somerset justices' petition to Charles asking for him to issue a declaration, and Laud's letter to Bishop Piers all provide important evidence to suggest that the decision to reissue the *Book of Sports* moved from the king himself. The evidence suggests that Charles was contemplating issuing his own Declaration of Sports long before Laud wrote to Piers, and that he was considering issuing an amended version of his father's Declaration. When Charles published his own Declaration in October 1633, it was, aside from the preamble, identical to James' earlier Declaration in all respects except that Charles added a paragraph in which he specifically licensed 'the Feasts of the Dedication of the Churches commonly called Wakes'.[133] It is surely no coincidence that Charles' letter to Phelips only referred to wakes or that Laud's letter to Piers similarly only asked about how wakes were regarded and kept and did not ask about or refer to any other forms of revelry. The paragraph in the Declaration concerning wakes stated that:

> because of late in some Counties of Our Kingdome, Wee finde that vnder pretence of taking away abuses, there hath been a generall forbidding, not onely of ordinary meetings, but of the Feasts of the Dedication of the Churches, commonly called Wakes. Now our expresse will and pleasure is, that these Feasts, with others, shall bee obserued.[134]

This is clearly a reference to the events in Somerset, again indicating their importance in the decision to reissue the Declaration and Charles' concern with proceedings there. Reflecting what Charles had written to Phelips in May 1633, the amending paragraph stated that justices were to see that any disorders were either prevented or punished, but that 'all neighbourhood and freedom, with manlike and lawful exercises be used'. Laud's letter to Piers and the amending paragraph of the 1633 Declaration merely echoed what Charles had himself written to Phelips in May 1633, suggesting that Charles was behind both the letter and the amendment. Furthermore, the fact that the letter enquired exclusively about wakes and that the amendment exclusively concerned wakes suggests that Charles was already intending to reissue the Declaration by early October, if not before, but that he was taking time to consider adding the specific reference to wakes which he subsequently did decide to include. The enquiry to Piers about wakes and the express inclusion of wakes in the 1633 Declaration are almost certainly linked. This also makes the fact that Charles issued the Declaration before Laud heard back from Piers more explicable. If Laud's enquiries to Piers had moved from Laud himself, then one would have expected Laud to have waited for a response. However, if Charles was already minded to issue the Declaration with the inclusion of a specific licence for wakes, it seems credible to suggest that, having instructed Laud to get more information, the king then decided to go ahead with his plan anyway and issued the revised Declaration without waiting for Piers' report to arrive.

The relationship between Charles and Laud was a complex one, but the pair largely shared the same aims and assumptions in terms of religious policy.[135] We will never know what conversations took place between the two men concerning the decision to issue the 1633 Declaration, but there is no evidence to suggest that Charles was not his own man in this matter, and the notion that Laud manipulated Charles into publishing the *Book of Sports* should be treated with caution. It is just as, if not more, likely that the decision to issue an amended version of his father's *Book of Sports* moved from Charles himself. One thing is clear: in issuing the revised Declaration, Charles, unlike his father, meant it to be enforced. His Declaration instructed that it should be published 'by order from the Bishops, through all the Parish Churches of their seuerall Diocesse respectiuely'.[136] As with other matters, Charles regarded the reading of his Declaration as a test of obedience. Indeed, the newswriter Edward Rossingham told Viscount Scudamore in September 1634, 'the question will not be whether that sporting upon the Sunday be lawful yea or no, but whether they do not ... disobey the command of authority'.[137] Charles' decision to enforce his *Book of Sports* was to create considerable disaffection and was to have profound and far-reaching consequences.

6

Enforcement and reaction
Choosing between the 'Commandments of God and Man'

James I's Declaration of Sports had been unpopular, both with puritans and with many more moderate Protestants, and he had wisely decided not to press its enforcement. By the time that Charles I issued his revised Declaration in 1633, political, social and religious tensions had increased considerably and the reaction was correspondingly more intense. Moreover, Charles fully intended to enforce his Declaration and the reading of it became a test of loyalty to the Crown.[1] As early as December 1633, Strafford, the Lord Deputy of Ireland, was informed by a source in England that: 'Here begins to be much difference in opinion about the book; for though it be the same verbatim that was publish'd in King James's time, yet it is commanded to be read in all the churches here and in the Country.'[2]

The Declaration required that the bishops should ensure its publication in every parish church, but it did not stipulate how it was to be published or who was required to read it. Indeed, Archbishop Ussher said that his understanding of the Declaration was 'that there was no clause therein commanding the ministers to read the book, but if it were published in the church by the clerk or churchwardens, the king's command is performed'.[3] Similarly, Thomas Wilson, the rector of Otham in Kent, who was brought before the church courts for refusing to read the Declaration, explained that he 'refused to read the Book ..., not out of any contempt of any Authority, but as being commanded by no Law, for the Kings Majesty doth not in the Book command or appoint the Minister to read it'.[4] Nonetheless, it was widely assumed that the minister should read it to his congregation and in some areas the reading of it by ministers became a test of compliance. Peter Heylyn pointed out that the bishops were given the task of publishing the Declaration and that, if they then instructed the parish minister to read it, the minister was duty bound to obey. He also pointed out that many churchwardens in country parishes could not read and should therefore not 'be imployed in publishing such Declarations, which require a more knowing man than a silly villager'.[5] Even so, not all of the bishops forced ministers to read the Declaration. When the Dorchester minister, John White, refused to read it, he avoided punishment when the churchwardens got someone else to read it on a Friday morning while White was away and the church was empty.[6] Although clergy and churchwardens were asked to certify that the Declaration had been published, they were rarely asked by whom it had been published.[7] Such loopholes were exploited by ministers who were reluctant to read the Book. William Price, a godly minister in the diocese of Peterborough, compromised his principles by allowing the parish clerk to read the Declaration at the end of divine service, while he put his fingers in his ears in order to signal his disapproval.[8] When Humphry Chambers, an otherwise conformist, moderate clergyman, was so anguished by the Declaration's licensing of mixed dancing that he felt he could not read it, his bishop sent a surrogate to read it instead, so that 'the distraction thereof may not afford ground for a Romish jubilee or schismatical triumph'.[9] However, whereas some bishops connived at such avoidance, others were keen to make sure that the incumbent had read and published the *Book of Sports* personally.[10] As Thomas Fuller recorded, 'all bishops urged not the reading of the book with rigour alike, nor punished the refusal with equal severity'.[11] Some enforced it strictly, some half-heartedly and some not at all.

As perhaps further evidence that reissuing the *Book of Sports* was the king's idea, Archbishop Laud himself did not enforce it rigorously. At his trial, Laud admitted that he had punished some ministers who failed to read the Declaration, but he explained that he had had to take some action because 'His Majesty having commanded this, I could do little if I had not so much as inquired what was done'. He stated that, in some instances, he 'gave time to them which had not read it, and then never asked more after it', and he pointed out that in those few instances where ministers were punished with suspension it was because the ministers had done other things that merited disciplinary action in addition to failing to read the Declaration.[12] Laud's assertions are supported by the surviving evidence. Following the printing of the Declaration, Laud wrote a letter to all the bishops in the Southern Province instructing them to use 'all diligence' in ensuring that the *Book of Sports* was published in their various parishes and to acquire copies of it in order to have them ready for publication. However, he did not stipulate how it should be published or by whom.[13] Laud's detractors portrayed him as a zealous pursuer of godly ministers who used the *Book of Sports* to entrap and punish them. Prynne accused Laud of having compiled the Declaration himself and, even though Laud's letter to the bishops gave no such instruction, claimed that: 'This Book he enjoyned all Ministers to read and publish openly in the church in time of Divine Service.' Prynne went on to assert that:

those who out of conscience refused to read it in this kinde were by his means suspended, excommunicated, prosecuted in the High-Commission, Sequestred from their Livings, yea many of them enforced to desert their Cures and depart the Kingdome; this book being made a snare onely to entrap or suppresse most of the painfull, godly, preaching Ministers throughout the Realm.[14]

Prynne claimed that Laud was responsible for the suspension and excommunication of 'many hundred Godly Ministers'.[15] In fact, Laud did not pursue a strict policy of enforcement at all.[16] In 1634 he censured only four ministers who refused to read the *Book of Sports*, while many other ministers in the Canterbury diocese refused to read it and yet went unpunished. The four who were censured: Richard Culmer of Goodnestone, John Player of Kennington, Thomas Hieron of Hernhill and Thomas Gardner of St Mary, Sandwich, were all well-known non-conformists who Heylyn described as 'troublesome persons ... who publickly opposed all establisht orders, neither conforming to his Majesties Instructions, nor the canons of the Church, nor the Rubricks in the publick Liturgy'.[17] Even so, Laud did not suspend any of them before first giving them time in which to reform. Gardner duly promised to conform and was not prosecuted further, even though it appears that he was never actually made to read the Declaration. The other three were suspended after failing to conform.[18] When they petitioned Laud to have their suspensions lifted, he, clearly exasperated by their continuing obstinacy, responded 'that if they knew not how to obey, he knew as little how to grant' and he refused to lift their suspensions.[19] Yet, aside from these ministers, Laud suspended only one other minister who refused to read the *Book of Sports*: Thomas Wilson of Otham, who was suspended in 1635. Like those censured in 1634, Wilson was also a non-conformist who had disobeyed in other matters. He was called before the High Commission in April 1635, but failed to attend on the appointed days.[20] At Laud's trial, the Archbishop pointed out that Wilson was suspended 'when he would neither obey, nor keep in his tongue' and, although Wilson was deprived of his living for almost four years, Laud made clear that 'it was not for not reading this book'.[21] Laud pointed out at his trial that far more ministers were punished in other dioceses, and he commented, justifiably, on his own enforcement of the *Book of Sports* that: 'my proceeding was far from rigour'.[22] Indeed, Thomas Valentine, the rector of Chalfont St Giles, having been suspended by the Dean of the Court of Arches for not reading the Declaration, petitioned Laud to have his suspension lifted. Laud made it clear that he had not intended ministers to be censured purely for failing to read the *Book of Sports* and told Valentine 'that he would stand right in your opinion except some other matter appeared against him'. Valentine's suspension was duly revoked.[23] Thomas Fuller, no apologist for Laud, confirmed that 'as for the archbishop of Canterbury, much was his moderation in his own diocess, silencing but three (in whom also a concurrence of other noncomformities) through the whole extent thereof'.[24]

Whereas Laud did not enforce the *Book of Sports* strictly, others did. The most rigorous enforcers were Bishop Piers of Bath and Wells, Bishop Curle of Winchester and, in particular, Matthew Wren, the Bishop of Norwich. Wren not only enquired in his visitation articles whether the *Book of Sports* had been published, but also by whom.[25] Indeed, Wren enquired about the reading of the Declaration in his visitation courts as well as his visitation articles.[26] He discovered that a large number of his clergymen had not read it, and responded by ordering sixty ministers of whom he 'had most doubt of' non-conformity to duly read the Declaration. Those who refused to comply were immediately suspended.[27] Years later, in the hope that they might get Wren impeached, a petition was sent to parliament signed by hundreds of inhabitants of the diocese of Ely, where Wren had become bishop after his time at Norwich. It accused Wren, *inter alia*, of 'pressing the reading of the booke of sports and recreacions ... whereby the common prophancion of the Lord's daie with beastlie drunkenness lascivious dauncings, quarrellings and fightings ... hath been exceedinglie encouraged'.[28] The articles of impeachment against Wren accused him of forbidding afternoon sermons on Sundays and of forcing ministers to read the *Book of Sports* 'publikely in their Churches' and of suppressing those ministers who refused to do so.[29] At his trial in 1641, Wren acknowledged that he had suspended thirty ministers, sixteen of whom were later also excommunicated. Yet, although Wren's policy of enforcement was much stricter than that of his fellow bishops, he too seems to have targeted ministers whom he suspected of non-conformity generally, and did not punish ministers purely for refusing to read the *Book of Sports*.[30]

Bishop Piers suspended at least twenty-five ministers who refused to read the Declaration in their churches.[31] Again, in at least some instances, Piers seems to have singled out ministers because of their non-conformity in others matters too.[32] Like Wren, Piers was accused at his trial of forbidding afternoon sermons and of suspending ministers who had refused to read the *Book of Sports*. In addition, in a specific reference to Piers' report on wakes of November 1633, his articles of impeachment further alleged that:

> To countenance which Revels, the sayd Bishop (in opposition to the orders of the Judges of Assize, and Justices of Peace of Somerset-shire, for the suppressing of Sport and Revels, and their Petition to the King to that purpose) did call before him divers Ministers of his Diocese, and presented unto them a writing in

approbation and commendations of the sayd Sports and Revells: whereunto many of the sayd Ministers subscribed their names, by the Bishops perswasions; which writing the sayd Bishop sent up to the Arch-Bishop of Canterbury, who after the receipt thereof suppressed the Justices Petition. And shortly after the book for sports and Revels on the Lords day was published.[33]

This article was wrong in its chronology in that the Declaration of Sports was issued before Piers' report was ever sent. Nonetheless, the fact that his involvement in the genesis of the *Book of Sports*, and in its enforcement, featured in accusations made against him so many years later is a testament to the lasting resentment over the Declaration's publication and the suspension of ministers who refused to read it.

Bishop Curle of Winchester was similarly later castigated for his enforcement of the *Book of Sports*. Prynne claimed that, after Wren and Piers, Curle 'was the most violent enforcer of this Booke on the Clergie', and accused Curle of suspending five ministers in a single day for refusing to publish it.[34] However, Curle, Piers and Wren were notable exceptions among the episcopacy. Most others adopted Laud's approach and were very moderate in their enforcement of the Declaration. For example, although Bishop Goodman of Gloucester suspended some ministers who persistently refused to read the Declaration, they were suspended for just a week in order to allow time for a neighbouring minister to read the book in place of the suspended incumbent.[35] In similar fashion, Bishop Coke of Bristol avoided suspending John White of Dorchester for refusing to read the *Book of Sports* when, much to White's annoyance, it was read by someone else. John Bancroft, Bishop of Oxford, did require ordination candidates to give their views on the *Book of Sports* and suspended three ministers who refused to read it, but, again, it seems that other factors may have led to these suspensions. Overall, although there is evidence to suggest that pressure was put on ministers to read the book, Bancroft did not punish many, if any, for not doing so.[36] In the diocese of Peterborough, even though it was reported that at least sixty ministers had refused to read it, none were censured. In Ely, Bishop White did not enforce the Declaration rigorously, despite the fact that he had earlier written works attacking Brabourne and puritan sabbatarianism. In London, Bishop Juxon thought it was sufficient that the Declaration had been published even if it had not been read by the minister personally. Juxon did suspend one minister who refused to read it, but, again, this appears to have been because of the minister's non-conformity in other matters and not because of this particular offence.[37]

Some bishops did not censure any ministers for failing to read the *Book of Sports* and made no efforts to ensure its publication beyond distributing copies of it to their parishes for publication.[38] Although Bishop Davenant of Salisbury ordered ministers to read the *Book of Sports*, he did not return the names of those of his clergy who refused to do so, declaring: 'I will never turn accuser of my brethren.'[39] Yet, only Bishop Potter of Carlisle, appears to have actually hindered the Declaration's publication. The courts in Carlisle actively discouraged ministers from reading the Declaration and Bishop Potter reputedly said that 'if it were sent to his diocese, he would slight it and urge none of his Jurisdiction to read it'.[40]

The enforcement of the *Book of Sports* by the bishops was, therefore, far from uniform. Nonetheless, most bishops ordered its publication and it was generally enforced. Robert Sanderson accepted that the king's Declaration settled the argument of the lawfulness of sports on Sundays and, although he still pleaded for their moderate use, he commended the use of recreations that refreshed the body such as 'Shooting, Leaping, pitching the Barre, Stoole-ball &c.'.[41] Regardless of how vigorously or otherwise they enforced it, most bishops did not question the Declaration's content. We can only speculate as to why their enforcement of the *Book of Sports* was so piecemeal. Certainly, many more ministers refused to read it than were ever suspended or censured. Even though the Declaration was not at odds with the Church's traditional view of Sunday observance, by 1633 the whole question of how people should spend the Lord's Day had become extremely contentious. The influence of puritan sabbatarianism on many clergy had made it a potentially explosive issue and most bishops wisely chose not to exacerbate the situation needlessly. Most seem to have recognised that the reading of the *Book of Sports* would be unpalatable for many of their clergy and, although they instructed that it should be published and they provided their parishes with copies of the Declaration, most chose not to force ministers to read it personally. Of those who were censured, none appear to have been punished over refusing to read the *Book of Sports* alone. All those who *were* censured appear to have been notorious non-conformists, and Prynne was right to claim that the *Book of Sports* was used to trap staunchly puritan ministers.[42] The refusal of troublesome non-conformists to read the *Book of Sports* was something that the bishops could use against them. However, the bishops were reluctant to enforce the *Book of Sports* more generally because they did not want to antagonise otherwise conforming clergy.

The examination of the Declaration's enforcement reveals that many ministers across the country refused to read it. Many moderate clergymen felt uncomfortable with the idea of promoting dancing and other revels from the pulpit, even if they did not otherwise subscribe to puritan sabbatarianism. Many anguished over whether they should obey their royal and ecclesiastical masters and read the *Book of Sports* to their congregations, or take a stand and refuse to do so. This dilemma is well illustrated by Nicholas Estwick's correspondence with Samuel Ward, master of Sidney Sussex, Cambridge. Estwick, the rector of Workton in

Northamptonshire, wrote to his friend seeking advice on what to do. He told Ward that the *Book of Sports* 'hath caused much distraction & griefe in many honest mens hearts in our Diocesse which have read it; and many there be to the number almost of three score (as I have beene told) which have refused to publish it.'[43] He did not question the morality of the Christian Sabbath, yet he was not sure whether or not the *Book of Sports* actually profaned the Sabbath, explaining that: 'albeit I have laboured in the point: yet I am not satisfied, but do hange in suspense whether Recreations on ye Lords day be lawful or not.' In particular, Estwick was unhappy at the thought of condoning dancing, Whitsun ales and May games, explaining that: 'I do vehemently suspect that some of theis in our countrie townes are seldome or never used on that day, if at any time without sin & many times with great disorder, and I can scarcely believe, that this & the sanctification of ye Saboth are compatible in our villages.' Estwick did not see such ales or games as sinful in themselves, or regard the holding of them as itself a clear profanation of the Sabbath, but they were all too often the occasions of sin and disorder and it was that which would profane the Lord's Day. Estwick was clearly uneasy about the Declaration, but was mindful of his duty of obedience to the king, stating that: 'if a godly Constantine commands me to publish his Constitutions which are not condemned by the Church ... in this case I may publish his pleasure.' He further mused that: 'If the soveraigne Magistrate commands me to reade his decree in the Church though the contents be such as I in conscience cannot approve, & I am not enforced to assent to it I may lawfully do it.'[44] Nonetheless, he told Ward that if he had been ordered personally to read the Declaration:

> I would have run the same hazard with those which have refused to publish the booke, for albeit I would be loath to suffer for disobedience to mans lawes in point of ceremonie, yet it would not trouble my conscience, to suffer for matters of that great consequence, which do so muche concerne Gods glorie & worship, as ye due sanctification of ye Saboth day.[45]

Estwick did not read the *Book of Sports* himself, but got someone else to do so in order to comply with the requirement that it should be published in his church. Yet he worried that more scrupulous ministers would not connive in such a thing and would resist its publication altogether. He feared that 'this scrupulocity would lay ye foundation of disorder & confusion both in the Church & Common-wealth'.[46] Ward reassured Estwick that 'a minister with safety of conscience, may publish in his church, being commanded by sovereign authority such edicts, the contents whereof he doth not approve in his owne conscience' and told him that recreations on Sundays were lawful and did not break the 'law of the Sabbath'. Indeed, Ward assured Estwick that there was no harm in 'honest Recreations', and reassured Estwick that 'our Saviour was present att a feast on the Sabbath day'.[47] The *Book of Sports* was not, then, at odds with the Church's teaching, even if, on a practical level, the fact that honest recreations could often turn into occasions of sin greatly troubled Estwick and others.

Many ministers were as tortured as Estwick was over the decision of whether to obey the king's command and read his Declaration or to follow their consciences and refuse to do so.[48] A significant minority made their objections clear and either refused to read it at all, or did read it but then preached against it.[49] Thomas Crosfield recorded in his diary in December 1633 that: 'The Declaration for lawfull recreations upon the Sabbath much exagitated by precise men, denied to be red by Mr Rogers ... because ... they pretend it opens a gap to much licentiousness.'[50] Christopher Rogers, the Principal of New Inn Hall, Oxford, was one of those 'precise men' and he and his fellow puritan ministers were indeed outraged. Not only did they refuse to read the Declaration, but some even opted to emigrate rather than comply with its publication. Hugh Peter, who himself went into voluntary exile for a number of years, recorded that:

> my reason for myself and others to go, was merely not to offend Authority in that difference of Judgment; and had not the Book for Encouragement of Sports on the Sabbath come forth, many had staid.[51]

Many more stayed and exploited the loopholes within the Declaration, which, although it required that it should be published, did not prohibit people from preaching against it. Bartholomew Safford, the rector of Enmore in Somerset, read the Declaration but then declared: 'whatsoever the Kinge is pleased to have donne, yeat the Kings of heaven commaundeth us to keepe the sabbath.'[52] After reading the Declaration, Stephen Dennison, rector of St Katherine Cree, read out the ten commandments and told his congregation: 'Dearly Beloved, you have heard now the Commandments of God and Man, obey which you please', while Thomas Spratt of Beaminster told his congregation that 'there is no one commanded to use these recreations ... but these laws are left to everyone's choice ... therefore I do advise you rather to obey God's laws.[53] John Wildgoose of St Peter le Bailey in Oxford preached that the Lord's Day should be kept holy even though 'the king had made laws against it', and Henry Page of Ledbury in Herefordshire preached against the Declaration, telling his congregation that playing sports on Sundays was as sinful as working on Sundays and that it was 'as lawfull for a woman to spinne her wheel or for a man to goe to plough or Cart as for a man on the Sabboth daye to dance the deuilishe round'.[54]

One of Exeter's leading and most zealous puritans, Ignatius Jurdain, 'did much reforme the open profaning of the Sabbath' during his time as Exeter's mayor and, 'by his zeal and vigilancy', intervened to stop 'profane pastimes [which] were then much used' on Sundays.[55] Jurdain was outraged by the *Book of Sports* and wrote to the Bishop of Exeter asking him 'to moove the King for the calling in of his book set out for sports upon Sundaies, or to shew his letter to the King, which he did'. Charles was so offended by Jurdain's letter that 'in a great Anger [he] said he would hang him', and the bishop then had to beg the king not to punish Jurdain.[56] L'Estrange later claimed that of all Charles' injunctions, there was not 'one Royal Edict, during all King Charles his reign, resented with equal regret' and there is no doubt that the book's publication and enforcement offended many people beyond the ranks of puritans like Jurdain.[57] Bulstrode Whitelocke recorded that 'much difference of Opinion was also preached and published, touching the Observation of the Lords day' and that the republishing of the *Book of Sports* 'was not very pleasing to many, who were no Puritans', and that it 'gave great distast to many, both others, as well as those who were usually termed Puritans'.[58] Even if there was not overt opposition, there was unhappiness in many parishes over the 'morris book' and the fact that 'the Kinge did alowe of that which god did forbid, meaninge that the king had of late comaunded sportes to be used upon sondaies after evening prayer'.[59] The wife of the rector of Thistleton, Rutland, rejected the idea that sports were being licensed in order to keep people away from alehouses, saying that it was:

> like the pope allows stews [brothels] to avoid fornication. And we may not do evil that good may come of it.[60]

The Declaration's enforcement also upset many ordinary folk and, in Buckinghamshire, one woman cursed the Dean of the Court of Arches, 'to the pit of hell' for suspending two ministers for failing to read the *Book of Sports*.[61] Nehemiah Wallington regarded various calamities which he claimed were meted out as punishments by God to those who profaned the Sabbath and wrote about the *Book of Sports* that 'this booke of Declaration was as dry fewell, to which fire being put quickly flamed forth that it made those that were filthy to be more filthy being inraged to take more liberty'.[62]

The *Book of Sports* was, though, popular among the many people who cherished their traditional way of life and the few opportunities they had for communal revels. Edmund Reeve commented on 'the happiness of the times when the feasts now commanded were duely observed' and asked who 'doe not daily complaine that, since wakes have been neglected, love between people of neighbour parishes hath very greatly decayed, and since Whitsun feasts have ceased love among the people of every parish hath unexpressibly waxen cold?'[63] However, in others the *Book of Sports* prompted a completely negative reaction. Thomas May later claimed that, although the Declaration permitted 'sports, and pastimes of jollity and lightnesse ... to the Country people' on Sundays, it was counter productive in that 'many men who had been before loose and carelesse, began ... to enter into a more serious consideration of it, and were ashamed to be invited by the authority of Church-men, to that which [was] ... a thing of infirmity'.[64] One such was Richard Conder, who recalled how he had been addicted to football as a young man, despite the parish minister's attempts to stop him and his friends playing football after church:

> til one sabbath morning, our good minister acquainted his hearers, that he was very sorry to tell them, that by order of the King and Council, he must read them the following paper or turn out of his living. This was the Book of Sports forbidding the minister or church-wardens or any other to molest or discourage the youth in their manly sports and recreations on the Lord's Day etc. When our minister was reading it, I was seized with a chill and horror not to be described. Now, thought I, iniquity is established by a law, and sinners are hardened in their sinful ways! What sore judgements are to be expected upon so wicked and guilty a nation![65]

Others were worried that people would abuse the licence given to them to revel, and that disorders or the fragmentation of authority would result. It was reported that the Declaration made 'masters of families complain exceedingly they cannot contain their servants from excursions into all profane sports and pastimes on the Lord's Day'.[66] Some JPs attempted to curb revels despite the Declaration's publication. At the Sessions in Bury St Edmunds, Justice Cole announced that he would indict any minister who encouraged Sunday recreations and, in Maidstone, justices attempted to stop youths indulging in Sunday recreations.[67] Despite the Declaration's licensing of the setting up of maypoles, the maypole at Cerne Abbas was chopped down in 1635 and made into a ladder.[68]

Yet, although the *Book of Sports* caused considerable distress and opposition, it *was* published in the majority of parishes and was welcomed by those who valued their traditional recreations. Inevitably, the voices and views of the mass of the common, illiterate people go largely unrecorded. Only those who got embroiled in confrontations or affrays were likely to find their way into the records, and it is impossible to gauge how representative they were. The loud clamour of puritans attacking traditional festivity for its immorality, and the concerns about disorders occurring at revels that were voiced by justices whose role it was to uphold law and order, have understandably given greater and undue prominence to the opposition to such revels. In many places and for many people wakes and ales remained popular and continued to enjoy support. Although the records cannot show us the scale of the support for traditional revelry, several pieces of evidence nonetheless hint at its continuing popularity. For example, when Edward Williams of Shaftesbury was presented for preaching against the *Book of Sports* in May 1634, the presentment was underwritten by ten parishioners.[69] The very fact that orders had to be made repeatedly in an attempt to try to suppress revels, and that puritan writers continually complained about such festivities, indicates that they were still very common in many parts of the country. Despite the best efforts of puritans and justices, in much of the country the common people remained stubbornly attached to their traditional way of life. In their petition to Charles I in August 1633, the twenty-five Somerset justices complained that the spreading rumour that orders against wakes and revels were to be revoked had been enough to prompt people to once again organise church ales, bid ales and clerk ales, which 'for the most part [had] for a long time been foreborne and not used'.[70] Francis Cheynell claimed that it was 'the great grievance in every parish' that there was 'a prophane and ignorant multitude who are all borne with a Pope in their belly, and are not yet redeemed from their grosse superstition and vaine Conversation which they received by Tradition from their Fathers'.[71] Edmund Calamy similarly complained that 'the Bulk of our people are wicked ... They are unreformed themselves; and it is no wonder they are so opposite to a thorow Reformation.'[72] Writing in 1643, William Mewe bemoaned the people's continuing love for 'whitsun-Ales-Lords-day sports' and the fact that they seemed 'resolved ... to engage their lives, liberties, to maintain these pleasing devotions'.[73]

The combined pressures of puritan sabbatarianism, the concerns on the part of justices to maintain social order, and the move away from traditional fundraising through ales towards a system of rates had led to a decline in ales in many places, as Piers' letter to Laud had acknowledged.[74] However, there is evidence to suggest that, just as the 1625 Act for better Sunday observance may have led to a decline in traditional revels, the publication of the *Book of Sports* led to a revival in traditional festivity in some parts of the country. This suggests that the Declaration gave people the courage to hold revels again who had, in recent years, felt oppressed by the forces which had been trying to suppress them.

In Devon, a county where puritan influence had long been strong and where many parishes had abandoned the traditional revels, the Caroline *Book of Sports* came too late to save wakes and ales in most parishes, but in other parts of the country it prompted a revival of festive traditions.[75] In the west Dorset village of Symondsbury, a maypole was once again erected and, in Dundry in north Somerset, a maypole was similarly set up next to the churchyard in May 1634. David Underdown's research suggests that there had not been a maypole in Dundry for many years and that there, and elsewhere in north Somerset, traditional festivities and recreations, which had been common before 1600, had gone into abeyance in many places before enjoying a revival in the 1630s, most probably following the publication of Charles' *Book of Sports*.[76] Similarly, at Birchington in Kent, where the churchwardens had paid to take down the maypole in 1606, a maypole was once again erected in 1636.[77] Many of the revels recorded in the 1630s at Montacute, Beercrocombe and elsewhere in Somerset were a revival of revels now licensed by the Declaration.[78] Parishes in other parts of the country also appear to have revived ales in the 1630s, such as in South Newington in Oxfordshire and in Great Marlow, where a church ale was held in 1639 instead of imposing a rate. During the 1630s traditional customs were supported by Laudian clergymen such as John Lothwaite in Norfolk, who enthusiastically read the *Book of Sports* and actively supported Sunday football matches, and Henry Hannington in Kent, who cut short the Sunday service to make way for drinking and dancing.[79] The Laudian minister, Thomas Laurence of Bemerton, 'caused a Maypole to be set up at his door and also in the same place a bowling green and kitling alley, it being adjoining to the churchyard, wherein every Sabbath day here was dancing, bowling and kitling'. Laurence praised dancing as 'very fit for recreation' and personally paid the fiddlers to play.[80] The *Book of Sports* was certainly good news for minstrels, such as Thomas Hellyer of Aldermaston, who said he felt 'bound to pray' for Archbishop Laud 'because he was the means of setting forth the Book of Recreations, which helped him to some money'.[81]

Richard Conder spoke of the 'sore judgements' he expected God to visit upon those who profaned the Sabbath as a result of the *Book of Sports*, and Denis Bond recorded in his diary how someone carting a maypole one Sunday in May 1639 was killed when the cart overturned and that 'the woman at Wilton which was to give the entertainment for the drinking the same day scalded her child in a milk pan that it died: this was done on the Lord's day.'[82] Writing in 1636, Henry Burton cited numerous examples of people he claimed had been similarly punished by God for breaking the Sabbath. Challenging those who 'have bene so audacious, as to affirme, the profanation of the Lords day by Maygames, Daunces, Maypoles, Wakes ... (especially after evening Prayer) to be no sin' he described many incidents of people being injured or killed after revelling on Sundays.[83] Furthermore, he claimed that the *Book of Sports* had encouraged such profanations. For example, he claimed that a young Enfield woman 'hearing of the liberty, which was given by the booke, which was published for sports, would needs goe daunce, so long as shee could stand on her leggs; she daunced so long, that thereof within 2 or 3 dayes shee dyed.'[84] Burton similarly claimed that in Woolston, where the godly minister had curtailed traditional revelry, 'upon the publication of this booke in printe, many of the inhabitants the springe following, were imboldened to set up Maypoles, Morricedaunce, and a Whitson ale, continuing their rude revelling a weeke together'. With evident relish, Burton went on to claim that God later punished them for their wickedness, when the room where the ale had been brewed caught fire and the barn where the revels had been held burned down along with thirteen houses 'most of whose inhabitants were actors or abetters in the same'.[85] Burton cited numerous examples of people being punished for abusing the Sabbath, many of whom, he claimed, had been led into their sin following the reading of the *Book of Sports*, such as the hapless man in Thurlow in Suffolk who held a feast for friends on a Sunday 'for joy of the publishing of the Booke for sports' and who was then 'the next day pressed to death, by the suddaine fall of a faggot stack'.[86] Burton's *Divine Tragedie* not only supports the suggestion that the Caroline *Book of Sports* caused a revival in festivities in several areas and that it encouraged people to take part in such revelry, but, given that he gave examples from places right across the country, it also suggests the widespread, popular nature of such festivity.

Although some revels do appear to have been revived, others had never been stopped, even if the pressures to suppress them had increased in the early 1600s. Many wakes and ales were held in the 1630s and, even if they were generally in gradual decline, the *Book of Sports* seems to have revived such revels in some areas or, at the very least, to have slowed down the rate of their decline. In the West Country, Justices still had to deal with people who became disorderly at revels, such as the youths at Dartmouth in 1634, who drank so much that 'they could not stand so steady as the [may]pole did'.[87] The JPs in Somerset appear to have been so cowed by Charles' rejection of their petition and by how Richardson was dealt with that, in 1638, they were reluctant even to deal with the disorderly aspects of ales and failed to punish a number of 'unruly people' attending a bid ale.[88]

The battle of pens

W.B. Whitaker wrote of Brabourne's *Defence of that most Ancient, and Sacred ordinance of Gods, the Sabbath Day* that it was part of 'a regular battle of pens' between the opposing sides over the question of Sunday observance.[89] Yet, in the years immediately following the publication of the *Book of Sports* there was an imbalance in what was printed. The 'battle of pens' was initially a rather one-sided affair. Although Heylyn later wrote that the *Book of Sports* 'was no sooner published then it was followed and pursued with such loud outcries as either the Tongues or Pens of the sabbatarians could raise against it', in fact relatively few people had the temerity to attack it in print during the 1630s.[90] One of the few who did was William Prynne, who complained about the 'many prophane and erroneous, impious books' that appeared 'against the very morality of the Sabbath' and attacked the bishops for having 'shut up the mouthes of sundry or our most godly, powerfull, painefull Preachers'.[91] Prynne was referring to the censuring of non-conformist ministers who refused to publish the Declaration, but he may also have had in mind the suppression of sabbatarian works during the 1630s. No sabbatarian works were legally published between 1633 and 1641.[92] Although a few unauthorised works did appear during these years, only works attacking and undermining puritan sabbatarianism were actually authorised. The most significant of these works were Francis White's *Treatise of the Sabbath-Day* of 1635, his *Examination and Confutation of a Lawlesse Pamphlet* of 1637 and Peter Heylyn's *History of the Sabbath* of 1636.

Following the publication of Brabourne's *Defence*, the king commanded Francis White, the Bishop of Ely, to write a work countering Brabourne's argument. In his *Treatise of the Sabbath-Day*, White attacked Brabourne's 'Sabbatarian errour' of arguing that Saturday was the Christian Sabbath, and then widened his attack to encompass 'Sunday-Sabbatizers' who sought to prohibit honest recreations on Sundays.[93] Although White said it was sacrilegious to use 'vitious and unlawfull' recreations on the Lords day, he maintained that it was perfectly permissible for 'honest and lawfull' recreations to be 'exercised upon some part of the Christian Holy-day'.[94] He claimed that 'Sunday Sabbatarians' believed that 'to use any civill recreation on the Lord's Day, is a sinne of as evill quality, As Murder, Adultery, Incest, False Witnesse, Theft' and cited examples of ministers who variously preached that Sunday bowling and bell-ringing were as sinful as murder and that 'to make a Feast ... on the Lords-day, is a great a sinne, as for a father to take a knife and cut his childes throat'.[95] He challenged those 'sabbatizers' who argued that the fourth commandment was a moral and perpetual precept and asserted that 'Sunday is grounded upon Apostolicall Authority: and not upon the Law given in Mount Sinai.'[96] White claimed that, given that the apostles had altered the Sabbath from Saturday to Sunday, Sunday was established as the Christian Sabbath by the Church and not by the fourth commandment. He similarly argued that the use of recreation 'in such manner as the Law of the Church, and of the State permitteth: is no sinne, and ... is not a transgression of any precept of the ... Decalogue.'[97] White highlighted the fact that the sabbatarianism of the radical Protestants was far stricter than the traditional sabbatarianism of the Church, which had permitted lawful recreations on Sundays provided people fulfilled their religious duty by first attending church.[98] White also claimed that it was sensible for the Church to allow people some recreations on holy days, arguing that 'if they should (upon Puritan principles) restraine them wholly from all repast: the Holy-day would be more unwelcome to them than the plough-day.'[99]

White was, of course, selective in his use of earlier works and the teachings of the Church, and manipulated his material to portray sabbatarians as judaizers.[100] Yet, his argument that puritan views represented a new kind of English sabbatarianism was fundamentally sound. White's assertion that the moderate use of recreations was permissible on Sundays was in keeping with the established traditions and teachings of the Church and he was right to argue that those who sought to ban such recreations on religious grounds were indeed 'novell sabbatarians'.[101] Those who argued that such recreations were a profanation of the Sabbath were indeed arguing for a new, stricter form of sabbatarianism.

White's lengthy treatise attacking the sabbatarianism that many people in England now adhered to, coming in the wake of the enforcement of the *Book of Sports*, prompted a strong reaction among the people that he was targeting. As Fuller put it:

> expressions fell from his pen, whereat many strict people ... took great distaste. Hereupon books begat books, and controversies on this subject were multiplied.[102]

In an unlicensed tract, Henry Burton responded by challenging White's assertion that the Lord's Day was instituted by the Church and argued instead 'that the keeping of the Lords Day is grounded upon, and commanded in the fourth Commandment, and so is not of human institution'.[103] Burton cited the *Homily of the place and time of Prayer* in support of his argument and denied that the Homily could be open to 'private interpretation ... of a sort of factions Sabbatarian Novellists'.[104] Burton argued that:

> the Lords day is come in place of the old Sabbath: ... if the fourth Commandement command the Sabbath day to be kept perpetually in all ages (as sayeth our Homily) and that Sabbath day of the Iewes is now come in place of the old, and is the Christians Sabbath day: then of necessity, doth the fourth Commandement command us Christians to keep the Lords day, as our new Sabbath day.[105]

He attacked White's distinction between 'vitious and unlawfull' recreations and 'honest and lawfull' ones as 'poore and pitifull shifts and shufflings'.[106] Burton condemned all recreations on Sundays and, in particular, he criticised the 'promiscuous meetings of wanton youth in their May-games, setting up of May-poles, dancing about them, dancing the Morice, and leading the ringdance, and the like' as 'obscene, or lascivious and voluptuous pastimes'.[107]

The issue of the status of Sunday as the Christian Sabbath and of how it should be observed now became even more of a theological football than before. The puritans had sought to elevate the status of Sunday and to demand a far stricter observance than had previously been the case. Indeed, George Walker, rector of St John the Evangelist, Watling Street, argued that the law of the Sabbath was binding on all Christians until the end of the world and said that, even though the Christian Sabbath had been moved from Saturday to Sunday, 'the moralitie and perpetuity of the law require that every circumstance of the Sabbath, and every particular Sabbath duty, should at all times remain the same perpetual and unchangable'.[108] In arguing this, Walker and his fellow puritans distorted the teaching and past practice of the English Church. Equally, Laudians and anti-puritans now exaggerated their own case and similarly distorted earlier writings and sermons in order to link puritanism with sabbatarianism such that people who advocated a stricter observance of Sunday, but who were otherwise orthodox, moderate Protestants, were likely to be labelled as puritans and at odds with both the Church hierarchy and the Crown.

White responded to Burton's unlicensed tract by publishing *An Examination and Confutation of a Lawlesse Pamphlet*, in which he again argued that the Lord's Day was not the 'litterall Sabbath of the fourth Commandement' and that Sunday and other holy days were 'left by the authoritie of God's Word, to the libertie of Christ's Church to be determined'.[109] He attacked 'Novell Teachers' for 'converting [Sunday] into a Legall Sabbath' and for 'Affirming that all bodily exercise, and all civill passe-time and Recreation, (although the same be sober and honest) is simply unlawfull, upon all houres of the Lord's Day'.[110] He stated that people had long debated issues of Sabbath observance and, claiming the king's approval for his earlier treatise, sought to settle people 'in a firme resolution, never to bee distracted with Sabbatarian fancies any more'.[111]

White played an important role in identifying puritans with a novel, overly-strict form of sabbatarianism that was contrary to the traditions of the Church, yet the most prominent figure in the attack against puritan sabbatarians was Peter Heylyn. In 1634 Heylyn organised the translation and publication of a lecture on the doctrine of the Sabbath that John Prideaux, Professor of Divinity at Oxford, had delivered in 1622.[112] Prideaux's lecture argued that the fourth commandment was partly moral and partly ceremonial. It touched on the question of recreations, stating that 'wee are permitted Recreations (of what sort soever) which serve lawfully to refresh our spirits, and nourish mutuall neighbourhood'. Even though recreations had not been the focus of Prideaux's sermon, it was this aspect that Heylyn stressed when he wrote a preface to Prideaux's *Doctrine of the Sabbath*, presenting Prideaux's work as if it were a defence of the recently reissued *Book of Sports*.[113] Prideaux was an orthodox Calvinist and fierce anti-Arminian. Heylyn deliberately used the preface to imply support for the *Book of Sports* from moderate, establishment Calvinists such as Prideaux.[114] In his preface, Heylyn said that the debate over the Sabbath was the most ancient controversy in the Church's history and implied that it was radical Protestants who had reignited that debate and had tried to introduce a new form of sabbatarianism, claiming that 'immediately upon the Reformation of Religion in these western parts, the Controversy broke out afresh'.[115] He argued that, on Sundays, 'all Recreations whatsoever are to be allowed which honestly may refresh the spirits, and encrease mutuall love and neighbourhood amongst us'. He particularly praised wakes for promoting 'good neighbourhood' along with dancing, shooting and wrestling 'and all other Pastimes, not by Law prohibited, which either exercise the body, or revive the minde'.[116]

Charles I then commissioned Heylyn to write his vast work on the history of the Sabbath. This distorted the history of sabbatarianism in such a way that it was portrayed as a feature of puritanism alone and as totally alien to mainstream religion. *Puritan* sabbatarianism was indeed different and much stricter than the traditional sabbatarianism of the English Church, but Heylyn's work suggested that all sabbatarianism was unorthodox.[117] Heylyn challenged the notion that the *Homily of the place and time of Prayer* created a 'Lords day Sabbath', arguing that the *Homily* required people to commit their 'whole selves body and soule' to the performance of the religious duties required of them, but that this did not mean that people 'should spend the day wholly in heavenly exercises; for then there were no time allowed us to eat and drinke.'[118] He argued that the Homily required people to give themselves wholly to God's worship during the time on the Lord's Day that was allocated to His worship, but that it did not require people to spend the *whole* day in holy exercises. Therefore, people should devote themselves completely to God's worship during divine service, but they were then free to spend the rest of the Lord's Day in 'dancing, shooting, leaping, vaulting, may-games, and meetings of good neighbourhood'.[119] Heylyn accused Nicholas Bownd of being 'the Founder of these Sabbatariancies' and, as Rogers had done, he accused Bownd of causing the spread of a false sabbatarianism.[120] He claimed that:

> in the yeere 1595, some of that faction which before had laboured with small profit, to overthrow the Hierarchy and government of this Church of England; now set themselves on worke to ruinate all the orders of it: to beate downe at one blow all dayes and times, which by the wisdome and authority of the Church, had beene appointed for Gods service, and in the steed thereof to erect a Sabbath, of their owne devising.[121]

He claimed that it was the publication in 1595 of Bownd's *Doctrine of the Sabbath* that led to the spread of sabbatarianism.[122] Although Heylyn's portrayal of all forms of sabbatarianism as unorthodox was misleading, he was nonetheless correct to highlight the extreme nature of Bownd's sabbatarianism. He argued that such sabbatarianism was contrary to the traditions and precepts of the Church and that the Sabbath of the fourth commandment was 'an institute peculiar to the Iewish Nation'.[123] Heylyn maintained that the Lord's Day should not be subject to the rigours of the Jewish Sabbath and that, consequently, it was wrong to forbid people from indulging in 'lawful pleasures and honest recreations'.[124] He condemned those people who had made the Lord's day into 'their new Saint Sabbath' and who had embraced 'new Sabbath doctrines' and commended the king for his action 'to suppresse those rigours, which some, in maintenance of their Sabbath-Doctrines, had pressed upon this Church, in these latter dayes'.[125] Heylyn further praised Charles for publishing the *Book of Sports*, thereby 'licensing on that day, those Lawful Pastimes, which some, without authority from Gods Word, or from the practice of Gods Church, had of late restrained'.[126]

Other writers similarly defended sports on Sundays, and linked sabbatarianism with puritanism. Robert Sanderson accused sabbatarians of being like Scribes and Pharisees who were sowing division within the Church as: 'they creep into houses, in a shape of sanctimony ... cast a snare upon the silly consciences of men, making concision in the Church of the Lord, and so the middle wall of partition which Christ hath broken down, they do renew, and this doing, shew themselves to be the deceitfull workers.'[127] John Pocklington accused zealous sabbatarians of being like Trypho the Jew and of using a 'sword to cut off all sports and recreations on their Sabbath'.[128] Pocklington argued that sabbatarians were wrong to refer to the Lord's Day as the Sabbath, and condemned their adoration of the 'idoll Sabbath'.[129] Christopher Dow, the rector of Battle in Sussex, wrote two works in this period which defended the use of recreations on Sundays. Dow claimed that the fourth commandment 'extends to us Christians, as well as to the Jewes in as much as to consecrate some part of our time to God'.[130] Yet, Dow argued that only part of the day had to be given over to worship and that people were free to use 'honest and seemly recreations, after the publike dutyes of the Day are finished'.[131] Dow attacked Burton's *Divine Tragedy Lately Acted*, accusing Burton of presuming to know God's mind in portraying accidents that had befallen people on Sundays as acts of God's judgment.[132] Dow denied that morris dancing and maypoles were heathen, and defended the *Book of Sports*, arguing 'that such as refuse to publish it accordingly, are justly punished, and their punishment no cruelty, or unjust persecution'.[133]

These works served to link puritans with the very concept of sabbatarianism to a much greater degree than before. Puritans had, of course, been associated with moves to suppress recreations long before the publication of the *Book of Sports* and the works defending it. As early as the mid-1590s the word 'puritan' had become a term used to abuse people who were against traditional revels, as it had been used against Richard Baxter's father when he had intervened to try to stop minstrels playing at a revel.[134] In 1629, for example, John Earle wrote that the fiddler who played at Whitsun ales 'hates naturally the puritan as an enemy to this mirth'.[135] However, the works of Heylyn, White, *et al* made the connection between sabbatarianism and puritanism even stronger and, in so doing, they further polarised attitudes and increased the divisions within Caroline society.

Poets and playwrights also contributed to the offensive against sabbatarians and the elements in society that were threatening the festive culture.[136] In 1633 Ben Jonson produced two plays celebrating rural pleasures. *The King's Entertainment at Welbeck* included a country wedding in which the bride was 'dressed like an old May-Lady' and *A Tale of a Tub* made several favourable references to wakes and ales.[137] In *Coelum Britanicum* (1634), Thomas Carew praised Charles I for protecting traditional revelry for the sake of religion.[138] *Annalia Dubrensia*, a collection of verses by various poets who emphasised the value of traditional revelry and attacked those who sought to suppress it, was published in 1636. In it John Trussell bewailed recent attacks on wakes, writing:

> The countrie Wakes, and whirlings have appeer'd
> Of late, like forraine pastimes: Carnivalls,
> Palme and Rush-bearing, harmelesse Whitson-ales
> Running at Quintain, May-games, generall Playes,
> By some more nice, then wise of latter dayes,
> Have in their Standings, Lectures, Exercises,
> Beene so reprov'd, traduc'd, condemn'd for vices
> Profane, and heathenish, ... so that now
> All Publike merriments, I know not how,
> Are questioned for their lawfulnesse; whereby
> Societie grew sicke; was like to die.[139]

John Ballad commended Trussell for boldly trying 'to stop those itching mouthes' which were clamouring against 'harmlesse sports'.[140] In 'A Congratulatory Poem', Robert Dover warned that, if people were to abandon their sports and pastimes, then, much to the detriment of the nation, they would be likely to be unfit and to turn to drinking rather than other active exercise. He condemned the 'refined Clergie' who attacked mixed dancing and other recreations and praised those who continued in their sports.[141]

The greatest literary defender of traditional festivity during this period was the poet, Robert Herrick. Herrick's most famous work, *Hesperides*, was not actually published until 1648, but he wrote the series of poems throughout the 1630s and 1640s, and used many of them to extol the virtues of rural pastimes and the value to the countryside community of traditional festivity. In 'Corinna's, Going A Maying', Herrick referred to the *Book of Sports* as 'The Proclamation made for May', and celebrated the rites associated with the traditional holiday of May Day.[142] In 'The Wake', Herrick suggested that wakes kept the common people amused and, with a certain amusement at the ruder sort's lack of sophistication, he recorded the simple attractions for them, writing:

> Tarts and Custards, Creams and Cakes,
> Are the Junketts still at Wakes:
> Unto which the Tribes resort,
> Where the business is the sport:
> Morris-dancers thou shalt see,
> Marian too in Pagentrie:
> And a Mimick to devise
> Many grinning properties.
> Players there will be, and those
> Base in action as in clothes:
> Yet with strutting they will please
> The incurious Villages.[143]

Although Herrick acknowledged that there was often disorder and violence at such wakes, he claimed wakes provided a way for country folk to be good neighbours, to drink together and to resolve disputes through mutual reconciliation:

> But the anger ends all here,
> Drencht in Ale, or drown'd in Beere.
> Happy Rusticks, best content
> With the cheapest Merriment:
> And possesse no other feare,
> Then to want the Wake next Yeare.[144]

In contrast to the works of writers celebrating the traditional festive culture, John Milton's *Comus*, a masque which was performed in 1634, implicitly criticised the liberty granted to people to dance and revel. Milton was not against well-controlled, decent revelry enjoyed at appropriate times, but was critical of unbridled festivity which could occasion sin.[145] The masque contains numerous coded attacks on Charles I's court and on Laud and his religious policies. Comus himself is portrayed as a very ungodly figure who corrupts people into licentiousness. The literary convention was to celebrate the rising of the sun, yet here Comus celebrates the sun going down and the world descending into night, with order being put to bed and replaced with disorder and heathenish revelry. Comus' speech is a dark hymn to debauchery in which he praises 'merry wakes and pastimes', and implicitly attacks those who would suppress such 'revelrie, Tipsie dance, and Jollitie' for their 'sowre Severitie' and their 'morall babble'.[146] *Comus* was a covert attack on the licence to revelry; more overt criticism was risky.

Indeed, there were very few overtly pro-sabbatarian works published in this period, and none were authorised. In addition to *A Brief Answer to a Late Treatise of the Sabbath Day* (1635), Burton published *A Divine Tragedie Lately Acted* (1636), and *For God and the King* (1636); William Prynne produced *Newes from Ipswich* (1636); Robert Bolton published *Some General Directions for a Comfortable Walking with God* (1638) and George Walker published *The Doctrine of the Sabbath* (1638). They all argued that the Sabbath was divinely instituted, defended the moral and perpetual nature of the fourth commandment, and denied that any recreations were permissible on Sundays. They attacked the publication of the king's Declaration, which Burton claimed had been like putting fuel on a fire and had encouraged people to provoke God's anger, and which Prynne claimed had turned the Lord's Day into the Devil's Day.[147]

Many other works attacking the *Book of Sports* and Sunday recreations would have appeared if the political climate had been different, but censorship and the punishment of openly non-conformist clergy discouraged people from publishing pro-sabbatarian works. A large number of anti-Laudian pamphlets and works challenging the writings of White and Heylyn were circulating in manuscript form during the 1630s, but very few made it into print during this period.[148] The puritan, John Vicars, recorded in 1636 that: 'Manuscripts are now the best help God's people have to vindicate the truth, printing being nowadays prohibited to them', and Prynne later claimed that the printing presses were 'locked up and strictly watched by Lawd and the Bishops ... in opposition to the Anti-Sabbatarian Pamphlets'. Controls were certainly tightened. In 1637 the Star Chamber ruled that the number of printers in England should be limited to just twenty-three and people in possession of illegal presses were to be harshly punished.[149] The licenser, Samuel Baker censored a commentary by William Jones which dealt with Sabbath observance, and Laud had passages in other works either censored or altered to remove references to the 'Sabbath' or to make them more hostile to the idea of strict Sunday observance.[150] Sir Edward Dering later complained that: 'All this wholesome doctrine was expunged lest it should mar a ball, a wake or a morris dance upon the Lord's Day.'[151]

Well over thirty religious books, and maybe many more, were interfered with or stopped at the press between 1625 and 1640 and it was dangerous to openly challenge the official line on Sunday observance.[152] Burton was punished for publishing his works attacking Francis White and ecclesiastical policy, along with William Prynne and John Bastwick, who had also published works attacking Laudian policies. In fact, censorship at this time was not as tightly controlled as the authorities would have liked. Nonetheless, people believed that the restrictions on printing were much tighter than they actually were, and this seems to have been sufficient to deter many would-be sabbatarian writers, who simply did not offer up their books for publication.[153] That situation changed as Charles I began to lose control of events and the controls on printing all too obviously began to break down. By 1641, realising that the Crown had lost control of the presses, and no longer fearing terrible consequences, sabbatarian writers were emboldened at last to publish their works, and there was a flood of sabbatarian tracts attacking the *Book of Sports* and traditional Sunday festivities.

With things now moving in the sabbatarians' direction, Richard Bernard, the rector of Batcombe in Dorset, condemned the 'books [that had] been written, and by licence passed the presse, to take away the morallity of the fourth Commandement'.[154] He rejected 'the opprobrious name of Sabbatarians' that had been applied to those who sought to uphold the commandment and insisted that it was a moral and perpetual precept and that the use of recreations on Sundays was a clear breach of it.[155] The puritan, William Gouge, attacked anti-sabbatarians for putting 'a knife to the throat of religion' and for branding those who observed the Sabbath properly 'with ignominious titles, as Precisions, Puritanes, Sabbatarians and Jewes'.[156] The writer and politician, George Abbot, similarly attacked what he described as 'primitive English Antisabbatarians' for being 'Patrons of impiety'. Declaring that 'God hateth rioting on the Sabbath', Abbot condemned those who wanted to permit dancing and other revels on Sundays.[157] George Hakewill wrote that even lawful recreations were forbidden on Sundays and the puritan, William Ames, similarly maintained that no sports should be played on the Lord's Day because they drew people's minds away from religion.[158] In a lengthy work on the morality of the fourth commandment, William Twisse argued that Christians were still bound by the commandment and attacked the use of sports on Sundays. Challenging the notion that wakes and ales promoted good neighbourliness, Twisse asked:

> whether Christian neighbourhood be not better maintained, in meeting together in the repeating of a Sermon ... then in meeting together at beare-baiting, or at a play, or at a maygame, or to look upon a morice dance.[159]

As Burton had done in 1636, Lewis Hughes and other writers cited examples of people struck by divine vengeance for playing or defending sports on Sundays; such as the man in Kingston who was apparently struck blind and dumb after rejoicing at the suspending of the local minister for not reading the *Book of Sports*. Hughes claimed that he would have needed to write a large volume 'to make mention of all the judgements that God hath shewed upon Sabbath breakers, since the *Book of Sports* was commanded to be read in Churches'.[160] In similar vein, Walker claimed that God continually showed his anger at Sabbath profanations:

> drowning some in their swimming, breaking the backs, armes, legs and necks of others in wrastling, striking with horrible lamenes and with deadly surfets, and sudden death, leapers, dancers, hunters, hawkers, riders, bowlers, and such like.[161]

The very fact that, as soon as the controls on the presses were lifted, so many such works were published is an indication of how important and divisive the question of Sabbath observance had become and the extent to which the *Book of Sports* had created lasting resentment. During Charles I's Personal Rule, the opposition to the *Book of Sports* was necessarily muted. Censorship and the widespread belief that the presses were tightly controlled had largely prevented opponents from attempting to publish sabbatarian and anti-Laudian works, and the lack of a parliament had denied people the platform from which to voice their opposition to the Declaration. All that changed with the rebellion in Scotland and the first Bishops' War. Charles I was forced to call a parliament in 1640 and the strength of feeling against the *Book of Sports* among many sections of Caroline society then became evident.

The *Book of Sports* and the Short and Long Parliaments

After eleven years without a parliament, during which time people had not had the opportunity to speak out against royal policies, parliament sat again in April 1640. The sitting of the Short Parliament afforded MPs their first opportunity to speak about the *Book of Sports*. The fact that a number of prominent MPs did so some seven years after its publication indicates how deeply it was resented. Francis Rous, the MP for Truro, objected to the fact that ministers had been made to read the 'booke concerning Mortice [sic] Danceinge on the Lords Day' and that some had faced suspension and excommunication. He claimed that they were unjustly punished because it could have been read by a clerk instead.[162] John Pym saw the publication and enforcement of the *Book of Sports* as 'a very greate grievance being ag[ains]t the foundacon of gover[n]m[en]t' and similarly condemned what he saw as the unjustified punishment of ministers who refused to read the Declaration.[163] Sir Walter Earle also attacked the suspension without warrant of ministers 'that read not the booke for pastimes', and the matter was one of the items listed in a report made for the House of Commons by the committee concerning innovations in religion.[164]

Charles I dissolved the Short Parliament in May 1640, but, following the defeat of English troops in the second Bishops' War, he was forced to call another parliament in November. The meeting of the Long Parliament once again enabled MPs to voice their grievances; and the *Book of Sports* continued to feature in their debates, indicating its profound impact. Puritans, in particular, had high hopes that the Long Parliament would undo the religious innovations that they believed Laud had introduced and hoped that it would also act to end the profanation of the Lord's Day. Richard Bernard dedicated his *Threefold Treatise of the Sabbath* to the Parliament and, in particular, to the Grand Committee of Religion, telling its members that they had been appointed by God to redress the errors of the anti-sabbatarians and to exalt 'the honour of Christ which by these men hath been so dishonoured'.[165] George Walker similarly welcomed the new Parliament and the changes that it heralded, writing: 'Now blessed be God for your happy Assembly in this most hopefull Parliament.'[166] Matthew Sylvester later observed that, even though MPs in the Long Parliament 'were of several Tempers as to Matters of Religion', they had various grievances which initially united them in calling for changes in government policy which included 'the Book for Dancing on the Lord's Day'.[167] Political and religious grievances combined in the Long Parliament, but, as John Morrill has demonstrated, it was religion that was the most important factor in determining MPs' actions.[168] While MPs by no means all shared the same views on Charles' religious policies, they were preoccupied by the future of religion in England, and the *Book of Sports* and Sunday observance was a recurring concern.

Once again, MPs attacked the *Book of Sports* and its enforcement. It was immediately included among the grievances that the House of Commons wanted redressed and MPs raised the cases of ministers who had been suspended for refusing to read it.[169] Not only did the Commons Committee for Religion recommend that several ministers should be restored to their livings, but it also enquired into the actions of other ministers who had shown fervent support for the Declaration. John Pocklington, whose *Sunday No Sabbath* had particularly offended the sabbatarians, was deprived of his living and his book was publicly burned: the same fate that had befallen Prynne's *Histrio-mastix* during the Personal Rule.[170] Puritan MPs then pushed for a strict sabbatarian discipline to be imposed upon the country.[171] On 8 September 1641 the Commons resolved that:

> the Lord's day should be duly observed and sanctified; that all dancing, or other sports either before or after divine service, be foreborne and restrained.[172]

Things moved more quickly still once parliament had set itself up as, in effect, an alternative government. In March 1643 MPs instructed the Lord Mayor of London to enforce proper Sabbath observance and the Mayor duly issued instructions that churchwardens and constables should 'not permit or suffer any person or persons in time of divine service, or at any time on the Lord's day ... to use any unlawful exercises or pastimes'.[173] Then, on 5 May 1643, Parliament ordered that the *Book of Sports* should be burned by the common hangman in Cheapside and that all copies of the book should be handed over to one of the sheriffs of London for burning.[174] Copies of the book were publicly burned five days later.

By this time, England had been plunged into civil war and the majority of MPs who continued to sit in the Long Parliament were keen to achieve much stricter Sabbath observance. The maypole and associated traditional festivity had almost become a symbol of the royalist cause and this may have spurred MPs on to try to eradicate it. In April 1644 an ordinance 'for the better observation of the Lords-Day' was passed which prohibited people from attending any 'Wake, ... Church-Ale, Dancing, Games, Sport or Pastime whatsoever', and further ordained that:

> because the prophanation of the Lords-day hath been heretofore greatly occasioned by May-Poles, (a Heathenish vanity, generally abused to superstition and wickedness) ... all and singular May-Poles, that are, or shall be erected, shall be taken down and removed ... And that no May-Pole shall be hereafter set up, erected or suffered to be within this Kingdome.[175]

In January 1645 Parliament established a Directory for the Public Worship of God, which declared that the whole of the Lord's Day had to be devoted to public and private worship and banned all sports and pastimes.[176] That October, Parliament ordered the excommunication of anyone who indulged in any form of recreation on the Lord's Day.[177]

By the time of this last ordinance, the first Civil War was all but over: a war which had torn England apart in the bloodiest and most divisive conflict that the country had ever seen. The factors that had led the country into such a terrible, prolonged conflict were many and varied, as were the reasons which determined people's allegiance. Yet, it is clear that religious belief and issues of culture were a major factor. Many parliamentarians wanted religious reform and, as MPs were trying to do through legislation at Westminster, they wanted to stamp out what they saw as profanations and to establish godly rule in the country; while many royalists wanted to preserve the established Church of England and to preserve their traditional way of life.

Traditional revelry and the question of allegiance

A vast amount has already been written about popular allegiance in the English Civil War and about the various factors that determined which side people supported – and, indeed, the extent to which people actively sided with one side or the other at all. It is beyond the scope of this book to provide a detailed examination of the question of allegiance, but it is important to consider the part which attitudes to traditional revelry and Sabbath observance may have played in determining loyalties in the 1640s. Links were certainly made after the war between support for traditional revelry and royalism; indeed, the maypole became something of a royalist totem. But can we be sure that attitudes to traditional festivity were necessarily a factor in determining allegiances at the war's outset?

David Underdown's study of early modern Somerset, Wiltshire and Dorset concluded that royalism was strongest in communities with strong social ties and an established hierarchy and which cherished their traditional festive culture. These areas tended to be in mixed farming and downland regions, where villages were much more nucleated. Where parishes were large and spread out, as in the woodland areas and cattle-grazing districts, social control by the local elite was less practical. Rapid economic change and the breaking down of communal solidarity which, in part, entailed the decline of traditional revels, provided fertile ground in which radical ideas could flourish. It was in these areas, Underdown argues, that there was strong support for Parliament.[178] Ann Hughes and others have rightly observed that Underdown's wood-pasture/sheep-corn dichotomy is too crude to fully explain allegiance to one side or the other. The links between economic activity, social structure and political attitudes were certainly more complex.[179] Nonetheless, the social structure and culture of particular areas were of considerable significance. So, too, was religious belief. Indeed, the two were often closely linked.

In general terms, whereas radical Protestants wanted to eradicate traditional festivity – which they saw as a vestige of the old Catholic religion preventing the godly reformation of society – religious conservatives retained a stubborn affection for that festive culture. Mark Stoyle cites the example of William Elliott, a respectable Exeter man who was both a fierce defender of traditional festive culture and antagonistic towards the 'puritant justices' who were trying to stamp it out. Elliott actively promoted the use of maypoles, church ales and Sunday gaming and fell foul of the local justices as a result. On one occasion, when Elliott was hauled before the justices for organising a prohibited church ale, he not only freely admitted selling ale but defiantly told the court that: 'he doth sell it and will sell it, for it is an aunciente custome that the wardens of the parish ... have used to sell drinke for the space of 3 hundred yeres, and it is for the good of the parishe.' As Stoyle observes, 'Elliott's opinions exude the true flavour of the religious and cultural conservatism which later underlay popular Royalism'.[180] But, how typical was Elliott? Are we right to conclude that men like Elliott saw their traditional way of life as under threat and that, when it later came to choosing sides, a desire to defend that way of life prompted them to support the king against Parliament?

Ronald Hutton has demonstrated that, among the gentry at least, a number of those who opposed the *Book of Sports* in the 1630s went on to support the king in the English Civil War.[181] For example, most of the Somerset justices who signed the petition against ales in 1633 were from leading royalist families. One of those justices, Sir John Stowell, not only signed the 1633 petition but also denounced Bishop Piers to the Commons in 1640, complaining that the bishop had punished a minister for 'preach[ing] twice upon Michaelmas Day to hinder church ales' and had excommunicated another 'for not reading [the] book of sports'.[182] Despite this, Stowell went on to be a staunch royalist in the Civil War. However, as Conrad Russell has observed, Stowell's opposition to the Somerset ales was almost certainly because of fears of disorder and, when it came to supporting the king or Parliament, his hatred of puritanism exceeded his concerns about the potential threat to social order posed by church ales.[183]

Indeed, we should not be surprised that the majority of Somerset justices who signed the 1633 petition against ales were royalists rather than parliamentarians, since, as the previous chapter demonstrated, most had not signed it out of any puritan sabbatarianism but because they either feared that ales might lead to violence or because they were opposed to Sir Robert Phelips and wanted to undermine his position. They were not motivated by religious zeal and, when they saw that the unfolding events of 1642 presented a much greater threat to the established order than any disorder at revels would ever do, they came out for the king. Similarly, many MPs who had initially backed attacks on royal policies pursued during the Personal Rule became alarmed by the radical direction which the Long Parliament was taking, and a royalist party within Parliament began to emerge. Consequently, many gentry who had been against revels in the 1630s because of their perceived threat to social order were now willing to show their support for the king because of the greater threat to the existing order posed by radical MPs and their supporters. They now had bigger fish to fry. Nonetheless, it is clear that their support for the king was, as Hutton points out, not due to a desire to preserve ales and traditional festivity.

Hutton also cites the examples of three men who had previously supported revelry in some form but who yet went on to support Parliament in the Civil War. The Essex MP, Sir Thomas Barrington, was a member of a leading Essex puritan family and a committed defender of parliamentary privileges and liberties during the 1640s. However, although Barrington was a puritan and staunch parliamentarian, his household accounts show that he not only condoned but actually hosted morris dancers, wassailers and other revellers at his house, Hatfield Broad Oak in Essex. This may seem a surprising thing for the leading member of a high profile puritan family to have done, but Barrington was not alone in this respect. Several puritan gentlemen saw it as a duty inherent upon people of their standing to host entertainers in order to amuse their households at the traditional festivals. That was not, quite the same thing as condoning unbridled public revelry on the Lord's Day, of course. Nonetheless, it is clear that, in Barrington's case, support for revelry clearly did not determine allegiance in the civil war.[184] George Wither, a poet who had written verse celebrating Rogationtide processions and Christmas revelry during the 1630s, and William Durham, who had defended dancing and May games in *Annalia Dubrensia*, similarly went on to become committed parliamentarians.[185] These cases clearly underscore Hutton's point that, at gentry level, attitudes to revels did not necessarily determine allegiance in the civil war. However, these three men may not have been typical. One can always find exceptions to every historical rule. For example, while most puritans were parliamentarians, some supported the king and, while the vast majority of Catholics were royalist, there were a few Catholics who nonetheless sided with Parliament. Out of 116 Catholic families in Lancashire none at all supported parliament, but in Yorkshire, out of a total of 157 Catholic families, ten did side with Parliament. Similarly, out of 132 Yorkshire puritan families, 24 were royalist and, out of 67 puritan families in Lancashire, seven supported the king.[186] But these Catholic parliamentarians and puritan royalists were the exceptions, not the rule.

The whole question of allegiance is complex and there are bound to be anomalies: just as there were a few Catholic parliamentarians and puritan royalists, so, too, there were some parliamentarians who had defended traditional revelry and some royalists who had earlier sought to suppress ales. However, it would appear that most of the men recorded as having supported traditional festivity in the 1630s went on to become royalists in the 1640s. For example, of the authors of *Annalia Dubrensia* who were still alive at the outbreak of the Civil War and whose allegiance is known, only William Durham supported Parliament. Many of the other contributors were ardent, active royalists. William Denny, for example, was imprisoned by Parliament at Windsor Castle for his work for the royalist cause. Owen Feltham, John Mennes, John Monson, John Trussell and Ferriman Rutter were all royalists, and William Davenant was knighted by Charles I at Gloucester in 1643 for his 'loyalty and poetry'.[187] Herrick, whose poetry championed traditional festivity, was also a committed royalist. Conversely, as discussed earlier in this chapter, Nehemiah Wallington, Thomas May, Francis Cheynell, Edmund Calamy and Denis Bond had all either explicitly condemned the *Book of Sports* or had otherwise attacked the people's attachment to what they saw as profanations and licentiousness; and they were all supporters of Parliament during the Civil War.[188] In a sermon delivered by the Exeter preacher, John Bond, during the summer of 1641, in which Bond identified an anti-Parliamentarian party of 'Anti-deliverancers', he claimed that those people who promoted Arminianism, Anti-sabbatarianism or 'licentious papers' were *'ten to one* ... Anti-Deliverancers'.[189] Therefore, even a contemporary firebrand such as Bond allowed for exceptions and for the fact that allegiance was not determined by particular beliefs in *every* case. Yet, he nonetheless believed that the majority of anti-sabbatarians and Arminians were enemies of Parliament and of the deliverance and reform that Parliament appeared to promise. When Richard Baxter recorded that 'the generality of the People through the land ... who were then called Puritans, Precisions, Religious Persons, that used to talk to God, ... and to follow Sermons ... and spend the Lord's Day in Religious Exercises ... adhered to the Parliament', and that the 'People that were for the King's Book, for Dancing and Recreation on the Lord's Days ... were against the Parliament', he similarly stated that this did not apply to *'all* or every *one'*. Yet, although, like Bond, Baxter acknowledged that there were exceptions, he made it clear that the majority of the godly were parliamentarian whereas the vast bulk of those who enjoyed their traditional revels were for the king.[190]

Even allowing for the exceptions, matters of allegiance were far from clear cut. People were undoubtedly motivated and influenced by a variety of factors. At the time of the dramatic unfolding of events in the early 1640s, contemporaries were themselves trying to explain why people were choosing to support one side or the other. Sermons, pamphlets and newssheets offered various motives for people's allegiances. For example, parliamentarian propaganda claimed that royalist gentry supported the king out of opportunism, 'hope of promotion' and 'hopes of future favour', and because they feared losing their privileged positions and trappings of wealth should the parliament win.[191] It accused 'many poore and ignorant people' of supporting the king 'because they feare the Parliament will take away their old Episcopal government, their old Cathedral service, their organs, altars, crossings of their children in Baptisme, and other such like customes'.[192] Conversely, royalist pamphlets stressed obligations of loyalty and the desire to defend the established Church. However, among these and other explanations and accusations, both sides also pointed to a desire to either defend or to reform the traditional festive culture and, in doing so, they ascribed motives to the ordinary people. This is important. So far, we have focussed on the motivations of those in positions of relative authority and privilege. In large part, of course, this is because we know much more about those at gentry level and above, and comparatively little about the views of ordinary people. Trying to establish with certainty and to prove one way or the other the reasons behind the different allegiances of the common people is an impossible task. To use Patrick Collinson's memorable phrase, it is 'like dissecting a raw egg'.[193] The voice of the ordinary people is largely silent and we cannot know their motives for certain. Yet, there is evidence, both in what was said about the royalist armies and in what ordinary people are recorded as actually having done at the time, that suggests that many humble royalists did make a link between supporting the king and resisting puritan reformation – and thus protecting their traditional way of life.

The puritan, Richard Baxter, certainly recognised a connection, commenting, as we have seen, that 'The Warre was begun in our streets before the King or Parliament had any Armies'. Indeed, as this book has demonstrated, arguments and conflicting attitudes over traditional revelry had aroused enormous passions in English society long before 1642. Baxter claimed that, even before the war, 'malignant hatred of seriousness in Religion, did work so violently in the rabble where I lived, that I could not stay at home with any probable safety of my life'.[194] Highlighting the impact of such divisions and the role played by the conflict over the licensing of sports on Sundays, in 1641 Robert Greville, Lord Brooke, referred to the *Book of Sports* as a 'sharp rasor ... with which they have since made great Divisions of heart'.[195] Such divisions continued with the outbreak of war. John Oldmixon, the eighteenth-century historian, noted that the 'Protestant and sober' people in Somerset had supported Parliament, whereas 'those Gentry and Peasantry who had oppos'd the putting down [of] Revels and Riots' had supported the king.[196] The parliamentarian author of *Britannicus His Pill to cure Malignancy* clearly linked royalism, or 'malignancy', with support for traditional festivity, urging his readers:

> Looke upon the persons that side with the King in this war ... almost generally Papists, Bishops and their adherents ... and none but know that his Majesties Store-house of Common Souldiers, he raiseth from the dark corners of the Land, where ignorance, blindnesse, and Libertinisme is prdominant and a pious godly ministery very scarcely to be heard of, where the Lords day is known by a few Common Prayers in the morning, and by dancing, drinking, and rioting about a May-Pole in the afternoon.[197]

Another parliamentarian pamphlet of 1642 claimed to inform its readers 'who are the malignant party of this kingdome' and went on to attack the actions of Laud and 'the Arminian party' before condemning the fact that, during the 1630s, 'pleasure was authorized, the Sabboth day profaned, to the great griefe of all true-hearted Protestants: and indeed what greater bondage could there be then this of Conscience'.[198] As we have seen, even before the outbreak of the Civil War, the puritan preacher, John Bond, had identified an anti-Parliamentarian party in Exeter. Among this group of 'Anti-Deliverancers' and 'delinquents' he numbered 'Anti-Sabbatarians' who 'have their May-poles and Church-ales, their Morish-dances, and Trojan-horses', and he concluded that there was 'now in this Kingdome, a Reforming and a Deforming party'.[199] At the war's height, Bond delivered another sermon in which he suggested that the fact that the Parliamentary forces had met with considerable opposition in Somerset was because 'Wakes, Revells, May-poles &c. ... so much abounded in those parts', indicating that the ordinary people there valued and wanted to protect them and understood that the king stood for their traditional revels and that Parliament was against them.[200] Richard Baxter also stated that 'the beggarly drunken Rowt' were for the king. He recorded that, at the outbreak of the Civil War, they 'openly reviled' the roundheads,

> And just as at their Shews, and Wakes, and Stage-plays, when the Drink and the Spirit of Ryot did work together in their Heads ... so was it with them now ... And when the Wars began, almost all these Drunkards went into the Kings Army.[201]

Several roundhead pamphleteers made reference to the fact that attachment to the traditional festive culture was a feature of royalism. For example, one parliamentarian pamphlet satirised royalists in Kent by printing a letter purporting to come from them which called for the resumption of merry-making on Sundays after church, with young men and maidens enjoying 'Cakes and Ale', and desiring to once again 'have a fidler on the Sabbath day'. It ended: 'let us serve God, after the old Protestant religion, and be merry together without preciseness.'[202]

In June 1644 the parliamentary diurnal, *The Spie*, claimed that royalists had made 'a Plea in the behalf of the vulgar Rabble, for Whitson-Ales and Morris-Dancing and Maypoles'. It went on to highlight the common people's attachment to traditional festivity, and the fact that they were willing to fight to defend it, claiming that: 'when they understand that [his Majestie] fights for such glorious Parcels of the Protestant Religion, they cannot chose but come in unto him, to helpe to defend these, and such like ancient Pagan Customes.'[203] In August 1645 *Mercurius Britanicus* attacked 'Cavaliers and Club-men', claiming that they stood for 'the old Vanities and Superstitions of the Fore-fathers ... and the wondrous old Heathen-Customes of Sunday-Pipings and Dancings, with the meritorious May-Poles, Garlands, Galliards, and jolly Whitsun-Ales'.[204] At least one royalist publication also alluded to a link between support for revels and allegiance to the king's cause: *The True Informer* published in 1643 referred to the royalist soldiers at the Battle of Edgehill 'who upon sight of the Enemies Colours ran as merrily down the hil, as if they had gone to a morris-dance'.[205]

But we do not need to rely solely on the writings of either parliamentarian or royalist propagandists. Some of the actions which ordinary royalists are recorded to have taken also point to a link in their minds between defending traditional revels and opposition to the puritans and parliamentarians. For example, on the eve of the Civil War it was widely reported that some people in the Oxford parish of Holywell had set up a maypole and attached 'the picture of a man in a Tub, and said that was a picture of a Roundhead'. They then shot at it with muskets.[206] Lady Brilliana Harley similarly recorded in June 1642 how at Ludlow and also at Croft 'they seet vp a May pole, and a thinge like a head vpon it ... and gathered a great many about it and shot at it in derision of roundheads'.[207] The link between recruitment to the royalist cause and the protection of traditional festivity was perhaps made most symbolically in Southwark in July 1642 when a copy of a proclamation concerning the commission of array was attached to a maypole in Southwark.[208] These events suggest that, at the very outset of the war, ordinary people saw the maypole and its associated festivity as under threat from the puritan and parliamentarian faction, and they deliberately used it to demonstrate their opposition. There was no stronger symbol of defiance. Collinson's comment that 'England's wars of religion began, in a sense, with a maypole' is well made.[209] The maypole became virtually synonymous with the royalist cause. Even after the conclusion of the first Civil War, the maypole remained a potent symbol of opposition to the parliamentarian cause, and maypoles formed rallying-points for popular royalist uprisings in May 1648 in Sussex, Kent, Suffolk and Cornwall.[210]

It has been argued that the *Book of Sports* was an issue which was essentially decided in 1640–41 and that it had little to do with the civil war which followed.[211] However, anxieties and anger over the *Book of Sports* and traditional revels continued to be a live issue during the months and years which followed. A petition of March 1642 from gentry in Rutland, for example, called for the 'stricter sanctification of the Lords day, and restraint of all prophanation thereof by Wakes'.[212] Similarly, a petition of April 1642, which purported to represent the views of the Cornish people but in fact represented the views of a small faction of Cornish puritans, called on Parliament to enact laws 'against the prophanation of the Sabbath or Lords day by Sports and Pastimes'.[213] Preaching at the Exeter Assizes in August 1642, the puritan minister Thomas Trescott called on the judges of the Western Circuit to enforce proper Sabbath observance, claiming that, far from being successfully suppressed, the Lords Day was being profaned 'by Bacchanalian Revellings, and Heathenish May-games ... which yet in some places are more zealously observed, and stood for, than ... the Lawes of God'.[214] The *Book of Sports* was not a dead issue.

Indeed, in 1643 William Mewe claimed that the people's love of 'Whitson-Ales-Lords-day sports' was one of the reasons that the country was being punished by God with the visitation of war upon the land.[215] Preaching to MPs in April 1643, William Greenhill similarly suggested that the war was a form of divine punishment for allowing the profanation of the Sabbath, and he told the assembled MPs that:

> The Book of Sports ... hath kindled a fire in our land, which is not like to be extinct till that Booke be burnt by publique Authority.[216]

The very next month Parliament did indeed order the burning of the *Book of Sports*, and its burning by the common hangman at Cheapside was widely reported.[217]

The issue of Sunday observance continued to exercise preachers and pamphleteers throughout the rest of the war. For example, in a sermon delivered to MPs in March 1644, the radical preacher, George Gillespie, declared that the 'licentiousnesse' of 'the Book of Sports, and other prophanations of the Lords day ... was most acceptable to the greatest part, and they have loved it so'. Gillespie, like Mewe and Greenhill, claimed that the war was a form of divine retribution for such profanations.[218] In July 1645 the puritan, John Ward, declared of the Arminian clergy that 'We have not forgotten what snares they laid for tender consciences, by pressing the reading [of] the book of Sports' and he condemned 'the corrupting of the manners of the people, by the Law of liberty on the Lords day'.[219] In Suffolk, where, in 1644, several ministers were brought before the Committees for Scandalous Ministers, the reading of the *Book of Sports* and the countenancing of recreations on Sundays featured prominently in the accusations made against them. For example, William Alcock, the Rector of Bettenham, was accused of readily publishing 'that Cursed booke' and the Vicar of Hoxne, Thomas Sayer, was charged with 'suffer[ing] vayne sports upon the Lord's dayes'. Among the charges made against Thomas Ambler, the Vicar of Wenhaston, it was stated that he 'hath defended the booke of sports upon the lords day' and that he had told 'some persons that desired his assistance towards the suppressinge of sports upon that day ... [that] they had nothing to do with it, [as] there was a book of liberty'.[220] The fact that the king's opponents in the Long Parliament felt it necessary, between September 1641 and October 1645, to issue a series of ordinances seeking to establish much stricter Sunday observance and to eradicate traditional revels also illustrates that the issue was one which was still very much alive throughout the 1640s.

The *Book of Sports* therefore cast a long shadow, and there was a link in the minds of many people between the royalist cause and the desire to preserve the traditional festive culture. The battle over Sunday recreations which had first been fought out in ink among the intellectual elites, and in the courts and in Parliament among the judicial and political elites was, finally, a factor in a bloody conflict in which vast numbers of ordinary people who had not been party to those more elevated debates found themselves all too closely involved. For many people, issues of religion and the maintenance or reformation of the established Church were bound up with conflicting attitudes over traditional revelry. The Civil War was, then, a cultural conflict as well as a religious and political one, and many on the royalist side do indeed appear to have been trying to defend their traditional way of life.

Conclusion

Although the royalists lost the Civil War, the execution of Charles I and the establishment of the Commonwealth did not settle the issue of Sunday observance. Nor did it represent the comprehensive defeat of popular revelry that Charles' puritan opponents had hoped for. Indeed, the godly found it necessary to continue to call for the suppression of wakes, May games and sports 'which trained up People to Vanity and Loosness long after the king's death'.[1] Reacting to continued revelry in parts of the country, Parliament – which had already enacted sabbatarian legislation during the 1640s – passed two further laws 'for the better observation of the Lords Day'. The 1650 Act repeated the prohibition on dancing on Sundays and the 1657 Act also banned, as the 1644 Act had done, 'Wakes, Revels, Wrestlings, Shootings, Leaping, Bowling, ... Church-Ales, May-Poles ... or any other Sports and Pastimes'.[2] In 1654 commissions of 'ejectors' were appointed to eject parish ministers judged to be 'scandalous, ignorant and insufficient'. The criteria for ejection included support for Sabbath-breaking and for wakes and morris dancing.[3] Initially, the number of ejections was small, but in 1655 Cromwell sent major-generals into the localities with orders to 'encourage and promote godliness, and discourage and discountenance all profaneness and ungodliness', including Sabbath-breaking. There was then a large-scale purge of ministers deemed unfit for office.[4]

Yet, despite these measures, traditional revels continued to take place during the Interregnum in various parts of the country, albeit to a much lesser extent than before.[5] In Devon, for example, the justices were outraged to be told that:

> certaine daies called Revell daies are yet observed in diverse parishes, which hath been heretofore the unhappy occasion of much profaneness and wickedness in letting out the corruptions of men into all manner of disorder, as drunkennes, swearing, fighting and playing at games expressly against the Word of God and contrary to the Statute.[6]

In 1652 people from the surrounding area collected in Woodborough, Wiltshire, and 'very disorderly danced the morris-dance' and, in the same year, a clergyman complained to the authorities that people in the Somerset parish of West Chinnock were regularly playing sports on Sundays, 'whereby God is highly discouraged'.[7] May Day continued to be celebrated in various parts of the country, as in Henley-in-Arden, in Warwickshire, where maypoles, morris dancing and 'other heathenish and unlawful customs' were used, and even in Hyde Park, where revellers gathered and 'much sin was committed by wicked meetings with fiddlers, drunkenness, ribaldry and the like'.[8] In April 1650, Nehemiah Wallington, recorded his distress at the failure of the authorities to prevent 'the profaning of the Lord's day'.[9] The fact that Parliament had to pass additional legislation in 1650 and 1657, and that Cromwell felt it necessary to despatch major-generals to enforce Sabbath observance and promote godliness, is an indication of the stubborn attachment many ordinary people had to traditional festivity.

During the course of the previous decades, the question of Sabbath observance and popular revelry had come, in large part, to define the political divisions within English society. The maypole continued to be one of the chosen symbols of opponents to the new regime, as was amply demonstrated in Wolverhampton in April 1653 when the dissolution of the Rump Parliament was celebrated by the erection of a maypole.[10] The attempts by the authorities to suppress traditional popular culture had met with opposition in many areas. Richard Baxter acknowledged that, despite some success in the puritan campaign to reform the people of Kidderminster, 'many ignorant and ungodly Persons ... were still among us'.[11] The puritan reformer, Robert Beake, suffered 'no small share of revilings' in his attempts to bring the people of Coventry to godliness.[12]

The country's puritan justices naturally supported attempts to reform their localities and to rid parishes of traditional Sunday revels, but many other JPs were at best half-hearted in supporting measures to suppress such festivity and some were deliberately obstructive. In November 1655 the major-general in charge of the east Midlands reported that 'what some justices in order to reformation do, others undo' and that 'wicked magistrates by reason of their number overpower the godly magistrates'.[13] Prior to the Civil War, many of these magistrates had supported such measures as a result of their concerns about social order, but such was the link that had been forged between the old order and traditional revelry that now the new regime wanted to suppress traditional revelry both on religious grounds and because of its potential to be used as a focus for royalist sedition, and many justices were reluctant to support them.[14]

The Restoration of the monarchy and the Commonwealth's failure also represented the restoration of traditional revelry and the failure of puritan sabbatarianism. Maypoles, long firmly linked with royalism, rapidly reappeared across the country and were used 'to vex the Presbyterians and Independents' and erstwhile supporters of the Republic.[15] In Oxford, the people were 'so violent for may-poles in opposition to the puritans that there was numbered twelve ... besides three or four morrises'.[16] The puritan, Adam Martindale, recorded how a 'rabble of prophane youths ... were encouraged to affront me, by setting up a May-pole in my way to the church, upon a little banke ... where, in times past, the Sabbath had beene wofully profaned'.[17] When Thomas Hall attempted to stop the erection of two maypoles at King's Norton, he was denounced as 'a preacher of false doctrine, and an enemy to the King'.[18] The apparent victory of traditional revelry over moral reform was keenly felt by radical Protestants who despaired that 'the Countrey, as well as the Town, abound with vanities; now the reins of Liberty and Licentiousness are let loose: May-poles, and Playes, and Juglers.'[19] These, and many more such examples, serve to underscore not only how deeply devoted large sections of the populace were to their traditional revels, but also how deeply they resented the attack that had been made upon them in the preceding years. The monarchy remained firmly linked to traditional festivity.

The Marquis of Newcastle urged the newly-restored Charles II to revive 'May-games, morris dancers, [and] the Lords of the May ... after evening prayer every Sunday and holy day'.[20] The king's progress through London in May 1660 included a maypole and morris dancers and, the following year, the Duke of York ordered sailors to help erect a giant maypole adorned with the royal coat of arms to replace the maypole that had been removed from the Strand in 1644.[21] The link between May games and the monarchy became even stronger during the course of Charles II's reign, as 'oak apples' and oak boughs – commemorating the king's escape after the Battle of Worcester – were incorporated into the traditional May garlands and celebrations.[22] Wakes, bull-baiting and other forms of revelry also clearly enjoyed a notable revival.[23]

Yet the victory of revelry over puritan reformation was not complete in that things did not return entirely to the situation before the Civil War. The long tradition of using ales to raise funds for parish churches remained more or less dead. Almost without exception, church ales were not revived at the Restoration.[24] Nor did Charles II seek to revive his father's *Book of Sports*. But, then, as Ronald Hutton rightly observes, he did not need to. Charles I had used his declaration, in part, as a test of loyalty with which to flush out radicals from within his Church. The Second Restoration Settlement of 1661–62 made a similar declaration redundant. Men like Baxter, Hall and Martindale were ejected from their livings without any need for a new *Book of Sports*.[25]

Some MPs persisted in trying to reintroduce sabbatarian legislation, seeking to ban wakes and other revels and to enforce strict Sunday observance on the English people. Yet, bills introduced to this end in

1662, 1663, 1664, 1667, 1670 and 1673 all failed.[26] Parliament did pass a bill for the better observance of the Lord's Day in 1677, which Charles II signed into law. However, although the Act prohibited trading on Sundays, it did not prohibit any recreations.[27] Earlier, in 1663, Charles II had issued a proclamation requiring people to attend church on Sundays and prohibiting: 'All meetings and Concourse of people out of their own parishes for any sports and pastimes whatsoever, and all unlawful exercises within their own parishes on the said day.'[28] Therefore, as the *Book of Sports* had done, it simply sought to prevent people from indulging in Sunday revels *outside their own parishes*.

* * *

In *The English Sabbath*, Kenneth Parker argues that there had been a long tradition of English sabbatarianism stretching back to the time of the medieval Church. He argues that puritan sabbatarianism was not a break with the past and claims, conversely, that it was Laud and his supporters who were the innovators in their attempts to licence revelry on Sundays. However, as this book has demonstrated, while Laudians like Peter Heylyn certainly exaggerated puritan claims, puritan sabbatarianism was radically different from the established view of Sunday observance. Parker grossly overplays sabbatarian tendencies within the English Church, whose hierarchy, both before and after the Restoration, was concerned principally with church attendance and was remarkably accommodating towards the people's desire for recreation on Sundays after church.[29] Although there had always been radical or zealous elements within the Church and wider society that had called for strict Sunday observance and for the suppression of popular recreations, they had never represented the mainstream view of either Church or state. The authorities certainly wanted people to cease non-essential work and to attend church and, particularly in the medieval period when it was most relevant, the government wanted to encourage Englishmen to practise their archery on Sunday afternoons. Beyond that, both Church and state were relaxed about how people spent the rest of their Sunday, provided their actions did not lead to disorder or sedition.

The puritan sabbatarianism that emerged during the course of the late sixteenth and early seventeenth century was far more all-encompassing than that which had been espoused by traditionalist clerics. The increasing stridency of puritan reformers coupled with growing concerns about social order on the part of many otherwise moderate justices turned village greens into cultural battlegrounds. The combined pressures of this new, hard-line form of sabbatarianism, concerns about social order and the stubborn attachment that many people had towards their traditional way of life created dangerous divisions and helped to polarise early Stuart society. As puritans came to be regarded as a serious threat to the authority of the Crown, and as they became ever more closely linked with moves to suppress traditional Sunday pastimes, first James I and then Charles I decided to engage in the debate and to identify the Crown with traditional festivity and popular culture. However, the cultural and religious divisions were so great that, far from resolving the issue, Charles I's decision to reissue the *Book of Sports* in 1633 made matters considerably worse, and his decision to enforce its publication created new enemies and contributed further to the deepening of divisions that spilled out into open conflict some years later.

Parker's work on the *English Sabbath* has been an important contribution to our knowledge of this period and of these important issues, but, as the present book has demonstrated, he fails to recognise the innovative nature and dramatic impact of puritan sabbatarianism. This book redresses the balance and reasserts the hugely divisive and novel nature of the puritan beliefs about Sunday observance. It has also challenged the assumption of all too many historians that Archbishop Laud was behind the reissuing of the *Book of Sports* – which appears in fact to have been very much the king's own work. As Tanner observed back in 1930, the sabbatarian controversy is indeed 'vastly more important than it appears at first sight'.[30] It contributed to the polarisation of early Stuart society and the reaction to it underscores the enormous political significance of popular festivity, as well as the religious divisions over Sunday observance. Understanding the issues surrounding the *Book of Sports* and the contemporary sabbatarian debate is vital to our understanding of the fractured nature of Caroline society.

Appendix

The text of the 1633 *Book of Sports*

The Kings Maiesties Declaration to His Subiects, concerning lawfull sports to bee vsed (London, 1633).

'By the King.

'Ovr Deare Father of blessed Memory, in his returne from Scotland, coming through Lancashire, found that his Subiects were debarred from Lawful Recreations upon Sundayes after Euening Prayers ended, and vpon Holy dayes: And Hee prudently considered, that if these times were taken from them, the meaner sort who labour hard all the weeke, should haue no Recreations at all to refresh their spirits. And after His returne, Hee farther saw that His loyall Subiects in all other parts of His Kingdome did suffer in the same kinde, though perhaps not in the same degree: And did therefore in His Princely wisedome, publish a Declaration to all his louing Subiects concerning lawfull Sports to be vsed at such times, which was printed and published by His royall Commandement in the yeere 1618. In the Tenor which hereafter followeth.

'By the King.

'Whereas vpon Our returne the last yere out of Scotland, We did publish Our Pleasure touching the recreations of Our people in those parts vnder our hand: For some causes Vs thereunto moouing, Wee have thought good to command these Our Directions then giuen in Lancashire with a few words thereunto added, and most applicable to these parts of Our Realmes, to bee published to all Our Subiects.

'Whereas Wee did iustly in Our Progresse through Lancashire, rebuke some Puritanes and precise people, and tooke order that the like vnlawfull carriage should not bee vsed by any of them hereafter, in the prohibiting and vnlawfull punishing of Our good people for the vsing their lawfull Recreations, and honest exercises vpon Sundayes and other Holy dayes, after the afternoone Sermon or Service: Wee now finde that two sorts of people wherewith that Countrey is much infested, (Wee meane Papists and Puritanes) haue maliciously traduced and calumniated those Our iust and honourable proceedings. And therefore lest Our reputation might vpon the one side (though innocently) haue some aspersion layd vpon it, and that vpon the other part of Our good people in that Countrey be misled by the mistaking and misinterpretation of Our meaning: We haue therefore thought good hereby to cleare and make Our pleasure to be manifested to all Our good People in those parts.

'It is true that at Our first entry to this Crowne, and Kingdome, Wee were informed, and that too truly, that Our County of Lancashire abounded more in Popish Recusants then any County of England, and thus hath still continued since to Our great regret, with little amendment, saue that now of late, in Our last riding through Our said County, Wee find both by the report of the Iudges, and of the Bishop of that diocesse, that there is some amendment now daily beginning, which is no small contentment to Vs.

'The report of this growing amendment amongst them, made Vs the more sorry, when with Our owne Eares We heard the generall complaint of Our people, that they were barred from all lawfull Recreation, & exercise vpon the Sundayes afternoone, after the ending of all Diuine Seruice, which cannot but produce two euils: The one, the hindering of the conuersion of many, whom their Priests will take occasion hereby to vexe, perswading them that no honest mirth or recreation is lawfull or tolerable in Our Religion, which cannot but breed a great discontentment in Our peoples hearts, especially of such as are peraduenture vpon the point of turning; The other inconuenience is, that this prohibition barreth the common and meaner sort of people from vsing such exercises as may make their bodies more able for Warre, when Wee or Our Successours shall haue occasion to vse them. And in place thereof sets vp filthy tiplings and drunkennesse, & breeds a number of idle and discontented speeches in their Alehouses. For when shall the common people haue leaue to exercise, if not vpon the Sundayes & holydaies, seeing they must apply their labour, & win their liuing in all working daies?

'Our expresse pleasure therefore is, that the Lawes of Our Kingdome, & Canons of Our Church be aswell obserued in that Countie, as in all other places of this Our Kingdome. And on the other part, that no lawfull Recreation shall bee barred to Our good People, which shall not tend to the breach of Our aforesaid Lawes, and Canons of Our Church: which to expresse more particularly, Our pleasure is, That the Bishop, and all other inferiour Churchmen, and Churchwardens, shall for their parts bee carefull and diligent, both to instruct the ignorant, and conuince and reforme them that are mis-led in Religion, presenting them that will not conforme themselues, but obstinately stand out to Our Iudges and Iustices: Whom We likewise command to put the Law in due execution against them.

'Our pleasure likewise is, That the Bishop of the Diocesse take the like straight order with all the Puritanes and Precisians within the same, either constraining them to conforme themselues, or to leave the County, according to the Lawes of Our Kingdome, and Canons of Our Church, and so to strike equally on both hands, against the contemners of Our Authority, and aduersaries of Our Church. And as for Our good peoples lawfull Recreation, Our pleasure likewise is, That after the end of Diuine Seruice, Our good people be not disturbed, letted, or discouraged from any lawful recreation, Such as dauncing, either men or women, Archery for men, leaping, vaulting, or any other such harmelesse Recreation, nor from hauing of May-Games, Whitson Ales, and Morris-dances, and the setting vp of Maypoles & other sports therewith vsed, so as the same be had in due & conuenient time, without impediment or neglect of Diuine Seruice: And that women shall haue leaue to carry rushes to the Church for the decoring of it, according to their old custome. But withal We doe here account still as prohibited all vnlawfull games to bee vsed vpon Sundayes onely, as Beare and Bullbaitings, Interludes, and at all times in the meaner sort of people by Law prohibited, Bowling.

'And likewise We barre from this benefite and liberty, all such knowne recusants, either men or women, as will abstaine from coming to Church or diuine Service, being therefore vnworthy of any lawfull recreation after the said Seruice that will not first come to the Church and serue God: Prohbiting in like sort the said Recreations to any that, though conforme in Religion, are not present in the Church at the Seruice of God, before their going to the said Recreations. Our pleasure likewise is, That they to whom it belongeth in Office, shall present and sharpely punish all such as in abuse of this Our liberty, will vse these exercises before the ends of all Diuine Seruices for that day. And We likewise straightly command, that euery person shall resort to his owne Parish Church to heare Diuine Seruice, and Parish by it selfe to vse the said Recreations after Diuine Seruice. Prohibiting likewise any Offensiue weapons to bee carried or used in the said times of Recreations. And Our pleasure is, That this Our Declaration shall bee published by order from the Bishop of the Diocesse, through al the Parish Churches, and that both Our Iudges of Our Circuit, and Our Iustices of Our Peace be informed thereof.

'Giuen at Our Mannour of Greenwich the foure and twentieth day of May, in the sixteenth yeere of Our Raigne of England, France and Ireland, and of Scotland the one and fiftieth.

'Now out of a like pious Care for the seruice of God, and for suppressing of any humors that oppose trueth, and for the Ease, Comfort & Recreation of Our well deseruing People, Wee doe ratifie and publish this Our blessed Fathers Declaration: The rather because of late in some Counties of Our Kingdome, Wee finde that vnder pretence of taking away abuses, there hath been a generall forbidding, not onely of ordinary meetings, but of the Feasts of the Dedication of the Churches, commonly called Wakes. Now our expresse will and pleasure is, that these Feasts with others shall bee obserued, and that Our Iustices of the peace in their seuerall Diuisions shall looke to it, both that all disorders there may be preuented or punised, and that all neighbourhood and freedome, with manlike and lawfull Exercises bee vsed. And Wee farther Command Our Justices of Assize in their seuerall Circuits, to see that no man doe trouble or molest any of Our loyall and duetifull people, in or for their lawfull Recreations, hauing first done their duetie to God, and continuing in obedience to Vs and Our Lawes. And of this Wee commande all Our Iudges, Iustices of Peace, as well within Liberties as without, Maiors, Bayliffes, Constables, and other Officers, to take notice of, and to see observed, as they tender Our displeasure. And Wee farther will, that publication of this Our Command bee made by order from the Bishops through all the Parish Churches of their seuerall Diocesse respectiuely.

'Giuen at Our Palace of Westminster the eighteenth day of October, in the ninth yeere of Our Reigne.

'God saue the King.'

Notes and references

Introduction

1 J.R. Tanner (ed.), *Constitutional Documents of the Reign of James I, 1603–1625* (Cambridge, 1930), p. 49.
2 For example, see: T.G. Barnes, 'County Politics and a Puritan Cause Célèbre: Somerset Churchales, 1633', in *TRHS*, Fifth Series, 9 (1959), pp. 103–22; D. Underdown, *Revel, Riot and Rebellion. Popular Politics and Culture in England 1603–1660* (Oxford, 1985), pp. 65–8; L.S. Marcus, *The Politics of Mirth. Jonson, Herrick, Milton, Marvell and the Defence of Old Holiday Pastimes* (Chicago, 1986), esp. pp. 106–7, 129–30 and 169–71; J. Davies, *The Caroline Captivity of the Church: Charles I and the Remoulding of Anglicanism* (Oxford, 1992), pp. 172–204; K. Sharpe, *The Personal Rule of Charles I* (New Haven and London, 1992), pp. 351–60; R. Hutton, *The Rise and Fall of Merry England. The Ritual Year, 1400–1700* (Oxford, 1994), pp. 196–8, 200–1 and 203–5; and R. Cust, *Charles I. A Political Life* (Longman, 2005), pp. 133 and 144.
3 L.A. Govett, *The King's Book of Sports* (London, 1890) was the last large-scale work devoted to the subject of the *Book of Sports*.
4 K.L. Parker, *The English Sabbath. A Study of doctrine and discipline from the Reformation to the Civil War* (Cambridge, 1988), *passim*.
5 J.H. Primus, *Holy Time. Moderate Puritanism and the Sabbath* (Mercer University Press, 1989), *passim*; A.N. Nelson (ed.), *Cambridge, REED* (Toronto, 1989), p. 369; K. Sharpe, *The Personal Rule of Charles I* (New Haven and London, 1992), p. 352; R. Cust, *Charles I. A Political Life* (Longman, 2005), p. 138.
6 W. Hunt, *The Puritan Moment. The Coming of Revolution in an English County* (Harvard, 1983), p. 145; L.A. Sasek (ed.), *Images of English Puritanism* (Louisiana State University Press, 1989), 1 and 4; D. Underdown, *Fire from Heaven. Life in an English Town in the Seventeenth Century* (Yale, 1992), p. 20; C. Durston and J. Eales (eds), *The Culture of English Puritanism, 1560–1700* (London, 1996), pp. 1–4; P. Lake, 'A Charitable Christian Hatred' in C. Durston and J. Eales (eds), *The Culture of English Puritanism, 1560–1700* (London, 1996), pp. 178–9; W. Lamont, *Puritanism and Historical Controversy* (London, 1996), p. 7; J. Spurr, *English Puritanism, 1603–1689* (London, 1998); J. Coffey and P. Lim (eds), *The Cambridge Companion to Puritanism* (Cambridge, 2008), pp. 1–5.

7 Coffey and Lim, *Cambridge Companion to Puritanism*, p. 5; Underdown, *Fire from Heaven*, pp. 20–1.
8 Perceval Wiburn, *A checke or reproof of M. Howlets vntimely shreeching in her Majiesties eares* (London, 1581), sig. 15v.
9 Hunt, *The Puritan Moment*, p. 146.
10 Quoted in Lamont, *Puritanism and Historical Controversy*, p. 3.
11 W.A. Mepham, 'Essex Drama Under Puritanism and the Commonwealth' in *The Essex Review*, Vol. 58 (1949), pp. 155–61 and 181–5; B. Lowe, 'Early Records of the Morris in England', in *Journal of the English Folk Dance & Song Society*, Vol. 7, No. 2 (1957), pp. 73–4.
12 P. Collinson, 'Elizabethan and Jacobean Puritanism as Forms of Popular Religious Culture' in C. Durston and J. Eales (eds), *The Culture of English Puritanism, 1560–1700* (London, 1996), p. 34; Alexandra Walsham's entry on Philip Stubbes in the *Oxford Dictionary of National Biography*, Vol. 53, p. 204. Collinson points out that Stubbes was not an 'ecclesiastical puritan' and Walsham similarly highlights the fact that Stubbes defended the structure of the established Church, but his attack on traditional festivity is certainly in keeping with the views of puritans and it is possible to view Stubbes as a puritan even if he was not among the most radical puritans who wanted to fundamentally alter the structure of the established Church.
13 Hunt, *The Puritan Moment*, p. 91; P. Seaver, *Wallington's World. A Puritan Artisan in Seventeenth-Century London* (Stanford, 1985), pp. 142–3; J. Eales, *Puritans and Roundheads. The Harleys of Brampton Bryan and the outbreak of the English Civil War* (Cambridge, 1990), p. 48; Durston and Eales, *Culture of English Puritanism*, p. 3; Spurr, *English Puritanism*, pp. 17–23; Coffey and Lim, *Cambridge Companion to Puritanism*, p. 1.
14 P. Collinson, *The Birthpangs of Protestant England. Religious and Cultural Change in the Sixteenth and Seventeenth Centuries* (London, 1988), p. 143.
15 See, for example, Matthew Sylvester, *Reliquiae Baxterianae* (London, 1696), pp. 1–3. Also: Spurr, *English Puritanism*, p. 17.
16 Coffey and Lim, *Cambridge Companion to Puritanism*, p. 3.
17 Durston and Eales, *Culture of English Puritanism*, pp. 8–9.

Chapter 1: 'Vain, stupid, profane games': Medieval attitudes to the playing of sports on the Sabbath and other holy days

1 A. Brandeis (ed.), *Jacob's Well. An English Treatise on the Cleansing of Man's Conscience* (Early English Text Society, London, 1900), pp. 105–6.
2 *Ibid.*, p. 105.
3 F. Heal, *Hospitality in Early Modern England* (Oxford, 1990), pp. 354–5; B. Harvey, 'Work and Festa Ferianda in Medieval England,' in *JEH*, Vol. XXIII, No. 4 (October, 1972), p. 305; R. Hutton, *The Rise and Fall of Merry England.The Ritual Year, 1400–1700* (Oxford, 1994), p. 46; J. Bennett, 'Conviviality and Charity in Medieval and Early Modern England', in *P&P*, 134 (1992), pp. 34–5; T.S. Henricks, *Disputed Pleasures. Sport and Society in Preindustrial England* (New York; Westport, Connecticut; and London, 1991), pp. 31–2; and R. Hutton, 'Seasonal Festivity in Late Medieval England: Some Further Reflections', in *English Historical Review*, 120:485 (2005), pp. 66–79.
4 See, for example, K. Thomas, 'Work and Leisure in Pre-Industrial Society,' in *P&P*, 29 (1964), pp. 52–3; J.M. Carter, *Medieval Games. Sports and*

Recreations in Feudal Society (New York; Westport, Connecticut; and London, 1992), p. 85.
5 Carter, *Medieval Games*, p. 99.
6 E. Muir, *Ritual in Early Modern Europe* (Cambridge, 1997), p. 60; Hutton, *Merry England*, p. 46.
7 E. Duffy, *The Stripping of the Altars. Traditional Religion in England 1400-1580* (New Haven and London, 1992), pp. 46–7.
8 *Ibid.*, pp. 41–2.
9 *Ibid.*, p. 42.
10 *Ibid.*
11 W. Rordorf, *Sunday. The History of the Day of Rest and Worship in the Earliest Centuries of the Christian Church* (London, 1968), pp. 154–5.
12 *Ibid.*, pp. 167–78; Harvey, 'Festa Ferianda', p. 289; E.C. Rodgers, *Discussion of Holidays in the Later Middle Ages* (New York, 1940), p. 29.
13 Rodgers, *Holidays*, pp. 30–1.
14 *Ibid.*, p. 29.
15 *Ibid.*, pp. 35, 37.
16 *Ibid.*, pp. 38–9.
17 *Ibid.*, pp. 39–40; Duffy, *Stripping of the Altars*, p. 42.
18 G.R. Owst, *Preaching in Medieval England. An Introduction to Sermon Manuscripts of the Period, c.1350–1450* (Cambridge, 1926), p. 4.
19 F.J. Furnivall (ed.), *Robert of Brunne's 'Handlyng Synne'* (London, 1901–1903), pp. 29–30.
20 *Ibid.*, p. 30.
21 P.H. Barnum (ed.), *Dives and Pauper* (Oxford, 1980), Vol. I, pp. 8, 9, and 33–4.
22 *Ibid.*, pp. 9-10, 274 and 290.
23 *Ibid.*, pp. 277-8.
24 *Ibid.*, p. 281.
25 *Ibid.*, p. 282.
26 G. Kristensson (ed.), *John Mirk's Instructions for Parish Priests* (Lund, 1974), pp. 119–20.
27 *Ibid.*
28 *Ibid.*
29 Rodgers, *Holidays*, p. 22.
30 *Jacob's Well*, p. 110.
31 Harvey, 'Festa Ferianda', pp. 293 and 303.
32 *Ibid.*, pp. 303–4.
33 *Ibid.*, p. 306.
34 *Ibid.*
35 *Ibid.*
36 *Ibid.*, pp. 306–7.
37 C. Harper-Bill, 'Who Wanted the English Reformation?', in *Medieval History*, Vol. 2, No. 1 (1992), p. 69.
38 For example, see Parker, *English Sabbath*, pp. 13–14 and Rodgers, *Holidays*, pp. 74–5. In 1413, the civil authorities, responding to a complaint by the Archbishop of Canterbury, passed an ordinance forbidding the barbers of the City of London from keeping their houses and shops open on Sundays and threatening them with a fine of 6s 8d for every contravention of the ordinance.

39 Kristensson, *Mirk*, p. 120; Harvey, 'Festa Ferianda', p. 307.
40 M.K. McIntosh, *Controlling Misbehaviour in England, 1370–1600* (Cambridge, 1998), p. 200.
41 *Handlyng Synne*, p. 145.
42 *Jacob's Well*, p. 134.
43 G.G. Coulton, *The Medieval Village* (Cambridge, 1925), p. 93.
44 *Handlyng Synne*, p. 156; Hutton, *Merry England*, p. 38.
45 For a detailed consideration of these and many other sports and pastimes enjoyed in this period, see J. Strutt, *The Sports and Pastimes of the People of England* (London, 1841).
46 Hutton, *Merry England*, p. 28.
47 Bennett, 'Conviviality and Charity', p. 37. Ales emerged during the fifteenth century as an important means of funding for parish churches. See R. Hutton, 'Seasonal Festivity in Late Medieval England', pp. 71–3.
48 *Ibid.*, pp. 20–1. For a discussion of help-ales and bride-ales and of charity ales generally, see Bennett's article.
49 *Ibid.*, p. 24.
50 A. Abram, *English Life and Manners in the Later Middle Ages* (London, 1913), p. 243.
51 Hutton, *Merry England*, p. 29.
52 Bennett, 'Conviviality and Charity', pp. 20–1.
53 P. Clark, *The English Alehouse. A Social History, 1200–1830* (London, 1983), p. 151.
54 Hutton, *Merry England*, p. 28.
55 E. Peacock, 'Church Ales,' in *The Archaeological Journal*, Vol. XL (March, 1883), p. 13.
56 Bennett, 'Conviviality and Charity', p. 34. Plymouth and Manchester were among the few towns that held ales.
57 C. Reeves, *Pleasures and Pastimes in Medieval England* (Stroud, 1995), pp. 154–5.
58 Strutt, *Sports and Pastimes*, p. 366.
59 Hutton, *Merry England*, pp. 29, 36 and 46; Strutt, *Sports and Pastimes*, pp. 364-6; Clark, *English Alehouse*, p. 25; Peacock, 'Church Ales', p. 10.
60 Peacock, 'Church Ales', p. 6.
61 Hutton, *Merry England*, p. 59.
62 Quoted in Peacock, 'Church Ales', p. 12.
63 Bennett, 'Conviviality and Charity', p. 41; Carter, *Medieval Games*, p. 109.
64 Carter, *Medieval Games*, p. 110.
65 Clark, *English Alehouse*, p. 25; Hutton, *Merry England*, pp. 29 and 59; Peacock, 'Church Ales', pp. 9 and 10; and Abram, *Life and Manners*, p. 243.
66 Bennett, 'Conviviality and Charity', p. 25.
67 Rodgers, *Holidays*, pp. 68–9.
68 Kristensson, *Mirk*, p. 120.
69 *Jacob's Well*, p. 105.
70 Mannyng, *Handlyng Synne*, pp. 36–8.
71 Quoted in Owst, *Preaching in Medieval England*, p. 180.
72 *Ibid.*, pp. 193–4; Rodgers, *Holidays*, p. 33.
73 *Jacob's Well*, p. 116.
74 Abram, *English Life and Manners*, pp. 235–6; T.S. Henricks, 'Sport and Social

History in Medieval England,' in *Journal of Sport History*, Vol. 9, No. 2, (Summer, 1982), p. 31; Henricks, *Disputed Pleasures*, p. 60.
75 McIntosh, *Controlling Misbehaviour*, pp. 104–5.
76 *Handlyng Synne*, p. 283.
77 See chapters three, four, five and six.
78 Peacock, 'Church Ales,' pp. 8–10.
79 Clark, *English Alehouse*, p. 33; Hutton, *Merry England*, p. 71.
80 13 Edward I, c. 6 (*The Statutes of the Realm*, vol. I, p. 98).
81 Kristensson, *Mirk*, p. 86.
82 *Handlyng Synne*, p. 283.
83 L.M. Clopper, *Drama, Play, and Game. English Festive Culture in the Medieval and Early Modern Period* (Chicago, 2001), p. 66.
84 Quoted in Clark, *English Alehouse*, p. 27.
85 Quoted in A.L. Poole, 'Recreations,' in A. L. Poole (ed.), *Medieval England*, Vol. II (revised edition), (Oxford, 1958), p. 625 and Henricks, 'Sport and Social History,' p. 30.
86 12 Richard II, c. 6 (*Stats. Realm*, vol. II, p. 57).
87 See: 11 Henry IV, c. 4; 17 Edward IV, c. 3; 11 Henry VII, c. 2; 19 Henry VII, c. 12; 3 Henry VIII, c. 13; 6 Henry VIII, c. 2; 6 Henry VIII, c. 13; 14 & 15 Henry VIII, c. 7 (*Stats. Realm*, vol. II, pp. 163, 462–3, 569, and 657; and vol. III, pp. 32–3, 123–4, 132–3 and 215–16); P.L. Hughes and J.F. Larkin (eds), *Tudor Royal Proclamations*, Vol. I, *The Early Tudors (1485–1553)* (New Haven and London, 1964), pp. 151–3 and 177–81.
88 3 Henry VIII, c. 13 (*Stats. Realm*, Vol. III, p. 32).
89 6 Henry VIII, c. 2 (*Stats. Realm*, Vol. III, p. 123).
90 Hughes and Larkin, *Tudor Royal Proclamations*, p. 178.
91 17 Edward IV, c. 3; 6 Henry VIII, c. 2 (*Stats. Realm*, Vol II, p. 462 and Vol. III, p. 123).
92 17 Edward IV, c. 3 (*Stats. Realm*, Vol. II, p. 462).
93 Henricks, 'Sport and Society,' p. 31; McIntosh, *Controlling Misbehaviour*, p. 101.
94 17 Edward IV, c. 3 (*Stats. Realm*, Vol. II, p. 463).
95 6 Henry VIII, c. 2 (*Stats. Realm*, Vol. III, p. 123).
96 For example, see: 12 Richard II, c. 6; 11 Henry IV, c. 4; 11 Henry VII, c. 2; and 19 Henry VII, c. 12 (*Stats. Realm*, Vol. II, pp. 57, 163, 569 and 657).
97 McIntosh, *Controlling Misbehaviour*, pp. 12–13.
98 *Ibid.*, p. 13.
99 Clark, *English Alehouse*, pp. 147–8.
100 McIntosh, *Controlling Misbehaviour*, p. 101.
101 Henricks, 'Sport and Social History,' p. 31; Henricks, *Disputed Pleasures*, p. 60.
102 Hutton, *Merry England*, p. 56.
103 Kristensson, *Mirk*, pp. 68–9.
104 Hughes and Larkin, *Tudor Royal Proclamations*, p. 152.
105 Abram, *English Life and Manners*, pp. 235–6.
106 P. Burke, *Popular Culture in Early Modern Europe* (revised edition, Aldershot, 1994), p. 217.
107 P. Jensen, *Religion and Revelry in Shakespeare's Festive World* (Cambridge, 2008), pp. 27–8.

Chapter 2: The impact of the break with Rome

1. L.A. Govett, *The King's Book of Sports* (London, 1890), pp. 20–1.
2. K.L. Parker, *The English Sabbath. A Study of doctrine and discipline from the Reformation to the Civil War* (Cambridge, 1988), pp. 26–7.
3. *Ibid.*, pp. 33–4.
4. R. Hutton, *The Rise and Fall of Merry England. The Ritual Year, 1400–1700* (Oxford, 1994), p. 74; W.B. Whitaker, *Sunday in Tudor and Stuart Times* (London, 1933), p. 13; C. Hill, *Society and Puritanism in Pre-Revolutionary England* (London, 1964), pp. 142–3.
5. Quoted in Whitaker, *Sunday in Tudor and Stuart Times*, pp. 13–14.
6. For a discussion of *The King's Book,* see: G. Bernard, *The King's Reformation: Henry VIII and the Remaking of the English Church* (Yale University Press, 2005), pp. 583–9.
7. Henry VIII, *A necessary doctrine and erudicion for any chrysten man* (London, 1543), sigs L5v–L6r.
8. Whitaker, *Sunday in Tudor and Stuart Times*, p. 16.
9. A.H. Lewis, *A Critical History of Sunday Legislation. From 321 to 1888 A.D.* (New York, 1888), pp. 92–3.
10. John Hooper, *A Declaration of the Ten Holy Commaundementes* (Zurich, 1549), sig. I4r.
11. Lewis, *A Critical History of Sunday Legislation*, p. 94.
12. *Ibid.*, p. 97.
13. Loades, *Mid-Tudor Crisis*, p. 146; D. Loades, *Mary Tudor. A Life* (Oxford, 1989), p. 208; A.H. Lewis, *Sunday Legislation*, p. 97.
14. P. Clark, *The English Alehouse. A Social History, 1200–1830* (London, 1983), p. 132.
15. W.P. Baker, 'The Observance of Sunday' in R. Lennard (ed.), *Englishmen at Rest and Play. Some Phases of English Leisure, 1558–1714* (Oxford, 1931), p. 84; A. Walsham, 'Godly Recreation: the problem of leisure in late Elizabethan and early Stuart society', in D.E. Kennedy, D. Robertson and A. Walsham (eds), *Grounds of Controversy. Three Studies in late 16th and early 17th century English polemics* (University of Melbourne, 1989), p. 12.
16. 33 Henry VIII, c. 9 (*The Statutes of the Realm*, Vol. III), pp. 837–41.
17. *Ibid.*; F.G. Emmison, *Elizabethan Life: Disorder* (Essex Record Office, 1970), p. 218.
18. D. Brailsford, *Sport and Society. Elizabeth to Anne* (London, 1969), p. 29.
19. Govett, *Book of Sports*, p. 49.
20. Sir Thomas Elyot, *The Boke Named The Gouvernor* (ed., Foster Watson, Everyman Library, 1907), pp. 112–13.
21. C.G. Cruickshank, *Elizabeth's Army* (Second edition, Oxford, 1966), p. 105.
22. Roger Ascham, *Toxophilus, the schole of shootinge conteyned in two bokes* (London, 1545), fols 14 and 40.
23. R. Hardy, *Longbow. A Social and Military History* (Third edition, Sparkford, 1992), p. 135.
24. Govett, *Book of Sports*, p. 49.
25. Hardy, *Longbow*, pp. 139–41.
26. J. Strutt, *The Sports and Pastimes of the People of England* (London, 1841), p. 269; T.S. Henricks, *Disputed Pleasures. Sport and Society in Pre-industrial England* (New York; Westport, Connecticut; and London, 1991), p. 88.

27 Brailsford, *Sport and Society*, p. 31.
28 Henricks, *Disputed Pleasures*, p. 88; Emmison, *Elizabethan Life*, p. 221; Elyot, *The Gouernor*, p. 113.
29 Robert Crowley, *One and thyrtye Epigrammes* (London, 1550), unpaginated.
30 Henricks, *Disputed Pleasures*, p. 89.
31 Strutt, *Sports and Pastimes*, p. 94; Henricks, *Disputed Pleasures*, pp. 73 and 89.
32 Brailsford, *Sport and Society*, p. 31.
33 *Ibid.*, p. 53; Henricks, *Disputed Pleasures*, p. 89; A.H. Dodd, *Elizabethan England* (London, 1973), pp. 150-1; Emmison, *Elizabethan Life*, pp. 225-6.
34 Elyot, *The Gouernor*, p. 113.
35 C. Haigh, *The Plain Man's Pathways to Heaven. Kinds of Christianity in Post-Reformation England, 1570-1640* (Oxford, 2007), p. 93.
36 Strutt, *Sports and Pastimes*, p. 257.
37 *Ibid.*, p. 258.
38 Whitaker, *Sunday*, p. 23; Strutt, *Sports and Pastimes*, p. 257.
39 Crowley, *One and thyrtye Epigrammes*, unpaginated.
40 Strutt, *Sports and Pastimes*, p. 282.
41 *Ibid.*, p. 283; J.A. Sharpe, *Early Modern England. A Social History, 1550-1760* (Second edition, London, 1997), p. 291.
42 33 Henry VIII, c. 9 (*The Statutes of the Realm*, Vol. III), p. 838.
43 M.K. McIntosh, *Controlling Misbehaviour in England, 1370-1600* (Cambridge, 1998), pp. 100-2; Emmison, *Elizabethan Life*, p. 218.
44 Henry VIII, *A Necessary Doctrine*, sig. M1r.
45 Elyot, *The Gouernor*, pp. 85-7.
46 E. Duffy, *The Voices of Morebath. Reformation and Rebellion in an English Village* (Yale, 2001), p. 120.
47 5 & 6 Edward VI, c. 4 (*The Statutes of the Realm*, Vol. IV, p. 133).
48 R. Hutton, *The Stations of the Sun. A History of the Ritual Year in Britain* (Oxford, 1996), p. 249.
49 A. Fletcher, *Tudor Rebellions* (Third edition, London, 1983), p. 40.
50 Fletcher, *Tudor Rebellions*, p. 54.
51 Hutton, *Stations of the Sun*, pp. 249-50.
52 Hutton, *Merry England*, p. 88.
53 *Ibid.*
54 Hutton, *Merry England*, pp. 89-90; Hutton, *Stations of the Sun*, pp. 83, 105-9.
55 Hutton, *Stations of the Sun*, p. 250.
56 Baker, 'Observance of Sunday', p. 83.
57 Hutton, *Merry England*, pp. 101-2.
58 Hutton, *Stations of the Sun*, p. 250; R. Hutton, 'The Local Impact of the Tudor Reformation', in C. Haigh (ed.), *The English Reformation Revised* (Cambridge, 1987), p. 131.
59 2 & 3 Philip & Mary, c. 9 (*The Statutes of the Realm*, Vol. IV), p. 285.

Chapter 3: The Reign of Elizabeth I and the battle over the Lord's Day

1 K.L. Parker, *The English Sabbath. A Study of Doctrine and Discipline from the Reformation to the Civil War* (Cambridge, 1988), p. 91.
2 *Ibid.*, p. 5.

3 A.H. Lewis, *A Critical History of Sunday Legislation. From 321 to 1888 A.D.* (New York, 1888), p. 99.
4 Parker, *English Sabbath*, p. 43.
5 W.B. Whitaker, *Sunday in Tudor and Stuart Times* (London, 1933), pp. 25–6.
6 Anon., *The seconde tome of homelyes ... set out by the authoritie of the Quenes Maiestie* (London, 1563), fol. 139.
7 *Ibid.*, fol. 140.
8 Parker, *English Sabbath*, pp. 43 and 46.
9 Alexander Nowell, *A Catechism* (ed. G.E. Corrie, Cambridge, 1853), p. iv.
10 *Ibid.*, pp. 128–9.
11 Parker, *English Sabbath*, p. 46.
12 Nowell, *Catechism*, p. 129.
13 *Ibid.*, pp. 129–30.
14 Parker, *English Sabbath*, pp. 47 and 90–1.
15 C. Hill, *Society and Puritanism in Pre-Revolutionary England* (London, 1964), p. 164.
16 R. Hutton, *The Rise and Fall of Merry England. The Ritual Year, 1400–1700* (Oxford, 1994), p. 126.
17 Thomas Cooper, *An Admonition to the People of England* (London, 1589), p. 57.
18 Hutton, *Merry England*, p. 127; K. Wrightson, *English Society, 1580–1680* (London, 1982), p. 210.
19 R.L. Greaves, *Society and Religion in Elizabethan England* (Minneapolis, 1981), pp. 413–14.
20 *Acts of the Privy Council of England* (New Series), Vol. XXII (1591–92) (London, 1901), pp. 548–9.
21 P. Clark, *English Provincial Society from the Reformation to the Revolution. Religion, Politics and Society in Kent, 1500–1640* (Harvester Press, 1977), p. 156; G. Williams, *Wales and the Reformation* (Cardiff, 1997), p. 322.
22 W.P. Baker, 'The Observance of Sunday', in R. Lennard (ed.), *Englishmen at Rest and Play. Some Phases of English Leisure, 1558–1714* (Oxford, 1931), p. 87; Hutton, *Merry England*, p. 127.
23 Parker, *English Sabbath*, p. 62.
24 *Ibid.*, p. 118; Hutton, *Merry England*, p. 127.
25 *Ibid.*, pp. 110–11; Hutton, *Merry England*, p. 127.
26 John Howson, *A Sermon Preached at St Maries in Oxford* (Oxford, 1602); Parker, *English Sabbath*, pp. 100–1; Hutton, *Merry England*, p. 137.
27 Hutton, *Merry England*, p. 128; R. Hutton, *The Stations of the Sun. A History of the Ritual Year in Britain* (Oxford, 1996), p. 253.
28 Cooper, *Admonition*, p. 57.
29 Parker, *English Sabbath*, pp. 52–5.
30 Hill, *Society and Puritanism*, p. 151.
31 Hutton, *Merry England*, p. 123.
32 T.S. Henricks, *Disputed Pleasures. Sport and Society in Pre-industrial England* (New York; Westport, Connecticut; and London, 1991), p. 87; D. Brailsford, *Sport and Society. Elizabeth to Anne* (London, 1969), p. 59.
33 Greaves, *Society and Religion*, p. 446; L.A. Govett *The King's Book of Sports* (London, 1890), pp. 70–1; J. Strutt, *The Sports and Pastimes of the People of England* (London, 1841), pp. 257–8.
34 Greaves, *Society and Religion*, p. 443.

35 *Ibid.*, p. 417.
36 *Ibid.*, p. 429; Hutton, *Merry England*, p. 124; Hutton, *Stations of the Sun*, p. 227.
37 Greaves, *Society and Religion*, pp. 426-7.
38 Govett, *Book of Sports*, pp. 23-4.
39 Whitaker, *Sunday*, p. 31.
40 P.L. Hughes and J.F. Larkin (eds), *Tudor Royal Proclamations*, Vol. II, *The Later Tudors (1553-1587)* (New Haven and London, 1969), pp. 359-62.
41 Govett, *Book of Sports*, pp. 23-4.
42 *Acts of the Privy Council of England* (New Series), Vol. X (1577-78) (London, 1895), p. 329.
43 R. Hardy, *Longbow. A Social and Military History* (Third edition, Sparkford, 1992), p. 141.
44 Parker, *English Sabbath*, p. 72.
45 *Ibid.*, p. 122.
46 *Ibid.*, p. 123.
47 *Ibid.*, pp. 123-8.
48 J.H. Primus, *Holy Time. Moderate Puritanism and the Sabbath* (Mercer University Press, 1989), pp. 37-53.
49 For example, see: Greaves, *Society and Religion*, pp. 395-408; Hill, *Society and Puritanism*, esp. pp. 142, 163-6 and 485; P. Collinson, *The Elizabethan Puritan Movement* (London, 1967), pp. 436-7; C. Durston and J. Eales (eds), *The Culture of English Puritanism, 1560-1700* (London, 1996), p. 23; M.M. Knappen, *Tudor Puritanism. A Chapter in the History of Idealism* (Chicago, 1939), p. 442.
50 Greaves, *Society and Religion*, p. 404.
51 Collinson, *Godly People*, p. 439.
52 Richard Greenham, *The Workes* (London, 1599), pp. 335-6; Nicholas Bownd, *The Doctrine of the Sabbath* (London, 1595), pp. 68-9.
53 Greenham, *The Workes*, p. 336; Bownd, *Doctrine of the Sabbath*, pp. 107-9 and 115-17.
54 Greenham, *The Workes*, p. 383.
55 *Ibid.*, p. 385.
56 Bownd, *Doctrine of the Sabbath*, pp. 32-3.
57 William Perkins, *A Golden Chaine* (London, 1591), sig. H7v.
58 Bownd, *Doctrine of the Sabbath*, p. 48.
59 *Ibid.*, p. 92.
60 *Ibid.*, p. 93.
61 *Ibid.*, p. 132.
62 *Ibid.*, p. 133.
63 *Ibid.*, pp. 134-5.
64 *Ibid.*, p. 135.
65 *Ibid.*, pp. 136-7.
66 For example, see: Heinrich Bullinger, *Fiftie Godlie And Learned Sermons* (London, 1577), p. 140; George Gifford, *A Catechisme* (London, 1583), sigs F7v-F8r; Peter Martyr, *The common places of the most famous and renowned divine Doctor Peter Martyr* (London, 1583), p. 375; Perkins, *A Golden Chaine*, sigs I2r-I3v; Zacharius Ursinus, *The Summe of Christian Religion* (Oxford, 1587), p. 944; Humphrey Roberts, *An Earnest Complaint* (1572), Epistle.

NOTES TO PAGES 53-55

67 George Estye, *A Most Sweete and Comfortable Exposition, upon the ten commaundements* (London, 1602), sig. M8v; Thomas Lovell, *A Dialogue between Custom and Veritie* (London, 1581), Epistle (sigs A4r–A4v).
68 John Field, *A Godly Exhortation by Occasion of the Late Judgement of God, shewed at Parris-Garden* (London, 1583), p. 4. Also see Arthur Dent, *The Plaine Mans Path-way to Heaven* (London, 1601), pp. 138–9.
69 Humphrey Roberts, *An Earnest Complaint* (London, 1572), Epistle.
70 Perkins, *A Golden Chaine*, sigs I3r–I3v; Adam Hill, *The Crie of England* (London, 1595), p. 21.
71 Leonard Wright, *A Summons for Sleepers* (London, 1589), p. 28.
72 William Kethe, *A Sermon made at Blandford Forum* (London, 1571), p. 9.
73 Hill, *Crie of England*, p. 16; Gifford, *Catechisme*, sig. F8r; Dent, *Plaine Mans Path-way*, pp. 138–9; Philip Stubbes, *The Anatomie of Abuses* (London, 1583), Preface to the Reader, and sigs L2v, M3v and N8r; Hugh Roberts, *The Day of Hearing* (Oxford, 1600), sigs K3r–K4v.
74 Stubbes, *Anatomie of Abuses*, sig. P6r. Football was indeed often the occasion of considerable violence. In 1599, for example, a football match held at White Notley in Essex resulted in violence and 'bludshedd contrary to her Majesties peace'; see: A. Walsham, 'Godly Recreation: the problem of leisure in late Elizabethan and early Stuart society', in D.E. Kennedy, D. Robertson and A. Walsham (eds), *Grounds of Controversy. Three Studies in late 16th and early 17th century English polemics* (University of Melbourne, 1989), p. 15.
75 Field, *A godly exhortation*, unpaginated; Bownd, *Doctrine of the Sabbath*, pp. 134–5.
76 P. Collinson, *The Birthpangs of Protestant England. Religion and Cultural Change in the Sixteenth and Seventeenth Centuries* (London, 1988), p. 107; P. Clark, *The English Alehouse. A Social History, 1200–1830* (London, 1983), p. 157.
77 Dent, *Plaine Mans Path-way*, pp. 35–6 and 71; Thomas Beard, *The Theatre of God's Judgements* (London, 1597), p. 367.
78 Martyr, *The Common Places*, Part II, pp. 497–502.
79 Stubbes, *Anatomie of Abuses*, sigs M7v–O3r; John Northbrooke, *A Treatise wherein Dicing, Dauncing, Vaine Playes or Enterludes, with Other Idle Pastimes Commonly Used on the Sabbath Day, are Reproved* (London, 1579), pp. 57–9; Christopher Fetherstone, *A dialogue agaynst light, lewde, and lasciuious dauncing* (London, 1582), sigs D4r–D5r; Samuel Bird, *A Friendlie Communication or Dialogue betweene Paule and Demas* (London, 1580), pp. 36–7.
80 Thomas Lovell, *A Dialogue between Custom and Veritie* (London, 1581), Epistle (sig. A4v).
81 Stubbes, *Anatomie of Abuses*, sigs M8r–M8v.
82 Peter Martyr, *Common Places*, Part I, p. 504.
83 Fetherstone, *Lascivious dauncing*, sigs C7r–C8v.
84 John Stockwood, *A Very Fruitful Sermon* (London, 1579), p. 27; Fetherstone, *Lascivious dauncing*, sig. C4v.
85 Stockwood, *A Very Fruitful Sermon*, p. 27.
86 Richard Carew, *The Survey of Cornwall* (London, 1602), pp. 69–70.
87 Stubbes, *Anatomie of Abuses*, sigs M6v–M7r.
88 Lovell, *Dialogue between Custom and Veritie*, sig. C2r.

89 Stubbes, *Anatomie of Abuses*, sig. M5r.
90 C. Marsh, *Popular Religion in Sixteenth-century England* (London, 1998), p. 97.
91 J.C. Cox, *Churchwardens' Accounts from the Fourteenth Century to the Close of the Seventeenth Century* (London, 1913), p. 284; J. Goring, *Godly Exercises or the Devil's Dance? Puritanism and Popular Culture in pre-Civil War England* (London, 1983), p. 12.
92 Fetherstone, *Lascivious dauncing*, sig. D7v; Roberts, *Day of Hearing*, sigs K4r-K4v; Stubbes, *Anatomie of Abuses*, sig. M3v.
93 Roberts, *Day of Hearing*, sigs K7r-K7v.
94 Fetherstone, *Lascivious dauncing*, sig. D7v.
95 Stubbes, *Anatomie of Abuses*, sig. M4r.
96 D. Cressy, *Bonfires and Bells. National Memory and the Protestant Calendar in Elizabethan and Stuart England* (London, 1989), pp. 21-2; Hutton, *Stations of the Sun*, p. 229.
97 Roberts, *Day of Hearing*, sig. K5v.
98 C. Haigh, 'The Continuity of Catholicism in the English Reformation', in C. Haigh (ed.), *The English Reformation Revised* (Cambridge, 1987), p. 206.
99 John Terry, *The Triall of Truth* (Oxford, 1600), pp. 125-6; John Field, *A Caveat for Parsons Howlet* (London, 1581), p. 53.
100 Northbrooke, *A Treatise*, p. 12; Roberts, *Day of Hearing*, sigs K7v-K8r.
101 Hill, *Crie of England*, pp. 2-3; Wright, *Summons for Sleepers*, p. 26; Lovell, *Dialogue between Custom and Veritie*, Epistle (sigs A6r-A6v).
102 Roberts, *Day of Hearing*, sig. K3v; Thomas White, *A Sermon Preached at Pawles Crosse on Sunday, the Thirde of November 1577 in the Time of the Plague* (London, 1578), p. 47; Field, *A Godly Exhortation*, unpaginated.
103 Hutton, *Merry England*, pp. 113-14; Hutton, *Stations of the Sun*, pp. 250-1.
104 Hutton, *Merry England*, pp. 118-20; Hutton, *Stations of the Sun*, p. 253.
105 Cox, *Churchwardens' Accounts*, pp. 281-91; Cressy, *Bonfires and Bells*, p. 21.
106 William Harrison, *A Description of England* (ed. F.J. Furnivall, London, 1877), p. 134.
107 M.K. McIntosh, *Controlling Misbehaviour in England, 1370-1600* (Cambridge, 1998), pp. 2-3; Durston and Eales, *Culture of English Puritanism*, pp. 24-5.
108 Ursinus, *Summe of Christian Religion*, p. 942.
109 Robert Cleaver, *A Godly Form of Household Governement* (London, 1598), p. 329; Peter Martyr, *A briefe Treatise concerning the use and abuse of Dauncing* (London, 1580?), sig. B2r.
110 Hill, *Crie of England*, pp. 62-3.
111 P. Griffiths, *Youth and Authority. Formative Experience in England, 1560-1640* (Oxford, 1996), pp. 34-7.
112 Durston and Eales, *Culture of English Puritanism*, p. 25.
113 C. Marsh, *Popular Religion in Sixteenth-century England* (London, 1998), p. 97; Griffiths, *Youth and Authority*, p. 145.
114 Greaves, *Society and Religion*, p. 427.
115 Clark, *English Provincial Society*, pp. 235-8 and 249.
116 Hutton, *Merry England*, pp. 119-20 and 145-6.
117 Greaves, *Society and Religion*, pp. 439-40.
118 *Ibid.*, p. 411; Hutton, *Stations of the Sun*, p. 254; F.G. Emmison, *Elizabethan Life: Disorder* (Essex Record Office, 1970), p. 224.

119 Hutton, *Merry England*, p. 139; Hutton, *Stations of the Sun*, p. 254; Greaves, *Society and Religion*, pp. 411 and 467.
120 Hutton, *Merry England*, p. 139; Greaves, *Society and Religion*, p. 468.
121 Govett, *Book of Sports*, p. 25.
122 Whitaker, *Sunday*, p. 39.
123 Greaves, *Society and Religion*, p. 411.
124 D.C. Beaver, *Parish Communities and Religious Conflict in the Vale of Gloucester, 1590-1690* (Harvard, 1998), pp. 125-6 and 136-7.
125 J.H.E. Bennett and J.C. Dewhurst (eds), *The Quarter Sessions Records with other Records of the Justices of the Peace for the County Palatine of Chester, 1559-1760* (Record Society of Lancashire and Cheshire, 1940), p. 50.
126 Greaves, *Society and Religion*, pp. 412 and 426; Hill, *Society and Puritanism*, p. 178; Hutton, *Merry England*, p. 138; C. Haigh, *English Reformations. Religion, Politics and Society under the Tudors* (Oxford, 1993), p. 280.
127 Hutton, *Stations of the Sun*, p. 235; Greaves, *Society and Religion*, p. 426; Hill, *Society and Puritanism*, p. 178; Hutton, *Merry England*, p. 138.
128 Goring, *Godly Exercises*, p. 3; Hutton, *Merry England*, p. 142.
129 Roberts, *Day of Hearing*, K6v.
130 Clark, *English Provincial Society*, p. 157; Parker, *English Sabbath*, p. 88.
131 Goring, *Godly Exercises*, p. 20; John Deacon, *A Treatise, intituled; Nobody is My Name* (London, 1585), sig. E5v.
132 Hutton, *Stations of the Sun*, p. 254.
133 Griffiths, *Youth and Authority*, p. 139. See also C. Haigh, *The Plain Man's Pathways to Heaven. Kinds of Christianity in Post-Reformation England, 1570-1640* (Oxford, 2007), p. 93.
134 Whitaker, *Sunday*, pp. 89-90; Beaver, *Vale of Gloucester*, p. 123.
135 Greaves, *Society and Religion*, pp. 418 and 442.
136 Goring, *Godly Exercises*, p. 9.
137 Hutton, *Merry England*, pp. 134-7.
138 Collinson, *Godly People*, pp. 441-3.
139 Hill, *Society and Puritanism*, p. 485.

Chapter 4: James I's 'dancing book' and the politicisation of 'Saint Sabbath'

1 Thomas Rogers, *The Catholic Doctrine of the Church of England* (ed. by J.J.S. Perowne, Cambridge, 1954), pp. 18, 187 and 322.
2 *Ibid.*, pp. 18, 89-90 and 315.
3 *Ibid.*, pp. 18-19.
4 *Ibid.*, pp. 19-20.
5 *Ibid.*, p. 20.
6 Nicholas Bownd, *Sabbathum Veteris et Novi Testamenti: or, The True Doctrine of the Sabbath* (London, 1606), sig. A3r.
7 W.P. Baker, 'The Observance of Sunday' in R. Lennard (ed.), *Englishmen at Rest and Play. Some Phases of English Leisure, 1558-1714* (Oxford, 1931), p. 99.
8 K.L. Parker, *The English Sabbath. A Study of doctrine and discipline from the Reformation to the Civil War* (Cambridge, 1988), pp. 94-5.
9 P. Collinson, *Godly People. Essays on English Protestantism and Puritanism* (London, 1983), pp. 441-2; Parker, *English Sabbath*, pp. 95-7; K.L. Parker, 'Thomas Rogers and the English Sabbath: The Case for a Reappraisal', in

Church History, Vol. 53, No. 3 (1984), pp. 344–6; R. Hutton, *The Rise and Fall of Merry England. The Ritual Year, 1400–1700* (Oxford, 1994), p. 165.

10 Rogers, *Catholic Doctrine of the Church of England*, p. 315; J.H. Primus, *Holy Time. Moderate Puritanism and the Sabbath* (Mercer University Press, 1989), pp. 84–5.

11 Nicholas Bownd, *Doctrine of the Sabbath* (London, 1595), sig. A4r.

12 R.L. Greaves, 'The Origins of English Sabbatarian Thought', in *Sixteenth Century Journal*, XII, No. 3 (1981), p. 33.

13 L. Racaut, 'The 'Book of Sports' and Sabbatarian Legislation in Lancashire, 1579–1616', in *Northern History*, Vol. XXXIII (1979), pp. 86, 87.

14 S.R. Gardiner, *History of England from the Accession of James I to the Outbreak of the Civil War, 1603–42* (Vol. III) (London, 1883), p. 248; C.R Cole and M.E. Moody (eds), *The Dissenting Tradition* (Ohio, 1975), p. 87.

15 Victoria County History, *Lancashire*, Vol. II, p. 58.

16 Gardiner, *History of England*, p. 248; Parker, *English Sabbath*, p. 140.

17 R.C. Richardson, *Puritanism in North-West England. A Regional Study of the Diocese of Chester to 1642* (Manchester, 1972), p. 5.

18 R.C. Richardson, 'Puritanism and the Ecclesiastical Authorities: The Case of the Diocese of Chester', in B. Manning (ed.), *Politics, Religion and the English Civil War* (London, 1973), p. 3.

19 Quoted in Richardson, 'Puritanism and Ecclesiastical Authorities', p. 3 and Richardson, *Puritanism in North-West England*, p. 18.

20 Richardson, 'Puritanism and Ecclesiastical Authorities', p. 3 and Richardson, *Puritanism in North-West England*, p. 18.

21 Richardson, 'Puritanism and Ecclesiastical Authorities', pp. 3–4.

22 Richardson, *Puritanism in North-West England*, pp. 18–19.

23 Ernest Axon, 'The King's Preachers in Lancashire, 1599–1845', in *Transactions of the Lancashire and Cheshire Antiquarian Society*, Vol. 56 (1941–42), p. 67.

24 J.E.C. Hill, 'Puritans and the 'Dark Corners of the Land', *Transactions of the Royal Historical Society*, Fifth Series, Vol. 13 (London, 1963), p. 90. See also: S. Hindle, 'Custom, Festival and Protest in Early Modern England: The Little Budworth Wakes, St Peter's Day, 1596', in *Rural History*, Vol. 6, No. 2 (1995), p. 161; and E. Baldwin *et al* (eds), *Cheshire including Chester. REED* (Toronto, 2007), p. 842.

25 L. Racaut, 'Book of Sports' and Sabbatarian Legislation', pp. 74–5; Richardson, *Puritanism in North-West England*, p. 11.

26 Parker, *English Sabbath*, p. 141; F.R. Raines (ed.), *The Journal of Nicholas Assheton* (Manchester, 1848), footnote, p. 42; R. Hollingworth, *Mancuniensis, or an History of the Towne of Manchester* (Manchester, 1839), p. 88.

27 Parker, *English Sabbath*, p. 141.

28 *Ibid.*

29 *Ibid.*, p. 142.

30 L. Racaut, 'Book of Sports' and Sabbatarian Legislation', pp. 74–5.

31 *Ibid.*, p 77; and J. Harland, *The Lancashire Lieutenancy under the Tudors and Stuarts*, Volume II (two volumes, Manchester, Chetham Society, 1859), *passim*.

32 Parker, *English Sabbath*, p. 143; L. Racaut, 'Book of Sports' and Sabbatarian Legislation', *passim*, esp. pp 76–9.

33 Parker, *English Sabbath*, p. 146.

34 J. Tait (ed.), *Lancashire Quarter Sessions Records*, Vol. I, *Quarter Session Rolls, 1590–1606* (London and Manchester, 1917), pp. xviii, 11 and 14.
35 Parker, *English Sabbath*, p. 143; F.R. Raines (ed.), *Chetham Miscellanies* (Chetham Society, 1875), Vol. 5, p. 2.
36 Raines, *Chetham Miscellanies*, p. iii.
37 Parker, *English Sabbath*, p. 143; Richardson, *Puritanism in North-West England*, p. 147.
38 Tait, *Lancashire Quarter Sessions*, p. 51.
39 E. Baines, *The History of the County Palatine and Duchy of Lancaster* (two volumes, London, 1868–70), p. 183.
40 Parker, *English Sabbath*, pp. 144–5.
41 Tait, *Lancashire Quarter Sessions*, pp. 11, 14, 175, 189, 216 and 226.
42 Raines, *Chetham Miscellanies*, p. 4.
43 B.W. Quintrell (ed.), *Proceedings of the Lancashire Justices of the Peace at the Sheriff's Table During Assizes Week, 1578–1694* (The Record Society of Lancashire and Cheshire), Vol. CXXI (1981), pp. 72–3; D.J. Wilkinson, 'Performance and Motivation amongst the Justices of the Peace in Early Stuart Lancashire', in *Transactions of the Historic Society of Lancashire and Cheshire*, CXXXVIII (1989), p. 54; L. Racaut, 'Book of Sports' and Sabbatarian Legislation', pp. 82–6.
44 B.W. Quintrell (ed.), *Proceedings of the Lancashire Justices*, p. 73.
45 L. Racaut, 'Book of Sports' and Sabbatarian Legislation', p. 85.
46 *Ibid.*, pp. 85–6.
47 P. Collinson, *The Elizabethan Puritan Movement* (London, 1967), p. 406; L. Racaut, 'Book of Sports' and Sabbatarian Legislation', pp. 80–1; Richardson, 'Puritanism and Ecclesiastical Authorities', p. 15.
48 Parker, *English Sabbath*, p. 148; R.S. France (ed.), *A Lancashire Miscellany*, Volume 109 (The Record Society of Lancashire and Cheshire, 1965), p. 29.
49 Parker, *English Sabbath*, p. 151.
50 Raines, *Journal of Nicholas Assheton*, p. 34.
51 *Ibid.*, pp. 41–2; D. Underdown, *Revel, Riot and Rebellion. Popular Politics and Culture in England, 1603–1660* (Oxford, 1985), p. 65.
52 John Barwick, *A Summarie Account of ... Thomas late Lord Bishop of Duresme* (London, 1660), p. 80; G.H. Tupling, 'The Causes of the Civil War in Lancashire', in *Transactions of the Lancashire and Cheshire Antiquarian Society*, Vol. 65 (1955), pp. 10–11; Hutton, *Merry England* (Oxford, 1994), p. 168.
53 Barwick, *A Summarie Account*, pp. 80–1.
54 *Ibid.*, p. 81.
55 *Ibid.*
56 *Ibid.*
57 Ernest Axon (ed.), *Manchester Sessions. Notes of Proceedings before Oswald Mosley (1616–1630), Nicholas Mosley (1661–1672), and Sir Oswald Mosley (1734–1739)*, Volume I, 1616–1622–3 (Manchester, 1901), pp. xxiv–xxvi.
58 *Ibid.*
59 *Ibid.*
60 *Ibid.*, pp. xxvi–xxvii.
61 James I, *The Kings Majesties Declaration to his Subjects, Concerning Lawful Sports to Be Used* (London, 1618), p. 1.
62 *Ibid.*, p. 7.

63 Parker, *English Sabbath*, p. 153.
64 N. McDowell, 'The stigmatizing of Puritans as Jews in Jacobean England: Ben Jonson, Francis Bacon and the *Book of Sports* controversy' in *Renaissance Studies*, Vol. 19, No. 3 (June, 2005), pp. 348–9 and 351. (Traske later recanted and was released from prison after just eighteen months, presumably because it was felt that he was no longer a threat and that he had served his purpose as an example of state discipline).
65 McDowell, 'The stigmatizing of Puritans as Jews', *passim*, esp. pp. 349 and 359.
66 C. Hill, *Society and Puritanism in Pre-Revolutionary England* (London, 1964), p. 159; R. Ashton (ed.), *James I by his Contemporaries* (London, 1969), p. 186.
67 A. Wilson, *The History of Great Britain, Being the Life and Reign of King James the First* (London, 1653), p. 106.
68 P. Cunningham (ed.), *Extracts from the accounts of the revels at court : in the reigns of Queen Elizabeth and King James I* (London, 1842), pp. xxxiv, 203, 204, 211; W.B. Whitaker, *Sunday in Tudor and Stuart Times* (London, 1933), p. 70; *CSPD, 1611–1618*, p. 512; J. Nichols, *The Progresses, Processions, and Magnificent Festivities of King James the First*, Vol. III (London, 1828), p. 26; L.A. Govett, *The King's Book of Sports* (London, 1890), p. 16.
69 C.H. McIlwain (ed.), *The Political Works of James I* (Cambridge, 1918), p. 48; Ashton, *James I by his Contemporaries*, p. 2.
70 Ashton, *James I by his Contemporaries*, pp. 2, 3, 8, 10, 63, 230 and 249; *Calendar of State Papers Venetian, 1617–1619*, pp. 258–9; Wilson, *History of Great Britain*, p. 104.
71 *CSPV, 1617–1619*, p. 259.
72 Ashton, *James I by his Contemporaries*, p. 64; L.S. Marcus, *The Politics of Mirth. Jonson, Herrick, Milton, Marvell and the Defence of Old Holiday Pastimes* (Chicago, 1986), p. 43.
73 McIlwain, *The Political Works of James I*, pp. 43, 48 and 49.
74 T.S. Henricks, *Disputed Pleasures. Sport and Society in Pre-industrial England* (New York; Westport, Connecticut; and London, 1991), p. 155.
75 J.F. Larkin and P.L. Hughes (eds), *Stuart Royal Proclamations, Volume I, Royal Proclamations of King James I, 1603–1625* (Oxford, 1973), p. 14.
76 HMC *Twelfth Report*, Appendix, Part IV, *The Manuscripts of the Duke of Rutland* (1888), Vol. I, pp. 390–1 (my italics).
77 Parker incorrectly assumed that the instructions issued to constables came from the king rather than local magistrates. Consequently, he wrongly concluded that James had sought to ban piping and dancing on Sundays. This led Parker to claim that the 1618 *Book of Sports* contradicted James' 1603 proclamation and instructions, whereas the 1603 Proclamation did not contradict the 1618 Declaration at all. See Parker, *English Sabbath*, pp. 117 and 153. Phebe Jensen has similarly assumed that these instructions merely clarified James' proclamation. See P. Jensen, *Religion and Revelry in Shakespeare's Festive World* (Cambridge, 2008), p. 198.
78 E.K. Chambers, *The Elizabethan Stage*, Vol. II (Oxford, 1923), pp. 267–9.
79 Marcus, *The Politics of Mirth*, p. 25.
80 Chambers, *Elizabethan Stage*, Vol. II, pp. 267–9.
81 Marcus, *The Politics of Mirth*, p. 4.

82 H.M. Shire, *Song, Dance and Poetry of the Court of Scotland under King James VI* (Cambridge, 1969), pp. 68, 91–2.
83 McIlwain, *The Political Works of James I*, p. 27.
84 James I, *Declaration ... concerning Lawfull Sports* (1618), pp. 4–5.
85 Ashton, *James I by his Contemporaries*, p. 186. In 1605 James, whose passion for hunting has already been noted, even defined his kingly activities as the hunting of 'witches, prophets, puritans, dead cats and hares' – See: A. Stewart, *The Cradle King. A Life of James VI and I* (London, 2003), p. 181.
86 McIlwain, *The Political Works of James I*, p. 24.
87 F. Shriver, 'Hampton Court Re-visited: James I and the Puritans' in *Journal of Ecclesiastical History*, Vol. 33, No. I (January, 1982), p. 66.
88 Hill, 'Puritans and the "Dark Corners of the Land"', p. 91.
89 Richardson, 'Puritanism and Ecclesiastical Authorities', p. 15.
90 James I, *Declaration ... concerning Lawfull Sports* (1618), p. 2.
91 Marcus, *The Politics of Mirth*, p. 113.
92 Ashton, *James I by his Contemporaries*, pp. 187–8.
93 Hill, *Society and Puritanism*, p. 193.
94 *CSPD, 1611–1618*, p. 608.
95 Thomas Fuller, *The Church History of Britain* (ed. J. Nicholls, three volumes, London, 1837), Vol. III, pp. 271–3.
96 P. Griffiths, *Youth and Authority. Formative Experience in England, 1560–1640* (Oxford, 1996), p. 57, n.175.
97 *CSPD, 1619–1623*, p. 276.
98 *Oxford Dictionary of National Biography* (Oxford, 2004), Vol. 4, p. 462.
99 See the discussion below on Parliament and bills designed to enforce stricter Sabbath observance.
100 Lewis Bayly, *The Practice of Pietie directing a Christian how to walke, that he may please God* (London, 1616), pp. 311 and 448–50.
101 P.A. Welsby, *George Abbot, the Unwanted Archbishop, 1562–1633* (London, 1962), p. 85; E.F. Slafter, *The Character and History of the Book of Sports, 1618–1643* (Boston, 1905), pp. 9–10.
102 Parker, *English Sabbath*, p. 160.
103 K. Fincham (ed.), *Visitation Articles and Injunctions of the Early Stuart Church*, Volume I (Church of England Record Society, 1994), p. 152.
104 J. Fielding, 'Arminianism in the Localities: Peterborough Diocese, 1603–1642', in K. Fincham (ed.), *The Early Stuart Church, 1603–1642* (London, 1993), pp. 100–1.
105 M. Stoyle, *From Deliverance to Destruction. Rebellion and Civil War in an English City* (Exeter, 1996), p. 29.
106 Hutton, *Merry England*, p. 174; Underdown, *Revel, Riot and Rebellion*, p. 66.
107 Underdown, *Revel, Riot and Rebellion*, p. 66.
108 J.I. Harris, 'Lucy Robartes's 'A meditation uppon the Lords day': A Puritan Palimpsest and English Sabbatarianism', in *The Seventeenth Century*, Vol. XXIII, No. 1 (Spring, 2008), pp. 14 and 31. Note: Harris quotes the penultimate word of the verse as 'Rests', when it is in fact 'Riots'.
109 HMC *Reports on the Manuscripts of the Duke of Buccleuch and Queensbury*, Vol. III (London, 1926), pp. 213–14.
110 HMC *Report on the Manuscripts of Lord Montagu of Beaulieu* (London, 1900), pp. 94–5.
111 *Ibid.*

NOTES TO PAGES 85–89   185

112 Fielding, 'Arminianism in the Localities', p. 101.
113 HMC *Report on the Manuscripts of Lord Montagu of Beaulieu* (London, 1900), p. 95.
114 HMC *Manuscripts of the Duke of Buccleuch and Queensbury*, Vol. III, pp. 211–12.
115 *Ibid.*, p. 208.
116 *Ibid.*, p. 209.
117 *Ibid.*, pp. 209–10.
118 Parker, *English Sabbath*, p. 157; HMC *Manuscripts of the Duke of Buccleuch and Queensbury*, Vol. III, p. 211.
119 HMC *Reports on the Manuscripts of the Duke of Buccleuch and Queensbury*, Vol. I (London, 1899), p. 254; Fielding, 'Arminianism in the Localities', p. 102.
120 Fielding, 'Arminianism in the Localities', p. 102.
121 J. Kent, 'Attitudes of Members of the House of Commons to the Regulation of 'Personal Conduct' in Late Elizabethan and Early Stuart England', in *Bulletin of the Institute of Historical Research*, Vol. 46 (1973), pp. 42–5 and 62.
122 Fletcher, *Reform in the Provinces*, p. 267.
123 George Widley, *The Doctrine of the Sabbath* (London, 1604), sigs A2v–A2r.
124 C. Hill, 'Seventeenth-century English Society and Sabbatarianism' in J.S. Bromley and E.H. Kossman (eds), *Britain and the Netherlands*, Vol. II (1964), p. 89.
125 *The Journals of the House of Commons*, Vol. I, pp. 260, 261 and 267; D.H. Wilson (ed.), *The Parliamentary Diary of Robert Bowyer, 1606–1607* (University of Minnesota Press, 1971), pp. 8 and 34.
126 M.F. Bond (ed.), *The Manuscripts of the House of Lords, Volume XI* (New Series), *Addenda, 1514–1714* (London, 1962), p. 96.
127 Whitaker, *Sunday in Tudor and Stuart Times*, p. 104; Hutton, *Merry England*, p. 156; E.R. Foster (ed.), *Proceedings in Parliament, 1610, Volume 2, House of Commons* (London, 1966), p. 408; Parker, *English Sabbath*, p. 129.
128 *Commons Journal*, pp. 467–8 and 483. Montagu's support is unsurprising given his later conflict with John Williams.
129 Hill, *Society and Puritanism*, p. 156.
130 C. Haigh, The Plain Man's Pathways to Heaven. Kinds of Christianity in Post-Reformation England, 1570–1640 (Oxford, 2007), p. 93.
131 *Commons Journal*, p. 476.
132 HMC, *Report on the Manuscripts of Reginald Rawdon Hastings*, Vol. IV (ed.) F. Bickley (1947), p. 265.
133 *Ibid.*, p. 266.
134 P. Collinson, 'Elizabethan and Jacobean Puritanism as Forms of Popular Religion Culture', in C. Durston and J. Eales (eds), *The Culture of English Puritanism, 1560–1700* (London, 1996), p. 37.
135 HMC, *Hastings*, pp. 266–7.
136 *The Journals of the House of Lords*, Vol. II, p. 710.
137 Parker, *English Sabbath*, p. 131.
138 HMC, *Hastings*, pp. 278–9.
139 *Ibid.*, pp. 279–80.
140 *Commons Journal*, pp. 511 and 514; W. Notestein, F.H. Relf and H. Simpson (eds), *Commons Debates, 1621*, Vol. IV (London, 1935), p. 33; Hutton, *Merry England*, p. 171.

141 Notestein et al, *Commons Debates*, Vol. II, pp. 104–5.
142 *Ibid.*, p. 82.
143 Notestein et al, *Commons Debates*, Vol. IV, p. 52; Notestein et al, *Commons Debates*, Vol. II, p. 82.
144 *Commons Journal*, p. 521.
145 Notestein et al, *Commons Debates*, Vol. IV, p. 53.
146 Notestein et al, *Commons Debates*, Vol. II, p. 95.
147 *Ibid.*, p. 96.
148 W. Prest, *The Inns of Court under Elizabeth I and the Early Stuarts, 1590–1640* (London, 1972), p. 184.
149 Notestein et al, *Commons Debates*, Vol. V, p. 501.
150 Notestein et al, *Commons Debates*, Vol. II, p. 96; Notestein et al, *Commons Debates*, Vol. IV, p. 63; Parker, *English Sabbath*, p. 171.
151 Notestein et al, *Commons Debates*, Vol. IV, p. 33.
152 *Ibid.*, p. 76.
153 James I, *Declaration ... Concerning Lawfull Sports* (1618), p. 6.
154 *CSPD, 1619–1623*, p. 276.
155 *Commons Journal*, pp. 671, 673 and 678.
156 Parker, *English Sabbath*, p. 174.
157 *Ibid.*
158 *Ibid.*
159 Bayly, *Practice of Pietie*, p. 400.
160 *Ibid.*, pp. 432–3.
161 *CSPD, 1619–1623*, p. 276.
162 P.A. Welsby, *Lancelot Andrewes, 1555–1626* (London, 1964), pp. 25–7.
163 Parker, *English Sabbath*, pp. 99–102 and 108; Barwick, *A Summarie Account*, p. 81.
164 Welsby, *Lancelot Andrewes*, p. 28.
165 K. Fincham (ed.), *Visitation Articles and Injunctions of the Early Stuart Church*, Vol. I (1994), p. 1; Parker, *English Sabbath*, p. 119.
166 For other examples of Jacobean bishops enquiring about unlawful games, see E. Baldwin et al (eds), *REED: Cheshire including Chester* (University of Toronto, 2007), pp. 4–5.
167 Parker, *English Sabbath*, pp. 119–20. Bishop Morton of Chester similarly enquired if bull-baitings, bear-baitings, May games, morris dances, ales or any 'such like prophane' pastimes were held on the Sabbath 'to the hinderance of Praiers, Sermons or other godly exercises'; see: E. Baldwin, *REED: Cheshire including Chester*, p. 5.
168 Fincham (ed.), *Visitation Articles*, pp. 11, 21 and 37.
169 Parker, *English Sabbath*, p. 120.
170 HMC, *Hastings*, pp. 266–7, 278–9; Hutton, *Merry England*, p. 155.
171 Hutton, *Merry England*, p. 155.
172 R. Halley, *Lancashire: Its Puritanism and Nonconformity*, Vol. I (Manchester, 1869), p. 234; Welsby, *George Abbot*, p. 85.
173 Nichols, *Progresses, Processions* (Vol. III), p. 397.
174 Axon (ed.), *Manchester Sessions*, p. xxvii.
175 Fincham (ed.), *Visitation Articles*, p. 152.
176 See, for example, William Burton, *An Abstract of the Doctrine of the Sabbaoth* (London, 1606), pp. 20–1; Fielding, 'Arminianism in the Localities', p. 100; William Harrison, *Differnce of Hearers* (London, 1614), Epistle and

pp. 138 and 140; W. Hunt, *The Puritan Moment. The Coming of Revolution in an English County* (Harvard, 1983), p. 140; John Sprint, *Propositions, tending to prove the neccessarie use of the Christian Sabbaoth, or Lord's Day* (London, 1607), pp. 10 and 26; Widley, *Doctrine of the Sabbath*, pp. 57, 99, 100–4, 106, 108–9; Hutton, *Merry England*, p. 156;
177 Harrison, *Difference of Hearers*, pp. 138 and 140.
178 Jeremy Goring, *Godly Exercises or the Devil's Dance? Puritanism and Popular Culture in pre-Civil War England* (London, 1983), p. 6.
179 Thomas Broad, *Three Questions Answered* (Oxford, 1621), Introduction and *passim*.
180 Marcus, *The Politics of Mirth*, pp. 96–8.
181 *Ibid.*, pp. 94–5; Hutton, *Merry England*, pp. 164–5.
182 M. Jamieson (ed.), *Ben Jonson. Three Comedies* (London, 1966), Prologue and p. 429.
183 Marcus, *The Politics of Mirth*, pp. 113–118.
184 Collinson, 'Elizabethan and Jacobean Puritanism', pp. 41–2; L. Marcus, 'Politics and Pastoral: Writing the Court on the Countryside', in K. Sharpe and P. Lake (eds), *Culture and Politics in Early Stuart England* (London, 1994), p. 152.
185 Marcus, *The Politics of Mirth*, pp. 50–8.
186 Thomas Coryate, *Coryats Crambe* (London, 1611), sigs E2v–E4v.
187 Collinson, 'Elizabethan and Jacobean Puritanism', p. 35.
188 Whitaker, *Sunday in Tudor and Stuart Times*, p. 81; A. Fletcher, *Reform in the Provinces. The Government of Stuart England* (New Haven and London, 1986), p. 268.
189 C. Hill, *Society and Puritanism*, p. 184; Whitaker, *Sunday in Tudor and Stuart Times*, p. 76.
190 Whitaker, *Sunday in Tudor and Stuart Times*, p. 76.
191 Edmund Rudierd, *The Thunderbolt of Gods Wrath* (London, 1618), Epistle dedicatory. See also W. Crashaw, *The Sermon Preached at the Crosse* (London, 1609), pp. 171–2. Crashaw called on the Lord Mayor of London and other magistrates to stop abuses of the Sabbath such as 'May-games and Morice dancers, by Wakes and Feasts'.
192 Hutton, *Merry England*, p. 159.
193 *Ibid.*, p. 158.
194 Hill, 'Seventeenth-Century English Society and Sabbatarianism', pp. 88–9.
195 Griffiths, *Youth and Authority*, p. 222.
196 Hutton, *Merry England*, pp. 172, 173–4.
197 C.J. Sisson, *The Lost Plays of Shakespeare's Age* (Cambridge, 1936), pp. 190–1, 193–6.
198 HMC Seventh Report, Appendix, p. 675.
199 Goring, *Godly Exercises*, p. 5; Underdown, *Revel, Riot and Rebellion*, pp. 52–3.
200 Sisson, *Lost Plays*, p. 163.
201 Underdown, *Revel, Riot and Rebellion*, p. 60.
202 See Hutton, *Merry England*, pp. 163–4.
203 Goring, *Godly Exercises*, p. 21; M. Ingram 'Puritans and the Church Courts, 1560–1640', in C. Durston and J. Eales (eds), *The Culture of English Puritanism, 1560–1700* (Basingstoke, Macmillan, 1996), p. 82.

Chapter 5: *The Book of Sports* and the reign of Charles I: From a 'pious Statute' to 'bloody civil war'

1. Richard Baxter, *A Holy Commonwealth* (London, 1659), p. 457.
2. J. Morrill, *The Nature of the English Revolution* (London, 1993), pp. 33–44.
3. Matthew Sylvester, *Reliquiae Baxterianae* (London, 1696), p. 31.
4. T. Fuller, *The Church History of Britain*, ed. J. Nicholls (Three volumes, London, 1837), Vol. III, p. 379.
5. *Ibid.*, p. 379.
6. John Ley, *Sunday A Sabbath* (London, 1641), sig. C3v.
7. K. Sharpe, *The Personal Rule of Charles I* (New Haven and London, 1992), p. 359.
8. See chapters 3 and 4.
9. See: C. Russell, *Crisis of Parliaments* (Oxford, 1972), pp. 298–9; C. Russell, *Parliaments and English Politics, 1621–1629* (Oxford, 1979), pp. 145–203; and R.E. Ruigh, *The Parliament of 1624: Politics and Foreign Policy* (Harvard University Press, 1971), *passim*.
10. S.R. Gardiner (ed.), *Debates in the House of Commons in 1625* (London, 1873), p. 14; M. Jansson and W. Bidwell (eds), *Proceedings in Parliament 1625* (Yale, 1987), p. 232.
11. *Commons Journal* (Vol. I), pp. 799, 800, 825, 827, 842 and 846; Russell, *Parliaments and English Politics*, p. 234; Jansson, *Proceedings in Parliament*, pp. 78 and 80.
12. K.L. Parker, *The English Sabbath. A Study of doctrine and discipline from the Reformation to the Civil War* (Cambridge, 1988), p. 176.
13. *Ibid.*, pp. 174–5.
14. A.J. Stephens (ed.), *The Statutes relating to Ecclesiastical and Eleemosynary Institutions* (two volumes, London, 1845), Vol. I, pp. 537–8. The italics are mine.
15. Walter Yonge, *The Diary of Walter Yonge, Esq.* (The Camden Society, London, 1848), p. 84; William Prynne, *Histrio-mastix* (London, 1633), p. 241.
16. Henry Burton, *For God and the King* (Amsterdam, 1636), p. 57; Henry Burton, *The Law and the Gospel Reconciled* (London, 1631), p. 56; Henry Burton, *A Brief Answer to a Late Treatise on the Sabbath Day* (Amsterdam, 1635), p. 28.
17. Prynne, *Histrio-mastix*, p. 241.
18. William Twisse, *Of the Morality of the Fourth Commandment* (London, 1641), p. 143.
19. Burton, *A Brief Answer*, pp. 28–9.
20. James I, *The Kings Majesties Declaration to his Subjects, Concerning Lawful Sports to Be Used* (London, 1618), p. 7.
21. J. Spurr, *English Puritanism, 1603–1689* (London, 1998), pp. 84–5.
22. E.S. Cope, *Politics Without Parliaments, 1629–1640* (London, 1987), p. 58; R. Hutton, *The Rise and Fall of Merry England. The Ritual Year, 1400–1700* (Oxford, 1994), p. 189. See also: A. Walsham, 'Godly Recreation: the problem of leisure in late Elizabethan and early Stuart society', in D.E. Kennedy, D. Robertson and A. Walsham (eds), *Grounds of Controversy. Three Studies in late 16th and early 17th century English polemics* (University of Melbourne, 1989), pp. 32–3.
23. D. Pickering (ed.), *The Statutes At Large*, Vol. VII (1783), p. 320.

24 Hutton, *Merry England*, p. 189.
25 Samuel Bachiler, *The Campe Royall* (London, 1629), epistle to the reader.
26 The orders banning wakes and ales in Dorset, Somerset and Devon are discussed in some detail in the section on the Somerset controversy later in this chapter; for the maypole, see Hutton, *Merry England*, p. 189.
27 Baxter was born on 12 November 1615; Sylvester, *Reliquiae Baxterianae*, pp. 1–3.
28 Nicholas Breton, *Fantasticks seruing for a perpetuall prognostication* (London, 1626).
29 Michael Drayton, *The Muses Elizium* (London, 1630), p. 11.
30 Thomas Broad, *Tractatus de Sabbato* (n.p., 1627); Edward Brerewood, *A Learned Treatise of the Sabaoth* (Oxford, 1630), pp. 37–8; Edward Brerewood, *A Second Treatise of the Sabbath* (Oxford, 1632), pp. 9, 14–15, 20–1 and 38–9.
31 Robert Cleaver, *A Declaration of the Christian Sabbath* (London, 1625), *passim*, especially the epistle dedicatory for the references to adversaries of the Sabbath and to innovations.
32 Richard Byfield, *The Doctrine of the Sabbath Vindicated* (London, 1631), p. 107.
33 Edward Elton, *Gods Holy Mind* (London, 1625), pp. 89–90 and 106.
34 Robert Bolton, *Some Generall Directions* (London, 1626), pp. 155 and 157.
35 Burton, *Law and Gospel Reconciled*, p. 65.
36 Griffith Williams, *The True Church* (London, 1629), p. 303. Williams was a maverick character who held a number of controversial views. He was appointed to the prebend at Westminster shortly before publishing *The True Church*. Despite his sabbatarian stance, which was at odds with the mainstream Church's view, he went on to be appointed as Bishop of Ossory in 1641 and to support the royalist cause in the Civil War.
37 *Ibid.*, pp. 307–8.
38 Theophilus Brabourne, *A Discourse Upon the Sabbath Day* (London, 1628), *passim*, especially pp. 1–63, 68–75 and 100–238.
39 Theophilus Brabourne, *A Defence of that most Ancient, and Sacred ordinance of Gods the Sabbath Day* (London, 1632), *passim*.
40 *Ibid.*, sigs B1r–B1v, D1v and p. 355.
41 *Ibid.*, p. 257.
42 *Ibid.*, sigs A2v–A3v.
43 *Ibid.*, sig. A4v.
44 *Ibid.*, pp. 609–10.
45 Peter Heylyn, *Cyprianus Anglicus or the Life of Archbishop Laud* (London, 1668), pp. 257–8.
46 B. Ball, '"Through Darkness to Light." Post-Restoration Sabbatarianism: Survival and Continuity', in R. Bonney and D.J.B. Trim (eds), *The Development of Pluralism in Modern Britain and France* (Bern, 2007), p. 114.
47 Heylyn, *Cyprianus Anglicus*, pp. 257–8; Francis White, *A Treatise of the Sabbath Day* (London, 1635), sig. A2v; Parker, *English Sabbath*, p. 199.
48 White, *Treatise*, *passim*; Francis White, *An Examination and Confutation of a Lawless Pamphlet* (London, 1637), sigs A2r–A4r. These works are discussed further in the section on the 'battle of pens' in chapter seven.
49 Heylyn, *Cyprianus Anglicus*, p. 258; William Prynne, *Canterburies Doome* (London, 1646), p. 148; C. Hill, *Society and Puritanism in Pre-Revolutionary*

England (London, 1964), p. 197; J. Davies, *The Caroline Captivity of the Church: Charles I and the Remoulding of Anglicanism* (Oxford, 1992), pp. 176–7. Strangely, Prynne referred to Brabourne's 1628 work, and not the later work which contained the dedication to Charles I.

50 Hamon L'Estrange, *The Reign of King Charles* (London, 1656), pp. 132–3.
51 F.S. Boas (ed.), *The Diary of Thomas Crosfield* (Oxford, 1935), p. 66.
52 Hutton, *Merry England*, p. 193.
53 William Prynne, *A Briefe Polemicall Dissertation* (London, 1654), sig. A2r.
54 Prynne, *Histrio-mastix*, to the Christian reader.
55 *Ibid.*, pp. 229, 232–3 and 239.
56 *Ibid.*, pp. 241 and 243.
57 *Ibid.*, pp. 252–3.
58 W. Lamont, *Marginal Prynne, 1600–1669* (London, 1962), p. 29.
59 Lamont, *Marginal Prynne*, p. 31.
60 *Ibid.*, p. 33; L.S. Marcus, *The Politics of Mirth. Jonson, Herrick, Milton, Marvell and the Defence of Old Holiday Pastimes* (Chicago, 1986), p. 169.
61 Fuller, *Church History*, Vol. III, p. 376.
62 T.G. Barnes, 'County Politics and a Puritan Cause Célèbre: Somerset Churchales, 1633', in *TRHS*, Fifth Series, 9 (1959), pp. 105–6.
63 *Ibid.*, pp. 108–9.
64 The Quarter Session records for Cornwall and for Dorset before 1660 do not survive (see D. Underdown, *Revel, Riot and Rebellion. Popular Politics and Culture in England, 1603–1660* (Oxford, 1985), p. 49 – footnote), therefore I have confined the comparison of orders against West Country ales to those made in Devon and Somerset. An order from the Dorset Assizes held in July 1631 does survive in which ales were suppressed due to 'soundry misdemeanours and disorders yeerely happeninge by occasion of the keepinge of publique revels, churchales, clerkes ales and other ales of like nature', but this order made no reference to any issues of religion. See J.S. Cockburn (ed.), *Western Circuit Assize Orders, 1629–1648* (London, 1976) p. 33.
65 Barnes cites various orders for Somerset (Barnes, 'County Politics', p. 109, footnote 1), but in doing so refers to a Somerset order of 1596 and cites as his reference: Prynne, *Canterburies Doome*, p. 152. However, the transcribed order printed by Prynne on that page is in fact the 1594 order. The reference that Barnes gives for the 1594 order (SP 16/96 No. 7) is in fact the 1628 petition to Judge Denham. Cases concerning ales were brought before Somerset justices in 1596, but the Somerset Record Office does not have any record of any specific order being made against the holding of church ales in 1596. Barnes also omits the 1612 Somerset order and he refers to a Devon order of 1606. Again, there was a case in Devon in 1606 concerning disorder at an ale, but no order prohibiting ales was made that year. However, an order was made by the Devon bench against ales in 1607.
66 DRO, *Quarter Sessions Order Book, Volume I (1592–1600)*, fols 125–126.
67 Prynne, *Canterburies Doome*, p. 152.
68 *Ibid.*, p. 153. The manslaughters recorded at these ales were referred to in the previous chapter.
69 M. Stoyle, *Loyalty and Locality. Popular Allegiance in Devon during the English Civil War* (Exeter, 1994), p. 218.
70 Prynne, *Canterburies Doome*, pp. 153–4; A.H.A. Hamilton, *Quarter Sessions from Queen Elizabeth to Queen Anne* (London, 1878), p. 115; Cockburn,

Western Circuit Assize Orders, footnote on pp. 3–4; Heylyn, *Cyprianus Anglicus*, p. 256.
71 Parker, *English Sabbath*, p. 182 (N.B. Parker here fails to list a number of orders – including the 1595 Devon order, which *was* sabbatarian, and he incorrectly dates the 1608 order as 1607 and the 1632 order as 1631); Prynne, *Canterburies Doome*, p. 52.
72 Barnes, 'County Politics', p. 109.
73 SRO, Q/SR 13/71.
74 SRO, Q/503 folio 394.
75 Prynne, *Canterburies Doome*, p. 154; Hutton, *Merry England*, p. 189; Barnes, 'County Politics', pp. 109–10.
76 Barnes, 'County Politics', pp. 109–10.
77 Thomas Trescott, *The Zealous Magistrate* (London, 1642), pp. 25–6. Although orders for Cornwall do not survive, it would appear from Richard Carew's Survey of Cornwall that, at least at the beginning of the seventeenth century, attempts were being made to suppress ales, but that they continued to be popular here too. See Richard Carew, *The Survey of Cornwall* (London, 1602), pp. 68–71.
78 Cockburn, *Western Circuit Assize Orders*, p. 46.
79 Prynne, *Canterburies Doome*, p. 128. As Hill observes, it is more likely that such children were conceived 'after' wakes and ales rather that actually 'at' them: C. Hill, 'Seventeenth-century English Society and Sabbatarianism', in J.S. Bromley and E.H. Kossman (eds), *Britain and the Netherlands*, Vol. II (1964), p. 98 (footnote no. 2).
80 See Barnes, 'County Politics' for a comprehensive discussion of the events, circumstances and consequences of the ales controversy in Somerset.
81 Prynne, *Canterburies Doome*, p. 132.
82 *Ibid.*, p. 132.
83 J. Stokes (ed.), *Somerset, REED* (Toronto, 1996), p. 978. The Prayer Book was annexed to the Act of Uniformity. Consequently, the rubrics in the Prayer Book were held to have the force of statute law.
84 P.E. Kopperman, *Sir Robert Heath. Window on an Age* (Royal Historical Society, 1989), p. 240.
85 F. Hargrave (ed.), *A complete collection of state-trials, and proceedings for high-treason* (London, 1776), p. 399; H.R. Trevor-Roper, *Archbishop Laud, 1573–1645* (Second edition, London, 1962), pp. 110–11; C. Carlton, *Archbishop William Laud* (London, 1987), p. 78.
86 Barnes, 'County Politics', p. 111.
87 *Ibid.*, pp. 111–13; Trevor-Roper, *Archbishop Laud*, p. 157.
88 *CSPD*, 1633–34, p. 20.
89 Barnes, 'County Politics', p. 113.
90 SRO, DD/PH 222, fol. 120.
91 SRO, DD/PH 222, fol. 126.
92 Barnes, 'County Politics', p. 115.
93 SP 16/255 No. 39. The petition was accompanied by a copy of Richardson's order revoking the earlier orders against ales and also by copies of three orders made against ales in previous years. However, curiously, the copies included with the petition were not copies of Somerset orders, but were copies of the Devon orders against ales of 1600, 1615 and 1627. It is not clear why this should have been the case.

94 Barnes, 'County Politics', p. 116 (footnote).
95 Ibid., pp. 116-17.
96 Parker, *English Sabbath*, p. 188.
97 Heylyn, *Cyprianus Anglicus*, p. 257. See also Prynne, *Canterburies Doome*, p. 148. Laud was similarly suspected of engineering the dismissal of Sir Robert Heath as chief justice of the Common Pleas, but his role in Heath's dismissal was overplayed. See: P.E. Kopperman, *Sir Robert Heath*, pp. 236-44; and T.G. Barnes, 'Cropping the Heath: the Fall of a Chief Justice, 1634', in *Historical Research*, Vol. 64, No. 155 (October, 1991), pp. 337-9 and 342.
98 Davies, *Caroline Captivity*, pp. 177-8.
99 Prynne, *Canterburies Doome*, pp. 52, 128 and 148; Burton, *For God and the King*, p. 59; White, *An Examination and Confutation*, p. 132; Davies, *Caroline Captivity*, p. 176; Peter Heylyn, *A Briefe and Moderate Answer* (London, 1637), p. 80; Christopher Dow, *Innovations Unjustly Charged Upon the Present Church and State* (London, 1637), pp. 74-5.
100 Barnes, 'County Politics', p. 119; Parker, *English Sabbath*, pp. 189-90; R. Cust, *Charles I. A Political Life* (Longman, 2005), p. 138; Sharpe, *Personal Rule*, pp. 354-5; Davies, *Caroline Captivity*, p. 176.
101 SP 16/255 No. 39.
102 Barnes, 'County Politics', p. 119; Parker, *English Sabbath*, p. 189.
103 D. Underdown (ed.), *William Whiteway of Dorchester, His Diary* (Dorset Record Society, Vol. 12, 1991), p. 132; J. Stokes (ed.), *Somerset, REED* (Toronto, 1996), p. 979.
104 SP 16/247 No. 24.
105 SP 16/250 No. 20.
106 Ibid.
107 SP 16/255 No. 39.
108 SP 16/250 No. 20.
109 J. Bliss and W. Scott (eds), *The Works of William Laud* (seven volumes, Oxford, 1847-60), IV, pp. 251 and 253.
110 SP 16/248 No. 12.
111 Davies, *Caroline Captivity*, p. 176.
112 Prynne, *Canterburies Doome*, p. 148.
113 Davies, *Caroline Captivity*, p. 176.
114 Ibid., 204; Trevor-Roper, *Archbishop Laud*, pp. 156 and 158-9.
115 Bliss, *Works of William Laud*, IV, p. 255; Ibid., III, p. 307.
116 Davies, *Caroline Captivity*, pp. 180 and 204; Hill, *Society and Puritanism*, p. 159.
117 See chapter six on the enforcement of the 1633 Declaration.
118 K. Sharpe, *The Personal Rule of Charles I*, pp. 191 and 197; K. Sharpe, *Remapping Early Modern England. The Culture of Seventeenth-Century Politics* (Cambridge, 2000), p. 173.
119 Davies, *Caroline Captivity*, p. 180.
120 Hamon L'Estrange, *The Reign of King Charles* (London, 1656), p. 133; Davies, *Caroline Captivity*, p. 175; Hill, *Society and Puritanism*, p. 159.
121 A.N. Nelson (ed.), *Cambridge, REED* (Toronto, 1989), p. 660. This could be a reference to Francis White who was the Bishop of Ely at the time and who also, at Charles' request, wrote *A Treatise of the Sabbath Day* (London, 1635). However, it is almost certainly a reference to Laud. The fact that

Priest was also accused of using 'vnfitting speches ... abowte the Alters and orgins in the Churches' would also suggest that he was referring to Laud.

122 J.I. Harris, 'Lucy Robartes's 'A meditation uppon the Lords day': A Puritan Palimpsest and English Sabbatarianism', in *The Seventeenth Century*, Vol. XXIII, No. 1 (Spring, 2008), p. 10. It should be noted, however, that this is a copy of the 1618 and not the 1633 *Book of Sports*, which is the only copy in the library at the Robarte's house at Lanhydrock. If it is, as seems highly likely, a reference to Laud, it is interesting that he is referred to as 'B.L.' and not 'A.L.', as he was Archbishop of Canterbury by the time that the 1633 *Book of Sports* was issued.

123 Anon., *The Bishops Potion* (London, 1641), pp. 1–3. See also chapter six, footnote 128. Laud then vomited a copy of *Sunday No Sabbath*, and when asked by his doctor if he had 'made' that also, the sick Laud replied: 'No, Doctor Pocklington made it, but I licenced it'.

124 G. Donaldson, *The Making of the Scottish Prayer Book of 1637* (Edinburgh, 1954), pp. 52–6, 60–6, 78–9 and esp. 80–1.

125 Davies, *Caroline Captivity*, p. 174.

126 Marcus, *Politics of Mirth*, p. 128.

127 J. Richards, '"His Nowe Majesty" and the English Monarchy: The Kingship of Charles I before 1640', in *Past and Present*, 113 (1986), p. 76.

128 Sharpe, *Remapping Early Modern England*, pp. 173–4. In a recent article, Mark Kishlansky has similarly asserted that '[Charles'] handbook was the *Basilikon Doron*'. See M. Kishlansky, 'Charles I: A Case of Mistaken Identity', in *P&P*, Vol. 189, No. I (November, 2005), p. 50.

129 *Ibid.*, p. 176.

130 Given Archbishop Abbot's opposition to the 1618 *Book of Sports*, as Fincham and Tyacke have observed, Abbot's death in August 1633 removed a potential obstacle to the reissuing of the Declaration of Sports. See K. Fincham and N. Tyacke, *Altars Restored. The Changing Face of English Religious Worship, 1547-c.1700* (Oxford, 2007), p. 144.

131 White, *An Examination and Confutation*, p. 132; Heylyn, *A Briefe and Moderate Answer*, p. 80.

132 C. Petrie (ed.), *The Letters, Speeches and Proclamations of King Charles I* (London, 1935), p. 200.

133 Charles I, *The Kings Majesties Declaration to his Subjects, Concerning Lawful Sports to Be Used* (London, 1633), pp. 15–16.

134 *Ibid.* It is not clear why Charles should have been so interested in wakes, but his letter to Phelips, the letter he instructed Laud to write to Piers and the 1633 Declaration itself all make it clear that he was particularly concerned that wakes should be protected. It may be that, because they were the Feasts of the Dedication of the churches, he saw them as revels that had a particular connection to the Church and should therefore be preserved.

135 Cust, *Charles I*, pp. 133–43.

136 Charles I, *Declaration ... Concerning Lawful Sports*, p. 17.

137 Sharpe, *Personal Rule*, p. 359.

Chapter 6: Enforcement and reaction: Choosing between the 'Commandments of God and Man'

1. J. Davies, *The Caroline Captivity of the Church: Charles I and the Remoulding of Anglicanism* (Oxford, 1992), p. 183.
2. L.A. Govett, *The King's Book of Sports* (London, 1890), p. 121.
3. E. Hawkins (ed.), *Travels in Holland, the United Provinces, England, Scotland and Ireland by Sir William Brereton* (London, 1844), pp. 139–40.
4. George Swinnock, *The Life and Death of Mr. Tho. Wilson* (London, 1672), p. 74.
5. Heylyn, *Cyprianus Anglicus*, p. 295.
6. D. Underdown (ed.), *William Whiteway of Dorchester, His Diary* (Dorset Record Society, Vol. 12, 1991), p. 147.
7. Davies, *Caroline Captivity*, p. 198.
8. T. Webster, *Godly Clergy in Early Stuart England. The Caroline Puritan Movement, c.1620–1643* (Cambridge, 1997), p. 229.
9. Sharpe, *Personal Rule*, p. 359.
10. K. Fincham (ed.), *Visitation Articles and Injunctions of the Early Stuart Church*, Vol. 1 (Church of England Record Society, 1994), p. 91; K. Fincham (ed.), *Visitation Articles and Injunctions of the Early Stuart Church*, Volume 2 (Church of England Record Society, 1998), pp. xviii-xix, 147 and 206; Webster, *Godly Clergy*, p. 206.
11. Fuller, *Church History*, p. 378.
12. J. Bliss and W. Scott (eds), *The Works of William Laud* (Oxford, 1847–60), Vol. IV, pp. 253–5.
13. *Ibid.*, pp. 329–30.
14. Prynne, *Canterburies Doome*, p. 128.
15. *Ibid.*, p. 153.
16. Davies, *Caroline Captivity*, pp. 185–7.
17. Heylyn, *Cyprianus Anglicus*, p. 308. Culmer was a staunch puritan and was a violent iconoclast during the 1640s – see J. Spraggon, *Puritan Iconclasm during the English Civil War* (Woodbridge, 2003), p. 185.
18. Davies, *Caroline Captivity*, pp. 185–6.
19. Heylyn, *Cyprianus Anglicus*, p. 10.
20. M. Jansson (ed.), *Proceedings in the Opening Session of the Long Parliament, Volume I: 3 November–19 December 1640* (New York, 2000), p. 368 (footnote no. 2).
21. See list of Articles against Wilson in Swinnock, *The Life and Death of Mr. Tho. Wilson*, pp. 67–91; Bliss, *Works of William Laud*, IV, p. 254.
22. *Ibid.*, p. 253.
23. Sharpe, *Personal Rule*, p. 356.
24. Fuller, *Church History*, p. 378. Fuller speaks here of Laud silencing three ministers, but, with the inclusion of Thomas Wilson, the number appears to have been four.
25. Fincham, *Visitation Articles*, Vol. 2, p. 147.
26. Davies, *Caroline Captivity*, p. 188.
27. *Ibid.*
28. W.M. Palmer (ed.), *Episcopal Visitation Returns for Cambridgeshire, 1638–1665* (Cambridge, 1930), p. 73; Hutton, *Merry England*, p. 197.
29. William Prynne, *The Anitpathie of the English Lordly Prelacie* (London, 1641), pp. 268–9.

30 Davies, *Caroline Captivity*, p. 188.
31 Hutton, *Merry England*, p. 196; Davies, *Caroline Captivity*, pp. 188–9.
32 Davies, *Caroline Captivity*, p. 189.
33 Prynne, *Anitpathie of the English Lordly Prelacie*. The pagination of this section of the book is irregular and this page is unpaginated. It can be found between the pages numbered 290 and 291.
34 *Ibid*.
35 Davies, *Caroline Captivity*, p. 191.
36 *Ibid*., p. 191; K. Fincham, 'Episcopal Government, 1603–1640' in K. Fincham (ed.), *The Early Stuart Church, 1603–1642* (London, 1993), p. 85.
37 Davies, *Caroline Captivity*, pp. 192–3; Webster, *Godly Clergy*, p. 206.
38 Davies, *Caroline Captivity*, p. 194.
39 *Ibid*., pp. 194–5.
40 *Ibid*., p. 195; Hutton, *Merry England*, p. 196.
41 Robert Sanderson, *A Soveraigne Antidote against Sabbatarian Errours* (London, 1636), pp. 23 and 25.
42 Prynne, *Canterburies Doome*, p. 128.
43 Tanner. MS. 71, f.186r: Estwick to Ward, 23 January 1634.
44 *Ibid*., f.186v.
45 *Ibid*., f. 186r.
46 *Ibid*., f.186v.
47 Parker, *English Sabbath*, p. 193.
48 Cope, *Politics without Parliaments*, p. 60.
49 Davies, *Caroline Captivity*, pp. 185–95; Hill, *Society and Puritanism*, pp. 193–4; Webster, *Godly Clergy*, p. 229; M. Ingram 'Puritans and the Church Courts, 1560–1640' in C. Durston and J. Eales (eds), *The Culture of English Puritanism, 1560–1700* (Basingstoke, Macmillan, 1996), p. 89; R. Marchant, *The Puritans and the Church in the Diocese of York, 1560–1642* (London, 1960), pp. 81–5 and 97–8.
50 *Diary of Thomas Crosfield*, p. 68.
51 Parker, *English Sabbath*, p. 194.
52 M. Stieg, *Laud's Laboratory. The Diocese of Bath and Wells in the Early Seventeenth Century* (London, 1982), p. 292.
53 Parker, *English Sabbath*, pp. 194–5; Davies, *Caroline Captivity*, pp. 198–9; Ingram 'Puritans and the Church Courts, p. 89.
54 Davies, *Caroline Captivity*, p. 174; Sharpe, *Personal Rule*, p. 365; C. Hill, 'Seventeenth-century English Society and Sabbatarianism' in J.S. Bromley and E.H. Kossman (eds), *Britain and the Netherlands*, Vol. II (1964), p. 98; D.N. Klausner (ed.), *Herefordshire, Worcestershire. REED* (Toronto, 1990), pp. 143–4.
55 Ferdinando Nicolls, *The Life and Death of Mr Ignatius Jurdain* (London, 1654), pp. 6 and 13.
56 *William Whiteway Diary*, p. 135; Nicolls, *Ignatius Jurdain*, sig. A2v (epistle dedicatory).
57 Hamon L'Estrange, *The Reign of King Charles* (London, 1656), p. 133.
58 Bulstrode Whitelocke, *Memorials of the English Affairs* (London, 1682), pp. 16, 17 and 18.
59 Underdown, *Revel, Riot and Rebellion*, p. 30; Stieg, *Laud's Laboratory*, p. 293.
60 C. Haigh, The Plain Man's Pathways to Heaven. Kinds of Christianity in Post-Reformation England, 1570–1640 (Oxford, 2007), p. 116.

61 CSPD., 1635, p. 40.
62 D. Booy (ed.), The Notebooks of Nehemiah Wallington, 1618-1654. A Selection (Aldershot: Ashgate, 2007), pp. 99-100 and 119-25.
63 K. Fincham and N. Tyacke, Altars Restored. The Changing Face of English Religious Worship, 1547-c.1700 (Oxford, 2007), p. 147.
64 Thomas May, The History of Parliament of England (London, 1647), pp. 23-4.
65 M. Spufford, Contrasting Communities. English Villagers in the Sixteenth and Seventeenth Centuries (Cambridge, 1974), pp. 231-2.
66 Hill, Society and Puritanism, p. 187.
67 Davies, Caroline Captivity, p. 200; Cope, Politics without Parliaments, pp. 58-9.
68 Hutton, Merry England, p. 198. There is only one reference to Cerne's maypole in the records and it is therefore not clear if the maypole had stood there for many years before being cut down in 1635, or if it had been set up only shortly before. See: R. Conklin et al (eds), Dorset, Cornwall. REED (Toronto, 1999), p. 338.
69 CSPD, 1634-35, p. 2.
70 SP 16/255 No. 39.
71 Francis Cheynell, Sions memento, and Gods alarum (London, 1643), p. 38.
72 Edmund Calamy, Englands looking-glasse (London, 1642), p. 56.
73 William Mewe, The robbing and spoiling of Jacob and Israel (London, 1643), p. 27.
74 Stoyle, Loyalty and Locality, pp. 215-17; SP 16/250 No. 20.
75 Stoyle, Loyalty and Locality, p. 217.
76 Underdown, Revel, Riot and Rebellion, pp. 86-8.
77 J.M. Gibson (ed.), Kent. REED (Toronto, 2002), Vol. I, p. xci.
78 Underdown, Revel, Riot and Rebellion, p. 99.
79 Ibid., p. 67.
80 L. Marcus, 'Politics and Pastoral: Writing the Court on the Countryside', in K. Sharpe and P. Lake (eds), Culture and Politics in Early Stuart England (London, 1994), p. 154.
81 CSPD, 1633-34, p. 460.
82 Spufford, Contrasting Communities, p. 231; Sharpe, Personal Rule, p. 358.
83 Henry Burton, A Divine Tragedie Lately Acted (Amsterdam, 1636), sig. A3v.
84 Ibid., p. 6.
85 Ibid., pp. 7-8.
86 Ibid., p. 14.
87 Hutton, Merry England, p. 198.
88 Barnes, 'County Politics', p. 120.
89 W.B. Whitaker, Sunday in Tudor and Stuart Times (London, 1933), p. 132.
90 Heylyn, Cyprianus Anglicus, p. 260.
91 William Prynne, Newes From Ipswich (Ipswich, 1636), unpaginated.
92 Parker, English Sabbath, p. 217.
93 White, A Treatise of the Sabbath Day, dedication, sig. A2v and p. 235.
94 Ibid., pp. 229-30 and 255.
95 Ibid., pp. 240 and 235-6.
96 Ibid., pp. 280-1.
97 Ibid., p. 241.
98 Ibid., p. 233.

99 Ibid., p. 266.
100 Parker, *English Sabbath*, p. 200; P. Lake, 'The Laudians and the Argument from Authority', in B.Y. Kunze and D.D. Brautigam (eds), *Court, Country and Culture. Essays on Early Modern British History in Honor of Perez Zagorin* (New York, 1992), pp. 160–5 and 171–3.
101 White, *A Treatise of the Sabbath Day*, p. 207.
102 Fuller, *The Church History of Britain*, Vol. III, p. 373.
103 Burton, *A Brief Answer to a Late Treatise*, p. 5.
104 Ibid., p. 13.
105 Ibid., p. 16.
106 Ibid., pp. 22–3.
107 Ibid., p. 23.
108 George Walker, *The Doctrine of the Sabbath* (Amsterdam, 1638), p. 52.
109 White, *Examination ... of a Lawless Pamphlet*, pp. 4, 7, 44–5, 46 and sig. A3r.
110 Ibid., pp. 4–5.
111 Ibid., pp. 14–16.
112 Hutton, *Merry England*, pp. 193–4.
113 John Prideaux, *The Doctrine of the Sabbath* (London, 1634), p. 39; A. Milton, 'The creation of Laudianism: a new approach', in T. Cogswell, R. Cust and P. Lake (eds), *Politics, Religion, and Popularity in Early Stuart Britain* (Cambridge, 2002), pp. 162–84.
114 A. Milton, 'Licensing, Censorship, and Religious Orthodoxy in Early Stuart England, in *The Historical Journal*, 41, 3 (1998), p. 648.
115 Prideaux, *Doctrine of the Sabbath*, sigs A1r and A2v.
116 Ibid., sig. C1v.
117 Milton, 'Creation of Laudianism', p. 172; Hutton, *Merry England*, p. 194.
118 Peter Heylyn, *The History of the Sabbath. Second Book* (London, 1636), p. 247.
119 Ibid., pp. 245, 247–8, 249.
120 Peter Heylyn, *The History of the Sabbath. First Book* (London, 1636), p. 101.
121 Heylyn, *History of the Sabbath, Second Book*, p. 250.
122 Ibid., p. 250.
123 Heylyn, *History of the Sabbath, First Book*, p. 171.
124 Heylyn, *History of the Sabbath, Second Book*, pp. 164 and 251.
125 Ibid., p. 258; and Heylyn, *History of the Sabbath, First Book*, sig. A3r.
126 Heylyn, *History of the Sabbath, First Book*, sig. A4r.
127 Sanderson, *A Soveraigne Antidote*, sig. A4r.
128 John Pocklington, *Sunday No Sabbath* (London, 1636), p. 38. Pocklinton most probably wrote *Sunday No Sabbath* in a move to gain Laud's favour and to seek advancement within the Church – see: K. Fincham and N. Tyacke, *Altars Restored. The Changing Face of English Religious Worship, 1547–c.1700* (Oxford, 2007), p. 155.
129 Ibid., pp. 4–6 and 9.
130 Christopher Dow, *A Discourse of the Sabbath* (London, 1636), p. 25.
131 Ibid., pp. 46 and 53–4.
132 Ibid., pp. 10–11.
133 Christopher Dow, *Innovations Unjustly Charged Upon the Present Church and State* (London, 1637), pp. 86, 76–7.
134 J. Goring, *Godly Exercises or the Devil's Dance? Puritanism and Popular*

Culture in pre-Civil War England (London,1983), p. 20; Matthew Sylvester, *Reliquiae Baxterianae* (London, 1696), pp. 1-3.
135 Goring, *Godly Exercises or the Devil's Dance?*, p. 20.
136 There is not space in this book to discuss the works of poets and playwrights in any depth. For further reading, see Marcus, *Politics of Mirth*, passim.
137 Hutton, *Merry England*, p. 194.
138 *Ibid.*
139 Matthew Walbancke, *Annalia Dubrensia* (London, 1636), sig. B2r.
140 *Ibid.*, sig. D4v.
141 Robert Dover, 'A Congratulatory Poem', in *Annalia Dubrensia*.
142 Robert Herrick, *Hesperides* (London, 1648), p. 75.
143 *Ibid.*, pp. 300-1.
144 *Ibid.*, p. 301.
145 M. Butler, *The Stuart Court Masque and Political Culture* (Cambridge, 2008), pp. 354-5.
146 John Milton, *A maske presented at Ludlow Castle* (London, 1637), pp. 4-5 and 28.
147 Burton, *A Divine Tragedie Lately Acted*, p. 2; Prynne, *Newes from Ipswich*, unpaginated.
148 Milton, 'Licensing, Censorship, and Religious Orthodoxy', p. 641. See also: H. Pierce, *Unseemly Pictures. Graphic Satire and Politics in Early Modern England* (Yale, 2008). pp. 29-32 and 82-103.
149 K. Fincham (ed.), *The Early Stuart Church, 1603-1642* (London, 1993), p. 16; Prynne, *A Briefe Polemicall Dissertation*, Sig. A2v; H. Pierce, *Unseemly Pictures*, p. 102.
150 D. Cressy, *England on Edge. Crisis and Revolution, 1640-1642* (Oxford, 2006), pp. 284-5; Hill, *Society and Puritanism*, p. 192; Hutton, *Merry England*, p. 193.
151 Hill, *Society and Puritanism*, p. 192.
152 Milton, 'Licensing, Censorship, and Religious Orthodoxy', p. 644.
153 Milton, 'Licensing, Censorship, and Religious Orthodoxy', pp. 636-7, 642 and 650.
154 Richard Bernard, *A Threefold Treatise of the Sabbath* (London, 1641), sig. A2v.
155 *Ibid.*, pp. 223, 88, 91, 92, 93, 228, 231 and 232-3.
156 William Gouge, *The Sabbaths Sanctification* (London, 1641), sig. A2r and p. 30.
157 George Abbot, *Vindiciae Sabbathi* (London, 1641), sig. A3v, and pp. 64, 65 and 87.
158 George Hakewill, *A Short but Cleare Discourse* (London, 1641), p. 29; William Ames, *The Marrow of Sacred Divinity* (London, 1642), p. 298.
159 Twisse, *Morality of the Fourth Commandment*, p. 244.
160 Lewes Hughes, *Signes from Heaven* (London, 1642), p. 10.
161 George Walker, *The Doctrine of the Holy Weekly Sabbath* (London, 1641), p. 158.
162 E. Cope (ed.), *Proceedings of the Short Parliament of 1640* (London, 1977), p. 147; J.D. Maltby (ed.), *The Short Parliament (1640) Diary of Sir Thomas Aston* (London, 1988), p. 7.
163 Cope, *Proceedings of Short Parliament*, p. 151; Maltby, *Diary of Thomas Aston*, pp. 8, 54, 94 and 256.

164 Maltby, *Diary of Thomas Aston*, p. 87; Cope, *Proceedings of Short Parliament*, pp. 203–4.
165 Bernard, *A Threefold Treatise*, sigs A3r–A3v.
166 Walker, *The Doctrine of the Holy Weekly Sabbath*, sig. A3r.
167 Sylvester, *Reliquiae Baxterianae*, p. 18.
168 J. Morrill, 'The Religious Context of the English Civil War', in *Transactions of the Royal Historical Society*, 5th Series, Vol. 34 (1984), *passim*.
169 Hutton, *Merry England*, p. 200; Jansson, *Proceedings in Long Parliament*, pp. 368, 372, 373 and 377.
170 Hutton, *Merry England*, p. 200.
171 C. Durston, 'Puritan Rule and the Failure of Cultural Revolution, 1645–1660', in C. Durston and J. Eales (eds), *The Culture of English Puritanism, 1560–1700* (London, 1996), p. 213; Milton, 'The creation of Laudianism', p. 175.
172 Daniel Neal, *The History of the Puritans* (Five volumes, London, 1822), Vol. II, p. 419.
173 *Ibid.*, Vol. III, p. 36.
174 Thomason Tract, 669.f.7[12]: Die Veneris 50. Maij. 1643.
175 C.H. Firth and R.S. Rait (eds), *Acts and Ordinances of the Interregnum, 1642–1660* (three volumes, London, 1911), Vol. I, pp. 420–1.
176 *Ibid.*, Vol. I, p. 599.
177 Whitaker, *Sunday in Tudor and Stuart Times*, p. 155.
178 Underdown, *Revel, Riot and Rebellion*, pp. 5, 40, 44, 82, 88–9, 95–6 and 179.
179 A. Hughes, 'Local History and the Origins of the Civil War', in R. Cust and A. Hughes (eds), *Conflict in Early Stuart England. Studies in Religion and Politics, 1603–1642* (London, 1989), pp. 241–3; See also M. Ingram, *Church Courts, Sex and Marriage in England, 1570–1640* (Cambridge, 1987), pp. 101–2 and Stoyle, *Loyalty and Locality*, p. 215.
180 Stoyle, *Loyalty and Locality*, pp. 220–1.
181 Hutton, *Merry England*, pp. 204–5.
182 A.H.A. Hamilton (ed.), *The Notebook of Sir John Northcote* (London, 1877), p. 102.
183 C. Russell, *The Fall of the British Monarchies, 1637–1642* (Oxford, 1991), p. 223.
184 W.A. Mepham, 'Essex Drama Under Puritanism and the Commonwealth' in *The Essex Review*, Vol. 58 (1949), pp. 155–61 and 181–5; B. Lowe, 'Early Records of the Morris in England', in *Journal of the English Folk Dance & Song Society*, Vol. 7, No. 2 (1957), pp. 73–4; *Oxford Dictionary of National Biography* [ODNB] (Oxford, 2004), Vol. 4, pp. 82–4.
185 Hutton, *Merry England*, p. 205; *ODNB*, Vol. 59, pp. 872–80 and Vol. 17, p. 406. Note that, although Durham celebrated May games, unlike other poems in *Annalia Dubrensia*, Durham's verse was not explicitly anti-Puritan. He may have become more radical in the years after *Annalia Dubrensia's* publication. The *ONDB* records that by 1642 he was 'a strong puritan'. It is possible that Durham's puritan beliefs developed and strengthened over time.
186 J.T. Cliffe, *The Yorkshire Gentry from the Reformation to the Civil War* (London, 1969), pp. 343–4; B.G. Blackwood, *The Lancashire Gentry and the Great Rebellion, 1640–1660* (Manchester, 1978), p. 65. Of those Puritans in England who were royalist in the 1640s, most were so only in the second

civil war; there were very few puritan royalists between 1642 and 1646 – see: P.R. Newman, *The Old Service: Royalist regimental colonels and the Civil War, 1642–1646* (Manchester, 1993), p. 15.

187 C. Whitfield (ed.), *Robert Dover and the Cotswold Games* (London, 1962), pp. 99–220; and *ODNB*, Vol. 15, pp. 254–60; Vol. 19, pp. 278–81; Vol. 37, pp. 812–15; and Vol. 38, pp. 676–7.

188 *ODNB*, Vol. 6, pp. 507–9; Vol. 9, pp. 485–9; Vol. 11, pp. 385–6; and Vol. 37, pp. 559–61.

189 John Bond, *A Doore of Hope* (London, 1641), p. 10 (my italics). Also, see M. Stoyle, *From Deliverance to Destruction: Rebellion and Civil War in an English City* (Exeter, 1996), pp. 50 and 168–70.

190 Sylvester, *Reliquiae Baxterianae*, p. 31.

191 J. Cokayne, *Englands Troubles Anatomized* (London, 1644), p. 47; England and Wales, *A Plea for the Parliament* (London, 1642), pp. 9–10.

192 Edmund Calamy, *Englands Antidote against the Plague of Civil War* (London, 1645), pp. 3–4.

193 P. Collinson, *The Birthpangs of Protestant England* (London, 1988), p. 152.

194 Richard Baxter, *A Holy Commonwealth* (London, 1659), pp. 456–7.

195 Robert Greville, *A discourse, opening the nature of that episcopacie which is exercised in England* (London, 1641), pp. 96–7.

196 John Oldmixon, *The History of England During the Reign of the Royal House of Stuart* (London, 1730), p. 208.

197 Britannicus, *Britannicus His Pill to cure Malignancy* (London, 1644), p. 7. I am very grateful to Mark Stoyle for giving me this reference.

198 Anon., *A New Remonstrance where is declared who are the Malignant Party* (London, 1642), p. A3r.

199 Bond, *Doore of Hope*, pp. 7, 10, 24, 29, and 93–5.

200 John Bond, *Occasus Occidentalis* (London, 1645), p. 31; Stoyle, *Loyalty and Locality*, p. 222.

201 Sylvester, *Reliquiae Baxterianae*, p. 42.

202 Thomason Tract, E. 258 (11): *Perfect Occurrences of Parliament, 3–10 January 1645*; Stoyle, *Loyalty and Locality*, p. 221.

203 Thomason Tract, E. 52 (12): *The Spie, 20–25 June 1644*; Stoyle, *Loyalty and Locality*, pp. 221–2.

204 Thomason Tract, E.298[24]: *Mercurius Britanicus, 25 August–1 September 1645*.

205 James Howell (?), *The True Informer who in the following discovrse or colloqvie discovereth unto the world the chiefe causes of the sad distempers in Great Britanny* (Oxford, 1643), p. 31.

206 Anon., *A sad warning to all prophane, malignant spirits* (London, 1642), pp. 3–4; Anon., *True New Newes* (London?, 1642), pp. 4–5; John Vicars, *A Looking-Glasse for Malignants* (London, 1643), p. 13; A. Clark (ed.), *The Life and Times of Anthony Wood, i: 1632–1653* (Oxford, 1891), p. 49; Underdown, *Revel, Riot and Rebellion*, p. 177.

207 T.T. Lewis (ed.), *The Letters of the Lady Brilliana Harley, Wife of Sir Robert Harley* (London, 1854), p. 167.

208 K. Lindley, *Popular Politics and Religion in Civil War London* (Aldershot, 1997), p. 211.

209 Collinson, *Birthpangs of Protestant England*, p. 141.

210 Hutton, *Merry England*, p. 210; R. Ashton, *Counter Revolution. The Second*

Civil War and its Origins, 1646–48 (London, 1994), p. 376; and M. Stoyle, *West Britons: Cornish Identities and the Early Modern British State* (Exeter University Press, 2002), p. 128.
211 Hutton, *Merry England*, pp. 204–5.
212 Thomason Tract, 669.f.6 (1): *A Copie of the Petition presented to the Kings Majesty by the high Sheriffe, accompanied with many hundreds of Gentlemen and Free-holders of the County of Rutland* (London, 1642).
213 Anon., *The Humble Petition of the Knights, Justices of the Peace, Gentlemen, Ministers, Free-holders and others of the Countie of Cornwall* (London, 1642), p. 2. I am very grateful to Mark Stoyle for giving me this reference.
214 Thomas Trescott, *The Zealous Magistrate* (London, 1642), p. 25; Stoyle, *Loyalty and Locality*, p. 226.
215 William Mewe, *The Robbing and Spoiling of Jacob and Israel Considered* (London, 1643), p. 27.
216 William Greenhill, *The Axe at the Root* (London, 1643), pp. 21–2.
217 Thomason Tract, 669.f.7 [12]: *Die Veneris 50 Maij. 1643*; Thomason Tract, E. 101 [24]: *Certaine Informations from Severall Parts of the Kingdome*, 8–15 May 1643; Thomason Tract, E. 101 [15]: *Mercurius Civicus*, 4–11 May 1643; Richard Culmer, *Cathedrall newes from Canterbury* (London, 1644), p. 7. Some copies of the *Book of Sports* were also burned by the Exchange at Cornhill – see Thomason Tract, E. 249 [6]: *A Perfect Diurnall of the Passages in Parliament*, 8–15 May 1643.
218 George Gillespie, *A Sermon Preached before the Honourable House of Commons* (London, 1644), pp. 18–19.
219 John Ward, *The Good-will of Him that Dwelt in the Bush* (London, 1645), p. 17. See also: John Taylor, *A Dog's Elegy* (London, 1644), p. 7; Samuel Gibson, *The Ruine of the Authors and Fomentors of Civill Warres* (London, 1645), pp. 25–6; and Anon., *A Declaration of a Strange and Wonderfull Monster* (London, 1646), p. 4.
220 Clive Holmes (ed.), *The Suffolk Committees for Scandalous Ministers, 1644–1646* (Suffolk Record Society, Vol. XIII, 1970), pp. 32, 75 and 76. See also: pp. 19, 34, 37, 52, 61, 69, 70, 71, 77–8, 79, 85, 88 and 92.

Conclusion

1 George Fox, *A journal or historical account of the life, travels, sufferings, Christian experiences and labour of love in the work of the ministry, of ... George Fox* (London, 1694), p. 25. Here the non-conformist Fox describes how, in 1649, he lobbied magistrates and judges to suppress wakes and May games.
2 C.H. Firth and R.S. Rait (eds), *Acts and Ordinances of the Interregnum 1642–1660* (three volumes, London, 1911), Vol. II, pp. 385 and 1162–3.
3 J. Spurr, *English Puritanism, 1603–1689* (London, 1998), p. 118. See also J. Miller, *After the Civil Wars. English Politics and Government in the Reign of Charles II* (Longman, Harlow, 2000), p. 130.
4 C. Durston, 'Puritan Rule and the Failure of Cultural Revolution, 1645–1660', in C. Durston and J. Eales (eds), *The Culture of English Puritanism, 1560–1700* (London, 1996), pp. 217–18; Spurr, *English Puritanism*, p. 118.

5 R. Hutton, *The Rise and Fall of Merry England. The Ritual Year, 1400–1700* (Oxford, 1994), p. 221.
6 A.H.A. Hamilton, *Quarter Sessions from Queen Elizabeth to Queen Anne* (London, 1878), p. 161.
7 D. Underdown, *Revel, Riot and Rebellion. Popular Politics and Culture in England, 1603–1660* (Oxford, 1985), p. 263; Durston, 'Puritan Rule', p. 221.
8 Durston, 'Puritan Rule', p. 223.
9 P.S. Seaver, *Allington's World. A Puritan Artisan in Seventeenth-Century London* (Stanford University Press, 1985), p. 149.
10 Underdown, *Revel Riot and Rebellion*, p. 269.
11 Matthew Sylvester, *Reliquiae Baxterianae* (London, 1696), p. 85.
12 Durston, 'Puritan Rule', p. 231.
13 *Ibid.*, pp. 220–1.
14 Underdown, *Revel, Riot and Rebellion*, p. 259.
15 Hutton, *Merry England*, p. 223; Underdown, *Revel, Riot and Rebellion*, pp. 274–5; T.S. Henricks, *Disputed Pleasures. Sport and Society in Pre-industrial England* (New York; Westport, Connecticut; and London, 1991), p. 106.
16 Hutton, *Merry England*, p. 223.
17 R. Parkinson (ed.), *The Life of Adam Martindale, Written by Himself* (The Chetham Society, Manchester, 1845), p. 156.
18 Underdown, *Revel, Riot and Rebellion*, p. 275.
19 Henry Jessey, *The Lords Loud Call to England* (London, 1660), p. 24 – quoting from a letter dated 7 May 1660. The town referred to is Newcastle.
20 Hutton, *Merry England*, p. 233.
21 James Heath, *The Glories and Magnificent Triumphs of the Blessed Restitution of His Sacred Majesty K. Charles* (London, 1662), p. 206; Hutton, *Merry England*, pp. 225–6; and P. Rogers, 'The Maypole in the Strand: Pope and the Politics of Revelry', in *British Journal of Eighteenth-Century Studies*, Vol. 28, No. 1 (2005), pp. 83 and 85.
22 Underdown, *Revel, Riot and Rebellion*, p. 283.
23 *Ibid.*, pp. 280–1; Hutton, *Merry England*, pp. 229–30 and 238–9; L.S. Marcus, *The Politics of Mirth. Jonson, Herrick, Milton, Marvell and the Defence of Old Holiday Pastimes* (Chicago, 1986), p. 262; E. Griffin, *England's Revelry. A History of Popular Sport and Pastimes, 1660–1830* (Oxford, 2005), pp. 41–2 and 59–67; and Durston, 'Puritan Rule', p. 231.
24 Hutton, *Merry England*, p. 229; R. Hutton, *The Stations of the Sun. A History of the Ritual Year in Britain* (Oxford, 1996), p. 257.
25 Hutton, *Merry England*, p. 231.
26 *Ibid.*, pp. 232–3.
27 K.L. Parker, *The English Sabbath. A Study of doctrine and discipline from the Reformation to the Civil War* (Cambridge, 1988), p. 219; Hutton, *Merry England*, pp. 232–3.
28 Charles II, *A Proclamation for the Observation of the Lords Day* (London, 1663).
29 Parker, *English Sabbath*, p. 219.
30 J.R. Tanner (ed.), *Constitutional Documents of the Reign of James I, 1603–1625* (Cambridge, 1930), p. 49.

Bibliography

Primary Sources

I. Manuscripts

BODLEIAN LIBRARY
Tanner. MS. 71.

DEVON RECORD OFFICE
Quarter Session Order Books, Volumes 1–6 (1592–1633).

NATIONAL ARCHIVES
SP 16/96 No. 7.
SP 16/96 No. 7 (i).
SP 16/247 No. 24.
SP 16/248 No. 12.
SP 16/250 No. 20.
SP 16/255 No. 39.
SP 16/255 No. 39 (i).
SP 16/255 No. 39 (ii).
SP 16/255 No. 39 (iv).
ASSI 24/20 LH 36.

SOMERSET RECORD OFFICE
Q/SR 2/118.
Q/SR 3/71.
Q/So3, fol. 394.
Q/SR 61(i)/52.
DD/PH 222, fol. 120.

II. Reports of the Historical Manuscripts Commission

HMC *Reports on the Manuscripts of the Duke of Buccleuch and Queensbury*, Vol. I (London, 1899).
HMC *Reports on the Manuscripts of the Duke of Buccleuch and Queensbury*, Vol. III (London, 1926).
HMC *Report on the Manuscripts of Lord Montagu of Beaulieu* (London, 1900).
HMC, *Report on the Manuscripts of Reginald Rawdon Hastings*, Vol. IV, (ed.) F. Bickley (1947).
HMC *Seventh Report*, Appendix.
HMC *Twelfth Report*, Appendix, Part IV, *The Manuscripts of the Duke of Rutland* (1888), Vol. I.

III. Records of Early English Drama
Bristol, M.C. Pilkington (ed.), (Toronto, 1997).
Cambridge, A.N. Nelson (ed.), (Toronto, 1989).
Cheshire including Chester, E. Baldwin *et al* (eds), (Toronto, 2007).
Chester, L.M. Clopper (ed.), (Toronto, 1979).
Coventry, R.W. Ingram (ed.), (Toronto, 1981)
Cumberland, Westmoreland, Gloucestershire, A. Douglas and P. Greenfield (eds), (Toronto, 1986).
Devon, J.M. Wasson (ed.), (Toronto, 1986).
Dorset, Cornwall, R. Conklin, S.L. Joyce *et al* (eds), (Toronto, 1999).
Herefordshire, Worcestershire, D.N. Klausner (ed.), (Toronto, 1990).
Kent, J.M. Gibson (ed.), (Toronto, 2002).
Lancashire, D. George (ed.), (Toronto, 1991).
Newcastle-upon-Tyne, J.J. Anderson (ed.), (Toronto, 1982).
Norwich 1540–1642, D. Galloway (ed.), (Toronto, 1984).
Oxford, J.R. Elliott *et al* (eds), (Toronto, 2004).
Shropshire, J.A.B. Somerset (ed.), (Toronto, 1994).
Somerset, J. Stokes (ed.), (Toronto, 1996).
Sussex, C. Louis (ed.), (Toronto, 2000).
York, A.F. Johnston and M. Rogerson (eds), (Toronto, 1979).

IV. Books
George Abbot, *Vindiciae Sabbathi* (London, 1641).
Thomas Adams, *The Happines of the Church* (London, 1618).
Richard Allestree, *The Whole Duty of Man* (London, 1661).
William Ames, *The Marrow of Sacred Divinity* (London, 1642).
Anon., *A Declaration of a Strange and Wonderfull Monster* (London, 1646).
Anon., *A New remonstrance wherein is declared who are the malignant party of this kingdome* (London, 1642).
Anon., *A sad warning to all prophane, malignant spirits* (London, 1642).
Anon., *Britannicus His Pill to cure Malignancy* (London, 1644).
Anon., *The humble petition of the knights, iustices of the peace, gentlemen, ministers, free-holders and others of the countie of Cornwall* (London, 1642).
Anon., *The Bishops Potion* (London, 1641).
Anon., *The seconde tome of homelyes ... set out by the authoritie of the Quenes Maiestie* (London, 1563).
Anon., *True New Newes* (London?, 1642).
Roger Ascham, *Toxophilus, the schole of shootinge conteyned in two bokes* (London, 1545).
Gervase Babington, *Certaine Plaine, briefe, and comfortable Notes upon euerie Chapter of Genesis* (London, 1592).
Gervase Babington, *A Very Fruitful Exposition of the Commandments* (1583).
Gervase Babington, *A Verie Fruitful Exposition of the Commandements* (London, 1615).
Gervase Babington, *The Workes of Gervase Babington* (London, 1615).
Samuel Bachiler, *The Campe Royall* (London, 1629).
James Balmford, *Three Posicions Concerning the Authoritie of the Lordes Daye* (London, 1607).
Peter Barker, *A Judicious and Painefull Exposition upon the Ten Commandements* (London, 1624).
Robert Barnes, *A supplicacion vnto the most gracyous prynce H. the viij* (London, 1534).
P.H. Barnum (ed.), *Dives and Pauper* (two volumes, Oxford, 1980).

John Barwick, *A Summarie Account of ... Thomas late Lord Bishop of Duresme* (London, 1660).
John Bastwick, *The Severall Humble Petitions of D. Bastwick, M. Burton, W. Prynne ... to the Humble House of Parliament* (London, 1641).
Stephen Bateman, *The new arival of the three gracis, into Anglia Lamenting the abusis of this present age* (London, 1580).
Richard Baxter, *A Holy Commonwealth* (London, 1659).
R. Bayley, *The Life of William Now Lord Archbishop of Canterbury* (London, 1643).
L. Bayly, *The Practice of Piety. Directing a Christian How to Walke, that He May Please God* (London, 1616).
Thomas Beard, *The Theatre of God's Judgements* (London, 1597).
Thomas Becon, *The Principles of Christian Religion* (London, 1553).
Thomas Becon, *A New Postil* (London, 1566).
Thomas Becon, *The Demaundes of Holy Scripture* (London, 1577).
Thomas Becon, *Catechism with other pieces written by him in the reign of Edward VI* (Cambridge, 1844).
Henry Bedel, *A Sermon Exhortyng to Pitie the Poore* (London, 1573).
Richard Bernard, *A Double Catechisme* (Cambridge, 1607).
Richard Bernard, *A Threefold Treatise of the Sabbath* (London, 1641).
Samuel Bird, *A Friendlie Communication or Dialogue betweene Paule and Demas* (London, 1580).
Robert Bolton, *Some Generall Directions* (London, 1626).
Robert Bolton, *Some General Directions* (London, 1638).
John Bond, *A Doore of Hope* (London, 1641).
John Bond, *Occasus Occidentalis* (London, 1645).
Nicholas Bownd, *The Doctrine of the Sabbath* (London, 1595).
Nicholas Bownd, *Sabbathum Veteris et Novi Testamenti: or, The True Doctrine of the Sabbath* (London, 1606).
Theophilus Brabourne, *A Discourse Upon the Sabbath Day* (London, 1628).
Theophilus Brabourne, *A Defence of that most Ancient, and Sacred ordinance of Gods the Sabbath Day* (London, 1632).
John Bradford, *Godly Meditations uppon the ten Commaundmentes* (London, 1567).
William Bradshaw, *A Protestation of the Kings Supremacie* (Amsterdam?, 1605).
A. Brandeis (ed.), *Jacob's Well. An English Treatise on the Cleansing of Man's Conscience* (Early English Text Society, London, 1900).
Edward Brerewood, *A Learned Treatise of the Sabaoth* (Oxford, 1630).
Edward Brerewood, *A Second Treatise of the Sabbath* (Oxford, 1632).
Nicholas Breton, *Fantasticks seruing for a perpetuall prognostication* (London, 1626).
John Bridges, *A sermon, preached at Paules Crosse on the Monday in Whitson weeke Anno Domini, 1571* (London, 1571).
Britannicus, *Britannicus His Pill to cure Malignancy* (London, 1644).
Thomas Broad, *Three Questions Answered* (Oxford, 1621).
Thomas Broad, *Tractatus de Sabbato* (n.p., 1627).
Matthew Bryan, *A Perswasive to the Stricter Observation of the Lords Day* (London, 1686).
Heinrich Bullinger, *Fiftie Godlie And Learned Sermons* (London, 1577).
Edmund Bunny, *The Whole Summe of Christian Religion* (London, 1576).
Henry Burton, *The Law and the Gospel Reconciled* (London, 1631).
Henry Burton, *A Brief Answer to a Late Treatise on the Sabbath Day* (Amsterdam, 1635).

Henry Burton, *A Divine Tragedie Lately Acted* (Amsterdam, 1636).
Henry Burton, *For God and the King* (Amsterdam, 1636).
William Burton, "The Anatomie of Belial" in *Workes* (London, 1602).
William Burton, *An Abstract of the Doctrine of the Sabbaoth* (London, 1606).
Richard Byfield, *The Doctrine of the Sabbath Vindicated* (London, 1631).
Edmund Calamy, *Englands looking-glasse* (London, 1642).
Edmund Calamy, *Englands Antidote against the Plague of Civil War* (London, 1645).
Richard Carew, *The Survey of Cornwall* (London, 1602).
Thomas Cartwright, *A Confutation of the Rhemists Translation* (Leyden, 1618).
Charles I, *The Kings Majesties Declaration to his Subjects, Concerning Lawful Sports to Be Used* (London, 1633).
Charles II, *A Proclamation for the Observation of the Lords Day* (London, 1663).
Francis Cheynell, *Sions memento, and Gods alarum* (London, 1643).
Robert Cleaver, *A Godly Form of Household Governement* (London, 1598).
Robert Cleaver, *A Declaration of the Christian Sabbath* (London, 1625).
J. Cokayne, *Englands Troubles Anatomized* (London, 1644).
Thomas Coryate, *Coryats Crambe* (London, 1611).
John Cosin, *A Collection of Private Devotions* (London, 1627).
Thomas Cooper, *An Admonition to the People of England* (London, 1589).
William Crashawe, *The Sermon Preached at the Cross* (London, 1609).
William Crashawe, *Milke for Babes, or, A North-Countrie Catechisme* (London, 1618).
Robert Crowley, *One and thyrtye Epigrammes* (London, 1550).
Richard Culmer, *Cathedrall newes from Canterbury* (London, 1644).
John Deacon, *A Treatise, intituled; Nobody is My Name* (London, 1585).
Thomas Dekker, *The Seven Deadly Sins of London*, (ed.) H.F.B. Brett-Smith (Oxford, 1922).
Arthur Dent, *The Plaine Mans Path-way to Heaven* (London, 1601).
Edward Dering, *Workes* (London, 1597).
Edward Dering, *A brief & necessary instruction, verye needful to bee knowen of all householders ... A briefe and necessarie catechisme* (London, 1605).
Simonds D'Ewes, *A Compleat Journal* (London, 1693).
John Dod, *A Treatise or exposition upon the ten commandements* (London, 1603).
John Dod, *A Plaine and Familiar Exposition of the Ten Commandments* (London, 1604).
Christopher Dow, *A Discourse of the Sabbath* (London, 1636).
Christopher Dow, *Innovations Unjustly Charged Upon the Present Church and State* (London, 1637).
Michael Drayton, *The Muses Elizium* (London, 1630).
W.H. Dunham and S. Pargelis, *Complaint and Reform in England, 1436–1714. Fifty Writings of the Time on Politics, Religion, Society, Economics, Architecture, Science, and Education* (New York, 1938).
Edward Elton, *Gods Holy Mind* (London, 1625).
Sir Thomas Elyot, *The Boke Named The Gouvernor*, ed. Foster Watson (Everyman Library, 1907).
England and Wales, *A Plea for the Parliament* (London, 1642).
George Estye, *A Most Sweete and Comfortable Exposition, upon the ten commaundements* (London, 1602).
George Estye, *Certaine Godly and learned Expositions upon divers parts of scripture* (London, 1603).

John Falconer, *A Brief Refutation of John Traskes Judaical and Novel Fancyes* (Saint Omer, English College Press, 1618).
Christopher Fetherstone, *A dialogue agaynst light, lewde, and lasciuious daunting* (London, 1582).
Dudley Fenner, *Certain Godly and Learned Treatises* (Edinburgh, 1592).
John Field, *A Caveat for Parsons Howlet* (London, 1581).
John Field, *A Godly Exhortation by Occasion of the Late Judgement of God, shewed at Parris-garden* (London, 1583).
Abraham Fleming, *The Footepath of Faith* (London, 1581).
George Fox, *A journal or historical account of the life, travels, sufferings, Christian experiences and labour of love in the work of the ministry, of ... George Fox* (London, 1694).
T. Fuller, *The Church History of Britain*, ed. J. Nicholls, (three volumes, London, 1837).
T. Fuller, *The Appeal of Injured Innocence* (London, 1659).
F.J. Furnivall (ed.), *Robert of Brunne's 'Handlyng Synne'*, (London, 1901-1903).
Nicholas Gibbons, *Questions and Disputations* (London, 1601).
Samuel Gibson, *The Ruine of the Authors and Fomentors of Civill Warres* (London, 1645).
George Gifford, *A Catechisme* (London, 1583).
Anthony Gilby, *A Pleasaunt Dialogue, Betweene a Souldier of Barwicke, and an English Chaplaine* (London?, 1581).
George Gillespie, *A Sermon Preached before the Honourable House of Commons* (London, 1644).
Stephen Gosson, *The Schoole of Abuse* (London, 1579).
William Gouge, *The Sabbaths Sanctification* (London, 1641).
Richard Greenham, *The Workes*, (London, 1599).
William Greenhill, *The Axe at the Root* (London, 1643).
Robert Greville, *A discourse, opening the nature of that episcopacie which is exercised in England* (London, 1641).
George Hakewill, *A Short but Cleare Discourse* (London, 1641).
Thomas Hall, *Funebria Florae, the Downfall of May-games* (London, 1660).
William Harrison, *Difference of Hearers* (London, 1614).
William Harrison, *A Description of England*, ed. F.J. Furnivall (London, 1877).
James Heath, *The Glories and Magnificent Triumphs of the Blessed Restitution of His Sacred Majesty K. Charles* (London, 1662).
Henry VIII, *A necessary doctrine and erudicion for any chrysten man* (London, 1543).
Robert Herrick, *Hesperides* (London, 1648).
Peter Heylyn, *The History of the Sabbath* (London, 1636).
Peter Heylyn, *A Briefe and Moderate Answer* (London, 1637).
Peter Heylyn, *Cyprianus Anglicus or the Life of Archbishop Laud* (London, 1668).
Adam Hill, *The Crie of England* (London, 1595).
William Hinde, *A Faithfull Remonstrance Of The Holy Life and Happy Death of Iohn Bruen of Bruen Stapleford in the County of Chester* (London, 1641).
Thomas Holland, *A Sermon Preached at St Pauls* (Oxford, 1601).
John Hooper, *A Declaration of the Ten Holy Commaundementes* (Zurich, 1549).
James Howell (?), *The True Informer who in the following discovrse or colloqvie discovereth unto the world the chiefe causes of the sad distempers in Great Britanny* (Oxford, 1643).
John Howson, *A Sermon preached at St Maries in Oxford* (Oxford, 1602).
Lewes Hughes, *Signes from Heaven* (London, 1642).

E. Hyde, *The History of the Rebellion and the Civil Wars in England*, (W. Dunn-Macray (ed.), six volumes, Oxford, 1888).
M. Jamieson (ed.), *Ben Jonson. Three Comedies* (London, 1966).
James I, *The Kings Majesties Declaration to his Subjects, Concerning Lawful Sports to Be Used* (London, 1618).
James I, *The effect of certaine branches of the statute made in anno 33. Henrici VIIJ touching the maintenance of artillery, and the punishment of such as vse vnlawfull games* (London, 1625).
Henry Jessey, *The Lords Loud Call to England* (London, 1660).
Richard Jones, *A Briefe and Necessarie Catechisme* (London, 1583).
White Kennett, *Parochial Antiquities* (Oxford, 1695).
William Kethe, *A Sermon Made at Blandford Forum* (London, 1571).
John King, *Lectures upon Ionas* (Oxford, 1597).
John Knewstub, *The Lectures of John Knewstub* (London, 1577).
G. Kristensson (ed.), *John Mirk's Instructions for Parish Priests* (Lund, 1974).
William Lambard, *The Duties of Constables* (London, 1583).
Hamon L'Estrange, *The Reign of King Charles* (London, 1656).
John Ley, *Sunday A Sabbath* (London, 1641).
Thomas Lovell, *A Dialogue between Custom and Veritie* (London, 1581).
Peter Martyr, *A briefe Treatise concerning the use and abuse of Dauncing* (London, 1580?).
Peter Martyr, *The common places of the most famous and renowmed diuine Doctor Peter Martyr* (London, 1583).
Thomas May, *The History of Parliament of England* (London, 1647).
T. May, *The History of the Parliament of England*, ed. F. Meseres (London, 1812).
C.H. McIlwain (ed.), *The Political Works of James I* (Cambridge, 1918).
William Mewe, *The robbing and spoiling of Jacob and Israel Considered* (London, 1643).
John Milton, *A maske presented at Ludlow Castle* (London, 1637).
Anthony Munday, *A Second and Third Blast of Retrait from Plaies* (London, 1580).
Wolfgang Musculus, *Commonplaces* (London, 1563).
Ferdinando Nicolls, *The Life and Death of Mr Ignatius Jurdain* (London, 1654).
John Norden, *A Sinfull Mans Solace* (London, 1585).
J. Northbrooke, *Spiritus est vicarious Christi in terra, A Treatise wherein Dicing, Dauncing, Vaine Playes or Enterludes, with Other Idle Pastimes Commonly Used on the Sabbath Day, are Reproved* (London, 1579).
Alexander Nowell, *A Catechism* (ed. G.E. Corrie, Cambridge, 1853).
Robert Parsons, *A Brief Discours Contayning Certayne Reasons Why Catholiques Refuse to Goe to Church* (Doway, 1580).
William Perkins, *A Golden Chaine* (London, 1591).
William Perkins, *A Commentarie or Exposition upon the Five First Chapters of the Epistle to the Galatians* (Cambridge, 1604).
William Perkins, *A godly and learned exposition or commentarie vpon the three first chapters of the Reuelation* (London, 1606).
William Perkins, *The Whole Treatise of the Cases of Conscience* (Cambridge, 1606).
John Pocklington, *Sunday No Sabbath* (London, 1636).
John Prideaux, *The Doctrine of the Sabbath* (London, 1634).
William Prynne, *Histrio-mastix* (London, 1633).
William Prynne, *Newes From Ipswich* (Ipswich, 1636).
William Prynne, *The Anitpathie of the English Lordly Prelacie* (London, 1641).

William Prynne, *Canterburies Doome* (London, 1646).
William Prynne, *A Briefe Polemicall Dissertation* (London, 1654).
Francis Quarles, *Emblemes* (London, 1635).
Robert of Brunne, *Handlyng Synne*, ed. F.J. Furnivall (Early English Text Society, London, 1901).
Hugh Roberts, *The Day of Hearing* (Oxford, 1600).
Humphrey Roberts, *An Earnest Complaint* (London, 1572).
John Rogers, *The Summe of Christianite* (1580?).
Richard Rogers, *Seven Treatises* (London, 1603).
Thomas Rogers, *The Catholic Doctrine of the Church of England*, ed. J.J.S. Perowne (Cambridge, 1954).
Edmund Rudierd, *The Thunderbolt of Gods Wrath* (London, 1618).
Robert Sanderson, *A Soveraigne Antidote against Sabbatarian Errours* (London, 1636).
Robert Some, *A Godly Treatise* (London, 1588).
William Smith, *The Vale-Royall of England or, The County Palatine of Chester Illustrated* (London, 1656).
John Sprint, *Propositions, tending to prove the necessarie use of the Christian Sabbaoth* (London, 1607).
John Stockwood, *A Very Fruitful Sermon* (London, 1579).
John Stow, *The Survay of London* (London, 1598).
Philip Stubbes, *The Anatomie of Abuses* (London, 1583).
George Swinnock, *The Life and Death of Mr. Tho. Wilson* (London, 1672).
Matthew Sylvester, *Reliquiae Baxterianae* (London, 1696).
John Taylor, *A Dog's Elegy* (London, 1644).
John Terry, *The Triall of Truth* (Oxford, 1600).
Thomason Tract, 669.f.6 (1): *A Copie of the Petition presented to the Kings Majesty by the high Sheriffe, accompanied with many hundreds of Gentlemen and Free-holders of the County of Rutland* (London, 1642).
Thomason Tract, 669.f.7[12]: *Die Veneris 50. Maij.* 1643.
Thomason Tract, E. 52 (12): *The Spie, 20–25 June 1644.*
Thomason Tract, E. 101 [15]: *Mercurius Civicus*, 4–11 May 1643.
Thomason Tract, E. 101 [24]: *Certaine Informations from Severall Parts of the Kingdome*, 8–15 May 1643.
Thomason Tract, E. 249 [6]: *A Perfect Diurnall of the Passages in Parliament*, 8–15 May 1643.
Thomason Tract, E. 258 (11): *Perfect Occurrences of Parliament, 3–10 January 1645.*
Thomason Tract, E.298[24]: *Mercurius Britanicus, 25 August–1 September 1645.*
Thomas Trescott, *The Zealous Magistrate* (London, 1642).
Richard Turnbull, *An exposition upon the canonicall epistle of Saint Iames* (London, 1592).
William Twisse, *Of the Morality of the Fourth Commandment* (London, 1641).
John Udall, *Obedience to the Gospell* (London, 1584).
Zacharius Ursinus, *The Summe of Christian Religion* (Oxford, 1587).
Laurence Vaux, *A Catechisme, or a Christian Doctrine, necessarie for children & ignorant people*, (Antwerp, 1574).
John Vicars, *A looking-glasse for malignants* (London, 1643).
John Vicars, *A sight of ye trans-actions of these latter years* (London, 1646).
J. Vicars, *England's Remembrancer* (London, 1641).
J. Vicars, *England's Parliamentarie Chronicle* (London, 1644–46).
W.B. (?), *The Yellovv Book* (London, 1656).
Matthew Walbancke, *Annalia Dubrensia* (London, 1636).

George Walker, *The Doctrine of the Sabbath* (Amsterdam, 1638).
George Walker, *The Doctrine of the Holy Weekly Sabbath* (London, 1641).
John Walsall, *A Sermon, preached at St Pauls Crosse* (London, 1578).
John Ward, *The Good-will of Him that Dwelt in the Bush* (London, 1645).
Francis White, *A Treatise of the Sabbath Day* (London, 1635).
Francis White, *An Examination and Confutation of a Lawless Pamphlet* (London, 1637).
Thomas White, *A Sermon Preached at Pawles Crosse on Sunday, the Thirde of November 1577* (London, 1578).
Bulstrode Whitelocke, *Memorials of the English Affairs* (London, 1682).
Richard Whitford, *A werke for housholders* (London, 1530).
Perceval Wiburn, *A checke or reproof of M. Howlets vntimely shreeching in her Majiesties eares* (London, 1581).
George Widley, *The Doctrine of the Sabbath* (London, 1604).
Griffith Williams, *The True Church* (London, 1629).
A. Wilson, *The History of Great Britain, Being the Life and Reign of King James the First* (London, 1653).
John Woolton, *The Castell of Christians* (London, 1577).
Leonard Wright, *A Summons for Sleepers* (London, 1589).
Thomas Young, *Dies Dominica* (Amsterdam?, 1639).

V. Editions of Documents

R. Ashton (ed.), *James I by his Contemporaries* (London, 1969).
Ernest Axon (ed.), *Manchester Sessions. Notes of Proceedings before Oswald Mosley (1616–1630), Nicholas Mosley (1661–1672), and Sir Oswald Mosley (1734–1739), Volume I, 1616–1622–3* (Manchester, 1901).
J.A.W. Bennett and H.R. Trevor-Roper (eds), *The Poems of Richard Corbett* (Oxford, 1955).
J.H.E. Bennett and J.C. Dewhurst (eds), *The Quarter Sessions Records with other Records of the Justices of the Peace for the County Palatine of Chester, 1559–1760* (Record Society of Lancashire and Cheshire, 1940).
J.H.E. Bennett and J.C. Dewhurst (eds), *Quarter Sessions Records, Chester, 1559–1760* (Record Society of Lancashire and Chester, 1940).
B.G. Blackwood, *The Lancashire Gentry and the Great Rebellion, 1640–1660* (Manchester, 1978).
J. Bliss and W. Scott (eds), *The Works of William Laud* (seven volumes, Oxford, 1847–60).
F.S. Boas (ed.), *The Diary of Thomas Crosfield* (Oxford, 1935).
M.F. Bond (ed.), *The Manuscripts of the House of Lords, Volume XI* (New Series), *Addenda, 1514–1714* (London, 1962).
D. Booy (ed.), *The Notebooks of Nehemiah Wallington, 1618–1654. A Selection* (Aldershot: Ashgate, 2007).
Calendar of State Papers Domestic: 1611–18; 1619–23; 1633–34; 1634–35.
Calendar of State Papers Venetian 1617–19.
A. Clark (ed.), *The Life and Times of Anthony Wood, Volume I: 1632–1653* (Oxford, 1891).
L.M. Clopper, *Drama, Play and Game. English Festive Culture in the Medieval and Early Modern Period* (Chicago, 2001).
J.S. Cockburn (ed.), *Western Circuit Assize Orders, 1629–1648* (London, 1976).
E. Cope (ed.), *Proceedings of the Short Parliament of 1640* (London, 1977).
Peter Cunningham (ed.), *Extracts from the Accounts of Revels at Court, in the reign of Queen Elizabeth and King James I* (London, 1842).

J.R. Dasent (ed.), *Acts of the Privy Council of England* (New Series) (London, 1896).
J. Earwaker, *The Court Leet Records of the Manor of Manchester* (Manchester, 1884).
Susan Ffarington (ed.), *The Farington Papers* (Chetham Society, 1856).
K. Fincham (ed.), *Visitation Articles and Injunctions of the Early Stuart Church, Volume 1* (Church of England Record Society, 1994).
K. Fincham (ed.), *Visitation Articles and Injunctions of the Early Stuart Church, Volume 2* (Church of England Record Society, 1998).
C.H. Firth and R.S. Rait (eds), *Acts and Ordinances of the Interregnum, 1642–1660* (three volumes, London, 1911).
E.R. Foster (ed.), *Proceedings in Parliament, 1610, Volumes 1 & 2, House of Lords* (London, 1966).
R.S. France (ed.), *A Lancashire Miscellany, Volume 109* (The Record Society of Lancashire and Cheshire, 1965).
F.J. Furnivall, *Harrison's Description of England in Shakspere's Youth, Being the Second and Third Books of His Description of Britaine and England* (London, 1877).
S.R. Gardiner (ed.), *Debates in the House of Commons in 1625* (London, 1873).
S.R. Gardiner (ed.), *The Constitutional Documents of the Puritan Revolution, 1625–1660* (Oxford, 1906).
M.J. Groombridge (ed.), *Calendar of Chester City Council Minutes, 1603–1642* (Blackpool, 1956).
A.H.A. Hamilton (ed.), *The Notebook of Sir John Northcote* (London, 1877).
A.H.A. Hamilton, *Quarter Sessions from Queen Elizabeth to Queen Anne* (London, 1878).
F. Hargrave (ed.), *A complete collection of state-trials, and proceedings for high-treason* (London, 1776).
J. Harland, *The Lancashire Lieutenancy under the Tudors and Stuarts* (Two Volumes, Manchester, Chetham Society, 1859).
E. Hawkins (ed.), *Travels in Holland, the United Provinces, England, Scotland and Ireland by Sir William Brereton* (London, 1844).
Clive Holmes (ed.), *The Suffolk Committees for Scandalous Ministers, 1644–1646* (Suffolk Record Society, Vol. XIII, 1970).
P.L. Hughes and J.F. Larkin (eds), *Tudor Royal Proclamations*, Vols. I, II and III, *The Early Tudors* (New Haven and London, 1964).
M. Jansson and W. Bidwell (eds), *Proceedings in Parliament 1625* (Yale, 1987).
M. Jansson (ed.), *Proceedings in the Opening Session of the Long Parliament, Volume I: 3 November–19 December 1640* (New York, 2000).
The Journals of the House of Commons.
The Journals of the House of Lords.
D.N. Klausner (ed.), *Wales*, Records of Early Drama (Toronto, 2005).
J.F. Larkin and P.L. Hughes (eds), *Stuart Royal Proclamations, Volume I, Royal Proclamations of King James I, 1603–1625* (Oxford, 1973).
J.F. Larkin (ed.), *Stuart Royal Proclamations, Volume II, Royal Proclamations of King Charles I, 1625–1646* (Oxford, 1983).
T.T. Lewis (ed.), *The letters of the Lady Brilliana Harley, Wife of Sir Robert Harley* (London, 1854).
J.D. Maltby (ed.), *The Short Parliament (1640) Diary of Sir Thomas Aston* (London, 1988).
J. Nichols, *The Progresses, Processions and Magnificent Festivities of King James the First* (London, 1828).

W. Notestein, F.H. Relf and H. Simpson (eds), *Commons Debates, 1621* (Seven volumes, London, 1935).
W.M. Palmer (ed.), *Episcopal Visitation Returns for Cambridgeshire, 1638–1665* (Cambridge, 1930).
R. Parkinson (ed.), *The Life of Adam Martindale, Written by Himself* (The Chetham Society, Manchester, 1845).
C. Petrie (ed.), *The Letters, Speeches and Proclamations of King Charles I* (London, 1935).
D. Pickering (ed.), *The Statutes At Large*, Vol. VII (1783).
B.W. Quintrell (ed.), *Proceedings of the Lancashire Justices of the Peace at the Sheriffs Table During Assizes Week, 1578–1694* (The Record Society of Lancashire and Cheshire), Vol. CXXI (1981).
F.R. Raines (ed.), *The Journal of Nicholas Assheton* (Manchester, 1848).
F.R. Raines (ed.), *Chetham Miscellanies*, Volume 5 (Chetham Society, 1875).
The Statutes of the Realm (twelve volumes, London, 1810–28).
A.J. Stephens (ed.), *The Statutes relating to Ecclesiastical and Eleemosynary Institutions* (two volumes, London, 1845).
J. Tait (ed.), *Lancashire Quarter Sessions Records*, Vol. I, *Quarter Session Rolls, 1590–1606* (London and Manchester, 1917).
J.R. Tanner (ed.), *Constitutional Documents of the Reign of James I, 1603–1625* (Cambridge, 1930).
T. Thomson (ed.), *Acts and Proceedings of the General Assemblies of the Kirk of Scotland, 1560–1618* (three volumes, Edinburgh, 1839–1845), Vol. III, *1593–1618*.
D. Underdown (ed.), *William Whiteway of Dorchester, His Diary* (Dorset Record Society, Vol. 12, 1991).
D.H. Wilson (ed.), *The Parliamentary Diary of Robert Bowyer, 1606–1607* (University of Minnesota Press, 1971).
Walter Yonge, *The Diary of Walter Yonge, Esq.* (The Camden Society, London, 1848).

Secondary Sources

I. Books

A. Abram, *English Life and Manners in the Later Middle Ages* (London, 1913).
A. Abram, *Social England in the Fifteenth Century. A Study of the Effects of Economic Conditions* (London, 1909).
J. Adair, *Puritans. Religion and Politics in Seventeenth-Century England and America* (Stroud, 1998).
S.D. Amussen and M.A. Kishlansky (eds), *Political Culture and Cultural Politics in Early Modern England* (Manchester, 1995).
A. Areangeli, *Recreation in the Renaissance. Attitudes towards Leisure and Pastimes in European Culture, c.1425–1675* (Basingstoke and New York, 2003).
R. Ashton, *The English Civil War. Conservatism and Revolution, 1630–1649* (Second edition, London, 1989).
R. Ashton, *Counter Revolution. The Second Civil War and its Origins, 1646–48* (London, 1994).
J. Aspin, *The British History Briefly Told; and a Description of the Ancient Customs, Sports and Pastimes of the English* (Second edition, London, 1840).
G.E. Aylmer, *Rebellion or Revolution? England from Civil War to Restoration* (Oxford, 1986).

E. Baines, *The History of the County Palatine and Duchy of Lancaster* (two volumes, London 1868–70).
J. Barbour and T. Quirk, *Essays on Puritans and Puritanism by Leon Howard* (Albuquerque, 1986).
T.G. Barnes, *Somerset, 1625–1640: A County's Government During the 'Personal Rule'* (Oxford, 1961).
D.C. Beaver, *Parish Communities and Religious Conflict in the Vale of Gloucester, 1590–1690* (Harvard, 1998).
G. Bernard, *The King's Reformation: Henry VIII and the Remaking of the English Church* (Yale University Press, 2005).
B.G. Blackwood, *The Lancashire Gentry and the Great Rebellion, 1640–1660* (Manchester, 1978).
M.W. Bloomfield, *The Seven Deadly Sins. An Introduction to the History of a Religious Concept, with Special Reference to Medieval English Literature* (Michigan, 1952).
D. Brailsford, *Sport and Society. Elizabeth to Anne* (London, 1969).
J. Brewer and J. Styles (eds), *An Ungovernable People. The English and their law in the seventeenth and eighteenth centuries* (London, 1980).
G. Brodie, *Constitutional History of the British Empire from the Accession of Charles I to the Restoration* (First published 1822. New edition, London, 1866).
P. Burke, *Popular Culture in Early Modern Europe* (revised edition, Aldershot, 1994).
M. Butler, *The Stuart Court Masque and Political Culture* (Cambridge, 2008).
C. Carlton, *Charles I: The Personal Monarch* (Second edition, London, 1995).
C. Carlton, *Archbishop William Laud* (London, 1987).
J.M. Carter, *Medieval Games. Sports and Recreations in Feudal Society* (New York; Westport, Connecticut; and London, 1992).
E.K. Chambers, *The Elizabethan Stage* (four volumes, Oxford, 1923).
P. Clark, *English Provincial Society from the Reformation to the Revolution. Religion, Politics and Society in Kent, 1500–1640* (Harvester Press, 1977).
P. Clark, A.G.R. Smith, N. Tyacke (eds), *The English Commonwealth 1547–1640. Essays in Politics and Society* (Leicester University Press, 1979).
P. Clark, *The English Alehouse. A Social History, 1200–1830* (London, 1983).
S. Clark, *The Elizabethan Pamphleteers. Popular Moralistic Pamphlets, 1580–1640* (East Brunswick, New Jersey, 1983).
J.T. Cliffe, *The Yorkshire Gentry from the Reformation to the Civil War* (London, 1969).
L.M. Clopper, *Drama, Play, and Game. English Festive Culture in the Medieval and Early Modern Period* (Chicago, 2001).
J. Coffey and P. Lim (eds), *The Cambridge Companion to Puritanism* (Cambridge, 2008).
C.R. Cole and M.E. Moody (eds), *The Dissenting Tradition* (Ohio, 1975).
P. Collinson, *The Elizabethan Puritan Movement* (London, 1967).
P. Collinson, *Godly People. Essays on English Protestantism and Puritanism* (London, 1983).
P. Collinson, *English Puritanism* (Historical Association, London, 1983).
P. Collinson, *The Birthpangs of Protestant England. Religion and Cultural Change in the Sixteenth and Seventeenth Centuries* (London, 1988).
E.S. Cope, *Politics Without Parliaments, 1629–1640* (London, 1987).
G.G. Coulton, *Social Life in Britain from the Conquest to the Reformation* (Cambridge, 1918).

G.G. Coulton, *The Medieval Village* (Cambridge, 1925).
J.C. Cox, *Churchwardens' Accounts from the Fourteenth Century to the Close of the Seventeenth Century* (London, 1913).
D. Cressy, *Bonfires and Bells. National Memory and the Protestant Calendar in Elizabethan and Stuart England* (London, 1989).
D. Cressy and L.A. Ferrell (eds), *Religion and Society in Early Modern England. A Sourcebook* (London, 1996).
D. Cressy, *England on Edge. Crisis and Revolution, 1640–1642* (Oxford, 2006).
C.G. Cruickshank, *Elizabeth's Army* (Second edition, Oxford, 1966).
R. Cust and A. Hughes (eds), *Conflict in Early Stuart England. Studies in Religion and Politics, 1603–1642* (London, 1989).
R. Cust, *Charles I. A Political Life* (Longman, 2005).
G. Davies, *The Early Stuarts, 1603–1660* (Oxford, 1959).
J. Davies, *The Caroline Captivity of the Church: Charles I and the Remoulding of Anglicanism* (Oxford, 1992).
J.T. Dennison, *The Market Day of the Soul: The Puritan Doctrine of the Sabbath in England, 1532–1700* (University Press of America, 1983).
A.H. Dodd, *Elizabethan England* (London, 1973).
G. Donaldson, *The Making of the Scottish Prayer Book of 1637* (Edinburgh, 1954).
E. Duffy, *The Stripping of the Altars. Traditional Religion in England, 1400–1580* (New Haven and London, 1992).
E. Duffy, *The Voices of Morebath. Reformation and Rebellion in an English Village* (Yale, 2001).
C. Durston and J. Eales (eds), *The Culture of English Puritanism, 1560–1700* (London, 1996).
L. Eachard, *The History of England* (Three volumes, London, 1707–18), Volumes I and II.
J. Eales, *Puritans and Roundheads. The Harleys of Brampton Bryan and the outbreak of the English Civil War* (Cambridge, 1990).
G. Eley and W. Hunt (eds), *Reviving the English Revolution Reflections and Elaborations on the Work of Christopher Hill* (London, 1988).
F.G. Emmison, *Elizabethan Life: Disorder* (Essex Record Office, 1970).
K. Fincham (ed.), *The Early Stuart Church, 1603–1642* (London, 1993).
K. Fincham and N. Tyacke, *Altars Restored. The Changing Face of English Religious Worship, 1547–c.1700* (Oxford, 2007).
A. Fletcher, *The Outbreak of the English Civil War* (London, 1981).
A. Fletcher, *Tudor Rebellions* (Third edition, London, 1983).
A. Fletcher and J. Stevenson (eds), *Order and Disorder in Early Modern England* (Cambridge, 1985).
A. Fletcher, *Reform in the Provinces. The Government of Stuart England* (New Haven and London, 1986).
W.H. Frere and C.E. Douglas, *Puritan Manifestoes. A Study of the Origin of the Puritan Revolt* (London, 1954).
R.H. Fritze and W.B. Robinson (eds), *Historical Dictionary of Stuart England, 1603–1689* (Westport, Connecticut and London, 1996).
S.R. Gardiner, *The Personal Government of Charles I, 1628–1637* (two volumes, London, 1877).
S.R. Gardiner, *History of England from the Accession of James I to the Outbreak of the Civil War, 1603–42* (ten volumes, London, 1883).
S.R. Gardiner, *The First Two Stuarts and the Puritan Revolution, 1603–1660* (New York, 1890).

J. Goring, *Godly Exercises or the Devil's Dance? Puritanism and Popular Culture in pre-Civil War England* (London, 1983).
L.A. Govett, *The King's Book of Sports* (London, 1890).
R.L. Greaves, *Society and Religion in Elizabethan England* (Minneapolis, 1981).
E. Griffin, *England's Revelry. A History of Popular Sport and Pastimes, 1660–1830* (Oxford, 2005).
P. Griffiths, *Youth and Authority. Formative Experience in England, 1560–1640* (Oxford, 1996).
C. Haigh, *Reformation and Resistance in Tudor Lancashire* (Cambridge, 1975).
C. Haigh (ed.), *The English Reformation Revised* (Cambridge, 1987).
C. Haigh, *English Reformations. Religion, Politics and Society under the Tudors* (Oxford, 1993).
C. Haigh, *The Plain Man's Pathways to Heaven. Kinds of Christianity in Post-Reformation England, 1570–1640* (Oxford, 2007).
Henry Hallam, *The Constitutional History of England* (two volumes, London, 1827).
R. Halley, *Lancashire: Its Puritanism and Nonconformity* (two volumes, Manchester, 1869).
R. Hardy, *Longbow. A Social and Military History* (Third edition, Sparkford, 1992).
T. Harris (ed.), *Popular Culture in England, c.1500–1850* (London, 1995).
F. Heal, *Hospitality in Early Modern England* (Oxford, 1990).
R.W. Heinze, *The Proclamations of the Tudor Kings* (Cambridge, 1976).
P.M. Hembry, *The Bishops of Bath and Wells, 1540–1640. Social and Economic Problems* (London, 1967).
T.S. Henricks, *Disputed Pleasures. Sport and Society in Pre-industrial England* (New York; Westport, Connecticut; and London, 1991).
C. Hill, *Puritanism and Revolution* (London, 1958).
C. Hill, *Society and Puritanism in Pre-Revolutionary England* (London, 1964).
C. Hill, *The Collected Essays of Christopher Hill, Vol. II, Religion and Politics in Seventeenth-century England* (Massachusetts, 1986).
C. Hill, *A Nation of Change and Novelty. Radical Politics, Religion and Literature in Seventeenth-Century England* (London, revised edition, 1993).
C. Hill, *Intellectual Origins of the English Revolution Revisited* (Oxford, 1997).
D. Hirst, *Authority and Conflict. England, 1603–1658* (London, 1986).
R. Hollingworth, *Mancuniensis, or an History of the Towne of Manchester* (Manchester, 1839).
R.A. Houlbrooke, *Church Courts and the People During the English Reformation, 1520–1570* (Oxford, 1979).
A. Hughes, *The Causes of the English Civil War* (London, 1991).
John Hughes and White Kennet (eds), *A Complete History of England* (three volumes, London, 1706), Vol. III.
D. Hume, *The History of Great Britain*, Volume I, *Containing the Reigns of James I and Charles I* (two volumes, Edinburgh, 1754).
W. Hunt, *The Puritan Moment. The Coming of Revolution in an English County* (Harvard and London, 1983).
R. Hutton, *The Rise and Fall of Merry England. The Ritual Year, 1400–1700* (Oxford, 1994).
R. Hutton, *The Stations of the Sun. A History of the Ritual Year in Britain* (Oxford, 1996).
R. Hutton, 'Seasonal Festivity in Late Medieval England: Some Further Reflections', in *English Historical Review*, 120:485 (2005), pp. 66–79.

P. Jensen, *Religion and Revelry in Shakespeare's Festive World* (Cambridge, 2008).
W.R.D. Jones, *The Tudor Commonwealth, 1529–1559* (London, 1970).
D. Katz, *Sabbath and Sectarianism in Seventeenth-Century England* (Leiden and New York, 1988).
W. Kennet, *The History of England from the Commencement of the Reign of Charles I to the end of the Reign of William III* (London, 1706).
M. Kishlansky, *A Monarchy Transformed. Britain, 1603–1714* (London, 1996).
M.M. Knappen, *Tudor Puritanism. A Chapter in the History of Idealism* (Chicago, 1939).
P.E. Kopperman, *Sir Robert Heath. Window on an Age* (Royal Historical Society, 1989).
R. Kraus, *History of the Dance in Art and Education* (New Jersey, 1969).
W. Lamont, *Marginal Prynne, 1600–1669* (London, 1962).
W. Lamont, *Puritanism and Historical Controversy* (London, 1996).
A.H. Lewis, *A Critical History of Sunday Legislation. From 321 to 1888 A.D.* (New York, 1888).
K. Lindley, *Popular Politics and Religion in Civil War London* (Aldershot, 1997).
D. Loades, *Mary Tudor. A Life* (Oxford, 1989).
D. Loades, *The Mid-Tudor Crisis, 1545–1565* (London, 1992).
T.B. Macaulay, *The History of England from the Accession of James the Second* (London, 1870).
D. MacCulloch, *The Later Reformation in England, 1547–1603* (London, 1990).
R. MacGillivray, *Restoration Historians and the English Civil War* (The Hague, 1974).
R. Marchant, *The Puritans and the Church Courts in the Diocese of York, 1560–1642* (London, 1960).
L.S. Marcus, *The Politics of Mirth. Jonson, Herrick, Milton, Marvell and the Defence of Old Holiday Pastimes* (Chicago, 1986).
C. Marsh, *Popular Religion in Sixteenth-century England* (London, 1998).
D. Mathew, *The Age of Charles I* (London, 1951).
J.S. McGee, *The Godly Man in Stuart England. Anglicans, Puritans, and the Two Tables, 1620–1670* (New Haven and London, 1976).
M.K. McIntosh, *Controlling Misbehaviour in England, 1370–1600* (Cambridge, 1998).
J. Miller, *After the Civil Wars. English Politics and Government in the Reign of Charles II* (Longman, Harlow, 2000).
A. Milton, *Catholic and Reformed. The Roman and Protestant Churches in English Protestant Thought, 1600–1640* (Cambridge, 1995).
J. Morrill, *The Nature of the English Revolution* (London, 1993).
E. Muir, *Ritual in Early Modern Europe* (Cambridge, 1997).
Daniel Neal, *The History of the Puritans* (five volumes, London, 1822).
P.R. Newman, *The Old Service: Royalist regimental colonels and the Civil War, 1642–46* (Manchester, 1993).
John Oldmixon, *Critical History of England* (two volumes, London, 1724–30).
John Oldmixon, *The History of England During the Reigns of the Royal House of Stuart* (London, 1730).
G.R. Owst, *Preaching in Medieval England. An Introduction to Sermon Manuscripts of the Period c.1350–1450* (Cambridge, 1926).
K.L. Parker, *The English Sabbath. A Study of doctrine and discipline from the Reformation to the Civil War* (Cambridge, 1988).
H. Pierce, *Unseemly Pictures. Graphic Satire and Politics in Early Modern England* (Yale, 2008).

W. Prest, *The Inns of Court under Elizabeth I and the Early Stuarts, 1590–1640* (London, 1972).
J.H. Primus, *Holy Time. Moderate Puritanism and the Sabbath* (Mercer University Press, 1989).
L. von Ranke, *A History of England Principally in the Seventeenth Century* (Six volumes, Oxford, 1875).
M. Rapin de Thoyras, *The History of England*, trans. N. Tindal (London, 1786).
B. Reay, *Popular Cultures in England, 1550–1750* (London, 1998).
L. Reeve, *Charles I and the Road to Personal Rule* (Cambridge, 1989).
C. Reeves, *Pleasure and Pastimes in Medieval England* (Stroud, 1995).
R.C. Richardson, *Puritanism in North-West England. A Regional Study of the Diocese of Chester to 1642* (Manchester, 1972).
E.C. Rodgers, *Discussion of Holidays in the Later Middle Ages* (New York, 1940).
W. Rordorf, *Sunday: the History of the Day of Rest and Worship in the Earliest Centuries of the Christian Church* (London, 1968).
R.E. Ruigh, *The Parliament of 1624: Politics and Foreign Policy* (Harvard University Press, 1971).
C. Russell, *The Crisis of Parliaments. English History, 1509–1660* (Oxford, 1971).
C. Russell (ed.), *The Origins of the English Civil War* (London, 1973).
C. Russell, *Parliaments and English Politics, 1621–1629* (Oxford, 1979).
C. Russell, *The Causes of the English Civil War* (Oxford, 1990).
C. Russell, *The Fall of the British Monarchies, 1637–1642* (Oxford, 1991).
L.A. Sasek, *Images of English Puritanism. A Collection of Contemporary Sources, 1589–1646* (Louisiana, 1989).
P.S. Seaver, *Wallington's World. A Puritan Artisan in Seventeenth-Century London* (Stanford University Press, 1985).
J.A. Sharpe, *Early Modern England. A Social History, 1550–1760* (Second edition, London, 1997).
K. Sharpe, *The Personal Rule of Charles I* (New Haven and London, 1992).
K. Sharpe, *Faction and Parliament: Essays on Early Stuart History* (Oxford, 1978).
K. Sharpe, *Remapping Early Modern England. The Culture of Seventeenth-Century Politics* (Cambridge, 2000).
H.M. Shire, *Song, Dance and Poetry of the Court of Scotland under King James VI* (Cambridge, 1969).
C.J. Sisson, *The Lost Plays of Shakespeare's Age* (Cambridge, 1936).
E.F. Slafter, *The Character and History of the Book of Sports, 1618–1643* (Boston, 1905).
J. Spraggon, *Puritan Iconoclasm during the English Civil War* (Woodbridge, 2003).
M. Spufford, *Contrasting Communities. English Villagers in the Sixteenth and Seventeenth Centuries* (Cambridge, 1974).
J. Spurr, *English Puritanism, 1603–1689* (London, 1998).
A. Stewart, *The Cradle King. A Life of James VI and I* (London, 2003).
M. Stieg, *Laud's Laboratory. The Diocese of Bath and Wells in the Early Seventeenth Century* (London, 1982).
L. Stone (ed.), *Social Change and Revolution in England, 1540–1640* (London, 1965).
M. Stoyle, *Loyalty and Locality. Popular Allegiance in Devon during the English Civil War* (Exeter, 1994).
M. Stoyle, *From Deliverance to Destruction: Rebellion and Civil War in an English City* (Exeter, 1996).

M. Stoyle, *West Britons: Cornish Identities and the Early Modern British State* (Exeter University Press, 2002).
J. Strutt, *The Sports and Pastimes of the People of England* (London, 1841).
K. Thomas, *Religion and the Decline of Magic. Studies in Popular Beliefs in Sixteenth- and Seventeenth-Century England* (London, 1971).
J.A.F. Thomson, *The Early Tudor Church and Society, 1485–1529* (London, 1993).
G.M. Trevelyan, *England Under the Stuarts* (Sixteenth edition, London, 1933).
W.B. Trevelyan, *Sunday* (London, 1908).
H.R. Trevor-Roper, *Archbishop Laud, 1573–1645* (Second edition, London, 1962).
N. Tyacke, *The Fortunes of English Puritanism, 1603–1640* (London, Friends of Dr. Williams's Library, 1989).
D. Underdown, *Revel, Riot and Rebellion. Popular Politics and Culture in England, 1603–1660* (Oxford, 1985).
D. Underdown, *Fire from Heaven. Life in an English Town in the Seventeenth Century* (Yale, 1992).
D. Underdown, *A Freeborn People: Politics and the Nation in Seventeenth-Century England* (Oxford, 1996).
Victoria County History, *Lancashire*.
T. Watt, *Cheap Print and Popular Piety, 1550–1640* (Cambridge, 1991).
T. Webster, *Godly Clergy in Early Stuart England. The Caroline Puritan Movement, c.1620–1643* (Cambridge, 1997).
P.A. Welsby, *George Abbot, the Unwanted Archbishop, 1562–1633* (London, 1962).
P.A. Welsby, *Lancelot Andrewes, 1555–1626* (London, 1964).
W.B. Whitaker, *Sunday in Tudor and Stuart Times* (London, 1933).
C. Whitfield (ed.), *Robert Dover and the Cotswold Games* (London, 1962).
S. Wilkins, *Sports and Games of Medieval Cultures* (Westport, 2002).
G. Williams, *Wales and the Reformation* (Cardiff, 1997).
D.H. Willson, *King James VI and I* (Oxford, 1956).
K. Wrightson and D. Levine, *Poverty and Piety in an English Village. Terling, 1525–1700* (New York and London, 1979).
K. Wrightson, *English Society, 1580–1680* (London, 1982).
Perez Zagorin, *The Court and Country: The Beginning of the English Revolution* (London, 1969).

II. Articles
Ernest Axon, 'The King's Preachers in Lancashire, 1599–1845', in *Transactions of the Lancashire and Cheshire Antiquarian Society*, Vol. 56 (1941–42), pp. 67–104.
M. Bailey, 'Rural Society', in R. Horrox (ed.), *Fifteenth Century Attitudes. Perceptions of Society in Late Medieval England* (Cambridge, 1994).
W.P. Baker, 'The Observance of Sunday.' in R. Lennard (ed.), *Englishmen at Rest and Play. Some Phases of English Leisure, 1558–1714* (Oxford, 1931).
T.G. Barnes, 'County Politics and a Puritan Cause Célèbre: Somerset Churchales, 1633', in *Transactions of the Royal Historical Society*, Fifth Series, 9 (1959), pp. 103–22.
T.G. Barnes, 'Cropping the Heath: the Fall of a Chief Justice, 1634', in *Historical Research*, Vol. 64, No. 155 (October, 1991), pp. 331–43.
B. Ball, '"Through Darkness to Light". Post-Restoration Sabbatarianism: Survival and Continuity', in R. Bonney and D.J.B. Trim (eds), *The Development of Pluralism in Modern Britain and France* (Bern, 2007), pp. 109–27.

G. Bernard, 'The Church of England c.1529–c.1642', in *History*, 75 (1990), pp. 183–206.

G. Bernard, 'The Making of Religious Policy, 1533–1546: Henry VIII and the Search for the Middle Way', in *The Historical Journal*, 41, 2 (1998), pp. 321–49.

J.M. Bennett, 'Conviviality and Charity in Medieval and Early Modern England', in *Past and Present*, 134 (1992), pp. 19–41.

O. Browstein, 'The Popularity of Baiting in England Before 1600: a Study in Social and Theatrical History', in *Educational Theatre Journal*, 21 (1969), pp. 237–50.

E. Carlson, 'The origins, function, and status of the office of churchwarden, with particular reference to the diocese of Ely', in M. Spufford, *The World of Rural Dissenters, 1520–1725* (Cambridge, 1995).

P. Collinson, 'Elizabethan and Jacobean Puritanism as Forms of Popular Religious Culture', in C. Durston and J. Eales (eds), *The Culture of English Puritanism, 1560–1700* (London, 1996).

P. Collinson, 'Merry England on the Ropes: The Contested Culture of the Early Modern English Town', in S. Ditchfield (ed.), *Christianity and Community in the West. Essays for John Bossy* (Aldershot: Ashgate, 2001), pp. 131–47.

G. Donaldson, 'The Scottish Church, 1567–1625', in A.G.R. Smith (ed.), *The Reign of James VI and I* (London, 1973), pp. 40–56.

C. Durston, 'Puritan Rule and the Failure of Cultural Revolution, 1645–1660', in C. Durston and J. Eales (eds), *The Culture of English Puritanism, 1560–1700* (London, 1996).

P.A. Fidler, '*Societas, Civitas* and Early Elizabethan Poverty Relief', in C. Carlton *et al* (eds), *State, Sovereigns & Society in Early Modern England* (Stroud, 1998).

J. Fielding, 'Arminianism in the Localities: Peterborough Diocese, 1603–1642', in K. Fincham (ed.), *The Early Stuart Church, 1603–1642* (London, 1993).

K. Fincham, 'Episcopal Government, 1603–1640', in K. Fincham (ed.), *The Early Stuart Church, 1603–1642* (London, 1993).

R.L. Greaves, 'The Origins of English Sabbatarian Thought', in *Sixteenth Century Journal*, XII, No. 3 (1981).

C. Haigh, 'The Continuity of Catholicism in the English Reformation', in C. Haigh (ed.), *The English Reformation Revised* (Cambridge, 1987).

C. Haigh, 'Anticlericalism and the English Reformation', in C. Haigh, (ed.), *The English Reformation Revised* (Cambridge, 1987).

C. Harper-Bill, 'Who Wanted the English Reformation?', in *Medieval History*, Vol. 2, No. 1 (1992), pp. 66–77.

J.I. Harris, 'Lucy Robartes's 'A meditation uppon the Lords day': A Puritan Palimpsest and English Sabbatarianism', in *The Seventeenth Century*, Vol. XXIII, No. 1 (Spring, 2008), pp. 1–33.

B. Harvey, 'Work and Festa Ferianda in Medieval England', in *Journal of Ecclesiastical History*, Vol. XXIII, No. 4 (October 1972), pp. 289–308.

F. Heal, 'The crown, the gentry and London: the enforcement of proclamation, 1596–1640', in C. Cross, D. Loades, and J.J. Scarisbrick (eds), *Law and Government Under the Tudors* (Cambridge, 1988).

T.S. Henricks, 'Sport and Social History in Medieval England', *Journal of Sport History*, Vol. 9, No. 2 (Summer, 1982), pp. 20–37.

C. Hill, 'Seventeenth-century English Society and Sabbatarianism', in J.S. Bromley and E.H. Kossman (eds), *Britain and the Netherlands*, Volume II (1964).

J.E.C. Hill, 'Puritans and the "Dark Corners of the Land"', in *Transactions of the Royal Historical Society*, Fifth Series, Volume 13 (London, 1963).

S. Hindle, 'Custom, Festival and Protest in Early Modern England: The Little Budworth Wakes, St Peter's Day, 1596', in *Rural History*, Vol. 6, No. 2 (1995), pp. 155–78.

A. Hughes, 'Local History and the Origins of the Civil War', in R. Cust and A. Hughes (eds), *Conflict in Early Stuart England. Studies in Religion and Politics, 1603–1642* (London, 1989).

R. Hutton, 'The Local Impact of the Tudor Reformation', in C. Haigh, *The English Reformation Revised* (Cambridge, 1987).

R. Hutton, 'Seasonal Festivity in Late Medieval England: Some Further Reflections', in *English Historical Review*, 120:485 (2005), pp. 66–79.

M. Ingram 'Puritans and the Church Courts, 1560–1640', in C. Durston and J. Eales (eds), *The Culture of English Puritanism, 1560–1700* (Basingstoke, Macmillan, 1996).

J. Kent, 'Attitudes of Members of the House of Commons to the Regulation of 'Personal Conduct' in Late Elizabethan and Early Stuart England', in *Bulletin of the Institute of Historical Research*, Volume 46 (1973).

M. Kishlansky, 'Charles I: A Case of Mistaken Identity', in *Past and Present*, Vol. 189, No. 1 (November, 2005), pp. 41–80.

P. Lake, 'The Laudians and the Argument from Authority', in B.Y. Kunze and D.D. Brautigam (eds), *Court, Country, and Culture. Essays on Early Modern British History in Honor of Perez Zagorin* (New York, 1992).

P. Lake, 'A Charitable Christian Hatred' in C. Durston and J. Eales (eds), *The Culture of English Puritanism, 1560–1700* (London, 1996).

B. Lowe, 'Early Records of the Morris in England', in *Journal of the English Folk Dance & Song Society*, Vol. 7, No. 2 (1957), pp. 61–80.

B. Manning, 'The Godly People', in B. Manning (ed.), *Politics, Religion and the English Civil War* (London, 1973).

L.S. Marcus, 'Politics and Pastoral: Writing the Court on the Countryside', in K. Sharpe and P. Lake (eds), *Culture and Politics in Early Stuart England* (London, 1994).

N. McDowell, 'The stigmatizing of Puritans as Jews in Jacobean England: Ben Jonson, Francis Bacon and the *Book of Sports* controversy' in *Renaissance Studies*, Vol. 19, No. 3 (June, 2005), pp. 348–63.

W.A. Mepham, 'Essex Drama Under Puritanism and the Commonwealth' in *The Essex Review*, Vol. 58 (1949), pp. 155–61 and 181–5.

A. Milton, 'Licensing, Censorship, and Religious Orthodoxy in Early Stuart England, in *The Historical Journal*, 41, 3 (1998), pp. 625–51.

A. Milton, 'The creation of Laudianism: a new approach', in T. Cogswell, R. Cust and P. Lake (eds), *Politics, Religion, and Popularity in Early Stuart Britain* (Cambridge, 2002), pp. 162–84.

M. Moisa and J. Bennett, 'Debate: Conviviality and Charity in Medieval and Early Modern England', *Past and Present*, 154 (February, 1997), pp. 223–42.

J. Morrill, 'The Religious Context of the English Civil War', in *Transactions of the Royal Historical Society*, Fifth Series, Volume 34 (1984), pp. 155–78.

D. Palliser, 'Urban Society', in R. Horrox (ed.), *Fifteenth Century Attitudes. Perceptions of Society in Late Medieval England* (Cambridge, 1994).

K. Parker, 'Thomas Rogers and the English Sabbath: The Case for a Reappraisal', in *Church History*, Volume 53, No. 3 (1984).

E. Peacock, 'Church Ales', *The Archaeological Journal*, Vol. XL (March, 1883), pp. 1–15.

A.L. Poole, 'Recreation', in A.L. Poole (ed.), *Medieval England*, Volume II (revised edition, Oxford, 1958).

L. Racaut, 'The 'Book of Sports' and the Sabbatarian Legislation in Lancashire, 1579–1616', in *Northern History*, Volume XXXIII (1997), pp. 73–87.
J. Richards, ' 'His Nowe Majesty' and the English Monarchy: The Kingship of Charles I before 1640', in *Past and Present*, 113 (1986), pp. 70–96.
R.C. Richardson, 'Puritanism and the Ecclesiastical Authorities. The Case of the Diocese of Chester', in B. Manning (ed.), *Politics, Religion and the English Civil War* (London, 1973).
P. Rogers, 'The Maypole in the Strand: Pope and the Politics of Revelry', in *British Journal of Eighteenth-Century Studies*, Vol. 28, No. 1 (2005), pp. 83–95.
F. Shriver, 'Hampton Court Re-visited: James I and the Puritans', in *Journal of Ecclesiastical History*, Volume 33, No. 1 (January, 1982), pp. 48–71.
M. Spufford, , 'Puritanism and Social Control?' in A. Fletcher and J. Stevenson (eds), *Order and Disorder in Early Modern England* (Cambridge, 1985).
K.L. Sprunger, 'English and Dutch sabbatarianism and the development of puritan social theology, 1600–1660', in *Church History*, 51 (1982), pp. 24–38.
J. Tait, 'The Declaration of Sports for Lancashire (1617)', in *English Historical Review*, XXXII (1917), pp. 561–8.
K. Thomas, 'Work and Leisure in Pre-Industrial Society', in *Past and Present*, 29 (1964), pp. 50–66.
H. Thurston, 'The Medieval Sunday', in *The Nineteenth Century*, 46 (July 1899).
G.H. Tupling, 'The Causes of the Civil War in Lancashire', in *Transactions of the Lancashire and Cheshire Anitquarian Society*, Vol. 65 (1955), pp. 1–32.
N. Tyacke, 'Puritanism, Arminianism and Counter-Revolution', in C. Russel (ed.), *The Origins of the English Civil War* (London, 1973).
N. Tyacke, 'Archbishop Laud', in K. Fincham (ed.), *The Early Stuart Church, 1603–1642* (London, 1993).
D. Underdown, 'Regional Cultures? Local Variations in Popular Culture during the Early Modern Period', in T. Harris (ed.), *Popular Culture in England, c.1500–1850* (London, 1995).
A. Walsham, 'Godly Recreation: the problem of leisure in late Elizabethan and early Stuart society', in D.E. Kennedy, D. Robertson and A. Walsham (eds), *Grounds of Controversy. Three Studies in late 16th and early 17th century English polemics* (University of Melbourne, 1989).
R. Whiting, 'Local Responses to the Henrician Reformation', in D. MacCulloch, *The Reign of Henry VIII. Politics, Policy and Piety* (London, 1995).
D.J. Wilkinson, 'Performance and Motivation amongst the Justices of the Peace in Early Stuart Lancashire', in *Transactions of the Historic Society of Lancashire and Cheshire*, CXXXVIII (1989).
K. Wrightson, 'Alehouses, Order and Reformation in Rural England, 1590–1660', in E. Yeo and S. Yeo (eds), *Popular Culture and Class Conflict, 1590–1914* (New Jersey, 1981).
D.L. Wykes, '"The Sabbaths ... spent before in idleness & the neglect of the word": the Godly and the use of time in their daily religion', in R.N. Swanson (ed.), *The Use and Abuse of Time in Christian History* (Studies in Church History, 37), (The Ecclesiastical History Society, 2002), pp. 211–21.

Index

A Necessary Doctrine and Erudition for any Christian Man see King's Book, The
Abbot, George 147
Abbot, George, Archbishop of Canterbury 82, 89, 91, 93, 193 (n. 130)
adultery 54
Agincourt, Battle of 31
Albrighton, Staffordshire 84
Alcock, William 158
Aldermaston, Berkshire 137
alehouses 7, 12, 13, 18, 30, 32, 40, 44, 48, 53, 54, 58, 60, 61, 71, 74, 80, 109, 119, 134, 166
ales (*see also* church ales, clerk ales, Easter-ales, bid-ales, bride-ales, help-ales, scot-ales and Whitsun-ales) xiv, xvi, 5, 16, 17, 18, 19, 23, 35, 36, 37, 44, 47, 53, 55, 57, 58, 59, 60, 61, 63, 70, 71, 73, 84, 86, 89, 90, 92, 94, 95, 96, 97, 98, 104, 110, 111, 112, 113, 114, 115, 116, 117, 119, 120, 132, 136, 137, 138, 144, 147, 152, 153, 156, 162, 186 (n. 167), 189 (n. 26), 190 (n. 64), 191 (n. 93)
Alton, Hampshire 104
Amberley, West Sussex 19
Ambler, Thomas 158
Ames, William 147
Anderton, John 72
Andrewes, Lancelot, Bishop of Winchester 92
Annalia Dubrensia 144, 153, 199 (n. 185)
archery xvii, 7, 8, 15, 18, 20, 21, 22, 23, 30, 31, 32, 47, 47–8, 50–1, 73, 76, 77, 82, 106, 131, 142, 160, 163, 167
Ascham, Roger 31
Ashburton, Devon 111
Ashton, Richard 72
Assheton, Edmund 70
Aylmer, John, Bishop of London 69

Bachiler, Samuel 104
backgammon *see* tables
badger-baiting 33
Baker, Samuel 146
ball games (*see also* club ball, handball, football, stoolball and trap-ball), 20, 73
Ballad, John 144
Banbury, Oxfordshire 46, 62
Bancroft, John, Bishop of Oxford 130
Bancroft, Richard, Archbishop of Canterbury 93
Barkley, Sir Charles 118
Barnes, Thomas 110, 112, 114, 116, 117, 120, 190 (n. 65)
Barnes, Richard, Bishop of Durham 44
Barrington, Sir Thomas 4, 152–3
Basilikon Doron 77, 79, 80
Bastwick, John 146
Batcombe, Dorset 147
Battle, Sussex 143
Baxter, Richard 100, 104, 105, 144, 154, 155, 156, 161, 162
Bayly, Lewis, Bishop of Bangor 82, 91, 92, 93; *The Practice of Pietie* 82, 92
Beake, Robert 161
Beaminster, Dorset, 133
bear-baiting xiv, xvi, 1, 30, 32, 33–4, 37, 44, 46, 48, 52, 53, 53–4, 57, 61, 70, 71, 72, 73, 75, 77, 78, 82, 87, 91, 92, 102, 106, 111, 147, 167, 186 (n. 167)
Beercrocombe, Somerset 137
Bemerton, Wiltshire 137
Bere Regis, Dorset 104
Bernard, Richard 147, 149; *Threefold Treatise of the Sabbath*, 149
Bettenham, Suffolk 158

INDEX

bid-ales (*see also* ales) xiv, 117, 136
Birchington, Kent 137
Bishops Potion, The 122
Black Death, The 13–14
Blackfriars, London 81
Bodmin, Cornwall 60
Bolton, Robert 106, 146; *Some General Directions for A Comfortable Walking With God* 146
Bond, Denis 137
Bond, John 154, 155–6
Bonner, Edmund, Bishop of London 37
Book of Homilies, The (*see also Homily of the Place and Time of Prayer*) xi, 41, 42, 43
Book of Sports (1617) (*see also* James I) 1, 74–6, 92, 93
Book of Sports (1618) (*see also* James I) 1, 5–6, 8, 66, 76, 78, 79, 80, 81, 82, 83, 84, 85, 86, 89, 90, 91, 93, 95, 98, 99, 102, 103, 110, 165, 183 (n. 77), 193 (n. 122); opposition to 81–2, 83–4, 89, 97, 126; support for 82–3, 83, 89–90; used to target puritans 98–9
Book of Sports (1633) (*see also* Charles I and Laud, William) 1, 2, 6, 8, 84, 100–1, 108, 112, 116, 126, 127, 128, 129, 130, 135, 136, 137, 138, 141, 148, 155, 157, 158, 162, 163, 164, 165–8, 193 (n. 122); burned by the common hangman 150, 158, 201 (n. 217); decision to publish 1, 6, 100–1, 108, 108–9, 116–25, 137, 164; enforcement of 126–31, 140, 140–1, 149, 152; opposition to 101, 131–5, 136, 137, 138–9, 145–6, 146, 147, 148, 149, 152, 154, 158; popularity of 134, 136, 137, 138, 143, 145, 154, 158; used to target puritans 2, 127, 131
bowling xiv, 15, 18, 19, 31, 32, 37, 44, 45, 53, 61, 62, 63, 66, 71, 72, 73, 77, 78, 82, 97, 106, 137, 148, 160, 167
Bownd, Nicholas 42, 49, 50, 51, 52, 54, 64, 66, 67, 68, 92, 94, 142; *Doctrine of the Sabbath* 50, 64, 66, 67, 68, 142
Bowyer, Sir William 97
Brabourne, Theophilus 106–8, 117, 123, 130, 138, 139, 189–90 (n. 49); *A Defence of that most Ancient, and Sacred ordinance of Gods, the Sabbath Day* 106–8, 117, 138, 139; *A Discourse Upon the Sabbath Day* 106
Bradshaw, John 72
Bramham, Yorkshire 81
Brerewood, Edward 105
Breton, Nicholas 105

bride-ales (*see also* ales) xiv, 16, 58
Bridgwater, Somerset 111
Britannicus His Pill to cure Malignancy 155
Bristol 62, 104
Broad, Thomas 94, 105; *Three Questions Answered* 94
Bromley, Edward, Justice 72, 75
Bromyard, John 13
Brook, Sir Thomas 84
Buckingham, George Villiers, Duke of 123
Buckinghamshire 48, 134
bull-baiting xiv, 15, 33–4, 52, 53, 61, 70, 71, 72, 73, 75, 77, 78, 87, 91, 92, 96, 102, 106, 111, 162, 167, 186 (n. 167)
Burghley, William Cecil, 1st Baron 48–9
Burton, Henry 103, 106, 116, 122, 137–8, 140, 143, 146, 147; *A Brief Answer to A Late Treatise of the Sabbath Day* 146; *A Divine Tragedie Lately Acted* 138, 143, 146
Burton, Robert 94
Bury St. Edmunds, Suffolk 135
Byfield, Richard 105

Caius, John 36
Calamy, Edmund 136, 153
Caldwell John, 69
Calvert, George 90
Calvin, John 25–6
Calvinism 3
cambuc xiv, 20
Canterbury 62
carding xiv, 15, 31, 32, 35, 53, 73, 77, 82
Carew, Richard, *Survey of Cornwall* 55, 64, 191 (n. 77)
Carew, Thomas 144; *Coelum Britanicum*, 144
casting of the stone 20, 21
Catholics 44, 48, 56, 61, 68–9, 69, 72, 74, 75, 80, 85, 90, 91, 153, 155, 165, 166; anti-Catholicism 3, 110
Cecil, Robert 72
censorship 101, 139, 146–7, 148
Cerne Abbas, Dorset 135, 196 (n. 68)
Chaderton, William, Bishop of Chester 70, 71
Chalfont St Giles, Buckinghamshire 128
Chambers, Humphry 127
Charles I 46, 99, 134, 136, 144, 145, 147, 153, 160, 164, 193 (n. 134); attitude to fourth commandment 121; attitude to puritans 118, 121, 165, 166; attitude to sports 121; *Book of Sports* (1633) 1, 84; decision to enforce the *Book of Sports* (1633) 1, 6, 100–1, 123, 125,

126; decision to publish the *Book of Sports* (1633) 6, 100, 101, 108, 109–10, 116, 117–18, 120, 122–5, 143, 164, 193 (n. 130); intervention in the Somerset ales controversy 114–15, 116, 123; offended by Brabourne's dedication in *A Defence of ... the Sabbath Day* 107, 189–90 (n. 49); support for Bill for better Sabbath observance 101–3, 104
Charles II 162, 163
Cheapside 76, 150
Cheshire 47, 60
chess 15, 18, 82
Chester, Corporation of 97; diocese of 69, 70, 75.
Cheynell, Francis 136, 153
Chudleigh, George 89
church attendance 7, 10, 12, 14, 15, 19, 22, 28, 29, 30, 40, 42, 43, 44, 47, 48, 49, 53, 61, 62, 68, 70, 71, 73, 75, 85, 87, 92–3, 102, 163, 167
church ales (*see also* ales) xiv, xvi, xvii, 16, 17, 35, 36, 43, 45, 55, 57, 58, 60, 64, 86, 87, 89, 90, 93, 96, 97, 98, 104, 109, 110, 111, 112, 113, 115, 117, 119, 136, 137, 150, 151, 152, 156, 160, 162, 190 (n. 64), 190 (n. 65)
church-houses 17, 19, 23, 35
churchyards 18, 19, 20, 23, 24, 35, 44, 63, 64, 93, 137
Civil War, the English 6, 100–1, 150, 151, 152, 154, 155, 157, 159, 160, 161, 162; allegiance in 6, 100, 101, 150, 151–9, 199 (n. 185), 199 (n. 186)
Cleaver, Robert 105; *Declaration of the Christian Sabbath* 105
clergy participating in or otherwise supporting May games and revels 23, 31, 44, 45, 63, 64, 137, 158
clerk ales xv, 111, 113, 117, 136, 190 (n. 64)
closh 21, 31
Clough, William, 81
club ball xv, 20
cock-fighting xv, 15, 20, 32, 33, 34, 52, 53, 54, 61, 71
Coffey, John 3, 5
Coke, George, Bishop of Bristol 130
Coke, Sir Edward 90
Coke, Sir John 114
Coldwell, John, Bishop of Salisbury 45
Coleford, Somerset 115
Collinson, Patrick 5, 155, 157, 170 (n. 12)
Commission of the Peace, Lancashire, purging of 69, 70, 72

Conder, Richard 135, 137
Constantine, Emperor 10
Cooper, Thomas, Bishop of Winchester 43–4, 45–6
Cope, Esther 103
Cornhill 36, 201 (n. 217)
Cornwall 14, 157, 190 (n. 64), 191 (n.77)
Coryate, Thomas 96
Coventry 161
Coventry, Thomas, Lord Keeper 116
Cox, Richard, Bishop of Ely 40, 43, 45; *Interpretations and Further Considerations of Certain Injunctions* 40, 43
Crewe, Sir Thomas 85
Croft, Herefordshire 157
Crosfield, Thomas 108, 133
Croydon, Surrey 82, 93
cudgels, playing with 85
Culmer, Richard 128, 194 (n. 17)
Curle, Walter, Bishop of Winchester 129, 130
Cust, Richard 117

dancing xiii, xiv, xvi, xvii, 5, 7, 9, 14, 15, 16, 18, 20, 23, 25, 28, 32, 35, 41, 44, 45, 46, 53, 54–5, 60, 61, 62, 63, 70, 71, 72, 73, 75, 76, 77, 78, 79, 82, 83, 84, 87, 88, 89, 90, 94, 95, 97, 98, 100, 103, 104, 106, 109, 127, 131–2, 133, 137, 140, 142, 144, 145–6, 146, 147, 148, 149, 150, 154, 155, 156, 160, 167
Davenant, John, Bishop of Salisbury 130
Davenant, William 153
Davies, Julien 116, 117, 120
John Deacon 63; *A Treatise, intituled; Nobody is My Name*, 63
Dedham Conference 49
dedication festivals (see wakes)
Deighton, Yorkshire 63
Dekker, Thomas 94–5; *If This Be not a Good Play, the Devil Is In It* 94–5
Denham, Sir John 111, 112
Dennison, Stephen 133
Denny, William 153
Dent, Arthur 53
Dering, Sir Edward 146
Devon 60, 63, 96, 97, 98, 104, 110, 111, 112, 136, 160, 189 (n. 26), 190 (n. 64), 190 (n. 65), 191 (n.71), 191 (n. 93)
dicing xv, 15, 21, 31, 32, 35, 37, 53, 73, 77, 82, 106
disorder, examples of 17, 33, 63, 138; fears over and condemnation of 4, 17, 18, 20, 22, 28, 30, 33, 35, 37–8, 40, 41, 45, 47, 55, 56, 57, 58, 59, 60, 61,

62, 63, 83, 85–6, 86, 96, 97, 98, 102, 110–11, 112, 115, 118, 119, 124, 132, 135, 152
Dives and Pauper 11–12
Donaldson, Gordon 122
Doncaster 62
Dorchester 127, 130
Dorset 104, 112, 114, 118, 151, 189 (n. 26), 190 (n. 64)
dove-ales (*see also* ales) 71
Dover, Robert 144
Dow, Christopher 117, 143
Drayton, Michael 105; *Muses Elizium* 105
drinking xiv, xv, 4, 16, 17, 18, 19, 22, 30, 45, 47, 53, 54, 55, 56, 60, 73, 74, 82, 84, 100, 106, 115, 145, 137, 155, 156, 166; condemnation of 12, 13, 14, 15, 28, 100, 129, 160, 161, 166; fears over 7, 22, 54, 55, 56, 61, 80, 86, 96, 98, 119
drinking cups 17
Duffy, Eamon 9
Dundry, Somerset 136
Durham, William 153, 199 (n. 185)
Dursley, Gloucestershire 104

Earle, John 144
Earle, Sir Walter 89, 148
East Midlands 161
Easter-ales (*see also* ales) xv, 16
Eaton Constantine, Shropshire 104
Edgehill, Battle of 156
Elizabeth I 46, 48, 49, 74, 86, 101
Elizabeth, daughter of James I 77
Elliott, William 151–2
Elton, Edward 105–6
Elverton, Derbyshire 16
Elyot, Thomas 31, 32, 33
Enfield 137
'Enormities of the Sabbath', The 70–1
Erasmus, Desiderius 33
Essex 60, 62, 153
Essex, Robert Devereux, 2nd Earl of 67
Estwick, Nicholas 131–3
Estye, George 52
Evers, Sir Francis 87
Exeter 19, 23, 83, 96, 111, 134, 151, 154, 156, 157

Fane, Sir Francis 85
Feltham, Owen 153
fencing 53, 77
Fetherstone, Christopher 54, 56
Field, John 54, 56
Fleet Prison 76, 82
Fleetwood, Edward 69

football 15, 20, 21, 32, 33, 35, 53, 57, 60, 63, 77, 88, 135, 137, 178 (n. 74)
Forster, William 69
fourth commandment, morally binding nature of 2, 10, 25–6, 27, 28, 39, 41, 42–3, 49, 52, 64, 67, 81, 92, 105, 105–6, 107, 108, 121, 139, 140, 141, 143, 146, 147
Frederick V, Elector Palatine 77
Fuller, Nicholas 87
Fuller, Thomas 50, 101, 110, 127, 128–9, 140
Fuller, William 47
Fuston, Yorkshire 83

gambling xv, 18, 21, 33, 34, 61, 71, 77, 100, 109; fears over and condemnation of 7, 15, 21–2, 22, 30, 32, 35, 47
Gardner, Thomas 128
Gifford, George 53
Gloucester 153
Gloucester, Vale of 61
gluttony 12, 28, 55, 96
Godwin, Francis, Bishop of Hereford 82, 94
Goodman, Godfrey, Bishop of Gloucester 130
Goodnestone, Kent 128
Gosson, Stephen 32
Gouge, William 81, 147
Grafton Underwood, Northamptonshire 84, 85
Great Bedwyn, Wiltshire 87
Great Marlow, Buckinghamshire 137
Greenham, Richard 50, 51, 52, 64, 92; *A Treatise of the Sabbath* 50
Grindal, Edmund, Archbishop of Canterbury 44
Guildford, Surrey 97
Greville, Robert, Lord Brooke 155
Greenhill, William 158
Gillespie, George 158

Hakewill, George 147
half-bowl xv, 21, 31
Hall, Thomas 162
Hampton Court Conference, 1604 80
handball xv, 15, 20
Handlyng Sinne see Mannyng of Brunne, Robert
Hannington, Henry 137
Harington, John 110, 116
Harley, Lady Brilliana 157
Harrison, William 57, 69, 94; *Difference of Hearers*, 94
harvest, working on holy days and

226   THE DEVIL'S BOOK

Sundays during harvest time 26, 28, 29, 40, 50, 51, 88
Hastings, Sir Francis 61, 86
hawking 23, 37, 48, 87, 148
Heath, Sir Robert 192 (n. 97)
help-ales (see also ales) xv, 16, 58
Hellyer, Thomas 137
Henley-in-Arden, Warwickshire 161
Henry VIII 26, 32, 35
Hentzner, Paul 33
Hernhill, Kent 128
Herrick, Robert 144–5, 153
Heylyn, Peter 68, 107, 108, 117, 123, 126–7, 128, 138, 139, 141–3, 144, 146, 163; *The History of the Sabbath* 139
Hieron, Thomas 128
High Commission 107
Hill, Adam 53, 58–9
Hill, Christopher 65, 191 (n. 79)
Hobart, Sir Henry, Lord Chief Justice 86
hobby horses xv, 36, 55
Hoghton Tower, Lancashire 73
Holywell, Oxford 157
Homily of the Place and Time of Prayer (see also *Book of Homilies, The*) 41–2, 140, 142
Hooper, John, 28, 36
Horninghold, Leicestershire 81
Horringer, Suffolk 64
Hoxne, Suffolk 158
Hugh, Bishop of Lincoln 12
Hughes, Ann 151
Hughes, Lewis 147
Hunt, William 4
hunting 7, 23, 37, 48, 61, 71, 77, 87, 148, 184 (n. 85)
hurling of stones 20
Hutton, Ronald 35, 103, 108, 152, 153

idleness, condemnation of 7, 10, 14, 18, 19, 28, 32; fears over 7, 10, 15, 26, 49, 50, 55, 56, 58–9, 106
idolatry 55, 76
illegitimate births, concerns over 56, 59, 191 (n. 79)
interludes *see* plays
Isham, Sir John 85

Jacob's Well, 7, 12, 18, 19, 23
James I xi, 1, 3, 46, 66, 79, 80, 86, 101, 122–3, 164; 1603 Proclamation, 78, 87, 90, 91, 92, 94, 183 (n. 77); attitude towards puritans 75, 79, 80, 90–1, 98, 99, 165, 166, 184 (n. 85); *Book of Sports* (1617) xi, 1, 74; *Book of Sports* (1618) xii, 1, 5–6, 102, 103, 124; lack of enforcement of *Book of Sports* (1618) 1, 76, 79, 93, 99, 103, 123, 125; reasons for issuing the *Book of Sports* (1618) 5, 76–80, 110; progress through Lancashire (1617) 1, 71, 73; support for sports and revels 73, 77–8, 78–9, 80, 91, 94, 184 (n. 85)
James, Duke of York 162
Jeffries, William 96
Jegon, Thomas, Archdeacon of Norwich 92
Jones, William 146
Jonson, Ben 95; *A Tale of the Tub* 144; *Bartholomew Fair* 95; *Pleasure Reconciled to Virtue* 95; *The King's Entertainment at Welbeck* 144
jousts 46
Juxon, William, Bishop of London 130
Jurdain, Ignatius 134
juggling 162

kailes *see* skittles
Keevil, Wiltshire 83
Kenilworth Castle, Warwickshire 46
Kennington 128
Kent 37, 44, 137, 156, 157
Kethe, William 53
Kett's Rebellion 1549, 36
Kidderminster, Worcestershire 161
King, John, Bishop of London 93
King's Book, The 27, 28, 35
King's Declaration to his Subjects, Concerning Lawful Sports to be Used see *Book of Sports*
Kingston, Surrey 147
Kirk, the (Church in Scotland) 78, 79
King's Norton 162
Kishlansky, Mark 193 (n. 128)

Lancashire 1, 44, 61, 68–70, 72, 74, 80, 81, 85, 96, 110, 165
Laneham, Robert 34
Langley, William 69
Lanhydrock, Cornwall 83–4, 121–2, 193 (n. 122)
Laud, William, Archbishop of Canterbury xii, xiii, 2, 113, 136, 137, 145, 146, 149, 155, 192 (n. 97), 192 (n. 121), 193 (n. 122), 193 (n. 123), 197 (n. 128); attitude to recreations and Sunday observance 121; enforcement of the *Book of Sports* 121, 127–9, 130, 194 (n. 24); role in the publication of the 1633 *Book of Sports* 6, 108, 113, 114, 116–25, 137, 163, 164

Laudians 2, 6, 137; caricatured beliefs of puritan opponents 2, 141, 163
Laurence, Thomas 137
Lea Marston, Warwickshire 84
leaping xv, xvii, 15, 28, 47, 75, 76, 77, 103, 131, 142, 148, 160, 167
Ledbury, Herefordshire 133
Leicester 60, 62
Ley, John 101
Lim, Paul 3, 5
Lincoln 44, 62
loggats xv, 20, 31
London 32, 34, 44, 47, 48, 57, 58, 60, 63, 64, 77, 81, 97, 113, 130, 150, 162
longbow *see* archery
Longdon, Worcestershire 96
Long Parliament 149–50, 152, 158
Lords of Misrule xvi, 36
Lords of the May xv, 162
Lothwaite, John 137
Lovell, Thomas 52–3, 55
Ludlow 157
Luther, Martin 25
L'Estrange, Hamon 108, 134

madding pole *see* maypoles
Maidstone 135
Maldon, Essex 63
Manchester 61, 68, 69
Mannyng of Brunne, Robert 11, 15, 18, 19, 20, 23
Marcus, Leah 122–3
Marlborough, Wiltshire 83
Marston, John 64
Martindale, Adam 162
Mary I 29, 34, 36, 37, 46, 57, 58
masques 77, 82, 109, 121, 145
Matthew, Tobias, Archbishop of York 92
May Day xvi, 16, 46, 55, 63, 96, 145, 161
May games xv, xvi, xvii, 5, 15, 16, 20, 23, 35, 36, 37, 43, 44, 45, 52, 53, 55, 56, 59, 60, 61, 62, 64, 70, 71, 73, 74, 76, 78, 82, 86, 87, 89, 90, 92, 94, 95, 96, 103, 104, 106, 109, 110, 112, 118, 132, 137, 140, 142, 144, 153, 157, 160, 162, 167, 186 (n. 167), 187 (n. 191), 201 (n. 1)
maypoles xvi, xvii, 36, 46, 52, 55, 56, 57, 62–3, 64, 76, 90, 95, 97, 103, 104, 105, 135, 136, 137, 138, 140, 143, 150, 151, 155, 156, 157, 160, 161, 161–2, 162, 167, 189 (n. 26), 196 (n. 68); as a heathen or pagan symbol 52, 55, 76, 150; as a symbol of royalism 150, 151, 157, 161, 161–2; as a symbol of traditional revelry 62–3, 97

May, Thomas, 135, 153
McDowell, Nicholas 76
Mencken, H.L. 4
Mennes, John 153
Mercurius Britannicus 156
Merry Devil of Edmonton, The 95
Mewe, William 136, 157, 158
Middlesex 44, 45, 47, 95
Midgley, Richard 69
minstrels *see* piping
Mirk, John 12, 18, 19, 23
Milton, John 145; *Comus*, 145–6
Monson John, 153
Montacute, Somerset 137
Montagu, James, Bishop of Bath and Wells 88–9, 93
Montagu, Sir Charles 86
Montagu, Sir Edward 84–6, 87, 88, 91, 185 (n. 128)
More, Sir Thomas 34
Morrill, John 149
morris dancing xv, xvi, 4, 36, 43–4, 44, 46, 55, 57, 62, 73, 76, 82, 87, 92, 96, 103, 105, 134, 138, 140, 143, 145, 146, 147, 148, 153, 156, 160, 161, 162, 167, 186 (n. 167); seen as heathenish 43, 55, 161
Morton, Thomas, Bishop of Chester 72, 73, 74, 75, 93, 186 (n. 167); drafted the first draft of the *Book of Sports* (1617) 74

Neile, Richard, Bishop of Lincoln 88
nine pins *see* skittles
Normanton, Rutland 63
Northbrooke, John 56
Northill, Bedfordshire 57
Norwich 63, 92, 129
Nowell, Alexander 48; *Catechism*, 42–3, 43
Northampton 83, 85, 86
Newcastle 202 (n. 19)

Okebrook, Derbyshire 16
Otham, Kent 126, 128
Oxfordshire 36
Oxford 44, 45, 133, 141, 162
Oldmixon, John 155

Page, Henry 133
pall-mall xvi, 77, 88
Paris Garden xvi, 48–9, 57
parish church, sanctity of 7, 18, 19–20, 23, 24, 44, 93
Parker, Matthew, Archbishop of Canterbury 40–1

Parker, Kenneth 1–2, 39, 76, 111, 117, 120, 163, 164, 183 (n.77), 191 (n.71); *English Sabbath, The* 163, 164
Parliament (*see also* Charles I), Acts and ordinances relating to Sunday observance and to traditional revels xi, xii, xiii, 7, 8, 14, 19, 21, 22, 23, 29, 30–1, 32–3, 35, 37, 40, 51, 60, 88, 102–4, 109, 136, 150, 158, 160, 161, 163; Statute of Artificers (1563) 59
Parliament, bills relating to Sunday observance and to traditional revels 48, 49, 82, 86–91, 92, 93, 99, 101–2, 162–3
Pasquils Palinodia 95
Perkins, William 51, 53, 64
Peter, Hugh 133
Peterborough 127, 130
Phelips, Sir Robert 114–15, 116, 118, 123, 124, 152, 193 (n.134)
Pickering, Sir John 85
Piers, William, Bishop of Bath and Wells 118–20, 124, 125, 129–30, 136, 152
Pilgrimage of Grace 1536, 26
pins *see* skittles
piping 44, 45, 53, 55, 61, 70, 71, 72, 73, 75, 78, 79, 84, 85, 96, 103, 105, 137, 144, 156, 161
pitching the bar xvi, 47, 105, 131
Player, John 128
playing at the caitch xvi, 77
plays (including interludes and stage plays) xv, 20, 30, 36, 44, 45, 46, 48, 52, 53, 57, 64, 75, 77, 78, 82, 87, 94, 95, 100, 102, 106, 109, 144, 147, 156, 162, 167
Pocklington, John xiii, 143, 149, 193 (n.123), 197 (n.128); *Sunday No Sabbath* 193 (n.123), 197 (n.128) *Sunday No Sabbath*, burned by the common hangman 149
poor relief/rating, provision of 57, 58, 59–60, 98, 119, 136
Popham, Sir John, Lord Chief Justice 60, 67
Potter, Barnaby Bishop of Carlisle, 131
preaching 4, 19, 26, 28, 29, 40, 44, 45, 67, 72, 75, 80, 93, 112, 128, 133, 136, 139, 152; puritan preachers sent to Lancashire 68–9
predestination 3
Price, William 127
Prideaux, John 141; *The Doctrine of the Sabbath* 141
Priest, James 121
Privy Council meetings held on Sundays 46, 77, 87, 121

promiscuity, concerns over and condemnation of 55, 56, 59
Prynne, William xii, 103, 104, 106, 108, 108–9, 113, 116, 117, 120, 121, 122, 127–8, 130, 131, 138–9, 146, 149, 189–90 (n.49), 190 (n.186); *Histrio-Mastix* xii, 106, 108–9, 149; *Histrio-Mastix* a factor in the decision to publish the 1633 *Book of Sports* 108–10, 117; *Histrio-Mastix* burned by the common hangman 109; *Newes From Ipswich* 146
puritans 1, 2, 7, 25, 36, 40, 46, 47, 49, 53, 54, 55, 58, 61, 63, 64, 65, 68–9, 70, 71, 72, 81, 82, 83, 86, 88, 94, 96, 97, 98, 101, 103, 104, 110, 111, 116, 118, 119, 121, 122, 126, 133, 134, 135, 136, 146, 147, 149, 152, 153, 157, 199 (n.186); criticised in the *Book of Sports* 74, 75, 80, 165, 166; antipathy towards 84, 85, 90, 91, 95, 97, 98, 100, 105, 121, 143–4, 151, 152, 155, 157, 161, 162; targeted 75, 76, 76–7, 78, 95, 99; *see also* Charles I and James I
puritanism, definition of 2–5, 63, 143–4
puritan sabbatarianism *see* sabbatarianism
Puttenham, George 64
Pym, John 90, 148

queckboard xvi, 21
quintain xvi, 144
quoits xvi, 15, 19, 20, 21, 31

Rainton, Nicolas, Lord Mayor of London 113
Ramsgate 63
Reeve, Edmund 134
Reeve, Robert 84
Restoration, The xiii, 161, 162, 163
Richardson, Sir Thomas, Lord Chief Justice xii, 112, 113–16, 117, 118, 138, 191 (n.93)
Robartes, 1st Earl of Radnor, family of *see* Lanhydrock, Cornwall
Roberts, Hugh 53, 55, 56
Roberts, Humphrey 53
Robin Hood xvi, 82
Rogers, Christopher 133
Rogers, Thomas xi, 64, 66, 67, 68, 70, 94, 98, 142; *Catholic Doctrine of the Church of England* 66, 94, 98
Romance of Merline 17
Rossingham, Edward 125
Rous, Francis 148
rowing 48

INDEX

Rudgwick, Sussex 64
Rudyard, Edmund 96
Rufford, Lancashire 63
Rump Parliament 161
running xvi, 15, 47, 77, 106, 144
rushbearing xvi, 71, 73, 75, 83, 87, 92, 144, 167
Russell, Conrad 152
Ruthven, Lord 79
Rutland 157
Rutter, Ferriman 153

sabbatarianism 1, 2, 6, 8, 11, 19, 24, 30, 39, 41, 42, 43, 46, 78, 139, 147, 154; puritan sabbatarianism xi, 2, 4, 5, 6, 12, 19, 24, 25, 39, 40, 42, 46, 48, 49, 50, 51, 57, 62, 63, 64–5, 66–8, 69, 70, 71, 76–7, 80, 81, 88, 91, 92, 93, 94, 97, 98, 99, 102, 105, 105–6, 107, 111, 112, 118, 123, 130, 131, 136, 139–41, 142–3, 144, 147, 152, 161, 163, 164
Safford, Bartholomew 133
Salford, Manchester 69, 70
Salisbury 97, 114
Sanderson, Robert 131, 143
Sandwich, Kent 128
Saye and Sele, William Fiennes, 1st Viscount 88
Sayer, Thomas 158
scot-ales (*see also* ales) xvi, 16, 18
Scottish Prayer Book 122
Scudamore, John, 1st Viscount 125
servile work, allowed on Sundays 10–11, 14, 27, 40; condemnation of work on Sundays 11, 12, 14, 66, 89; forbidden on Sundays 9, 10, 10–11, 13–14, 27, 43
Shaftesbury, Dorset 89, 136
Sharpe, Kevin 101, 117
Shepheards Pie, The 95
Shepherd, Thomas 89–90, 98
Sherfield, Henry 114
shooting *see* archery
Short Parliament 101, 148–9
shovegroat xvii, 62
shovel-board xvii, 62
Shrewsbury, Shropshire 62
Shrove Tuesday 33
silver games (*see also* May games) 55
singing 15, 18, 52
skittles xv, xvi, 21, 31, 32
Smith, Henry 97
Somerset xii, 1, 16, 60, 61, 63, 97, 98, 104, 108, 110, 111, 112, 113, 114, 115, 116, 117, 118, 120, 123, 124, 129, 133, 136, 137, 151, 152, 155 156, 161,
 189 (n. 26), 190 (n. 64), 190 (n. 65), 191 (n. 93)
Somerset justices, 1633 petition 115–16, 117, 118, 119–20, 124, 129–30, 136, 138, 152
Spie, The 156
Southampton 60
South Newington, Oxfordshire 137
Southwark, London xvi, 157
Spanish Armada, 1588 32
sports and revels, attempts to suppress sports and traditional revels held on Sundays xii, 1, 2, 4, 8, 20, 33, 36, 37–8, 39–40, 43–4, 52, 56, 57, 58, 60, 61, 63, 64, 70, 71, 72, 73, 74, 75, 76, 80, 81, 83, 85, 86, 90, 91, 95, 96, 97, 98, 104, 109, 110, 111–13, 115–16, 117, 118, 136, 138, 143, 146, 149–50, 151, 157, 161, 163, 164, 191 (n.77); leading to injury and death 17, 22, 33, 48, 56, 57, 85, 87–8, 96, 111, 115, 148, 178 (n.74); linked to Catholicism 40, 56; linked to paganism 40, 43, 52, 55, 56; popularity of 37, 62, 63, 64, 71, 90, 95, 97, 105, 110, 112, 119, 120, 134, 135–8, 144–5, 160, 161, 162
Spratt, Thomas 133
St Paul's churchyard, London 113
Staffordshire 97
Star Chamber xii, 76, 114, 146
Stockwood, John 53
Stogursey, Somerset 16
stoolball xvii, 61, 106
Stow, John 64
Stowell Sir John, 152
Stoyle, Mark 151–2, 200 (n. 197), 201 (n. 213)
Strafford, Thomas Wentworth, 1st Earl of 126
Strand, The, London 162
Stratford, Warwickshire 92, 97
Stubbes, Philip 53, 53–4; defined as a puritan 4–5, 170 (n. 12)
Suffolk 157
summer games *see* May games
summer poles *see* Maypoles
Sunday, examples of people divinely 'punished' for working or revelling on Sundays 12–13, 57, 92, 101, 137–8, 147–8, 157–8
Sunday, observance of 8, 9, 10, 11, 14, 18, 19, 20, 22, 23, 26–7, 27–8, 28, 29, 30, 33, 41, 43, 44, 45, 46, 47, 49–50, 50, 51, 52, 53, 61, 63, 78, 86, 87, 92, 101–2, 133, 149–50, 151, 157, 161, 166
Sussex 157

Symes, John 116
Sylvester, Matthew 149
Symondsbury, Dorset 136
Sydenham, Humphrey 60

tables xvii, 15, 18, 31, 53, 63, 77, 82
Tanner, J.R. 1, 6, 164
Taunton Castle, Somerset 112
taverns *see* alehouses
tennis xvi, xvii, 15, 19, 21, 22, 31, 32–3, 37, 46, 52, 53, 77, 88, 97, 106, 121
Terry, John 56
Tewkesbury, Gloucestershire 61, 63
Thames Valley 57
Thatcham, Berkshire 98
Thistleton, Rutland 134
throwing at cocks xvii, 34
throwing the sledge xvii, 47, 105
Thurlow, Suffolk 138
tipling *see* drinking
trap-ball 83
Traske, John xii, 76, 183 (n. 64)
Trescott, Thomas 112, 157
True Informer, The 156
Twisse, William 103, 147
Twyning, Gloucestershire 61
Tyndale, William 26
Trussell, John 144, 153

Ussher, James, Archbishop of Armagh 126
Underdown, David 136, 151

Valentine, Thomas 128
vaulting xvii, 15, 75, 76, 103, 142, 167
Vicars, John 146

wakes xii, xvii, 5, 7, 14, 16, 17, 18, 19, 23, 26, 35, 47, 48, 53, 55, 57, 58, 59, 60, 61, 70, 71, 82, 84, 85, 86, 87, 94, 95, 96, 97, 104, 109, 110, 111, 112, 113, 115, 118, 119–20, 124–5, 129, 134, 135, 136, 137, 138, 142, 144, 145, 146, 147, 150, 156, 157, 160, 162, 167, 187 (n. 191), 189 (n. 26), 193 (n. 134), 201 (n. 1)
Walker, George 141, 146, 148, 149; *The Doctrine of the Sabbath* 146
Wallington, Nehemiah 134, 154, 161
Walsham, Alexandra 170 (n. 12)
Walsingham, Sir Francis 69
Warbleton, Sussex 62
Ward, John 158

Ward, Samuel 131–3
Warrington, Cheshire 73
Wells, Somerset 98
Welsby, Paul 92
Wenhaston, Suffolk 158
West Chinnock, Somerset 161
Western Rebellion, 1549 35
Whitaker, W.B. 138
White Notley, Essex 64
White, Francis, Bishop of Ely 107–8, 117, 123, 130, 139–40, 140, 141, 144, 146, 192–3 (n. 121); *An Examination and Confutation of a Lawlesse Pamphlet* xiii, 139, 141; *A Treatise of the Sabbath Day* xii, 139
White, John 127, 130
Whitehall Palace 32, 34
Whiteway, William 118
Whitelocke, Bulstrode 134
Whitgift, John, Archbishop of Canterbury 45, 64, 67
Whitsun-ales (*see also* ales) xv, xvii, 16, 57, 76, 87, 95, 103, 104, 118, 132, 134, 136, 138, 144, 156, 157, 167
Wiburn, Percival 3
Widley, George 87; *The Doctrine of the Sabbath* 87
Wildgoose, John 133
Williams, Edward 136
Williams, Griffith 106, 189 (n. 36)
Williams, John 84–6, 91, 185 (n. 128)
Wilson, Thomas 126, 128, 194 (n. 24)
Wilton, Wiltshire 137
Wiltshire 151
Windsor Castle, 46 153
Wither, George 153
Wolverhampton 161
Woodborough, Wiltshire 161
Woolston 137
Workton, Northamptonshire 131–2
Worcester, Battle of 162
Wren, Matthew, Bishop of Norwich 129, 130
wrestling 7, 15, 18, 20, 23, 46, 47, 77, 105, 106, 142, 148, 160
Wright, Leonard 53
Wyatt's Rebellion, 1554 37
Wylye, Wiltshire 98, 99
Wymondham, Norfolk 36

Yonge, Walter 103, 104
young people, particular concerns about youthful misbehaviour 22, 59

BV133 .D68 2011 JUN 1 5 2012

Dougall, Alistair

The devil's book : Charles I, the Book of sports and Puritanism in Tudor and early Stuart England